CAMBRIDGE LI

Books of end..... ...y scholarly value

Philosophy

This series contains both philosophical texts and critical essays about philosophy, concentrating especially on works originally published in the eighteenth and nineteenth centuries. It covers a broad range of topics including ethics, logic, metaphysics, aesthetics, utilitarianism, positivism, scientific method and political thought. It also includes biographies and accounts of the history of philosophy, as well as collections of papers by leading figures. In addition to this series, primary texts by ancient philosophers, and works with particular relevance to philosophy of science, politics or theology, may be found elsewhere in the Cambridge Library Collection.

Observations on Man

The orphaned son of an Anglican clergyman, David Hartley (1705–57) was originally destined for holy orders. Declining to subscribe to the Thirty-Nine Articles, he turned to medicine and science yet remained a religious believer. This, his most significant work, provides a rigorous analysis of human nature, blending philosophy, psychology and theology. First published in two volumes in 1749, *Observations on Man* is notable for being based on the doctrine of the association of ideas. It greatly influenced scientists, theologians, social reformers and poets: Samuel Taylor Coleridge, who named his eldest son after Hartley, had his portrait painted while holding a copy. Volume 2 is particularly concerned with human morality and the duty and expectations of mankind. Here the author is keen to show that scientific observation is not necessarily in conflict with religious conviction.

Cambridge University Press has long been a pioneer in the reissuing of out-of-print titles from its own backlist, producing digital reprints of books that are still sought after by scholars and students but could not be reprinted economically using traditional technology. The Cambridge Library Collection extends this activity to a wider range of books which are still of importance to researchers and professionals, either for the source material they contain, or as landmarks in the history of their academic discipline.

Drawing from the world-renowned collections in the Cambridge University Library and other partner libraries, and guided by the advice of experts in each subject area, Cambridge University Press is using state-of-the-art scanning machines in its own Printing House to capture the content of each book selected for inclusion. The files are processed to give a consistently clear, crisp image, and the books finished to the high quality standard for which the Press is recognised around the world. The latest print-on-demand technology ensures that the books will remain available indefinitely, and that orders for single or multiple copies can quickly be supplied.

The Cambridge Library Collection brings back to life books of enduring scholarly value (including out-of-copyright works originally issued by other publishers) across a wide range of disciplines in the humanities and social sciences and in science and technology.

Observations on Man

His Frame, his Duty, and his Expectations

VOLUME 2

DAVID HARTLEY

CAMBRIDGE
UNIVERSITY PRESS

CAMBRIDGE
UNIVERSITY PRESS

University Printing House, Cambridge, CB2 8BS, United Kingdom

Published in the United States of America by Cambridge University Press, New York

Cambridge University Press is part of the University of Cambridge.
It furthers the University's mission by disseminating knowledge in the pursuit of
education, learning and research at the highest international levels of excellence.

www.cambridge.org
Information on this title: www.cambridge.org/9781108063616

© in this compilation Cambridge University Press 2013

This edition first published 1749
This digitally printed version 2013

ISBN 978-1-108-06361-6 Paperback

OBSERVATIONS

ON

MAN,

HIS

FRAME,

HIS

DUTY,

AND HIS

EXPECTATIONS.

In TWO PARTS.

By DAVID HARTLEY, M. A.

LONDON,

Printed by S. RICHARDSON;
For JAMES LEAKE and WM. FREDERICK,
Bookfellers in BATH:
And fold by CHARLES HITCH and STEPHEN AUSTEN,
Bookfellers in LONDON.

M.DCC.XLIX.

OBSERVATIONS

ON

M A N, &c.

PART the SECOND.

Containing OBSERVATIONS on
the DUTY and EXPECTATIONS of Mankind.

THE
CONTENTS
OF THE
SECOND PART.

C H A P. II.

Of the Truth of the Christian Religion.

ſtian

CHAP.

CHAP. III.
Of the Rule of Life.

SECT. I.
Of the Rule of Life, as deducible from the Practice and Opinions of Mankind.

SECT. II.
Of the Regard due to the Pleasures and Pains of Sensation, in forming the Rule of Life.

S E C T. III.

Of the Regard due to the Pleaſures and Pains of Imagination in forming the Rule of Life.

S E C T. IV.

Of the Regard due to the Pleaſures of Honour, and the Pains of Shame, in forming the Rule of Life.

S E C T.

S E C T. V.

Of the Regard due to the Pleasures and Pains of
Self-interest in forming the Rule of Life.

S E C T. VI.

Of the Regard due to the Pleasures and Pains of
Sympathy, in forming the Rule of Life.

S E C T.

CHAP.

CHAP. IV.

Of the Expectations of Mankind, here and hereafter, in confequence of their Obfervance or Violation of the Rule of Life.

SECT. I.

Of the Expectation of Individuals in the prefent Life.

SECT. II.

Of the Expectation of Bodies Poli ic, the *Jews* in particular, and the World in general, during the prefent State of the Earth.

S E C T. III.

Of a future State after the Expiration of this Life.

S E C T. IV.

Of the Terms of Salvation.

S E C T. V.

Of the final Happineſs of all Mankind in ſome diſtant future State.

C O N C L U S I O N.

OBSER-

OBSERVATIONS

ON

MAN, &c.

In TWO PARTS.

PART II.

Containing Observations on the Duty and Expectations of Mankind.

INTRODUCTION.

WHATEVER be our Doubts, Fears, or Anxieties, whether selfish or social, whether for Time or Eternity, our only Hope and Refuge must be in the infinite Power, Knowlege, and Goodness of God. And if these be really our Hope and Refuge, if we have a true practical Sense and Conviction of God's infinite Ability and Readiness to protect and bless us, an intire, peaceful, happy Resignation will be the Result, notwithstanding the Clouds and Perplexities wherewith we may fometimes be encompaffed. He who has brought us into this State, will conduct us through it : He knows all our Wants and Diftreffes : His infinite Nature will bear down all Oppofition from our Impotence, Ignorance, Vice, or Mifery : He is our Creator, Judge, and King, our Friend, and Father, and God.

And though the tranfcendent Greatnefs and Glorioufnefs of this Profpect may, at firft View, make our Faith ftagger, and incline us to difbelieve through Joy ; yet, upon farther Confideration, it feems rather to confirm and eftablifh itfelf on that Account ; for the more it exceeds our Gratitude and Comprehenfion, the more does it coincide with the Idea of that abfolutely perfect Being, whom the feveral Orders of imperfect Beings perpetually fuggeft to us, as our only Refting-place, the Caufe of Caufes, and the fupreme Reality.

However, on the other hand, it muft be acknowleged, that the Evils which we fee and feel are ftrong Arguments of the Poffibility of ftill greater Evils, of any finite Evils whatever, and of their Confiftency with the Divine Attributes. All Finites are equally nothing in refpect of infinite ; and if the infinite Power, Knowlege, and Goodnefs of God can permit the leaft Evil, they may permit any finite Degree of it, how great foever, for any thing that we know to the contrary. And this moft alarming Confideration cannot but compel every thinking Perfon to ufe his utmoft Endeavours, firft for his own Prefervation and Deliverance ; and then, in proportion to his Benevolence, for the Prefervation and Deliverance of others.

Nor can fuch a Perfon long hefitate what Method to take in the geneial. The Duties of Piety, Benevolence, and Self-government,. confidered in the general, have had fuch a Stamp fet upon them by all Ages and Nations, by all Orders and Conditions of Men, approve themfelves fo much to our Frame and

Confti

Conftitution, and are fo evidently conducive to both public and private Happinefs here, that one cannot doubt of their procuring for us not only Security, but our *Summum Bonum*, our greateft poffible Happinefs, during the whole Courfe of our Exiftence, whatever that be.

Thefe are the genuine Dictates of what is called Natural Religion. But we, who live in Chriftian Countries, may have recourfe to far clearer Light, and to a more definite Rule: The Chriftian Revelation is attefted by fuch Evidences hiftorical, prophetical, and moral, as will give abundant Comfort and Satisfaction to all who feek them earneftly. A future Life, with indefinite, or even infinite, Rewards and Punifhments, is fet before us in exprefs Terms, the Conditions declared, Examples related both to encourage our Hopes, and alarm our Fears, and Affureances of Affiftance and Mercy delivered in the ftrongeft and moft pathetic Terms.

Yet ftill there are Difficulties both in the Word of God, and in his Works; and thefe Difficulties are fometimes fo magnified, as to lead to Scepticifm, Infidelity, or Atheifm. Now, the Contemplation of our own Frame and Conftitution appears to me to have a peculiar Tendency to leffen thefe Difficulties attending Natural and Revealed Religion, and to improve their Evidences, as well as to concur with them in their Determination of Man's Duty and Expectations. With this View, I drew up the foregoing Obfervations on the Frame and Connexion of the Body and Mind; and, in Profecution of the fame Defign, I now propofe,

Firft, To proceed upon this Foundation, and upon the other Phænomena of Nature to deduce the Evidences for the Being and Attributes of God, and the general Truths of Natural Religion.

Secondly, Laying down all thefe as a new Foundation, to deduce the Evidences for Revealed Religion.

B 2   Thirdly,

Thirdly, To inquire into the Rule of Life, and the particular Applications of it, which refult from the Frame of our Natures, the Dictates of Natural Religion, and the Precepts of the Scriptures taken together, compared with, and cafting Light upon, each other. And,

Fourthly, To inquire into the genuine Doctrines of Natural and Revealed Religion thus illuftrated, concerning the Expectations of Mankind, here and hereafter, in confequence of their Obfervance or Violation of the Rule of Life.

I do not prefume to give a complete Treatife on any of thefe Subjects ; but only to borrow from the many excellent Writings, which have been offered to the World on them, fome of the principal Evidences and Deductions, and to accommodate them to the foregoing Theory of the Mind ; whereby it may appear, that though the Doctrines of Affociation and Mechanifm do make fome Alterations in the Method of reafoning on Religion, yet they are far from leffening either the Evidences for it, the Comfort and Joy of religious Perfons, or the Fears of irreligious ones.

Obſervations on Man, *his* Frame, *his* Duty, *and his* Expectations.

CHAP. I.

Of the Being and Attributes of God, and of Natural Religion.

PROP. I.

Something muſt have exiſted from all Eternity; or, There never was a Time when nothing exiſted.

OR, when we place ourſelves in ſuch an imaginary Point of Time, and then try to conceive how a World, finite or infinite, ſhould begin to exiſt, abſolutely without Cauſe, we find an inſtantaneous and irreſiſtible Check put to the Conception, and we are compelled at once to rejeCt the Suppoſition: So that the manner in which we rejeCt it, is a proper Authority for doing ſo. It is ſuperfluous, in this Caſe, to inquire into the Nature of this Check and RejeCtion, and Diſſent grounded thereon; ſince, after all our Inquiries, we

B 3 muſt

muſt ſtill find an inſuperable Reluctance to aſſent. The Suppoſition will not remain in the Mind, but is thrown out immediately; and I do not ſpeak of this, as what ought to follow from a proper Theory of Evidence and Aſſent, but as a Fact, which every Man feels, whatever his Notions of Logic be, or whether he has any or no; and I appeal to every Man for the Truth of this Fact. Now, no Truth can have a greater Reality to us, nor any Falſhood a greater Evidence againſt it, than this inſtantaneous, neceſſary Aſſent or Diſſent. I conclude, therefore, that there never was a Time when nothing exiſted; or, in other Words, that ſomething muſt have exiſted from all Eternity.

PROP. 2.

There cannot have been a mere Succeſſion of finite dependent Beings from all Eternity; but there muſt exiſt, at leaſt, one infinite and independent Being.

IF an infinite Succeſſion of finite dependent Beings be poſſible, let *M, N, O,* &c. repreſent the ſeveral Links of this Chain or Series; *N* is therefore the mere Effect of *M, O* of *N,* &c. as we deſcend; and as we aſcend, *M* is the Effect of *L, L* of *K,* &c. Each particular Being, therefore, is a mere Effect; and therefore the Suppoſition of ſuch a Succeſſion finite *à parte ante,* would be rejected immediately according to the laſt Propoſition, ſince *A,* the Firſt Term, would be an Effect abſolutely without a Cauſe. And the ſame thing holds, whatever Number of Terms be added *à parte ante.* If, therefore, an infinite Number be added (which I here ſuppoſe poſſible for Argument's ſake), ſo that the Series may become infinite *à parte ante,* the ſame Concluſion muſt be valid according to the Analogy of all mathematical Reaſonings

fonings concerning Infinites : Since we do not approach to the Poffibility of this Series in any Step of our Progrefs, but always remain in the fame State of utter Inability to admit it, we can never arrive thither ultimately. Where-ever the ultimate Ratio of Quantities, fuppofed then to be infinitely great or fmall, is different from that of the fame Quantities fuppofed to be finite, there is a perpetual Tendency to this ultimate Ratio in every Increafe or Diminution of the Quantities : It follows, therefore, that an infinite Succeffion of mere finite dependent Beings is impoffible to us; which relative Impoffibility, as I obferved before, is our *Ne plus ultra.* Though we fhould fancy relative Impoffibles to be poffible *in themfelves,* as it is fometimes phrafed, the utter Rejection, which forces itfelf again and again upon the Mind, when we endeavour to conceive them fo, fuppreffes all nafcent Tendencies to Affent.

The fame thing may be confidered thus : If there be nothing more in the Univerfe than a mere Succeffion of finite dependent Beings, then there is fome Degree of Finitenefs fuperior to all the reft ; but this is impoffible, fince no Caufe can be affigned for this Degree rather than any other : Befides, this fupreme finite Being will want a Caufe of its Exiftence, fince it is finite; which yet it cannot have, fince all the reft are inferior to it.

Or thus : If an infinite Succeffion of finite Beings be poffible, let us fuppofe it in Men : It will be neceffary, however, to fuppofe one or more Beings fuperior to Man, on account of the Exquifitenefs of his Frame of Body and Mind, which is far above his own Power to execute, and Capacity to comprehend : And if this Being or Beings be not infinite, we muft have recourfe to a fecond infinite Succeffion of finite Beings. But then it will be natural to fuppofe, that thefe Beings, though able to comprehend Man through their fuperior Faculties, cannot compre-

hend

hend themfelves, and fo on till we come to an infinite Being, who alone can comprehend himfelf.

There are many other Arguments and Methods of Reafoning, of the fame kind with thofe here delivered, which lead to the fame Conclufion; and they all feem to turn upon this, that as all finite Beings require a fuperior Caufe for their Exiftence and Faculties, fo they point to an infinite one, as the only real Caufe, himfelf being uncaufed. He is, therefore, properly denominated independent, felf-exiftent, and neceffa-rily-exiftent; Terms which import nothing more, when applied to the Deity, than the Denial of a fo-reign Caufe of his Exiftence and Attributes; notwith-ftanding that thefe Words, on account of their differ-ent Derivations, and Relations to other Words, may feem to have a different Import, when applied to the Deity.

If it be objected, that a Caufe is required for an infinite Being, as well as for a finite one; I anfwer, that though the Want of a Caufe for finite Beings, with other Arguments to the fame Purpofe, leads us neceffarily to the Confideration and Admiffion of an infinite one; yet, when we are arrived there, we are utterly unable to think or fpeak properly of him: However, one would rather judge, that, for the fame Reafon that all Finitenefs requires a Caufe, Infinity is incompatible with it.

If it be fuppofed poffible for a Man, through logi-cal and metaphyfical Perplexities, or an unhappy Turn of Mind, not to fee the Force of thefe and fuch-like Reafonings, he muft, however, be at leaft *in Æquilibrio* between the two oppofite Suppofitions of the Propofition; *viz.* that of an infinite Succeffion of finite dependent Beings, and that of an infinite independent Being. In this Cafe, the Teftimony of all Ages and Nations, from whatever Caufe it arifes, and of the Scriptures, in favour of the laft Suppofi-tion, ought to have fome Weight, fince fome Credibility

bility muſt be due to theſe, in whatever Light they be conſidered. If, therefore, they have no Weight, this may ſerve to ſhew a Man, that he is not ſo perfectly *in Æquilibrio*, as he may fancy. This Propoſition will alſo be confirmed by the following. My chief Deſign under it has been to produce the abſtract metaphyſical Arguments for the Exiſtence of an infinite independent Being. Some of theſe are more ſatisfactory to one Perſon, ſome to another; but in all there is ſomething of Perplexity and Doubt concerning the exact Propriety of Expreſſions, and Method of Reaſoning, and perhaps ever will be; ſince the Subject is infinite, and we finite. I have given what appears moſt ſatisfactory to myſelf; but without the leaſt Intention to cenſure the Labours of others upon this important Subject. If we underſtood one another perfectly, not only our Concluſions, but our Methods of arriving at them, would probably appear to coincide. In the mean time, mutual Candour will be of great Uſe for the preventing the ill Effects of this Branch of the Confuſion of Tongues.

P R O P. 3.

The infinite independent Being is endued with infinite Power and Knowlege.

THIS Propoſition follows from the foregoing; it being evident, that moſt or all the Ways there delivered, or referred to, for proving an infinite Being, do, at the ſame time, prove the Infinity of his Power and Knowlege. To ſuppoſe a Being without any Power, or any Knowlege, is, in effect, to take away his Exiſtence, after it has been allowed. And to ſuppoſe an infinite Being with only finite Power, or finite Knowlege, is ſo diſſonant to the Analogy of Language, and of the received Method of Reaſoning, that it muſt be rejected by the Mind.

But

But the Infinity of the Divine Power and Knowlege may alfo be proved in many independent Ways, and thefe Proofs may be extended, in a contrary Order, to infer the foregoing Propofition.

Thus, Firft ; When a Man confiders the feveral Orders of fentient and intelligent Beings below him, even in the moft tranfient Way, and afks himfelf whether or no Mankind be the higheft Order which exifts within the whole *Compafs of Nature*, as we term it, he cannot but refolve this Queftion in the Negative; he cannot but be perfuaded, that there are Beings of a Power and Knowlege fuperior to his own, as well as inferior. The Idea, the internal Feeling, of the actual Exiftence of fuch Beings forces itfelf upon the Mind, adheres infeparably to, and coalefces with, the Reflection upon the inferior Orders of Beings, which he fees. Farther, as we can perceive no Limits fet to the defcending Scale, fo it is natural, even at firft View, to imagine, that neither has the afcending Scale any Limits ; or, in other Words, that there actually exifts one, or more Beings, endued with infinite Power and Knowlege.

Secondly, When we contemplate the innumerable Inftances and Evidences of boundlefs Power, and exquifite Skill, which appear every-where in the Organs and Faculties of Animals, in the Make and Properties of the Vegetable and Mineral Kingdoms, in the Earth, Water, and Air of this Globe, in the heavenly Bodies, in Light, Gravity, Electricity, Magnetifm, the Attraction of Cohefion, &c. &c. with the manifeft Adaptations and Subferviencies of all thefe Things to each other, in fuch manner as to fhew both the moft perfect Knowlege of them, and of all their Properties, and the moft abfolute Command over them ; when we confider alfo that vaft Extent of thefe Effects of Power and Knowlege, which Telefcopes, Microfcopes, and the daily Obfervations and Experiments of Mankind, open to our View ; the real

3   Exiftence,

Exiftence, firft, of Power and Knowlege far beyond human Conception, and then, of thofe that are actually infinite, forces itfelf upon the Mind, by the clofe Connexion and indiffoluble Union between the feveral Ideas here mentioned.

For, Thirdly, Though no finite Being can comprehend more than the finite Effects of Power and Knowlege ; nay, though to fuppofe infinite Effects, *i. e.* an infinite Univerfe, is thought by fome to involve a Contradiction, to be the fame Thing as fuppofing an actually infinite Number ; yet it appears to me, that the other Branch of the Dilemma repels us with the greateft Force. To fuppofe a finite Univerfe, is to fuppofe a Stop where the Mind cannot reft ; we fhall always afk for a Caufe of this Finitenefs, and, not finding any, reject the Suppofition. Now, if the Univerfe be fuppofed infinite, this proves at once the abfolute Infinity of the Divine Power and Knowlege, provided we allow them to follow in a finite Degree, from the finite Evidences of Power and Knowlege, in that Part of the Univerfe which is prefented to our View.

As to the foregoing Objection to the Infinity of the Univerfe, we may obferve, that it arifes merely from the Finitenefs of our Comprehenfions. We can have no Conception of any thing infinite, nor of the Poffibility that any other Being, conceived by us, can conceive this, *&c. &c.* But all this vanifhes, when we come to confider, that there actually is, that there neceffarily muft be, an infinite Being. This Being may conceive his own infinite Works, and he alone can do it. His own infinite Nature, which we cannot but admit, is as much above Conception as the Infinity of his Works. And all apparent Contradictions, in thefe Things, feem to flow merely from our ufing the Words denoting Infinity, of which we can neither have any Idea, nor any Definition, but by equivalent Terms, like thofe Words of which we have

Ideas

Ideas or Definitions. In the fame manner as when the Conditions of an algebraic Problem are impoffible, the unknown Quantity comes out indeed by the Refolution of the Equation under an algebraic Form, as in other Cafes; but then this Form, when examined, is found to include an Impoffibility.

As the Infinity of the Divine Power and Knowlege may be deduced from that of the Univerfe, fo the laft may be deduced from the firft, fuppofed to be proved by other Arguments. And it may be obferved in general, upon all Inquiries into this Subject, that the Mind cannot bear to fuppofe either God or his Works finite, however unable we may be to think or fpeak of them properly, when they are fuppofed to be infinite.

Fourthly, As it appears from the Train of Reafoning ufed in this and the foregoing Propofition, that an infinite Being is abfolutely neceffary for the Exiftence of the vifible World, as its Creator ; fo the Confideration of this leads us to the Infinity of his Power and Knowlege. The Things created muft be merely paffive, and fubject intirely to the Will of him who created them. In like manner, all the Powers and Properties of created Things, with all the Refults of thefe, in their mutual Applications, through all Eternity, muft be known to him. And this follows in whatever manner we confider Creation, of which we can certainly form no juft Idea. It is evident, as juft now mentioned, that an Author of this World is abfolutely required ; alfo, that this Author muft have been from all Eternity. It is therefore moft natural for us to conclude, that there have been infinite Effects of his Almighty Power from all Eternity. But then this does not exclude Creations in Time, I mean of Things made from nothing. For it feems to me, that our narrow Faculties cannot afford us the leaft Foundation for fuppofing the Creation of Things from nothing impoffible to God.

Laftly,

Laftly, There is a great Acceffion of Evidence for the Infinity of the Divine Power and Knowlege, and for the Creation of all Things by God, and their intire Subjection to him, from the Declarations of the Scriptures to this Purpofe. This Acceffion of Evidence can fcarce be neceffary in this Age ; but, in the Infancy of the World, Revelation feems to have been the chief or only Foundation of Faith in any of the Divine Attributes. And even now, it cannot but be Matter of the greateft Comfort and Satisfaction to all good Men, to have an independent Evidence for thefe important Truths ; and that more efpecially, if their Minds have been at all perplexed with the metaphyfical Difputes and Subtleties, which are often ftarted on thefe Subjects.

P R O P. 4.
God is infinitely benevolent.

AS all the natural Attributes of God may be comprehended under Power and Knowlege, fo Benevolence feems to comprehend all the moral ones. This Propofition therefore, and the foregoing, contain the Fundamentals of all that Reafon can difcover to us concerning the Divine Nature and Attributes.

Now, in inquiring into the Evidences for the Divine Benevolence, I obferve, Firft, That as we judge of the Divine Power and Knowlege by their Effects in the Conftitution of the vifible World, fo we muft judge of the Divine Benevolence in the fame Way. Our Arguments for it muft be taken from the Happinefs, and Tendencies thereto, that are obfervable in the fentient Beings, which come under our Notice.

Secondly, That the Mifery, to which we fee fentient Beings expofed, does not deftroy the Evidences for the Divine Benevolence, taken from Happinefs, unlefs we fuppofe the Mifery equal or fuperior to the Happinefs A Being who receives three Degrees of
Happinefs,

Happinefs, and but one of Mifery, is indebted for two Degrees of Happinefs to his Creator. Hence our Inquiry into the Divine Benevolence is reduced to an Inquiry into the Balance of Happinefs, or Mifery, conferred, or to be conferred, upon the whole Syftem of fentient Beings, and upon each Individual of this great Syftem. If there be Reafon to believe, that the Happinefs which each Individual has received, or will receiye, be greater than his Mifery, God will be benevolent to each Being, and infinitely fo to the whole infinite Syftem of fentient Beings ; if the Balance be infinitely in favour of each Individual, God will be infinitely benevolent to each, and infinito-infinitely to the whole Syftem.

It is no Objection to this Reafoning, that we defire pure Happinefs, and prefer it to an equal Balance of Happinefs mixed with Mifery ; or that the Confideration of Mifery, amidft the Works of an infinitely benevolent Being, gives us Perplexity. For this Difappointment of our Defires, and this Perplexity, can amount to no more than finite Evils, to be deducted from the Sum total of Happinefs ; and our Obligations to the Author of our Beings muft always be in Proportion to this remaining Sum. We may add, that as this Difappointment and Perplexity are Sources of Mifery at prefent, they may, in their future Confequences, be much ampler Sources of Happinefs ; and that this feems to be the natural Refult of fuppofing, that Happinefs prevails over Mifery.

Thirdly, Since the Qualities of Benevolence and Malevolence are as oppofite to one another, as Happinefs and Mifery, their Effects, they cannot coexift in the fame fimple unchangeable Being. If therefore we can prove God to be benevolent, from the Balance of Happinefs, Malevolence muft be intirely excluded ; and we muft fuppofe the Evils, which we fee and feel, to be owing to fome other Caufe, however unable we

may

may be to affign this Caufe, or form any Conceptions of it.

Fourthly, Since God is infinite in Power and Knowlege, *i. e.* in his natural Attributes, he muft be infinite in the moral one alfo ; *i. e.* he muft be either infinitely benevolent, or infinitely malevolent. All Arguments, therefore, which exclude infinite Malevolence, prove the infinite Benevolence of God.

Laftly, As there are fome Difficulties and Perplexities which attend the Proofs of the Divine Self-exiftence, Power, and Knowlege, fo it is natural to expect, that others, equal, greater, or lefs, fhould attend the Confideration of the divine Benevolence. But here again Revelation comes in Aid of Reafon, and affords inexpreffible Satisfaction to all earneft and well-difpofed Perfons, even in this Age, after Natural Philofophy, and the Knowlege of Natural Religion, have been fo far advanced. In the early Ages of the World, Divine Revelation muft have been, almoft, the only influencing Evidence of the moral Attributes of God.

Let us now come to the Evidences for the Divine Benevolence, and its Infinity.

Firft, then, It appears probable, that there is an Over-balance of Happinefs to the fentient Beings of this vifible World, confidered both generally and particularly. For though Diforder, Pain, and Death, do very much abound every-where in the World, yet Beauty, Order, Pleafure, Life, and Happinefs, feem to fuperabound. This is indeed impoffible to be afcertained by any exact Computation. However, it is the general Opinion of Mankind, which is fome kind of Proof of the Thing itfelf. For fince we are inclined to think, that Happinefs or Mifery prevails, according as we ourfelves are happy or miferable (which both Experience, and the foregoing Doctrine of Affociation, fhew), the general Prevalence of the Opinion of Happinefs is an Argument of the

general

general Prevalence of the Thing itfelf. Add to this, that the Recollection of Places, Perfons, &c. which we have formerly known, is in general pleafant to us. Now Recollection is only the compound Veftige of all the Pleafures and Pains, which have been affociated with the Object under Confideration. It feems therefore, that the Balance muft have been in favour of Pleafure. And yet it may be, that fmall or moderate actual Pains are in Recollection turned into Pleafures. But then this will become an Argument, in another way, for the Prevalence of the Pleafures, and particularly of thofe of Recollection, *i. e.* mental ones. It appears alfo, that the Growth and Health of the Body infer the general Prevalence of Happinefs, whilft they continue. Afterwards, the mental Happinefs may overbalance the bodily Mifery.

Secondly, If we fhould lay down, that there is juft as much Mifery as Happinefs in the World (more can fcarce be fuppofed by any one), it will follow, that if the Laws of Benevolence were to take place in a greater Degree than they do at prefent, Mifery would perpetually decreafe, and Happinefs increafe, till, at laft, by the unlimited Growth of Benevolence, the State of Mankind, in this World, would approach to a paradifiacal one. Now, this fhews that our Miferies are, in a great meafure, owing to our want of Benevolence, *i. e.* to our moral Imperfections, and to that which, according to our prefent Language, we do and muft call *Ourfelves*. It is probable therefore, that, upon a more accurate Examination and Knowlege of this Subject, we fhould find, that our Miferies arofe not only in great meafure, but intirely, from this Source, from the Imperfection of our Benevolence, whilft all that is good comes immediately from God, who muft therefore be deemed perfectly benevolent. And fince the Courfe of the World, and the Frame of our Natures, are fo ordered, and fo adapted to each other, as to enforce Benevolence upon us, this is a

farther

farther Argument of the kind Intentions of an over-ruling Providence. It follows hence, that Malevolence, and confequently Mifery, muft ever decreafe.

Thirdly, All the Faculties, corporeal and mental, of all Animals, are, as far as we can judge, contrived and adapted both to the Prefervation and Well-being of each Individual, and to the Propagation of the Species. And there is an infinite Coincidence of all the feveral fubordinate Ends with each other, fo that no one is facrificed to the reft, but they are all obtained in the utmoft Perfection by one and the fame Means. This is a ftrong Argument for all the Divine Perfections, Power, Knowlege, and Goodnefs. And it agrees with it, that final Caufes, *i. e.* natural Good, are the beft Clue for guiding the Invention in all Attempts to explain the Œconomy of Animals.

Fourthly, As Order and Happinefs prevail in general more than their Contraries, fo when any Diforder, bodily or mental, does happen, one may obferve, in general, that it produces fome Confequences, which in the End rectify the original Diforder ; and the Inftances where Diforders propagate and increafe themfelves without vifible Limits, are comparatively rare. Nay, it may be, that all the apparent ones of this kind are really otherwife ; and that they would appear otherwife, were our Views fufficiently extenfive.

Fifthly, The whole Analogy of Nature leads us from the Confideration of the infinite Power and Knowlege of God, and of his being the Creator of all Things, to regard him as our Father, Protector, Governor, and Judge. We cannot therefore but immediately hope and expect from him Benevolence, Juftice, Equity, Mercy, Bounty, Truth, and all poffible moral Perfections. Men of great Speculation and Refinement may defire to have this analogical Reafoning fupported, and fhewn to be valid; and it is very ufeful to do this as far as we are able. But it carries great Influence previoufly to fuch logical Inquiries; and even after them, though they fhould not prove fatisfactory, a Perfon of a fober and well-difpofed Mind, would ftill find himfelf affected by it in no inconfiderable Degree. Such a Perfon would be compelled, as it were, to fly to the infinite Creator of the World in his Diftreffes, with Earneftnefs, and with fome Degree of Faith, and would confider him as his Father and Protector.

Sixthly, Whenever we come to examine any particular Law, Fact, Circumftance, &c. in the natural or moral World, where we have a competent Information and Knowlege, we find that every thing which has been, was right in refpect of the Sum total of Happinefs ; and that when we fuppofe any Change to have been made, which appears, at firft Sight, likely to produce more Happinefs ; yet, after fome Reflection, the Confideration of fome other Things neceffarily influenced by fuch a Change, convinces us, that the prefent real Conftitution of Things is beft upon the Whole. Books of Natural Hiftory and Natural Philofophy, and indeed daily Obfervation, furnifh abundant Inftances of this ; fo as to fhew, that, other Things remaining the fame, every fingle Thing is the moft conducive to general Happinefs, that it can be according to the beft of our Judgments. And though our Judgments are fo fhort and imperfect, that this cannot pafs for an abfolutely conclufive Evidence, yet it is very remarkable, that thefe imperfect Judgments of ours fhould lie conftantly on the fame Side. We have no Reafon to fuppofe, that a better Acquaintance with Things would give us Caufe to alter it, but far otherwife, as appears from the univerfal Confent of all that are inquifitive and learned in thefe Matters. And if there were a few Objections in the other Scale (which I believe Philofophers will fcarce allow), they can, at the utmoft, have no more than the fame imperfect Judgment to reft upon.

Seventhly,

Seventhly, Suppofing that every fingle Thing is, other Things remaining the fame, the moft conducive to Happinefs that it can be, then the real Deficiencies that are found in refpect of Happinefs, and which, at firft Sight, appear to arife from a proportional Deficiency in the Divine Benevolence, may be equally afcribed to a Deficiency in the Divine Power or Knowlege. For this wonderful, precife, minute Adaptation of every thing to each other is fuch an Argument for Benevolence in the moft unbounded Senfe, that one would rather afcribe, whatever Diforders there are in the Univerfe, to fome neceffary Imperfection in Things themfelves, furpaffing, if poffible, the Divine Power or Knowlege to rectify; this appearing to be the weaker Side of the Dilemma.

By a fingle Thing, in the two foregoing Paragraphs, I mean one that is fo comparatively; fo that I call not only a fingle Part of an Animal (which yet is a Thing decompounded, perhaps without Limits), but a whole Syftem of Animals, when compared with other Syftems, a fingle Thing. Now, to afk whether Happinefs could not be promoted, if the whole Univerfe was changed, is abfurd; fince it is probable, from what is already offered, that the Happinefs of the Univerfe is always infinitely great; the Infinity of the Divine Power and Knowlege requiring infinite Benevolence, *i. e.* the infinite Happinefs of the Creation, if Benevolence be at all fuppofed a Divine Attribute, as has been noted before.

Eighthly, Since the apparent Defects that are in Happinefs may, according to the laft Paragraph but one, be equally referred to fome fuppofed Defect in one of the principal Attributes of Power, Knowlege, or Goodnefs, it does even from hence appear probable, that thefe Defects are not owing to any Defect in any of them, *i. e.* that there are no fuch Defects in reality, but that all our Difficulties and Perplexities in thefe Matters arife from fome Mifapprehenfion of

our

our own, in Things that infinitely furpafs our Capacities; this Suppofition, whatever Reluctance we may have to it, being far the moft eafy and confiftent of any.

Ninthly, I remarked above, that the Exclufion of infinite Malevolence from the Divine Nature, does itfelf prove the infinite Benevolence of God. Let us fee what Arguments there are for this Exclufion. Now, Malevolence always appears to us under the Idea of Imperfection and Mifery; and therefore infinite Malevolence muft appear to us to be infinitely inconfiftent with the infinite Power and Knowlege proved, in the foregoing Propofition, to belong to the Divine Nature. For the fame Reafons, infinite Benevolence, which always appears to us under the Idea of Perfection and Happinefs, feems to be the immediate and neceffary Confequence of the natural Attributes of infinite Power and Knowlege: Since the wifhing Good to others, and the endeavouring to procure it for them, is, in us, generally attended with a pleafurable State of Mind, we cannot but apply this Obfervation to the Divine Nature, in the fame manner that we do thofe made upon our own Power and Knowlege. And to deny us the Liberty of doing this in the firft Cafe, would be to take it away in the laft, and confequently to reduce us to the abfurd and impoffible Suppofition, that there is no Power or Knowlege in the Univerfe fuperior to our own.

Tenthly, Malevolence may alfo be excluded in the following manner: If we fuppofe a Syftem of Beings to be placed in fuch a Situation, as that they may occafion either much Happinefs, or much Mifery, to each other, it will follow, that the Scale will turn more and more perpetually in favour of the Production of Happinefs: For the Happinefs which *A* receives from *B*, will lead him by Affociation to love *B*, and to wifh and endeavour *B*'s Happinefs, in return: *B* will therefore have a Motive, arifing from his De-

fire

fire of his own Happinefs, to continue his good Offices to *A*: Whereas the Mifery that *A* receives from *B*, will lead him to hate *B*, and to deter him from farther Injuries. This muft neceffarily be the Cafe, if we only admit, that every intelligent Being is actuated by the View of private Happinefs, and that his Memory and Trains of Ideas are of the fame kind with ours. Now, the firft Suppofition cannot be doubted, and to exclude the laft would be to forbid all Reafoning upon other intelligent Beings : Not to mention, that thefe two Suppofitions cannot, perhaps, be feparated, fince the Defire of Happinefs feems in us to be the mere Refult of Affociation, as above explained ; and Affociation itfelf the general Law, according to which the intellectual World is framed and conducted. Now this different Tendency of Benevolence and Malevolence, *viz.* of the firft to augment itfelf without Limits, of the latter to deftroy itfelf ultimately, appears to be a very ftrong Argument for the infinite Benevolence of God. For, according to this, Benevolence muft arife in all Beings, other things being alike, in proportion to their Experience of Good and Evil, and to their Knowlege of Caufes and Effects. One cannot doubt, therefore, but that infinite Benevolence is infeparably connected with the fupreme Intelligence : All the higher Orders of intellectual Beings have, probably, higher Degrees of it, in the general, and accidental Differences, as we call them, being allowed for ; and therefore the higheft Intelligence, the infinite Mind, muft have it in an infinite Degree ; and as every Degree of Benevolence becomes a proportional Source of Happinefs to the Benevolent, fo the infinite Benevolence of the Supreme Being is the fame thing with his infinite Perfection and Happinefs. In like manner, the Contemplation of the infinite Perfection and Happinefs of God is an inexhauftible Treafure of Happinefs to all his benevolent and devout Creatures ; and He is infinitely benevolent to them,

in

in giving them fuch Faculties, as, by their natural
Workings, make them take Pleafure in this Contemplation of his infinite Happinefs.

Eleventhly, A Reafon may be given not only confiftent with the infinite Benevolence of God, but even
arifing from it, why fome Doubts and Perplexities
fhould always attend our Inquiries into it, and Arguments for it, provided only that we fuppofe our prefent Frame to remain fuch as it is: For it appears
from the Frame of our Natures, as I fhall fhew hereafter, and was hinted in the laft Paragraph, that our
ultimate Happinefs muft confift in the pure and perfect Love of God ; and yet, that, admitting the prefent Frame of our Natures, our Love of God can
never be made pure and perfect without a previous
Fear of him. In like manner, we do, and muft,
upon our Entrance into this World, begin with the
Idolatry of external things, and, as we advance in it,
proceed to the Idolatry of ourfelves ; which yet are
infuperable Bars to a complete Happinefs in the Love
of God. Now, our Doubts concerning the Divine
Benevolence teach us to fet a much higher Value upon
it, when we have found it, or begin to hope that we
have ; our Fears enhance our Hopes, and nafcent
Love ; and all together mortify our Love for the
World, and our interefted Concern for ourfelves, and
particularly that Part of it which feeks a complete
Demonftration of the Divine Benevolence, and its Infinity, from a mere felfifh Motive ; till at laft we arrive at an intire Annihilation of ourfelves, and an abfolute Acquiefcence and Complacence in the Will of
God, which afford the only full Anfwer to all our
Doubts, and the only radical Cure for all our Evils
and Perplexities.

Twelfthly, It is probable, that many good Reafons
might be given, why the Frame of our Natures fhould
be as it is at prefent, all confiftent with, or even flowing from, the Benevolence of the Divine Nature ; and
yet

yet ſtill that ſome Suppoſition muſt be made, in which the ſame Difficulty would again recur, only in a leſs Degree. However, if we ſuppoſe this to be the Caſe, the Difficulty of reconciling Evil with the Goodneſs of God might be diminiſhed without Limits, in the ſame manner as mathematical Quantities are exhauſted by the Terms of an infinite Series. It agrees with this, that as long as any Evil remains, this Difficulty, which is one Species of Evil, muſt remain in a proportional Degree ; for it would be inconfiſtent to ſuppoſe any one Species to vaniſh before the reſt. However, if God be infinitely benevolent, they muſt all decreaſe without Limits, and conſequently this Difficulty, as juſt now remarked. In the mean time, we muſt not extend this Suppoſition of Evil, and of the Difficulty of accounting for it, to the whole Creation: We are no Judges of ſuch Matters ; and the Scriptures may, perhaps, be thought rather to intimate, that the Mixture of Good and Evil is peculiar to us, than common to the Univerſe, in the Account which they give of the Sin of our firſt Parents, in eating of the Tree of the Knowlege of Good and Evil.

Thirteenthly, Some Light may, perhaps, be caſt upon this moſt difficult Subject of the Origin of Evil, if we lay down the ſeveral Notions of infinite Goodneſs, which offer themſelves to the Mind, and compare them with one another, and with the Appearances of Things. Let us ſuppoſe then, that we may call that infinite Benevolence, which makes either,

1. Each Individual infinitely happy always. Or,

2. Each Individual always finitely happy, without any Mixture of Miſery, and infinitely ſo in its Progreſs through infinite Time. Or,

3. Each Individual infinitely happy, upon the Balance, in its Progreſs through infinite Time, but with a Mixture of Miſery. Or,

4. Each Individual finitely happy in the Courſe of its Exiſtence, whatever that be, but with a Mixture

of

of Mifery as before ; and the Univerfe infinitely happy upon the Balance.   Or,

5. Some Individuals happy and fome miferable upon the Balance, finitely or infinitely, and yet fo that there fhall be an infinite Overplus of Happinefs in the Univerfe.

All poffible Notions of infinite Benevolence may, I think, be reduced to fome one of thefe Five ; and there are fome Perfons who think, that the Infinity of the Divine Benevolence may be vindicated upon the laft and loweft of thefe Suppofitions.   Let us confider each particularly.

The Firft, *viz.* That each Individual fhould be always happy infinitely, is not only contrary to the Fact at firft View, but alfo feems impoffible, as being inconfiftent with the finite Nature of the Creatures. We reject it therefore as foon as propofed, and do not expect, that the Divine Benevolence fhould be proved infinite in this Senfe.   And yet were each Individual always finitely happy according to the next Suppofition, we fhould always be inclined to afk why he had not a greater finite Degree of Happinefs conferred upon him, notwithftanding the manifeft Abfurdity of fuch a Queftion, which muft thus recur again and again for ever.

The Second Suppofition is that which is moft natural as a mere Suppofition.   We think that pure Benevolence can give nothing but pure Happinefs, and infinite Benevolence muft give infinite Happinefs.   But it is evidently contrary to the Fact, to what we fee and feel, and therefore we are forced; though with great Unwillingnefs, to give up this Notion alfo.   It may, however, be fome Comfort to us, that if we could keep this, the fame Temper of Mind which makes us prefer it to the next, would fuggeft the Queftion, *Why not more Happinefs?* again and again for ever, as juft now remarked ; fo that we fhould not be fatisfied with it, unlefs our Tempers were alfo altered.   This, indeed,

indeed, would be the Cafe, becaufe, as I obferved before, all the Speciefes of Evil and Imperfection muft
vanifh together. But then this Confideration, by
fhewing that the endlefs Recurrency of the Queftion
above-mentioned, and the concomitant Diffatisfaction,
are Imperfections in us, fhews at the fame time, that
they are no proper Foundation for an Objection to the
Divine Benevolence.

The Third Suppofition is poffible in itfelf ; but then
it can neither be fupported, nor contradicted, by the
Facts. If there appear an unlimited Tendency towards the Prevalence of Happinefs over Mifery, this
may be fome Prefumption for it. But all our Judgments, and even Conjectures, are confined within a
fhort Diftance from the prefent Moment. A Divine
Revelation might give us an Affurance of it. And
it feems, that this Suppofition is, upon an impartial
View, equally eligible and fatisfactory with the foregoing. We eftimate every Quantity by the Balance,
by what remains after a Subtraction of its Oppofite ;
and if this be an allowed authentic Method, in the
feveral kinds of Happinefs, why not in Happinefs confidered in the Abftract ? But we muft not conclude,
that this is the genuine Notion of the Divine Benevolence. There may perhaps be fome Prefumptions
for it, both from Reafon and Scripture ; but I think
none, in the prefent Infancy of Knowlege, fufficient
to ground an Opinion upon. However, there feem
to be no poffible Prefumptions againft it ; and this
may encourage us to fearch both the Book of God's
Word, and that of his Works, for Matter of Comfort
to ourfelves, and Arguments whereby to reprefent his
moral Character in the moft amiable Light.

The Fourth Suppofition is one to which many
thinking, ferious, benevolent, and pious Perfons are
now much inclined. All the Arguments here ufed
for the Divine Benevolence, and its Infinity, feem to
infer it, or, if they favour any of the other Suppofitions,

fitions, to favour the Third, which may be faid to include this Fourth. There are alfo many Declarations in the Scriptures concerning the Goodnefs, Bounty, and Mercy of God to all his Creatures, which can fcarce be interpreted in a lower Senfe.

As to the Fifth Suppofition, therefore, it follows, that it is oppofed by the preceding Arguments, *i. e.* by the Marks and Footfteps of God's Goodnefs in the Creation, and by the Declarations of the Scriptures to the fame Purpofe. However, there are a few Paffages of Scripture, from whence fome very learned and devout Men ftill continue to draw this Fifth Suppofition ; they do alfo endeavour to make this Suppofition confiftent with the Divine Benevolence, by making a farther Suppofition, *viz.* that of Philofophical Liberty, as it is called in thefe Obfervations, or the Power of doing different Things, the previous Circumftances remaining the fame. And it is highly incumbent upon us to be humble and diffident in the Judgments which we make upon Matters of fuch Importance to us, and fo much above our Capacities. However, it does not appear to many other learned and devout Perfons, either that the Scripture Paffages alluded to are a proper Foundation for this Opinion, or that of Philofophical Free-will, though allowed, can afford a fufficient Vindication of the Divine Attributes.

Thefe Obfervations feem naturally to occur, upon confidering thefe five Suppofitions, and comparing them with one another, and with the Word and Works of God. But there is alfo another Way of confidering the Third Suppofition, which, as it is a Prefumption for it, though not an Evidence, agreeably to what was intimated above, I fhall here offer to the Reader.

Firft then, Affociation has an evident Tendency to convert a State of fuperior Happinefs, mixed with inferior Mifery, into one of pure Happinefs, into a paradifiacal one, as has been fhewn in the firft Part of
thefe

thefe Obfervations, *Prop.* 14. *Cor.* 9. Or, in other Words, Affociation tends to convert the State of the Third Suppofition into that of the Second.

Secondly, When any fmall Pain is introductory to a great Pleafure, it is very common for us, without any exprefs Reflection on the Power of Affociation, to confider this Pain as coalefcing with the fubfequent Pleafure, into a pure Pleafure, equal to the Difference between them ; and, in fome Cafes, the fmall Pain itfelf puts on the Nature of a Pleafure, of which we fee many Inftances in the daily Occurrences of Life, where Labour, Wants, Pains, become actually plea-fant to us, by a Luftre borrowed from the Pleafures to be obtained by them. And this happens moft parti-cularly, when we recollect the Events of our paft Lives, or view thofe of others. It is to be obferved alfo, that this Power of uniting different and oppofite Senfations into one increafes as we advance in Life, and in our intellectual Capacities ; and that, ftrictly fpeaking, no Senfation can be a Monad, inafmuch as the moft fimple are infinitely divifible in refpect of Time, and Extent of Impreffion. Thofe, therefore, which are efteemed the pureft Pleafures, may con-tain fome Parts which afford Pain ; and, converfely, were our Capacities fufficiently enlarged, any Senfa-tions connected to each other in the way of Caufe and Effect, would be efteemed one Senfation, and be de-nominated a pure Pleafure, if Pleafure prevailed upon the Whole.

Thirdly, As the Enlargement of our Capacities enables us thus to take off the Edge of our Pains, by uniting them with the fubfequent fuperior Pleafures, fo it confers upon us more and more the Power of enjoying our future Pleafures by Anticipation, by extending the Limits of the prefent Time, *i. e.* of that Time in which we have an Intereft. For the prefent Time, in a metaphyfical Senfe, is an indivifible Mo-ment ; but the prefent Time, in a practical Senfe, is

a

a finite Quantity of various Magnitudes, according to our Capacities, and, beginning from an indivisible Moment in all, seems to grow on indefinitely in Beings who are ever progressive in their Passage through an eternal Life.

Suppose now a Being of great Benevolence, and enlarged intellectual Capacities, to look down upon Mankind passing through a Mixture of Pleasures and Pains, in which, however, there is a Balance of Pleasure, to a greater Balance of Pleasure perpetually, and, at last, to a State of pure and exalted Pleasure made so by Association : It is evident, that his Benevolence to Man will be the Source of pure Pleasure to him from his Power of uniting the opposite Sensations, and of great present Pleasure from his Power of Anticipation. And the more we suppose the Benevolence and Capacities of this Being enlarged, the greater and more pure will his sympathetic Pleasure be, which arises from the Contemplation of Man. It follows therefore, that, in the Eye of an infinite Mind, Creatures conducted, as we think, according to the Third of the foregoing Suppositions, are conducted according to the Second, and these according to the First ; or, in other Words, that the First, Second, and Third, of the foregoing Suppositions, are all one and the same in the Eye of God. For all Time, whether past, present, or future, is present Time in the Eye of God, and all Ideas coalesce into one to him ; and this one is infinite Happiness, without any Mixture of Misery, *viz.* by the infinite Prepollence of Happiness above Misery, so as to annihilate it ; and this merely by considering Time as it ought to be considered in Strictness, *i. e.* as a relative Thing, belonging to Beings of finite Capacities, and varying with them, but which is infinitely absorbed in the pure Eternity of God. Now the Appearance of Things to the Eye of an infinite Being must be called their real Appearance in all Propriety. And tho' it be impossible

fible for us to arrive at this true Way of conceiving
Things perfectly, or directly, yet we shall approach
nearer and nearer to it, as our intellectual Capacities,
Benevolence, Devotion, and the Purity of our Happinefs, depending thereon, advance : And we seem
able, at present, to exprefs the real Appearance, in
the fame way as Mathematicians do ultimate Ratios,
to which Quantities ever tend, and never arrive, and
in a Language which bears a fufficient Analogy to
other Expreffions that are admitted. So that now (if
we allow the Third Suppofition) we may in fome
fort venture to maintain that, which at firft Sight
feemed not only contrary to obvious Experience, but
even impoffible, *viz.* that all Individuals are actually
and always infinitely happy. And thus all Difficulties
relating to the Divine Attributes will be taken away ;
God will be infinitely powerful, knowing, and good,
in the moft abfolute Senfe, if we confider Things as
they appear to him. And furely, in all Vindications
of the Divine Attributes, this ought to be the Light
in which we are to confider Things. We ought to
fuppofe ourfelves in the Centre of the Syftem, and to
try, as far as we are able, to reduce all apparent Re-
trogradations to real Progreffions. It is alfo the greateft
Satisfaction to the Mind thus to approximate to its
firft Conceptions concerning the Divine Goodnefs, and
to anfwer that endlefs Queftion, *Why not lefs Mifery,
and more Happinefs?* in a Language which is plainly
analogous to all other authentic Language, though it
cannot yet be felt by us on account of our prefent Imperfection, and of the Mixture of our Good with Evil.
Farther, it is remarkable, that neither the Fourth nor
Fifth Suppofitions can pafs into the Third, and that
the Fifth will always have a Mixture of Mifery in it,
as long as the *Principium Individuationis* is kept up.
And if this be taken away, the Suppofitions themfelves are deftroyed, and we intirely loft.

I have

I have been the longer in confidering the Divine Benevolence, on account of its Importance both to our Duty and Happinefs. There feems to be abundant Foundation for Faith, Hope, Refignation, Gratitude, Love. We cannot doubt but the Judge and Father of all the World will conduct himfelf according to Juftice, Mercy, and Goodnefs. However, I defire to repeat once more, that we do not feem to have fufficient Evidence to determine abfolutely for any of the Three laft Suppofitions. We cannot indeed but wifh for the Third, both from Self-intereft and Benevolence ; and its Coincidence with the Firft and Second, in the Manner juft now explained, appears to be fome Prefumption in favour of it.

PROP. 5.

There is but öne Being infinite in Power, Knowlege, and Goodnefs ; i. e. but one God.

FOR, if we fuppofe more than one, it is plain, fince the Attributes of infinite Power, Knowlege, and Goodnefs, include all poffible Perfection, that they muft be intirely alike to each other, without the leaft poffible Variation. They will therefore intirely coalefce in our Idea, *i. e.* be one to us. Since they fill all Time and Space, ⌈and are all independent, omnipotent, omnifcient, and infinitely benevolent,⌉ their Ideas cannot be feparated, but will have a numerical, as well as a generical, Identity. When we fuppofe other Beings generically the fame, and yet numerically different, we do at the fame time fuppofe, that they exift in different Portions of Time or Space ; which Circumftances cannot have Place in refpect of the fuppofed Plurality of infinite Beings. We conclude, therefore, that there is but one infinite Being, or God.

The Unity of the Godhead is alfo proved by Revelation, confidered as fupported by Evidences which
have

have no Dependence on Natural Religion. And as this Proof of the Unity is of great Importance even now, fo it was of far greater in antient Times, when the World was over-run with Polytheifm. And it is highly probable to me, that as the firft Notions of the Divine Power, Knowlege, and Goodnefs, which Mankind had, were derived from Revelation, fo much more were their Notions of the Unity of the Godhead.

P R O P. 6.

God is a Spiritual, or Immaterial Being.

SInce God is the Caufe of all Things, as appears from the foregoing Propofitions, he muft be the Caufe of all the Motions in the material World. If therefore God be not an immaterial Being, then Matter may be the Caufe of all the Motions in the material World. But Matter is a mere paffive Thing, of whofe very Effence it is, to be endued with a *Vis inertiæ*; for this *Vis inertiæ* prefents itfelf immediately in all our Obfervations and Experiments upon it, and is infeparable from it, even in Idea. When we confider any of the active Powers of Matter, as they are called, fuch as Gravitation, Magnetifm, Electricity, or the Attractions and Repulfions, which take place in the Cohefions and Separations of the fmall Particles of natural Bodies, and endeavour to refolve thefe into fome higher and fimpler Principles, the *Vis inertiæ* is always the common Bafis upon which we endeavour to erect our Solutions. For the active Party, which is fuppofed to generate the Gravitation, Magnetifm, &c. in the paffive one, muft have a Motion, and a *Vis inertiæ*, whereby it endeavours to perfift in that Motion, elfe it could have no Power; and, by Parity of Reafon, the paffive Party muft have a *Vis inertiæ* alfo, elfe it could neither make Refiftance to the active Party, nor imprefs Motion on foreign

5   Bodies.

Bodies. Let us proceed therefore as far as we pleafe in a Series of fucceffive Solutions, we fhall always find a *Vis inertiæ* inherent in Matter, and a Motion derived to it from fome foreign Caufe. If this Caufe be fuppofed Matter always, we fhall be carried on to an infinite Series of Solutions, in each of which the fame precife Difficulty will recur, without our at all approaching to the Removal of it. Whence, according to the mathematical Doctrine of ultimate Ratios, not even an infinite Series, were that poffible in this Cafe, could remove it. We muft therefore ftop fomewhere, and fuppofe the requifite Motion to be imparted to the fubtle Matter, by fomething, which is not Matter; *i. e.* fince God is the ultimate Author of all Motion, we muft fuppofe him to be immaterial.

The fame Thing may be inferred thus : If there be nothing but Matter in the World, then the Motions and Modifications of Matter muft be the Caufe of Intelligence. But even finite Intelligences, fuch as that of Man, for Inftance, fhew fo much Skill and Defign in their Conftitution, as alfo to fhew, that their Caufes, *i. e.* the appropriated Motions and Modifications of Matter, muft be appointed and conducted by a prior and fuperior Intelligence. The infinite Intelligence of God therefore, proved in the Third Propofition, fince it refults from the Motions and Modifications of Matter, requires another infinite Intelligence to direct thefe Motions, which is abfurd. God is therefore proved to be immaterial from his infinite Intelligence.

It is true, indeed, that our Senfes convey nothing to us but Impreffions from Matter; and, therefore, that we can have no exprefs original Ideas of any Things, befides material ones ; whence we are led to conclude, that there is nothing but Matter in the Univerfe. However, this is evidently a Prejudice drawn from our Situation, and an Argument taken merely from our
Igno-

Ignorance, and the Narrownefs of our Faculties. Since therefore, on the other hand, mere Matter appears quite unable to account for the fimpleft and moft ordinary Phænomena, we muft either fuppofe an immaterial Subftance, or elfe fuppofe, that Matter has fome Powers and Properties different and fuperior to thofe which appear. But this laft Suppofition is the fame in effect as the firft, though, on account of the Imperfection of Language, it feems to be different.

At the fame time it ought to be obferved, that if a Perfon acknowleges the infinite Power, Knowlege, and Goodnefs of God, the Proofs of which are prior to, and quite independent on, that of his Immateriality, this Perfon acknowleges all that is of practical Importance. But then, on the other hand, it is alfo to be obferved, That the Opinion of the Materiality of the Divine Nature has a Tendency to leffen our Reverence for it, and, confequently, to invalidate the Proofs of the Divine Power, Knowlege, and Goodnefs.

How far the Scriptures deliver the Immateriality of God in a ftrict philofophical Senfe, may perhaps be doubted, as their Style is in general popular. However, there is a ftrong Prefumption, that they teach this Doctrine, fince the popular Senfe and natural Interpretation of many fublime Paffages concerning the Divine Nature infer its Immateriality. There is therefore fome Evidence for this Attribute, to be taken from Revelation, confidered as ftanding upon its own diftinct Proofs.

COROLLARY. Since God is immaterial, Matter muft be one of the Works of his infinite Power. In the mean time, this does not feem to me to exclude the Poffibility of its having exifted from all Eternity. But then, neither have we, on the other hand, any Reafon to conclude, that the whole material Syftem, or any Part of it, could not have been created in Time. It is, perhaps, moft probable, *i. e.* fuitable to the

Divine

Divine Attributes, that infinite material Worlds have exifted from all Eternity. But it becomes us, in all thefe Things, to diftruft our own Reafonings and Conjectures to the utmoft.

PROP. 7.

God is an eternal and omniprefent Being.

GOD's Eternity, *à parte ante,* appears from the Second Propofition, in which his Independency is proved ; and the Eternity, *à parte poft,* is infeparably connected with that *à parte ante.* Both are alfo included in the Idea of infinite Power, or of infinite Knowlege ; and, indeed, when we fay, that God is eternal *à parte ante,* and *à parte poft,* we do, we can, mean no more, than to fay, that his Power and Knowlege extend to all Times. For we muft not conceive, or affirm, that he exifts in Succeffion, as finite Beings do ; through whofe Imaginations, or Intellects, Trains of Ideas pafs. All Time, as was faid before, is equally prefent to him, though in a Manner of which we cannot form the leaft Conception.

In like manner, by God's Omniprefence, or Ubiquity, we muft be underftood to mean, that his Power and Knowlege extend to all Places. For as Time, and its Exponent, the Succeffion of Ideas, is a Thing that relates merely to finite Beings ; fo Space and Place relate, in their original Senfe, to material ones only ; nor can we perceive any Relation that they bear to immaterial ones, unlefs as far as we feign a Refemblance between material and immaterial Beings, which is furely an inconfiftent Fiction. We cannot, therefore, difcover any Relation which Space or Place bear to the Divine Exiftence. It is a fufficient Acknowlegement both of God's Eternity and Omniprefence, that we believe his Power and Knowlege to extend to all Times and Places, though we be intirely at a Lofs how to conceive or exprefs the Manner of
.this

this infinite Extent of thefe Attributes. And there is a remarkable Agreement between innumerable Paffages of the Scriptures, and this practical Notion of God's Eternity and Omniprefence.

PROP. 8.

God is an immutable Being.

THIS follows from the Infinity of the Divine Power, Knowlege, and Goodnefs, *i. e.* from his infinite Perfection. For if the Divine Nature admitted of any Variation, it would alfo admit of different Kinds and Degrees of Perfection, and therefore could not always be infinitely perfect. This is the moft abftracted and philofophical Way of confidering the Divine Immutability. In a popular and practical Senfe, it excludes all that which we call inconftant, arbitrary, and capricious, in finite Beings; and becomes a fure Foundation for Hope, Truft, and Refignation. We may confider ourfelves as being at all Times, and in all Places, equally under the Direction and Protection of the fame infinite Power, Knowlege, and Goodnefs, which are fo confpicuous in the Frame of the vifible World.

PROP. 9.

God is a free Being.

THE Authors who have treated upon the Divine Nature and Attributes, ufually afcribe Liberty or Freedom to God, and fuppofe it to be of a Nature analogous to that Free-will which they afcribe to Man. But it appears to me, that neither the philofophical, nor popular Liberty, as they are defined below in the Fourteenth and Fifteenth Propofitions, can be at all applied to God. Thus, we can neither apply to God the Power of doing different Things, the

previous

previous Circumftances remaining the fame, nor a voluntary generated Power of introducing Ideas, or performing Motions; nor any thing analogous to either of thefe Powers, without the groffeft Anthropomorphitifm.

But Liberty is alfo ufed in another Senfe, *viz.* as the Negation of, and the Freedom from, a fuperior, compelling Force; and in this Senfe it may and muft be applied to the Deity; his Independency and Infinity including it. And in this Senfe it is contrary to the Notion of thofe Heathens, who fuppofed even God himfelf fubject to Fate.

Upon the Whole, if by Liberty, Freedom, or Freewill, be meant any thing great or glorious, God certainly has it; if otherwife, certainly not. Thus, if it mean Freedom from a fuperior compelling Caufe of any kind, as in the laft Paragraph, God certainly has it, he being the Caufe of Caufes, the univerfal, the one only Caufe. If it mean, that God could have made an Univerfe lefs perfect than that which actually exifts, he certainly has it not, becaufe this would make God lefs perfect alfo. And here it feems to be a Thing eftablifhed amongft Writers on this Matter, to maintain, that God is fubject to a moral Neceffity, and to the Perfection of his own Nature; which Expreffions, however, are to be confidered as nothing more than particular Ways of afferting the Infinity of the Divine Power, Knowlege, and Goodnefs. If it be faid, that God might have made a different Univerfe, equally perfect with that which now exifts, and that his Freedom confifts in this, the Anfwer feems to be, that we are intirely loft here, in the Infinities of Infinities, *&c. ad infinitum,* which always have exifted, and always will exift, with refpect to Kind, Degree, and every poffible Mode of Exiftence. One cannot, in the leaft, prefume either to deny or affirm this Kind of Freedom of God, fince the abfolute Perfection of God feems to imply both intire Uniformity,

and

and infinite Variety in his Works. We can here only
submit, and refer all to God's infinite Knowlege and
Perfection.

PROP. 10.

*Holiness, Justice, Veracity, Mercy, and all other
moral Perfections, ought to be ascribed to God
in an infinite Degree.*

I Have in the last Four Propositions treated of such
Attributes of the Divine Nature, as have a more
immediate Connexion with the natural ones of Independency, infinite Power, and infinite Knowlege. I
come now to those, that are deducible from, and ex-
planatory of the moral one, *viz.* of the Divine Benevolence.

The chief of these seem to be Holiness, Justice,
Veracity, and Mercy. These are ascribed to all earthly
Superiors, to whom we pay Respect and Love, and
therefore must belong, in the popular and practical
Sense, to him, who is the highest Object of Reverence
and Affection. Let us see how each is to be defined,
and what Relation they bear to Benevolence.

First, then, Holiness may be defined by moral
Purity and Rectitude. And these, when applied to
the Deity, can only denote the Rectitude of his
Actions towards his Creatures. If therefore he be
benevolent to all his Creatures, he cannot but have
moral Purity and Rectitude.

The same Thing may be considered thus: All
moral Turpitude in us proceeds from our selfish Fears
or Desires, made more irregular and impetuous through
our Ignorance, and other natural Imperfections. But
none of these Causes can take place with respect to the
Deity; he must therefore be free from all moral Turpitude.

Justice is that which gives to every one according
to his Deserts, at least as much as his good Deserts

require,

require, and not more than is fuitable to his evil ones. But this is evidently included in the Divine Benevolence, even according to the Fifth of the Suppofitions, mentioned *Prop.* 4. by thofe who defend that Suppofition, and, according to the Third and Fourth, by the common Confent of all, and the plain Reafon of the Thing. No Man can deferve more from his Creator than a Balance of Happinefs proportional to his Merit, which is the Fourth Suppofition ; and confequently the Divine Benevolence, according to the Third Suppofition, in which the Balance of Happinefs is infinite, includes ftrict Juftice, and infinitely more. And all this will hold equally, whether we define Defert in the popular, practical Way, by the three meritorious Principles of Action, Benevolence, Piety, and the moral Senfe, alone ; or by thefe, with the additional Suppofition of philofophical Liberty, if we embrace either the Third or Fourth Suppofitions. Philofophical Liberty is indeed neceffary for the Vindication of the Divine Benevolence and Juftice, according to the Fifth Suppofition, in the Opinion of moft of thofe who hold this Suppofition. But then they efteem it to be alfo fufficient for this Purpofe, and confequently maintain the Divine Juftice, into which we are now inquiring.

It may alfo be reckoned a Part of Juftice not to let Offenders go unpunifhed, or efcape with too flight a Degree of Punifhment ; the Order and Happinefs of the World, *i. e.* Benevolence, requiring, that frail Men fhould be deterred from Vice by the dreadful Examples of others, and mifchievous Perfons difarmed. However, this does not at all hinder, but that the fame Perfons, who are thus punifhed and difarmed, may afterwards receive a Balance of Happinefs, finite or infinite. And thus punitive Juftice may be reconciled to Bounty and Benevolence, according to the Third or Fourth Suppofitions.

Veracity

Veracity in Men is, the Obfervance of Truth, and Fidelity in all their Declarations and Promifes to others; and the Obligation to it arifes from its great Ufefulnefs in all the Intercourfes of Mankind with each other, and the extreme Mifchiefs which Fiction and Fraud occafion in the World. And it cannot be doubted, but that the Divine Benevolence, according to any of the Suppofitions above made, includes what is analogous to this moral Quality in Men.

In like manner, it cannot be doubted but that the Divine Benevolence includes Mercy, or all that Tendernefs to Offenders which the Order and Happinefs of the World will permit. Or, if the Fifth Suppofition made concerning the Divine Benevolence be found to exclude it, this will be a ftrong Argument for rejecting that Suppofition.

I have here fhewn in what manner we may vindicate thefe Attributes of the Divine Nature, from the Whole of Things, *i. e.* the Courfe of Events, both as they now appear in the prefent State, and as we expect they will appear in a future one. But God has alfo given us fufficient general Evidences of thefe his relative moral Attributes, from the prefent State alone; at the fame time that, if we extend our Views no farther, fome Difficulties and Perplexities will arife in refpect of certain Particulars. I will mention fome both of the Evidences and Difficulties in regard to each of thefe four Attributes of Holinefs, Juftice, Veracity, and Mercy.

It might be expected, that God, if he thought fit to inftitute a Religion by Revelation, fhould inftitute one in which Holinefs and moral Purity fhould be eminently injoined, and moral Turpitude prohibited in the moft awful Manner. And it is a remarkable Coincidence of Things, and Evidence of the Divine Purity, that the Jewifh and Chriftian Religions fhould both have this internal Proof, and the moft cogent external ones in their Favour. Whilft, on the contrary,

the

the impure Pagan Religions had all the external Marks of Fiction and Forgery.

The Voice of Confcience, or the moral Senfe, within a Man, however implanted or generated, injoining moral Rectitude, and forbidding moral Turpitude, and accordingly acquitting or condemning, rewarding or punifhing, bears Witnefs, in like manner, to the moral Rectitude of that univerfal Caufe from whom it muft proceed ultimately.

At the fame time there are Difficulties in Revealed Religion, and Deviations in the moral Senfe, much contrary to what we feem to expect from our firft Notions of the Divine Rectitude.

Since God is juft, we may expect that Virtue will be the Source of Happinefs, Vice that of Mifery, even in this World. And fo we find it in general ; at the fame time that there are many particular Exceptions of both Kinds,

The Veracity of God feems to engage him to take care, that all thofe Intimations which may be reckoned Calls and Cautions of Nature, fhould give us right Information ; alfo, that all Perfons who have the apparent Credentials of being fent from him, *i. e.* thofe of performing Miracles, fhould be in Truth fo fent. And all Things concur, in general, to verify both thefe Pofitions. There are, however, feveral particular Exceptions, as is well known.

Mercy requires, that fuch Perfons as repent and amend, fhould have Opportunities of frefh Trial, and of retrieving, afforded them. And this is remarkably fo in the general. Moft Men are tried again and again before their Healths, Fortunes, Credit, *&c.* become irrecoverable. And yet there are fome Inftances of extraordinary Severity upon the very firft Offence.

Now, it may be obferved of all thefe Inftances, that the general Tenor is fufficient to eftablifh the Attributes here afferted ; it being reafonable to expect, from our Ignorance of the prefent State, and much

more

more from that of the future one, that great Difficulties and Exceptions muſt occur to us. And as theſe unſearchable Judgments of God ſerve to humble us, and make us ſenſible of our Ignorance, they even concur with the general Tenor.

P R O P. 11.

God is to be conſidered by us, not only as our Creator, but alſo as our Governor, Judge, and Father.

THAT God is our Creator, is evident from the Three firſt Propoſitions; in which his Independency and infinite Power are eſtabliſhed, from the Neceſſity which we finite and dependent Beings have of an infinite and independent Creator: And this Appellation belongs to Him alone.

The Three following Appellations are firſt applied to earthly Superiors; and therefore belong to God only in an analogical Senſe. It is, however, a Senſe of infinite Importance to be acknowleged and regarded by us: Let us, therefore, ſee in what manner Analogies drawn from Language, and from the Phænomena of Nature, lead us to call God our Governor, Judge, and Father.

As God is our Creator, he has, according to the Analogy of Language, a Right to diſpoſe of us, to govern and judge us, and is alſo our Father in a much higher Senſe than our natural Parents, who are only occaſional Cauſes, as it were, of our Exiſtence. In like manner, his infinite Power and Knowlege intitle Him to be our Governor, and his infinite Benevolence to be our Father: The Intimations alſo which he gives of his Will, both in his Word and Works, and the Rewards and Puniſhments which he beſtows in the way of natural Conſequences, as we term it, all ſhew, that he is our Governor and Judge. And

as

as the moral Attributes afferted in the laft Propofition
may be deduced from thefe Appellations of Governor,
Judge, and Father, eftablifhed on independent Principles, fo they, when proved by their own peculiar
Evidences, infer thefe Appellations : All which may
be fummed up in this general Pofition, that the
Events of Life, and the Ufe of Language, beget fuch
Trains of Ideas and Affociations in us, as that we cannot but afcribe all morally good Qualities, and all ve-
nerable and amiable Appellations, to the Deity ; at
the fame time that we perceive the Meaning of our
Expreffions not to be ftrictly the fame, as when they
are applied to Men ; but an analogical Meaning,
however a higher, more pure, and more perfect one.
The Juftnefs of this Application is farther confirmed
by the common Confent of all Ages and Nations,
and by the whole Tenor of the Scriptures.

If it be faid, that fince this Method of fpeaking is
not ftrictly literal and true, but merely popular and
anthropomorphitical, it ought to be rejected ; I anfwer, that even the Attributes of Independency, Omnipotence, Omnifcience, and infinite Benevolence,
though the moft pure, exalted, and philofophical Appellations, to which we can attain, fall infinitely fhort
of the Truth, of reprefenting the Deity as he is, but
are mere popular and anthropomorphitical Expreffions.   And the fame might ftill be faid for ever of
higher and more pure Expreffions, could we arrive
at them : They would ever be infinitely deficient, and
unworthy of God.   But then it appears from the preceding Propofitions, and other Writings of a like Nature, that, if we will confider the Phænomena of the
World, and argue from them fufficiently, we muft
needs fee and acknowlege, that there is an infinite
Being, and that Power, Knowlege, and Goodnefs,
are his Character. We cannot get rid of this internal
Feeling and Conviction, but by refufing to confider
the Subject, and to purfue the Train of Reafoning,
which

which our own Faculties, or the preceding Inquiries of others, will lead us to. God is not to be esteemed an unreal Being, or destitute of all Character, because he is infinite and incomprehensible, or because we have not adequate Phrases whereby to denote his Existence and Attributes. On the contrary, his infinite Nature seems strongly to argue, that Existence, Power, Knowlege, and Goodness, do really and properly belong to him alone; and that what we call so here on Earth, in our first and literal Senses, are mere Shadows and Figures of the true Realities. And it would be in vain to bid us reject this Language, since it must recur again and again from the Frame of our Natures, if we pursue the Subject. In like manner, the relative moral Attributes of Holiness, Justice, Veracity, Mercy, &c. and the relative moral Appellations of Governor, Judge, and Father, &c. are inseparably connected with the Use of Language, and the Course and Constitution of the visible World. We see that things have happened, and must believe, that they will hereafter happen (*i. e.* in the general, and allowing for particular Exceptions, as above remarked), after such a manner as these Attributes and Appellations intimate to us : They are, consequently, a convenient and highly useful Method of ranging and explaining past Events, and predicting future ones, and therefore may be used for this Purpose; nay, they must be so used, since the Events of Life thus ranged, explained, and predicted by them, do necessarily suggest them to us, and impress upon us this their Use, admitting only the real Existence of God, and his infinite Power, Knowlege, and Goodness; which, as was just now shewn, cannot but be admitted, if Men will think sufficiently on the Subject. However, since the Use of these relative moral Attributes and Appellations is popular, and attended with particular Exceptions; whereas that of the Attributes of infinite Power, Knowlege, and Goodness, is more

phi-

philofophical and extenfive, it will be proper to bear this in Mind; and where there appears to be any Oppofition between the popular and philofophical Language, to interpret that in Subordination to this.

COROLLARY. The Doctrine of Providence, general and particular, may be confidered as a Confequence from the foregoing Attributes and Appellations of the Divine Nature. By general Providence, I mean the adjufting all Events to the greateft Good of the Whole; by particular, the adjufting all to the greateft Good of each Individual; and, confequently, by both together, the adjufting the greateft Good of the Whole, and of each Individual, to each other; fo that both fhall fall exactly upon the fame Point. However difficult this may feem, I take it to be the genuine Confequence of the foregoing Propofitions. Infinite Power, Knowlege, and Goodnefs, muft make our moft kind and merciful Father both able and willing to effect this: It does, therefore, actually take place, though we cannot fee it. However, that there are many Marks both of general and particular Providence, as thus explained, is fufficiently evident, and acknowleged by all: Both thefe appear alfo to be afferted in the Scriptures.

The following Obfervation affords a ftrong Evidence for a particular Providence. When a Perfon furveys the Events of his paft Life, he may find many, which have happened much contrary to natural Expectation, and his then Defires, which yet appear extremely beneficial and defirable at the now prefent Time, as alfo to have proceeded from natural Caufes then unknown to him. Now, we may conclude from hence, that God conceals the Tendencies and Refults of the Courfe of Nature at the then prefent Time, left we fhould truft in that, and forfake him; but difcovers them afterwards with their Harmonies and Ufes, that we may fee his Goodnefs, Knowlege, and Power, in them, and fo truft *him* in

future

future Perplexities. It is analogous to this, that the Scripture Prophecies are inexplicable before the Event, and often sufficiently clear afterwards.

PROP. 12.

The Manner of Reasoning here used, in respect of the Course and Constitution of Nature, has a Tendency to beget in us Love and Reverence towards God, and Obedience to his Will: Or, in other Words, There is a Religion of Nature properly so called.

NATURAL Religion appears to be used in different Senses by different Writers: However, they are all, I think, reducible to the Three that follow, and will all be found to coincide ultimately, though they may appear different at first View.

The First Sense, in which Natural Religion may be used, is that of this Proposition; in which it is put for that Love and Reverence towards God, and Obedience to his Will, which the Light of Nature, or the Consideration of the Works of God, injoins. In this Sense it is most properly opposed to, and contradistinguished from, Revealed Religion, or those Affections and Actions towards God, which the Scripture, or the Word of God, injoins.

Secondly, Natural Religion may be defined such a Regulation of the Affections and Actions as the moral Sense requires: For the moral Sense is Part of the Light of Nature, and of our natural Faculties, whether it be considered as an Instinct, or as the generated Result of external Impressions and our natural Frame taken together, according to what is delivered in the first Part of these Observations; and this moral Sense approves and commands, or disapproves and forbids, certain Dispositions of Mind, and bodily Actions flowing therefrom. It is also called the Law of first In-
scription

scription by many Perfons, and under that Term diftinguifhed from the Law of Revelation, which is fuppofed pofterior to it in Order of Time. Hence the fame Perfons confider the moral Senfe, or Law of firft Infcription, as the Foundation of Natural Religion : And, indeed, moft Perfons either exprefly adopt, or implicitly refer to, this Definition of Natural Religion in their Writings and Difcourfes. The heathen World, not having the immediate Light of Revelation, are fuppofed to have had nothing more than the mere Light of Nature, and mere Natural Religion ; and they feem to have been chiefly directed by the Senfe of what was fit, right, and proper, upon the Occafion, *i. e.* by the moral Senfe. Natural Religion may therefore, according to this way of confidering it, be properly defined by the moral Senfe.

Thirdly, Natural Religion may be defined by rational Self intereft; *i. e.* it may be called fuch a Regulation of our Affections and Actions, as will procure for us our *Summum Bonum*, or greateft poffible Happinefs. If we fuppofe the Inquiries of the Antients concerning the *Summum Bonum* to have been of a religious and moral Nature, then will this Definition be fuitable to their Notions. However, it has a very important Ufe, *viz.* that of compelling us to be attentive, i npartial, and earneft in the Inquiry.

I will now proceed, firft, to prove the Propofition, or to deduce Love and Reverence to God, and Obedience to his Will, from the preceding Method of Reafoning concerning the Courfe and Conftitution of Nature; and, fecondly, to fhew the perfect Agreement of all thefe Three Definitions of Natural Religion with each other.

Now it is, at once evident, that the Confideration of the infinite Power, Knowlege, and Goodnefs of God, of his Holinefs, Juftice, Veracity, and Mercy, and of his being our Creator, Governor, Judge, and Father, muft infpire us witn the higheft Love and

3   Re-

Reverence for him, and beget in us that Tendency to comply with his Will, which, according to the proper Use of Language, is called a Senfe of *Duty*, *Obligation*, of what we *ought* to do. It is evident alfo, that the Will of God muft be determined by his Attributes and Appellations. He muft there-fore will, that we fhould apply to him, as we do to earthly Superiors of the fame Character, puri-fying, however, and exalting our Affections to the utmoft; that we fhould be merciful, holy, juft, *&c.* in Imitation of him, and becaufe this is to concur with him in his great Defign of making all his Crea-tures happy; and laftly, that we fhould fo ufe the Pleafures of Senfe, and the Enjoyments of this World, as not to hurt ourfelves or others. There is therefore a Courfe of Action regarding God, our Neighbour, and ourfelves, plainly injoined by the Light of Na-ture ; or, in the Words of the Propofition, there is a Religion of Nature properly fo called.

I come, in the next Place, to fhew the Agreement of the Second and Third Definitions of Natural Reli-gion with the Firft, or with that of the Propofition.

Now, that Compliance with the moral Senfe coin-cides with Obedience to the Will of God, needs no Proof, it being the firft and immediate Dictate of the moral Senfe, that it is fit, right, and our neceffary Duty, to obey God, as foon as he is difcovered with the amiable and awful Attributes and Appellations above afcribed to him. There is, therefore, an intire Agreement between the Firft and Second Definitions. It may appear alfo, that the Firft Rule of Duty is neceffary to perfect the Second. For the moral Senfe, as will appear from the preceding Hiftory of its Rife and Growth, muft be vague and uncertain, and vary according to the various Circumftances of Life. But the moral Character of God, as delivered in the fore-going Propofitions, affords a plain Rule of Life,

applicable

applicable and precife in the various Circumftances of it. When, therefore, Obedience to the Will of God is eftablifhed by the moral Senfe, it does, in Return, become a Regulator to this, determine its Uncertainties, and reconcile its Inconfiftencies. And, agreeably to this, we may obferve, that the Perfection of the moral Senfe is, in general, proportional to the Perfection of our Notions of the Divine Nature; and that the Idolatry of the Heathens, and their Ignorance of the true God, muft have produced an utter Perverfion and Corruption of their moral Senfe, agreeably to the Declarations of the Scriptures ; which is a remarkable Coincidence of Reafon with Revelation.

In like manner, it needs no Proof, that rational Self-intereft, and Obedience to the Will of God, are the fame Thing. Our only Hope and Security, here and hereafter, muft be in our Obedience to him, who has all Power and all Knowlege. And thus the Firft and Third Definitions are found to be perfectly coincident. The Second and Third, therefore, *i. e.* the whole Three, are coincident alfo.

This Coincidence might be confirmed by numberlefs Inftances, were we to confider and compare together the Dictates of the moral Character of God, of our own moral Senfe, properly directed, and of rational Self-intereft in the feveral particular Circumftances of Life. But this would be to anticipate what I have to fay in the Third Chapter of this Second Part concerning the Rule of Life.

P R O P. 13.

Natural Religion receives great Light and Confirmation from Revealed.

IT feems to be the Opinion of fome Perfons, that Revealed Religion is intirely founded upon Natural ; fo that unlefs Natural Religion be firft eftablifhed upon its own proper Evidences, we cannot
proceed

proceed at all to the Proof of Revealed. If this were fo, Revealed Religion could not caft any Light or Evidence upon Natural, but what it had before received from it ; and confequently, this Propofition would be built upon that falfe Way of Reafoning which is called arguing in a Circle. But there are certainly independent Evidences for Revealed Religion, as well as for Natural ; they both receive Light and Confirmation from each other ; and this mutual Confirmation is a ftill farther Evidence for both. I will give a fhort Account of all thefe Particulars, that the Propofition may the more fully appear.

Firft, Natural Religion has independent Evidences. This has been the Bufinefs of the foregoing Propofitions, and particularly of the laft, to fhew. And indeed, it is acknowleged by all, unlefs they be Atheifts or Sceptics. We are certainly able to infer the Exiftence and Attributes of God, with our Relation and Duty to him, from the mere Confideration of Natural Phænomena, in the fame Manner as we do any Conclufions in Natural Philofophy. And though our Evidence here may not perhaps be demonftrative, it is certainly probable in the higheft Degree.

Secondly, Revealed Religion has alfo independent Evidences. For, if we allow the Miracles mentioned in the Old and New Teftaments, the Genuinenefs and Accomplifhment of the Prophecies contained therein, and the moral Charaĉters of Chrift, the Prophets and Apoftles, it will be impoffible not to pay the greateft Regard to the Doĉtrines and Precepts which they deliver, *i. e.* to Revealed Religion. We do, and we muft always give Credit to Perfons much fuperior to ourfelves in natural and moral Endowments. Thefe Endowments ftrike us with Awe and Reverence, engage our Attention, humble us, and put us into a teachable, flexible Difpofition. And I appeal to all thofe, who do really believe the Miracles and moral Charaĉters of Chrift, the Prophets and Apoftles, and the Accomplifhment of the Prophecies delivered by them, whether they do not immediately find themfelves in this humble, teachable Difpofition of Mind, upon confidering thefe Credentials cf a Divine Miffion, and that exclufively of all other Confiderations. As to thofe who do not fuppofe Chrift, the Prophets and Apoftles, to have had thefe Credentials, they can fcarce be proper Judges, what would be the genuine Confequence of a State of Mind, of a Belief, which they have not. However, one may appeal even to them, provided they will only fuppofe thefe Credentials true for a Moment, in order to fee what would then follow. And it is a ftrong Argument of the Juftnefs of this Reafoning, that all thofe who reject Revealed Religion, do alfo reject the Credentials, *i. e.* the Truth of the Scripture Hiftory. Revealed Religion is therefore built upon the Truth of the Scripture Hiftory ; *i. e.* upon the external Evidences commonly called hiftorical and prophetical. But thefe Evidences are to be tried in the fame Manner as the Evidences for any other Hiftory, and have no more Connexion with Natural Religion, and its Evidences, fuch, for Inftance, as thofe delivered in this Chapter, than the Evidences for the *Greek* or *Roman* Hiftory. So that Revealed Religion has Evidences, and thofe of the ftrongeft Kind, intirely independent on Natural Religion.

Thirdly, Natural Religion receives much Light and Confirmation from Revealed, agreeably to the Propofition here to be proved. This follows both becaufe Revealed Religion, now fhewn to have its independent Evidences, teaches the fame Doctrines concerning God, as I have remarked already in feveral Places, and delivers the fame Precepts to Man, in the general, as natural ; and becaufe thefe very independent Evidences, *viz.* the Miracles and moral Characters of Chrift, the Prophets and Apoftles, and the Accomplifhment of their Prophecies, have a direct

an d

and immediate Tendency to beget in us a deep Senſe and Convi&ion of a ſuperior Power, and of his Providence and moral Government over the World. So that if a Man ſhould either be ignorant of the Chain of Reaſoning by which the Exiſtence and Attributes of God and Natural Religion are proved from the Phænomena of the World, or ſhould, from ſome Depravation of Mind, intelle&ual or moral, be diſpoſed to call in queſtion this Chain of Reaſoning, in Whole or in Part ; he muſt however come to the ſame Concluſions, from the mere Force of the hiſtorical and prophetical Evidences in favour of the Scriptures. And this is a Thing of the utmoſt Importance to Mankind, there being many who are incapable of purſuing this Chain of Reaſoning, many who, though capable, are diſinclined to it, many who from their Vices have a contrary Inclination, and ſome who, ſeeing the Perplexity and Obſcurity that attend ſome ſubordinate Parts of this Reaſoning, are diſpoſed to doubt about the Whole. For though ſomething of the ſame Kind holds in reſpe& of the hiſtorical and prophetical Evidences for the Truth of the Scriptures, eſpecially of the laſt, yet, in general, theſe are more level to the Capacities of the inferior Ranks amongſt Mankind, and more ſimple and ſtriking, than the independent Evidences for Natural Religion ; and if they were but equally convincing, they would, however, make the Evidence double upon the Whole. Not to mention, that it is an inexpreſſible Satisfa&ion to the beſt Men, and the ableſt Philoſophers, thoſe who have the moſt intire Convi&ion from natural Reaſon, to have this new and diſtin& Support for ſuch important Truths. It may be added as an Argument in favour of the Reaſoning of this Paragraph, *i. e.* of the Propoſition here to be proved, to thoſe who believe Revealed Religion, that God has thought fit to teach Mankind Natural Religion chiefly by means of Revealed.

Fourthly,

Fourthly, Revealed Religion receives great Light and Confirmation from Natural. For if we suppose a Person to be first instructed in the Doctrines and Precepts of Natural Religion, and to be intirely convinced of their Truth and Fitness from the mere Light of Reason, and then to have the Scriptures communicated to him, the Conformity of these with his previous Notions would be a strong Evidence in their Favour, *i. e.* in favour of the Miracles, Prophecies, and those Doctrines which are peculiar to Revealed Religion. When, farther, he came to perceive, that many of the Writers of the Sacred Books lived when the Truths of Natural Religion were unknown to the rest of the World, and that many also were of so low a Rank in Life, that they cannot be supposed to have known even so much as the rest of the World did, by natural Means, he will be strongly inclined to allow them that supernatural Light which they claim, *i. e.* to allow their Divine Authority.

Lastly, The mutual Light and Confirmation which Natural and Revealed Religion cast upon each other, and the Analogy which there is between their proper Evidences, and even that between the several Obscurities and Perplexities that attend each, are a new Argument in favour of both, considered as united together, and making one Rule of Life, and the Charter of a happy Immortality. For Resemblance, Agreement, and Harmony of the Parts, are the peculiar Characteristics of Truth, as Inconsistency and Self-contradiction are of Fiction and Falshood.

P R O P.

PROP. 14.

Religion presupposes Free-will in the popular and practical Sense; i. e. it presupposes a voluntary Power over our Affections and Actions.

FOR Religion being the Regulation of our Affections and Actions according to the Will of God, it presupposes, that after this Will is made known to us, and we, in consequence thereof, become desirous of complying with it, a sufficient Power of complying with it should be put into our Hands. Thus, for Instance, since Religion commands us to love God and our Neighbour, it presupposes that we have the Power of generating these Affections in ourselves, by introducing the proper generating Causes, and making the proper Associations, *i. e.* by Meditation, religious Conversation, reading practical Books of Religion, and Prayer. Since Religion requires of us to perform beneficent Actions, and to abstain from injurious ones, also to abstain from all those Self-indulgences which would be hurtful to ourselves, it presupposes, either that we have a Power of so doing, or at least a Power of generating such Dispositions of Mind, as will enable us so to do. Farther, it presupposes that we have a Power of making perpetual Improvement in virtuous Affections and Actions, since this also is required of us by it. Still farther, since Religion requires of a Man this Regulation of his Affections and Actions, and since the Powers hitherto mentioned are all grounded upon a sufficient Desire thus to regulate himself, it must presuppose a Power of generating this sufficient Desire, and so on till we come to something which the Man is already possessed of, as Part of his mental Frame, either conferred in a supernatural Way, or acquired in the usual Course of Nature. For Religion, in requiring the Powers above-mentioned, requires also whatever pre-

vious

vious Powers are neceffary to the actual Exertion of thefe Powers. But all thefe Powers, of whatever Order they are, the laft excepted, are thofe Powers over our Affections and Actions, which I have, in the foregoing Part of this Work, endeavoured to derive from Affociation, and fhewn to be the fame with thofe which are commonly called voluntary Powers. It follows, therefore, that Religion requires voluntary Powers over our Affections and Actions, or Free-will in the popular and practical Senfe.

This may be illuftrated by the Confideration of the State of Madmen, Idiots, Children, and Brutes, in refpect of Religion. For as they are all efteemed to be incapable of Religion, and exempted from the Obligation thereof, fo the Reafon of this in all is evidently, that they are deftitute of the proper voluntary Powers over their Affections and Actions ; the Affociations requifite thereto having never been formed in Idiots, Children, and Brutes, and being confounded and deftroyed in Madmen. For fuppofe the Child to be grown up, and the Madman to recover his Senfes, *i. e.* fuppofe the Affociations requifite for the voluntary Powers to be generated or reftored, and Religion will claim them as its proper Subjects.

In like manner, it may be obferved, that when any Action is commended or blamed, this is always done upon Suppofition, that the Action under Confideration was the Effect of voluntary Powers. Thus, when a Man commits an Action otherwife blameable, through Inattention, Ignorance, or Difeafe, he is excufed on account of its being involuntary ; unlefs the Inattention, Ignorance, or Difeafe, were themfelves voluntary, and then the Blame remains. But Commendation and Blame are Ideas that belong to Religion : It appears therefore, that voluntary Powers muft belong to it alfo.

I afferted above, that Religion not only requires and prefuppofes the common voluntary Powers, by which

we

we perform and forbear Actions, and new-model our Affections, but also whatever else, voluntary or involuntary, is neceffary for the actual Exertion of thefe Powers. And the Connexion between thefe Points feems to be immediate and undeniable ; to require any Thing, muft be to require all that is neceffary for that Thing. And yet, fince all Men do not act up to the Precepts of Religion, it feems undeniable, on the other hand, that fome want fomething that is neceffary, immediately or mediately, for the actual Exertion of the proper voluntary Powers over their Affections and Actions. Now, I fee no way of extricating ourfelves from this Difficulty, but by fuppofing, that thofe who want this one neceffary Thing at prefent, will, however, obtain it hereafter, and that they who fhall obtain it at any diftant future Time, may be faid to have obtained it already, in the Eye of him to whom paft, prefent, and future, are all prefent, *who quickeneth the Dead, and calleth the Things that be not as though they were.* For that the Suppofition of Free-will, in the philofophical Senfe, cannot folve this Difficulty, will appear, I think, in the next Propofition.

COROLLARY. It may be reckoned fome Confirmation of Religion, that the voluntary Powers which it requires, according to this Propofition, are an evident Fact, and alfo that they are deducible from the Frame of our Natures, *i. e.* from our original Faculties, and the Law of Affociation, taken together. For thus Religion may be faid to harmonize with Obfervation, and with the Nature of Man, its Subject.

P R O P.

PROP. 15.

Religion does not prefuppose Free-will in the phi-
lofophical Senfe ; i. e. It does not prefuppofe a
Power of doing different Things, the previous
Circumftances remaining the fame.

FOR, Firft, It has been fhewn, in the foregoing
Part of this Work, that we do not, in Fact, ever
exert any fuch Power in the important Actions of our
Lives, or the ftrong Workings of our Affections, all
thefe being evidently determinable by the previous
Circumftances. There are therefore no Actions or
Affections left, except trifling and evanefcent ones, in
which Religion can prefuppofe philofophical Free-will,
or Liberty ; and even here the Evidence for it is
merely an *argumentum ab ignorantiâ.* But if Religion
requires philofophical Liberty at all, it muft require
it chiefly in the moft important Actions and Affections.
It does not therefore require it at all. We cannot fuppofe Religion to be at Variance with common Obfervation, and the Frame of our Natures.

Secondly, Some Reafons have been given already,
in the firft Part of this Work, and more will be added
in the next Propofition, to fhew that philofophical
Liberty cannot take place in Man, but is an Impoffibility. It is therefore impoffible, that Religion fhould
require it.

Thirdly, It appears from the Courfe of Reafoning
ufed under the foregoing Propofition, that all which
Religion does require and prefuppofe, is, firft, a fufficient Defire, Hope, Fear, Self-intereft, or other fuch-
like Motive, and then fufficient voluntary Powers,
whereby to regulate our Affections and Actions agreeably to the Will of God. But philofophical Liberty, or
the Power of doing different Things, the previous
Circumftances remaining the fame, is fo far from being

ing required, in order to our obtaining any of thefe Requifites, that it is inconfiftent with them. For the fufficient Defire, *&c.* unlefs it be given by God in a fupernatural Way, is of a factitious Nature, and follows the previous Circumftances with a rigorous Exactnefs; in like manner the voluntary Powers are all generated according to the Law of Affociation, which Law operates in a mechanical, neceffary Way, and admits of no Variations, while the Circumftances remain the fame ; all which is, I prefume, fufficiently evident to thofe who have well confidered the foregoing Part of this Work. Thefe Requifites are therefore inconfiftent with philofophical Liberty, inafmuch as this implies, that though there be a Defire fufficient to caufe the Exertion of the Will, this Exertion may or may not follow ; alfo, that though the voluntary Powers depending on this Exertion be completely generated by Affociation, they may or may not follow it in Fact. This Suppofition is indeed abfurd at firft Sight ; however, if it be admitted for a Moment, in order to fee what would follow, it is manifeft, that the Man will be rendered lefs able to comply with the Will of God thereby, and that it will not add to, but take away from, the Requifites propofed by Religion. Philofophical Liberty does not therefore help us to folve the Difficulty mentioned under the laft Propofition, but, on the contrary, increafes it.

If it fhould be faid, that we are not to fuppofe the Defire fufficient, and the voluntary Powers complete, and then farther to fuppofe, that thefe may or may not take Effect, but only to fuppofe Defire in general, fufficient or infufficient, and voluntary Powers in general, complete or incomplete, and that thus it will not be unreafonable to fuppofe, that they may or may not take Effect ; whence the manifeft Abfurdity mentioned in the laft Paragraph will be removed ; I anfwer, that this is to defert the Hypothefis of philofophical Liberty, the previous Circumftances being

fupſuppoſed different, that ſo their Conſequences may be different alſo. If any particular Degree of Deſire or voluntary Power be fixed upon, and all the other concurring Circumſtances of Body and Mind fixed likewiſe, *i. e.* if the previous Circumſtances be rigorouſly determinate, which is the Suppoſition of philoſophical Liberty, this one fixed, determinate Degree of Deſire, or voluntary Power, cannot have the two oppoſite Epithets of ſufficient and inſufficient, or of complete and incomplete, both predicated of it with Truth, define Sufficiency or Completeneſs as you pleaſe. Philoſophical Liberty does not therefore allow us to ſuppoſe Deſire or voluntary Power in general, in order that they either may or may not take Effect.

Fourthly, It will appear, that Religion does not preſuppoſe philoſophical Liberty, if we enter upon the Examination of thoſe Arguments which are commonly brought to ſhew that it does. Theſe are, that unleſs philoſophical Liberty be admitted, there will be no Foundation for Commendation or Blame, and conſequently no Difference between Virtue and Vice; that all Puniſhment for Actions, uſually called vicious, will be unjuſt; and that God will be the Author of ſuch Actions, which it is impious to ſuppoſe; inaſmuch as the Notion of popular Liberty is not ſufficient to obviate theſe Difficulties. Now, to this I anſwer, that there are two different Methods of Speaking, and, as it were, two different Languages, uſed upon theſe Subjects; the one popular, and, when applied to God, anthropomorphitical; the other philoſophical; and that the Notion of popular Liberty is ſufficient to obviate theſe Difficulties, while we keep to the popular Language alone; alſo, that the philoſophical Language does of itſelf obviate theſe Difficulties, while we keep to it alone; but that, if we mix theſe Languages, then, and not till then, inſuperable Difficulties will ariſe, as might well be expected. Let us conſider each of theſe Poſitions particularly.

Firſt then, I ſay that the Suppoſition of popular
Liberty

Liberty is fufficient to obviate the forementioned Difficulties, whilft we keep to the popular Language alone. For, in the popular Language, a Man is commended and blamed merely for the right or wrong Ufe of his voluntary Powers ; the firft is called Virtue, the laft Vice ; and Rewards and Punifhments are faid to be refpectively due to them. Thus, when a Man, having an Opportunity to do a beneficent Action, exerts an Act of Will, and, in Confequence thereof does it, he is commended for it ; it is called a Virtue, or a right Ufe of his voluntary Powers, and is faid to deferve a Reward ; whereas, had he, in like Circumftances, done a malevolent Action, he would have been blamed for it ; it would have been called a wrong Ufe of his voluntary Powers, or a Vice ; and a Punifhment inflicted upon him, in Confequence hereof, would have been faid to be juft. This is a mere Hiftory of the Fact, and a Narration of the Method in which the Words here confidered acquire their proper Senfes ; and I appeal to the general Tenor of Writings and Difcourfes for the Support of what is here afferted. If no voluntary Action be exerted, the Words Commendation, Right Ufe, Virtue, Reward, on one hand, alfo the Words, Blame, Wrong Ufe, Vice, Punifhment, on the other, become intirely unapplicable. If there be, and the Motive be good, fuppofe Piety or Benevolence, the firft Set of Words take place ; if the Motive be bad, the laft. Men, in the common Ufe of Language, never confider whether the Agent had it in his Power to have done otherwife, the previous Circumftances remaining the fame ; they only require, that he fhould have done a beneficent Action, from a benevolent Intention. If they find this, they will apply the Words, Commendation, Right Ufe, *&c.* And the fame holds in refpect of injurious Actions, and malevolent Intentions. The Agent will, in this Cafe, be blamed, and faid to be juftly punifhed, without any farther Inquiry. Sometimes, indeed, they do inquire farther, *viz.* into the

Original

Original of thefe Intentions. But then this comes to the fame Thing at laft ; for if thefe Intentions were generated voluntarily, it enhances the Commendation or Blame due to them ; if, in great meafure, involuntarily, abates it. Popular Liberty, or voluntary Powers, do therefore afford fufficient Foundation for Commendation and Blame, for the Difference between Virtue and Vice, and for the Juftice of punifhing Vice according to the popular Language. Where it is to be remarked, that whatever will juftify Punifhments inflicted by Men, will juftify thofe inflicted by God in like Circumftances, fince Juftice is afcribed to God only in a popular and anthropomorphitical Senfe.

And as popular Liberty fuffices for the forementioned Purpofes, whilft we ufe the popular Language, fo it vindicates God from the Charge of being the Author of Sin, according to the fame Language. For, according to this, all voluntary Actions are afcribed to Men, not to God ; but Sin, or Vice, always prefuppofes an Exertion of a voluntary Power, according to the popular Language ; therefore Sin muft be afcribed to Man, and not to God, as long as we continue to fpeak the popular Language.

Secondly, I fay, that if we keep to the philofophical Language alone, it will obviate all Difficulties, and enable us to talk confiftently and clearly upon thefe Subjects. For, according to this, Virtue and Vice are to Actions, what fecondary Qualities are to natural Bodies ; *i. e.* only Ways of expreffing the Relation which they bear to Happinefs and Mifery, juft as the fecondary Qualities of Bodies are only Modifications of the primary ones. And the fame may be faid of all the other Words belonging to the moral Senfe. Hence it follows, that, according to the philofophical Language, we are to confider all the moral Appellations of Actions as only denoting their Relation to natural Good and Evil, and that moral Good and Evil are only Compofitions and Decompofitions

of

of natural. There is, however, a Difference between moral Good and moral Evil, becaufe they are different and oppofite Compofitions; they may alfo be attended with different and oppofite Compofitions, from the Frame of our Natures, and Circumftances of our Lives, fuch as Commendation and Blame.

And as Juftice in God is, by the fame Language, exalted into Benevolence, he may inflict Punifhment, *i. e.* another Species of natural Evil, juftly, provided it be confiftent with Benevolence, *i. e.* with a Balance of Happinefs. Man may alfo inflict Punifhment juftly, provided he does it according to fome Definition of Juftice amongft Men, previoufly fettled and allowed, fuppofe Compliance with the Will of God, the Laws of Society, the greater Good of the Whole, *&c.*

Farther, Since all the Actions of Man proceed ultimately from God, the one univerfal Caufe, we muft, according to this Language, annihilate Self, and afcribe all to God. But then, fince Vice, Sin, *&c.* are only Modifications and Compofitions of natural Evil, according to the fame Language, this will only be to afcribe natural Evil to him; and, if the Balance of natural Good be infinite, then even this natural Evil will be abforbed and annihilated by it.

It may a little illuftrate what is here delivered, to remark, that as we fhould not fay of a fuperior Being, whofe Sight could penetrate to the ultimate Conftitution of Bodies, that he diftinguifhed Colours, but rather, that he diftinguifhed thofe Modifications of Matter which produce the Appearances of Colours in us, fo we ought not to afcribe our fecondary Ideas of Virtue and Vice to fuperior Intelligences, and much lefs to the fupreme.

Thirdly, I fay, that if we mix thefe two Languages, many Difficulties and Abfurdities muft enfue from this previous Abfurdity. Thus, if, retaining the popular Notions of moral Good and Evil, we fuppofe God, according

according to the philofophical Language, to be benevolent only, *i. e.* to regard only natural Good and
Evil, or to be the Author of all Actions, the Confequence will be impious   If we adhere to the philofophical Notions of Virtue and Vice, we muft not retain
the popular Notion of God's Juftice, inafmuch as Punifhment will then be unjuft; as it will alfo be, if we
join the popular Notion of God's Juftice with the philofophical one, of his being the Author of all Actions.
Laftly, if we allow Man to confider himfelf as the
Author of his own Actions, he muft alfo confider
Virtue and Vice according to the popular Notions, and
conceive of God as endued with the popular Attribute
of Juftice, in order to be incited to Virtue, and deterred from Vice; whereas, could Man really annihilate himfelf, and refer all to God, perfect Love would
caft out Fear, he would immediately become Partaker
of the Divine Nature, and, being one with God, would
fee him to be pure Benevolence and Love, and all that
he has made to be good.

The following Remark may perhaps contribute to
illuftrate this Matter. Virtue and Vice, Merit and
Demerit, Reward and Punifhment, are applied to voluntary Actions only, as before-mentioned. Hence
they are efteemed unapplicable to involuntary ones.
But involuntary Actions are neceffary by a Neceffity
ab extra, which is generally feen; and becaufe the
Neceffity *ab intra,* which caufes voluntary Actions,
is feldom feen, thefe are fuppofed not to be neceffary.
Hence not neceffary and neceffary, are put for. voluntary and involuntary, refpectively; and moral Appellations fuppofed peculiar to the firft, *i. e.* not neceffary; inconfiftent with the laft, *i. e.* neceffary. Hence,
when we come to difcover our Miftake, and to find,
that voluntary Actions are neceffary, an Inconfiftency
arifes; we apply moral Appellations to them as voluntary from a primary Affociation, deny thefe Appellations of them on account of their new Denomination

of

of neceffary, and a fecondary and tralatitious Affociation. Here then, if we can either perfift in our Miftake,
and ftill fuppofe voluntary Actions not to be neceffary,
or, finding this Miftake, can however perfift to apply
moral Appellations to fuch neceffary Actions as are
voluntary, from the primary Affociation; or, laftly, not being able to withftand the Force of the fecondary Affociation, whereby moral Appellations are
denied of neceffary Actions, voluntary as well as involuntary, can perceive that moral Good and Evil
are only Compofitions of Natural, *i. e.* if we can either
fee the whole Truth, or fhut our Eyes againft that
Part that offends us; no Difficulty will arife.

Philofophical Liberty is alfo fuppofed by fome neceffary, in order to folve the Origin of Evil, and to
juftify the Eternity of Punifhment; and the obviating
of thefe Difficulties is brought as an Argument in Support of it. Now here I obferve,

Firft, That the Origin of Evil may be made confiftent with the Benevolence of God, by fuppofing
that every Creature has a Balance of Happinefs; and,
confequently, fince this is a Suppofition highly probable, there feems to be little Need of philofophical
Liberty for this Purpofe.

Secondly, That, fince this Suppofition is highly probable, the Eternity of Punifhment is highly improbable; and, confequently, that philofophical Liberty
may be needlefs here alfo.

Thirdly, That philofophical Liberty will not folve
the Origin of Evil. The Method of Reafoning ufed
here is fome fuch as this. If Man have not philofophical Liberty, but always does the fame Thing,
where the previous Circumftances are the fame, then
all his Actions are to be referred to God; confequently,
if he have philofophical Liberty, all his Actions need
not be referred to God; he is an independent Creature
in fome Things, and is himfelf alone chargeable with
fome of his Actions. Let Man act wrong in thefe in-

I

dependent

dependent Cafes, and the Evil which follows will be chargeable upon Man, and not God; *i. e.* the Origin of Evil will be accounted for. But here it is to be obferved, that there are fome Evils, or Sufferings, which cannot be fuppofed to arife from the Abufe of Free-will in the Creature that fuffers, as in the Pains which happen to Children juft born, and to Brutes. Thefe Evils are not therefore chargeable upon *them.* If, therefore, they be chargeable upon Free-will, it muft be the Free-will of fome other Creature. But this is as great a Difficulty, as that which it is brought to folve ; and cannot be folved but by fuppofing that God gives a Balance of Happinefs to *A,* for what he fuffers from *B.* Now this Suppofition, in its full Extent, will folve the firft Difficulty, and make the Hypothefis of Free-will intirely unneceffary, as obferved above. But, befides this, it is to be confidered, that fince Free-will is thus the Occafion of introducing Evil into the World, the reftlefs, felfifh, objecting Creature will afk why he has Free-will, fince it is not this, but Happinefs, which *he* defires, and hoped from the Divine Benevolence, the Attribute now to be vindicated. He that produces any Caufe, does, in Effect, produce the Thing caufed. To give a Being a Power of making itfelf miferable, if this Being ufe that Power, is juft the fame Thing, in him who has infinite Power and Knowlege, as directly making him miferable ; and appears to be no otherwife confiftent with Benevolence to that Being, than upon Suppofition, that fuperior Happinefs is conferred upon him afterwards. Now this removes the Difficulty in the Cafe of Neceffity, as well as of Free-will, in the Eye of Reafon, of an infinite Being ; and clafhes lefs and lefs without Limits with the Imagination, as we advance in Intellect, Difintereftednefs, and abfolute Refignation to God.

If it be faid, that God could not but beftow Freewill upon his Creatures, I anfwer, that this is *gratis dictum,*

dictum, there not being the leaft Appearance of Evidence for it ; alfo, that it is making God fubject to a Neceffity fuperior to himfelf, which would be to raife a greater Difficulty than it folves. And, upon the Whole, we may conclude, that the Suppofition of Free-will, or Liberty, in the philofophical Senfe, does not at all help us to account for the Origin of Evil.

Fourthly, Since Free-will cannot account for finite Evil, much lefs can it account for infinite, *i. e.* for the Eternity of Punifhment. And indeed many, who receive Free-will, do, however, fee its Infufficiency for this Purpofe, and, in Confequence thereof, believe that the Punifhments of a future State will not be eternal. It is true, indeed, that the Arguments againft the Eternity of Punifhment are fhorter, ftronger, and clearer, upon the Suppofition of Neceffity, of God's being the real, ultimate Author of all Actions, than upon the Suppofition of Free-will. But then this feems, if all Things be duly confidered, to be rather a Prefumption in favour of the Doctrine of Neceffity, than otherwife.

The Invention and Application of the Hypothefis of Free-will, for the Vindication of the Divine Benevolence, has probably arifen from the Application of what paffes in human Affairs, in too ftrict a manner, to the Relation between the Creator and his Creatures ; *i. e.* to an Anthropomorphitifm of too grofs a Kind. Thus the Actions of a Son are free, in refpect of his Father ; *i. e.* though the Father can, and does influence the Son in many Things, yet the Son's Actions depend upon many Circumftances, Impreffions, Affociations, &c. in which the Father has no Concern. It will therefore be a fufficient Vindication of the Father's Benevolence to the Son, if he has taken care, that the Son fuffers nothing from the Things over which the Father has Power. What Evils happen to the Son, from Quarters where the Son is free in re-

fpect

spect of his Father, *i. e.* uninfluenced by him, these are no-ways to be referred to the Father. Now, it is very natural for humble and pious Men, in considering the Sins and Miseries of Mankind, to suppose that we have some such Powers independent of God; and that all the Evil, which happens to each Person, is to be derived from these independent Powers. But then this Notion should not be hastily and blindly embraced and maintained, without an Examination of the Fact, and of the Consistency of such a Notion with Piety, in other respects. The First of these Points I have already considered in the foregoing Part of this Work; the Last I shall now consider in the following Proposition.

PROP. 16.

The natural Attributes of God, or his infinite Power and Knowlege, exclude the Possibility of Free-will in the philosophical Sense.

FOR, to suppose that Man has a Power independent of God, is to suppose, that God's Power does not extend to all Things, *i. e.* is not infinite. If it be said, that the Power itself depends upon God, but the Exertion of it upon Man, the same Difficulty will recur; since the Exertion does not depend upon God, there will be something produced in the World, which is not the Effect of his Power; *i. e.* his Power will not extend to all Things, consequently not be infinite. And the same Thing holds, if we refine farther, and proceed to the Exertion of the Exertion, *&c.* If this depend upon Man, God's Power will be limited by Man's; if upon God, we return to the Hypothesis of Necessity, and of God's being the Author of all Things. However, the simplest and clearest Way is to suppose, that Power, and the Exertion of Power,

are

3

are one and the fame Thing ; for Power is never known but by its actual Exertion, *i. e.* is no Power till it be exerted. If, indeed, we fay that Man's Actions depend both upon God and himfelf, this feems at firft Sight to folve the Difficulty. Since they depend upon God, his Power may be infinite ; fince they depend on Man, they may be afcribed to *him.* But then the Thing in Man on which they depend, call it what you pleafe, muft either depend upon God or not ; if it does, Neceffity returns ; if not, God's infinite Power is infringed. And the fame Thing will hold, as it appears to me, in any other Way of ftating this Matter.

Again, to fuppofe that a Man may do either the Action *A*, or its Oppofite *a*, the previous Circum-ftances remaining the fame, is to fuppofe that one of them may arife without a Caufe ; for the fame pre-vious Circumftances cannot be the Caufe of the two oppofite Effects. Now, if any thing can arife without a Caufe, all Things may, by Parity of Reafon ; which is contrary to the Firft Propofition of this Chapter, or to the common Foundation upon which Writers have erected their Arguments for the Being and Attributes of God. To fay that Free-will is the Caufe, is an identical Propofition ; fince it is faying, that the Power of doing different Things, the previous Cir-cumftances remaining the fame, is the Caufe that this may be done, *viz.* that either *A* or *a* may follow the fame previous Circumftances. Or, if we put for phi-lofophical Free-will the Power of doing Things with-out a Caufe, it will be a Word of nearly the fame Im-port as Chance. For Chance is the Ignorance or De-nial of a Caufe. It will therefore be as unfit to afcribe a real Caufality to Free-will as to Chance.

And as Free-will is inconfiftent with the infinite Power of God, fo it is with his infinite Knowlege alfo. For infinite Knowlege muft include the Knowlege

of

of all future Things, as well as of all paft and prefent ones. Befides, paft, prefent and future, are all prefent with refpect to God, as has been obferved before. Infinite Knowlege muft therefore include Prefcience. But Free-will does not allow of Prefcience. Knowlege of all Kinds prefuppofes the Certainty of the Thing known ; *i. e.* prefuppofes that it is determined in refpect of Time, Place, Manner, *&c. i. e.* prefuppofes it to be neceffary. Thus, if we confider any thing as known certainly, or certain fimply, fuch as a mathematical Truth, a paft Fact, *&c.* we fhall find it to be neceffary, and that it cannot be otherwife than it now is, or was formerly ; which is the contrary to what is fuppofed of the Actions of Creatures endued with Free-will. Thefe Actions, therefore, cannot be known, or foreknown, not being the Objects of Knowlege.

The Maintainers of Neceffity do indeed deny, that there is any fuch Thing as Uncertainty at all ; unlefs as far as this is put relatively for the Limitation of Knowlege in any Being, fo that the Thing called Uncertain may or may not be, for any thing that this Being knows to the contrary. But if they do, for Argument's fake, allow fuch a Thing as abfolute Uncertainty, *i. e.* that a Thing either may or may not be, it is plain, that this abfolute Uncertainty muft include the Relative, *i. e.* exclude Knowlege and Foreknowlege. That Action of *B* which either may or may not be, cannot be known certainly to be by *A*, becaufe it may not be ; it cannot be known not to be, becaufe it may be. Suppofe *A* to make Conjectures concerning any future Action of *B*. Then this Action may or may not be, for any thing *A* knows to the contrary ; it alfo may or may not be in itfelf, provided there be any fuch thing as abfolute Uncertainty. Suppofe *A*'s Conjectures to pafs into a well-grounded Probability of a high Degree, that the Action will hap-

happen, then both the Relative and abfolute *may not*, are reduced to narrow Limits. Suppofe *A*'s Conjectures to arife to Knowlege, or Certainty, then both the relative and abfolute *may not*, vanifh. *A.* cannot know, or be certain, that a Thing will happen, at the fame time that it may or may not happen, for any thing that he knows to the contrary ; nor can a Thing be relatively certain, and abfolutely uncertain. *A*'s Foreknowlege does therefore imply relative Certainty ; this requires abfolute Certainty ; and abfolute Certainty is in exprefs Terms oppofite to philofophical Free-will. Foreknowlege is therefore inconfiftent with Free-will ; or rather Free-will, if it were poffible, would exclude Foreknowlege. It is not therefore poffible.

Nor does it alter the Cafe here to allege, that God's infinite Knowlege muft extend infinitely farther than Man's, and, confequently, may extend to Things uncertain in themfelves, fince the very Terms *Knowlege* and *uncertain* are inconfiftent. To make them confiftent, we muft affix fome new and different Senfe to one of them, which would be to give up either the Divine Foreknowlege or Free-will in reality, while we pretend in Words to maintain them. If God's Knowlege be fuppofed to differ fo much from Man's in this fimple effential Circumftance, that the Certainty of it does not imply the Certainty of the Thing known, we lofe all Conception of it. And if the fame Liberties were ufed with the Divine Power and Benevolence, we fhould lofe all Conception of the Divine Nature.

To which it may be added, that the Reafoning in the laft Paragraph but one, concerning the Knowlege of the Being *A*, is not at all affected, or altered, by his Rank, as to Intelligence. Suppofe his intellectual Capacities to be greater and greater perpetually, ftill all Things remain precifely the fame, without the

leaft

leaſt Variation. They will therefore, according to the Analogy of ultimate Ratios, remain preciſely the ſame, though his Knowlege be ſuppoſed infinite. It follows, therefore, that God's infinite and certain Knowlege, or his Foreknowlege, is as inconſiſtent with philoſophical Free-will, as Man's finite, but cer‑tain, Knowlege or Foreknowlege.

C H A P.

CHAP. II.

Of the Truth of the Chriſtian Religion.

TO believe the Chriſtian Religion, is to believe
that *Moſes* and the Prophets, *Chriſt* and his
Apoſtles, were endued with Divine Authority, that they had a Commiſſion from God to act and
teach as they did, and that he will verify their Declarations concerning future Things, and eſpecially thoſe
concerning a future Life, by the Event ; or, in other
Words, it is to receive the Scriptures as our Rule of
Life, and the Foundation of all our Hopes and Fears.
And as all thoſe who regulate their Faith and Practice
by the Scriptures are Chriſtians ; ſo all thoſe who diſ-
claim that Name, and paſs under the general Title of
Unbelievers, do alſo diſavow this Regard to the Scriptures. But there are various Claſſes of Unbelievers.
Some appear to treat the Scriptures as mere Forgeries ;
others allow them to be the genuine Writings of thoſe
whoſe Names they bear, but ſuppoſe them to abound
with Fictions, not only in the miraculous, but alſo
in the common Part of the Hiſtory ; others, again, allow this Part, but reject that ; and, laſtly, there are
others who ſeem to allow the Truth of the principal
Facts, both common and miraculous, contained in the
Scriptures, and yet ſtill call in queſtion its Divine
Authority, as a Rule of Life, and an Evidence of a
happy Futurity under Chriſt our Saviour and King.
He, therefore, that would ſatisfy himſelf or others in
the Truth of the Chriſtian Religion, as oppoſed by

theſe

thefe feveral Claffes of Unbelievers, muft inquire into
thefe Three Things :

First, The Genuinenefs of the Books of the Old
and New Teftaments.

Secondly, The Truth of the principal Facts contained in them, both common and miraculous. And,

Thirdly, Their Divine Authority.

I will endeavour, therefore, to ftate fome of the
chief Evidences for each of thefe important Points,
having firft premifed three preparatory Propofitions,
or Lemmas, whereby the Evidence for any one of
them may be transferred upon the other two.

P R O P. 17.

*The Genuinenefs of the Scriptures proves the Truth
of the principal Facts contained in them.*

FOR, Firft, It is very rare to meet with any genuine Writings of the hiftorical kind, in which
the principal Facts are not true ; unlefs where both
the Motives which engaged the Author to falfify, and
the Circumftances which gave fome Plaufibility to the
Fiction, are apparent ; neither of which can be alleged in the prefent Cafe with any Colour of Reafon.
Where the Writer of a Hiftory appears to the World
as fuch, not only his moral Senfe, but his Regard to
his Character and his Intereft, are ftrong Motives not
to falfify in notorious Matters ; he muft therefore
have ftronger Motives from the oppofite Quarter, and
alfo a favourable Conjuncture of Circumftances, before
he can attempt this.

Secondly, As this is rare in general, fo it is much
more rare, where the Writer treats of Things that
happened in his own Time, and under his own Cognizance or Direction, and communicates his Hiftory
to Perfons under the fame Circumftances. All which
may be faid of the Writers of the Scripture Hiftory.

That this, and the following Arguments, may be
applied

applied with more Eaſe and Clearneſs, I will here, in one View, refer the Books of the Old and New Teſtaments to their proper Authors. I ſuppoſe then, that the Pentateuch conſiſts of the Writings of *Moſes*, put together by *Samuel*, with a very few Additions ; that the Books of *Joſhua* and *Judges* were, in like manner, collected by him ; and the Book of *Ruth*, with the firſt Part of the Firſt Book of *Samuel*, written by him ; that the latter Part of the Firſt Book of *Samuel*, and the Second Book, were written by the Prophets who ſucceeded *Samuel*, ſuppoſe *Nathan* and *Gad*; that the Books of *Kings* and *Chronicles* are Extracts from the Records of the ſucceeding Prophets concerning their own Times, and from the public genealogical Tables, made by *Ezra* ; that the Books of *Ezra* and *Nehemiah* are Collections of like Records, ſome written by *Ezra* and *Nehemiah*, and ſome by their Predeceſſors ; that the Book of *Eſther* was written by ſome eminent *Jew*, in or near the Times of the Tranſaction there recorded, perhaps *Mordecai* ; the Book of *Job* by a *Jew* of an uncertain Time ; the *Pſalms* by *David*, and other pious Perſons ; the Books of *Proverbs* and *Canticles* by *Solomon*; the Book of *Eccleſiaſtes* by *Solomon*, or perhaps by a *Jew* of later Times, ſpeaking in his Perſon, but not with an Intention to make him paſs for the Author; the Prophecies by the Prophets whoſe Names they bear ; and the Books of the New Teſtament by the Perſons to whom they are uſually aſcribed. There are many internal Evidences, and in the Caſe of the New Teſtament many external Evidences alſo, by which theſe Books may be ſhewn to belong to the Authors here named. Or, if there be any Doubts, they are merely of a critical Nature, and do not at all affect the Genuineneſs of the Books, nor alter the Application of theſe Arguments, or not materially. Thus, if the Epiſtle to the *Hebrews* be ſuppoſed written, not by St. *Paul*, but by *Clement* or *Barnabas*, or any other of their Cotemporaries, the Evidence therein

given

given to the Miracles performed by Chriſt, and his Followers, will not be at all invalidated thereby.

Thirdly, The great Importance of the Facts mentioned in the Scriptures makes it ſtill more improbable, that the ſeveral Authors ſhould either have attempted to falſify, or have ſucceeded in ſuch an Attempt. This is an Argument for the Truth of the Facts, which proves the Genuineneſs of the Books at the ſame time, as I ſhall ſhew below in a diſtinct Propoſition. However, the Truth of the Facts is inferred more directly from their Importance, if the Genuineneſs of the Scriptures be·previouſly allowed. The ſame thing may be obſerved of the great Number of particular Circumſtances of Time, Place, Perſons, &c. mentioned in the Scriptures, and of the Harmony of the Books with themſelves, and with each other. Theſe are Arguments both for the Genuineneſs of the Books, and Truth of the Facts diſtinctly conſidered, and alſo Arguments for deducing the Truth from the Genuineneſs. And indeed the Arguments for the general Truth of the Hiſtory of any Age or Nation, where regular Records have been kept, are ſo interwoven together, and ſupport each other in ſuch a Variety of Ways, that it is extremely difficult to keep the Ideas of them diſtinct, not to anticipate, and not to prove more than the Exactneſs of Method requires one to prove. Or, in other Words, the Inconſiſtency of the contrary Suppoſitions is ſo great, that they can ſcarce ſtand long enough to be confuted. Let any one try this in the Hiſtory of *France* or *England*, *Greece* or *Rome*.

Fourthly, If the Books of the Old and New Teſtaments were written by the Perſons to whom they were aſcribed above, *i. e.* if they be genuine, the moral Characters of theſe Writers afford the ſtrongeſt Aſſurance, that the Facts aſſerted by them are true. Falſhoods and Frauds of a common Nature ſhock the moral Senſe of common Men, and are rarely met with,

except

except in Persons of abandoned Characters : How inconsistent then must those of the most glaring and impious Nature be with the highest moral Characters ! That such Characters are due to the sacred Writers, appears from the Writings themselves by an internal Evidence ; but there is also strong external Evidence in many Cases ; and indeed this Point is allowed in general by Unbelievers. The Sufferings which several of the Writers underwent both in Life and Death, in Attestation of the Facts delivered by them, is a particular Argument in favour of these.

Fifthly, The Arguments here alleged for proving the Truth of the Scripture History from the Genuineness of the Books, are as conclusive in respect of the miraculous Facts, as of the common ones. But besides this we may observe, that if we allow the Genuineness of the Books to be a sufficient Evidence of the common Facts mentioned in them, the miraculous Facts must be allowed also, from their close Connexion with the common ones. It is necessary to admit both or neither. It is not to be conceived, that *Moses* should have delivered the *Israelites* from their Slavery in *Egypt*, or conducted them through the Wilderness for Forty Years, at all, in such manner as the common History represents, unless we suppose the miraculous Facts intermixed with it to be true also. In like manner, the Fame of Christ's Miracles, the Multitudes which followed him, the Adherence of his Disciples, the Jealousy and Hatred of the Chief Priests, Scribes and Pharisees, with many other Facts of a common Nature, are impossible to be accounted for, unless we allow, that he did really work Miracles. And the same Observations hold in general of the other Parts of the Scripture History.

Sixthly, There is even a particular Argument in favour of the miraculous Part of the Scripture History, to be drawn from the Reluctance of Mankind to receive miraculous Facts. It is true, that this Reluctance

is

is greater in fome Ages and Nations than in others; and probable Reafons may be affigned why this Reluctance was, in general, lefs in antient Times than in the prefent (which, however, are Prefumptions that fome real Miracles were then wrought): But it muft always be confiderable from the very Frame of the human Mind, and would be particularly fo amongft the *Jews* at the Time of Chrift's Appearance, as they had then been without Miracles for Four hundred Years, or more. Now this Reluctance muft make both the Writers and Readers very much upon their Guard; and if it be now one of the chief Prejudices againft Revealed Religion, as Unbelievers unanimoufly affert, it is but reafonable to allow alfo, that it would be a ftrong Check upon the Publication of a miraculous Hiftory at or near the Time when the Miracles were faid to be performed; *i. e.* it will be a ftrong Confirmation of fuch an Hiftory, if its Genuinenefs be granted previoufly.

And, upon the Whole, we may certainly conclude, that the principal Facts, both common and miraculous, mentioned in the Scriptures, muft be true, if their Genuinenefs be allowed. The Objection againft all miraculous Facts will be confidered below, after the other Arguments for the Truth of the Scripture Miracles have been alleged.

The Converfe of this Propofition is alfo true; *i. e.* If the principal Facts mentioned in the Scriptures be true, they muft be genuine Writings. And though this converfe Propofition may, at firft Sight, appear to be of little Importance for the Eftablifhment of Chriftianity, inafmuch as the Genuinenefs of the Scriptures is only made ufe of as a Medium whereby to prove the Truth of the Facts mentioned in them, yet it will be found otherwife upon farther Examination. For there are many Evidences for the Truth of particular Facts mentioned in the Scriptures, fuch, for Inftance, as thofe taken from Natural Hiftory, and the

cotemporary

cotemporary profane Hiſtory, which no-ways preſuppoſe, but, on the contrary, prove the Genuineneſs of
the Scriptures; and this Genuineneſs, thus proved,
may, by the Arguments alleged under this Propoſition, be extended to infer the Truth of the reſt of the
Facts. Which is not to argue in a Circle, and to
prove the Truth of the Scripture Hiſtory from its
Truth; but to prove the Truth of thoſe Facts, which
are not atteſted by Natural or Civil Hiſtory, from
thoſe which are, by the Medium of the Genuineneſs
of the Scriptures.

PROP. 18.

*The Genuineneſs of the Scriptures proves their
Divine Authority.*

THE Truth of this Propoſition, as it reſpects the
Book of *Daniel*, ſeems to have been acknowleged by *Porphyry*, inaſmuch as he could no-ways invalidate the Divine Authority of this Book, implied
by the Accompliſhment of the Prophecies therein delivered, but by aſſerting, that they were written after
the Event, *i. e.* were Forgeries. But the ſame Thing
holds of many of the other Books of the Old and New
Teſtaments, many of them having unqueſtionable
Evidences of the Divine Foreknowlege, if they be allowed genuine. I reſerve the prophetical Evidences
to be diſcuſſed hereafter, and therefore ſhall only ſuggeſt the following Inſtances here, in order to illuſtrate
the Propoſition; *viz. Moſes*'s Prophecy concerning
the Captivity of the *Iſraelites*, of a State not yet
erected; *Iſaiah*'s concerning *Cyrus*; *Jeremiah*'s concerning the Duration of the *Babyloniſh* Captivity;
Chriſt's concerning the Deſtruction of *Jeruſalem*, and
the Captivity that was to follow; St. *John*'s concerning the great Corruption of the Chriſtian Church; and
Daniel's concerning the Fourth Empire in its Declenſion; which laſt was extant in *Porphyry*'s Time

at

at leaft, *i. e.* before the Events which it fo fitly reprefents.

The fame Thing follows from the Sublimity and Excellence of the Doctrines contained in the Scriptures. Thefe no-ways fuit the fuppofed Authors, *i. e.* the Ages when they lived, their Educations or Occupations ; and therefore, if they were the real Authors, there is a Neceffity of admitting the Divine Affiftance.

The Converfe of this Propofition, *viz.* that the Divine Authority of the Scriptures infers their Genuinenefs, will, I fuppofe, be readily acknowleged by all. And it may be ufed for the fame Purpofes as the Converfe of the laft. For there are feveral Evidences for the Divine Authority of the Scriptures, which are direct and immediate, and prior to the Confideration both of their Genuinenefs, and of the Truth of the Facts contained in them. Of this Kind is the Character of Chrift, as it may be collected from his Difcourfes and Actions related in the Gofpels. The great and manifeft Superiority of this to all other Characters, real and fictitious, proves, at once, his Divine Miffion, exclufively of all other Confiderations. Suppofe now the Genuinenefs of St. *Luke*'s Gofpel to be deduced in this Way, the Genuinenefs of the *Acts* of the Apoftles may be deduced from it, and of St. *Paul*'s Epiftles from the *Acts*, by the ufual critical Methods. And when the Genuinenefs of the *Acts* of the Apoftles, and of St. *Paul*'s Epiftles, is thus deduced, the Truth of the Facts mentioned in them will follow from it by the laft Propofition ; and their Divine Authority by this.

PROP.

P R O P. 19.

The Truth of the principal Facts contained in the Scriptures proves their Divine Authority.

THIS Propofition may be proved two Ways; Firft, exclufively of the Evidences of Natural Religion, fuch as thofe delivered in the laft Chapter; and, Seeondly, from the previous Eftablifhment of the great Truths of Natural Religion. And, Firft,

It is evident, That the great Power, Knowlege, and Benevolence, which appeared in Chrift, the Prophets and Apoftles, according to the Scripture Accounts, do, as it were, command Affent and Submiffion from all thofe who receive thefe Accounts as hiftorical Truths; and that, though they are not able to deduce, or have not, in fact, deduced the Evidences of Natural Religion; nay, though they fhould have many Doubts about them. The Frame of the human Mind is fuch, that the Scripture Hiftory, allowed to be true, muft convince us, that Chrift, the Prophets and Apoftles, were endued with a Power greater than human, and acted by the Authority of a Being of the higheft Wifdom and Goodnefs.

Secondly, If Natural Religion be previoufly eftablifhed, the Truth of the principal Facts of the Scriptures proves their Divine Authority in an eafier and more convincing manner.

For, Firft, the Power fhewn in the Miracles wrought by Chrift, the Prophets and Apoftles, the Knowlege in their Prophecies, and their good moral Characters, fhew them to be, in an eminent manner, the Children, Servants, and Meffengers, of him, who is now previoufly acknowleged to be infinite in Power, Knowlege, and Goodnefs.

Secondly, Chrift, the Prophets and Apoftles, make an exprefs Claim to a Divine Miffion. Now, it cannot be reconciled to God's moral Attributes of

Juftice,

Juſtice, Veracity, Mercy, &c. that he ſhould permit theſe Perſons to make ſuch a Claim falſly, and then endue them, or ſuffer them to be endued, with ſuch Credentials, as muſt ſupport ſuch a falſe Claim. Their Claim is not, therefore, a falſe one, if we admit their Credentials; or, in other Words, the Truth of the principal Facts mentioned in the Scriptures proves the Divine Miſſion of Chriſt, the Prophets, and Apoſtles, *i. e.* the Divine Authority of the Scriptures.

The ſame Obſervations may be made upon the Converſe of this Propoſition, as upon thoſe of the Two laſt.

And thus the Genuineneſs of the Scriptures, the Truth of the principal Facts contained in them, and their Divine Authority, appear to be ſo connected with each other, that any one being eſtabliſhed upon independent Principles, the other Two may be inferred from it. The Firſt and Second of theſe Points are, indeed, more evidently ſubſervient to the laſt, than the laſt is to them; for, if the laſt be allowed, it is at once all that the Believer contends for; whereas ſome Perſons appear to admit, or not to reject, the Firſt, or even the Second, and yet are ranked under the Title of Unbelievers. It is neceſſary to ſhew to ſuch Perſons, that the Firſt and Second infer each other mutually, and both of them the laſt; and it may be of ſome Uſe to ſhew, that the laſt infers the two Firſt in ſuch a way, as to caſt ſome Light upon itſelf, without arguing in a Circle; the Divine Authority of one Book being made to infer the Genuineneſs of another, or the Facts contained in it, *i. e.* its Divine Authority alſo.

Here it may not be amiſs to ſay ſomething concerning the Divine Inſpiration of the Scriptures. Now there are Three different Suppoſitions, which may be made concerning this Point.

The firſt and loweſt is, That all the Paſſages delivered by *Moſes* and the Prophets, as coming from
God,

God, and by the Evangelifts, as the Words of
Chrift, alfo the Revelation given to St. *John* in a
Divine Vifion, with all parallel Portions of Scripture,
muft be confidered as divinely infpired, and as having
immediate Divine Authority ; elfe we cannot allow
even common Authority to thefe Books ; but that
the common Hiftory, the Reafonings of the Apoftles
from the Old Teftament, and perhaps fome of their
Opinions, may be confidered as coming merely from
themfelves, and therefore, though highly to be regarded, are not of unqueftionable Authority. The
Arguments for this Hypothefis may be, that fince the
Scriptures have fuffered by Tranfcribers, like other
Books, a perfect Exactnefs in the Original, as to minute Particulars (in which alone it has fuffered, or
could fuffer, from Tranfcribers), is needlefs ; That
Mofes and the Prophets, the Evangelifts and Apoftles,
had natural Talents for writing Hiftory, applying the
Scriptures, reafoning, and delivering their Opinions ;
and that God works by natural Means, where there
are fuch ; That the Apoftles were ignorant of the true
Extent of *Chrift's* Kingdom for a confiderable Time
after his Refurrection, and perhaps miftaken about his
fecond Coming ; That God might intend, that nothing
in this World fhould be perfect, our bleffed Lord excepted ; That fome hiftorical Facts feem difficult to
be reconciled to one another, and fome Applications
of Paffages from the Old Teftament by the Writers
of the New, with their Reafonings thereupon, incon-
clufive and unfatisfactory ; That the Writers themfelves no-where lay claim to Infallibility, when fpeaking from themfelves ; and that *Hermas, Clemens Ro-
manus,* and *Barnabas,* who were apoftolical Perfons,
feem evidently to have reafoned in an inconclufive
Manner.

The Second Hypothefis is, That hiftorical Incidents of fmall Moment, with Matters of a Nature foreign to Religion, may indeed not have Divine Au-

thority ; but that all the reſt of the Scriptures, the
Reaſonings, the Application of the Prophecies, and
even the Doctrines of inferior Note, muſt be inſpired ;
elſe what can be meant by the Gifts of the Spirit, particularly that of Prophecy, *i. e.* of inſtructing others?
How can *Chriſt*'s Promiſe of the Comforter, who
ſhould lead his Diſciples into *all Truth*, be fulfilled?
Will not the very Eſſentials of Religion, the Divine
Miſſion of *Chriſt*, Providence, and a future State, be
weakened by thus ſuppoſing the ſacred Writers to be
miſtaken in religious Points? And though the Hiſtory and the Reaſonings of the Scriptures have the
Marks of being written in the ſame manner as other
Books, *i. e.* may ſeem not to be inſpired, yet a ſecret
Influence might conduct the Writers in every Thing
of Moment, even when they did not perceive it, or
reflect upon it themſelves ; it being evident from obvious Reaſonings, as well as from the foregoing
Theory, that the natural Workings of the Mind are
not to be diſtinguiſhed from thoſe, which a Being that
has a ſufficient Power over our intellectual Frame,
might excite in us.

　　The Third and laſt Hypotheſis is, That the whole
Scriptures are inſpired, even the moſt minute hiſtorical Paſſages, the Salutations, incidental Mention of
common Affairs, *&c.* The Arguments in favour of
this Hypotheſis are, That many Parts of Scripture appear to have double, or perhaps manifold Senſes ;
That not one Jot or Tittle of the Law (*i. e.* of the
whole Scriptures of both the Old and New Teſtaments, in an inlarged Way of Interpretation, which,
however, ſeems juſtifiable by parallel Inſtances) ſhall
periſh ; That the Bible, *i. e.* the Book of Books, as
we now have it, appears to have been remarkably diſtinguiſhed by Providence from all other Writings,
even of good *Jews* and Chriſtians, and to admit of a
Vindication in reſpect of ſmall Difficulties, and ſmall
ſeeming Inconſiſtencies, as well as of great ones, every

I　　　　　　　　　　　　　　　　　Day

Day more and more as we advance in Knowlege; and that Effects of the same Kind with Divine Inspiration, *viz.* the working of Miracles, and the Gift of Prophecy, subsisted during the Times of the Authors of the Books of the Old and New Testaments, and even in all, or nearly all, of these Writers; also, that they extended, in some Cases, to very minute Things.

I will not presume to determine which of these three Suppositions approaches nearest to the Truth. The following Propositions will, I hope, establish the first of them at least, and prove the Genuineness of the Scriptures, the Truth of the Facts contained in them, and their Divine Authority, to such a Degree, as that we need not fear to make them the Rule of our Lives, and the Ground of our future Expectations; which is all that is absolutely necessary for the Proof of the Christian Religion, and the Satisfaction and Comfort of religious Persons. I even believe, that the following Evidences favour the second Hypothesis strongly, and exclude all Errors and Imperfections of Note; nay, I am inclined to believe, that serious, inquisitive Men can scarce rest there, but will be led by the successive clearing of Difficulties, and unfolding of the most wonderful Truths, to believe the whole Scriptures to be inspired, and to abound with numberless Uses and Applications, of which we yet know nothing. Let future Ages determine. The evidently miraculous Nature of one Part, *viz.* the prophetical, disposes the Mind to believe the Whole to be far above human Invention, or even Penetration, till such time as our Understandings shall be farther opened by the Events which are to precede the second Coming of *Christ.* In the mean while, let Critics and learned Men of all Kinds have full Liberty to examine the sacred Books; and let us be sparing in our Censures of each other. *Let us judge nothing before the Time, until the Lord come; and then shall every Man have Praise of God.* Sobriety of Mind, Humility, and Piety, are requisite in

the

the Purfuit of Knowlege of every Kind, and much more in that of facred. I have here endeavoured to be impartial to each Hypothefis, and juft to hint what I apprehend each Party would or might fay in Defence of their own. However, *they are all Brethren,* and ought not to *fall out by the Way.*

P R O P. 20.

The Manner in which the Books of the Old and New Teflaments have b en handed down from Age to Age, proves both their Genuinenefs, and the Truth of the principal Facts contained in them.

FOR, Firft, It refembles the Manner in which all other genuine Books and true Hiftories have been conveyed down to Pofterity. As the Writings of the *Greek* and *Roman* Poets, Orators, Philofophers and Hiftorians, were efteemed by thefe Nations to be tranfmitted to them by their Forefathers in a continued Succeffion, from the Times when the refpective Authors lived, fo have the Books of the Old Teftament by the *Jewifh* Nation, and thofe of the New by the *Chriftians*; and it is an additional Evidence in the laft Cafe, that the primitive Chriftians were not a diftinct Nation, but a great Multitude of People difperfed through all the Nations of the *Roman* Empire, and even extending itfelf beyond the Bounds of that Empire. As the *Greeks* and *Romans* always believed the principal Facts of their hiftorical Books, fo the *Jews* and *Chriftians* did more, and never feem to have doubted of the Truth of any Part of theirs In fhort, whatever can be faid of the traditional Authority due to the *Greek* and *Roman* Writers, fomething analogous to this, and for the moft part of greater Weight, may be urged for the *Jewifh* and *Chriftian.* Now, I fuppofe that all fober-minded Men admit the Books
ufually

uſually aſcribed to the *Greek* and *Roman* Hiſtorians, Philoſophers, *&c.* to be genuine, and the principal Facts related or alluded to in them to be true, and that one chief Evidence for this is the general traditionary one here recited. They ought therefore to pay the ſame Regard to the Books of the Old and New Teſtaments, ſince there are the ſame or greater Reaſons for it.

Secondly, If we reconſider the Circumſtances recited in the laſt Paragraph, it will appear, that theſe traditionary Evidences are ſufficient ones ; and we ſhall have a real Argument, as well as one *ad hominem,* for receiving Books ſo handed down to us. For it is not to be conceived, that whole Nations ſhould either be impoſed upon themſelves, or concur to deceive others, by Forgeries of Books or Facts. Theſe Books and Facts muſt therefore, in general, be genuine and true ; and it is a ſtrong additional Evidence of this, that all Nations muſt be jealous of Forgeries for the ſame Reaſons that we are.

Here it may be objected, that as we reject the Prodigies related by the *Greek* and *Roman* Writers, though we admit the common Hiſtory, ſo we ought alſo to reject the Scripture Miracles. To this I anſwer,

Firſt, That the Scripture Hiſtory is ſupported by far ſtronger Evidences than the *Greek* or *Roman,* as will appear in the following Propoſitions.

Secondly, That many of the Scripture Miracles are related by Eye-witneſſes, and were of a public Nature, of long Duration, attended by great and laſting Effects, inſeparably connected with the common Hiſtory, and evidently ſuitable to our Notions of a wiſe and good Providence, which cannot be ſaid of thoſe related by the Pagan Writers.

Thirdly, That the Scripture Miracles not attended by theſe cogent Circumſtances are ſupported by their Connexion with ſuch as are ; and that after we have

admitted

admitted thefe, there remains no longer any Prefumption againft thofe from their miraculous Nature.

Fourthly, If there be any fmall Number found
amongft the Pagan Miracles, attefted by fuch-like
Evidences as the principal ones for the Scripture Miracles, I do not fee how they can be rejected ; but it
will not follow, that the Scripture Miracles are falfe,
becaufe fome of the Pagan ones are true.

P R O P. 21.

*The great Importance of the Hiftories, Precepts,
Promifes,Threatenings and Prophecies contained
in the Scriptures, are Evidences both of their
Genuinenefs, and of the Truth of the principal
Facts mentioned in them.*

THIS is one of the Inftances in which the Evidences for the Scriptures are fuperior, beyond
Comparifon, to thofe for any other antient Books.
Let us take a fhort Review of this Importance in its
feveral Particulars.

The Hiftory of the Creation, Fall, Deluge, Longe-
vity of the Patriarchs, Difperfion of Mankind, Calling of *Abraham*, Defcent of *Jacob* with his Family
into *Egypt*, and the Precepts of abftaining from
Blood, and o Maircumcifion, were of fo much Concern, either and nkind in general, or to the *Ifraelites*
in particularhat it fome of them of fo extraordinary a
Nature, as te am could not be an indifferent Matter
to the Peopɪ ˊ ongft whom the Account given of
them in *Genefis* was firft publifhed, whether they received them or not. Suppofe this Account to be firft
publifhed amongft the *Ifraelites* by *Mofes*, and alfo to
be then confirmed by clear, univerfal, uninterrupted
Tradition (which is poffible and probable, according
to the Hiftory itfelf), and it will be eafy to conceive,
upon this true Suppofition, how this Account fhould

be

be handed down from Age to Age amongst the *Jews,* and received by them as indubitable. Suppose this Account to be false, *i. e.* suppose that there were no such Evidences and Vestiges of these Histories and Precepts, and it will be difficult to conceive how this could have happened, let the Time of Publication be as it will. It early, the People would reject the Account at once for want of a clear Tradition, which the Account itself would give them Reason to expect. If late, it would be natural to inquire how the Author came to be informed of Things never known before to others.

If it be said, that he delivered them as communicated to him by Revelation (which yet cannot well be said on account of the many References in *Genesis* to the remaining Vestiges of the Things related), these surprising, interesting Particulars would at least be an Embarassment upon his fictitious Credentials, and engage his Cotemporaries to look narrowly into them.

If it be said, that there were many Cosmogonies and Theogonies current amongst the Pagans, which yet are evidently Fictions ; I answer, that these were, in general, regarded only as amusing Fictions ; however, that they had some Truths in them, either expressed in plain Words, or concealed in Figures; and that their Agreement with the Book of *Genesis,* as far as they are consistent with one another, or have any Appearance of Truth, is a remarkable Evidence in favour of this Book. It is endless to make all the possible Suppositions and Objections of this Kind ; but it appears to me, that the more are made, the more will the Truth and Genuineness of the Scriptures be established thereby.

It ought to be added, in relation to the Precepts of abstaining from Blood, and Circumcision, before-mentioned, that if the first was common to Mankind, or was known to have been so, the last peculiar to the Descendents of *Abraham,* at the Time of the Publi-

cation

cation of the Book of *Genesis*, this confirms it ; if otherwise, would contribute to make it rejected. If neither
the Practices themselves, nor any Vestiges of them,
subsisted at all, the Book must be rejected. The Difficulty of deducing thefe Practices from the Principles
of human Nature ought to be considered here ; as it
tends to prove their divine Original, agreeably to the
Accounts given of them in *Genesis*.

Let us next come to the Law of *Moses*. This was
extremely burdensome, expensive, severe, particularly upon the Crime of Idolatry, to which all Mankind were then extravagantly prone. and absurd, according to the common Judgment of Mankind, in
the Instances of forbidding to provide themselves with
Horses for War and commanding all the Males of
the whole Nation to appear at *Jerusalem* three times
in a Year. At the same time, it claims a Divine Authority every-where, and appeals to Facts of the moft
notorious Kinds, and to Customs and Ceremonies of
the moft peculiar Nature, as the Memorials of thefe
Facts. We cannot conceive, then, that any Nation,
with fuch Motives to reject, and fuch Opportunities
of detecting, the Forgery of the Books of *Exodus*,
Leviticus, *Numbers*, and *Deuteronomy*, should yet
receive them, and fubmit to this heavy Yoke. That
they fhould often throw it off in Part, and for a Time,
and rebel againft the divine Authority of their Law,
though fufficiently evidenced, is eafily to be accounted
for from what we fee and feel in ourfelves and others
every Day ; but that they fhould ever return and repent, ever fubmit to it, unlefs it had divine Authority,
is utterly incredible. It was not a Matter of fuch
fmall Importance, as that they could content themfelves
with a fuperficial Examination, with a lefs Examination than would be fufficient to detect fo notorious a
Forgery ; and this holds, at whatever time we fuppofe
thefe Books to be publifhed.

That

That the *Jews* did thus ſubmit to the Law of *Moſes*, is evident from the Books of the Old and New Teſtaments, if we allow them the leaſt Truth and Genuineneſs, or even from profane Writers ; nay, I may ſay, from the preſent Obſervance of it by the *Jews* ſcattered through all the Kingdoms of the World.

If it be ſaid, that other Nations have aſcribed Divine Authority to their Lawgivers, and ſubmitted to very ſevere Laws; I anſwer, Firſt, That the Pretences of Lawgivers amongſt the Pagans to Inſpiration, and the Submiſſion of the People to them, may be accounted for in the Degree in which they are found, from the then Circumſtances of Things, without having recourſe to real Inſpiration ; and particularly, that if we admit the patriarchal Revelations related and intimated by *Moſes*, and his own Divine Legation, it will appear, that the Heathen Lawgivers copied after theſe ; which is a ſtrong Argument for admitting them. Secondly, That there is no Inſtance amongſt the Pagans, of a Body of Laws being produced at once, and remaining without Addition afterwards; but that they were compiled by degrees, according to the Exigencies of the State, the Prevalence of a particular Faction, or the Authority of ſome particular Perſons, who were all ſtyled Lawgivers, as *Draco* and *Solon* at *Athens :* That they were made, in general, not to curb, but humour, the Genius of the People ; and were afterwards repealed and altered from the ſame Cauſes: Whereas the Body Politic of the *Iſraelites* took upon itſelf a complete Form at once, and has preſerved this Form in great meaſure to the preſent Time, and that under the higheſt external Diſadvantages ; which is an Inſtance quite without Parallel, and ſhews the great Opinion which they had of their Law, *i. e.* its great Importance to them.

If it be ſaid, that the Laws of the *Iſraelites* were not perhaps impoſed at once, but grew up by degrees,

as

as in other Nations, this will make the Difficulty of receiving the Books of *Exodus, Leviticus, Numbers,* and
Deuteronomy, in which the contrary, with all the particular Circumftances, is afferted, greater than ever.
In fhort, of all the Fictions or Forgeries that can happen amongft any People, the moft improbable is that
of their Body of Civil Laws ; and it feems to be utterly impoffible in the Cafe of the Law of *Mofes.*

The next Part of the Scriptures, whofe Importance
we are to confider, is the Hiftory contained in the
Books of *Joshua, Judges, Ruth, Samuel, Kings, Chronicles, Ezra,* and *Nehemiah,* and extending from the
Death of *Mofes* to the Re-eftablifhment of the *Jews*
after the *Babylonifh* Captivity, by *Ezra* and *Nehemiah.*
Now, in this Hiftory are the following important
Facts, moft of which muft be fuppofed to leave fuch
Veftiges of themfelves, either external vifible ones,
or inte nal in the Minds and Memories of the People,
as would verify them, if true ; make them be rejected,
if falfe. The Conqueft of the Land of *Canaan,* the
Divifion of it, and the Appointment of Cities for the
Priefts and Levites by *Joshua* ; the frequent Slave-
ries of the *Ifraelites* to the neighbouring Kings, and
their Deliverance by the Judges ; the Erection of a
Kingdom by *Samuel* ; the Tranflation of this Kingdom from *Saul*'s Family to *David,* with his Conquefts ;
the Glory of *Solomon*'s Kingdom ; the Building of the
Temple ; the Divifion of the Kingdom ; the idolatrous Worfhip fet up at *Dan* and *Bethel* ; the Captivity of the *Ifraelites* by the Kings of *Affyria* ; the
Captivity of the *Jews* by *Nebuchadnezzar* ; the Deftruction of their Temple ; their Return under *Cyrus,*
Rebuilding the Temple under *Darius. Hyftafpis,* and
Re-eftablifhment under *Artaxerxes Longimanus,* by
Ezra and *Nehemiah* ; Thefe Events are fome of
them the moft glorious, fome of them the moft fhame-
ful that can well happen to any People. How can we
reconcile Forgeries of fuch oppofite Kinds, and efpecially

cially as they are interwoven together ? But, indeed, the Facts are of ſuch Conſequence, Notoriety, and Permanency in their Effects, that neither could any particular Perſons amongſt the *Iſraelites* firſt project the Deſign of feigning them, nor their own People concur with ſuch a Deſign, nor the neighbouring Nations permit the Fiction to paſs. Nothing could make a jealous Multitude amongſt the *Iſraelites* or neighbouring Nations acquieſce, but the invincible Evidence of the Facts here alleged. And the ſame Obſervations hold of numberleſs other Facts of leſſer Note, which it would be tedious to recount ; and of miraculous Facts as much, or rather more than others. Beſides which, it is to be noted, that all theſe have ſuch various neceſſary Connexions with each other, that they cannot be ſeparated, as has been already remarked.

And all this will, I preſume, be readily acknowleged, upon Suppoſition that the ſeveral Books were publiſhed in or near the Times of the Facts therein recorded. But, ſay the Objectors, this will not hold in ſo ſtrong a manner, if the Books be publiſhed after theſe Times. Let us take an extreme Caſe then, and ſuppoſe all theſe hiſtorical Books forged by *Ezra.* But this is evidently impoſſible. Things of ſo important and notoriousa Kind, ſo glorious and ſo ſhameful to the People, for whoſe Sake they were forged, would have been rejected with the utmoſt Indignation, unleſs there were the ſtrongeſt and moſt genuine Footſteps of theſe Things already amongſt the People. They were therefore in part true. But many Additions were made by *Ezra*, ſay the Objectors. I anſwer, if theſe were of Importance, the Difficulty returns. If not, then all the important Facts are true. Beſides, what Motive could any one have for making Additions of no Importance ? Again, if there were any antient Writings extant, *Ezra* muſt either copy after them, which deſtroys the preſent Suppoſition ;

or

or differ from and oppofe them, which would betray
him. If there were no fuch antient Writings, the
People could not but inquire in Matters of Importance,
for what Reafons *Ezra* was fo particular in Things of
which there was neither any Memory, nor Account
in Writing. If it be faid, that the People did not regard what *Ezra* had thus forged, but let it pafs un-
contradicted ; this is again to make the Things of
fmall or no Importance. Befides, why fhould *Ezra*
write, if no one would read or regard ? Farther,
Ezra muft, like all other Men, have Friends, Enemies, and Rivals; and fome or all of thefe would have
been a Check upon him, and a Security againft him
in Matters of Importance.

If, inftead of fuppofing *Ezra* to have forged all
thefe Books at once, we fuppofe them forged fuccef-
fively, one, two, or three Centuries after the Facts related ; we fhall, from this intermediate Suppofition,
have (befides the Difficulty of accounting for fuch a
regular Succeffion of Impoftures in Matters fo important) a Mixture of the Difficulties recited in the
two preceding Paragraphs, the Sum total of which
will be the fame, or nearly the fame, as in either of
thofe Cafes. And, upon the Whole, the Forgery of
the Annals of the *Ifraelites* appears to be impoffible,
as well as that of the Body of their Civil Laws.

If it be faid, that the Hiftories and Annals of other
Nations have many Fictions and Falfhoods in them ;
I anfwer, that the fuperior Importance of the Events
which happened to the *Jewifh* Nation, and the miraculous Nature of many of them, occafioned their being recorded at the then prefent Times, in the way
of fimple Narration, the Command of God alfo concurring, as it feems ; and that thus all Addition, Variety, and Embellifhment, was prevented : Whereas
the Hiftories of the Originals of other Nations were
not committed to Writing till long after the Events,
after they had been corrupted and obfcured by numberlefs

berlefs Fables and Fictions, as is well known. There are many other Circumftances peculiar to the *Jewiſh* Hiftory, which eftablifh its Truth even in the minuteft Things, as I fhall fhew in the following Propofitions; and I hope the Reader will fee, in the Progrefs of the Argument, that the fame Method of Reafoning which proves the *Jewiſh* Hiftory to be rigoroufly exact, proves alfo, that the Hiftories of other Nations may be expected to be partly true, and partly falfe, as they are agreed to be by all learned and fober minded Men.

I pafs over the Books of *Eſther*, *Job*, the *Pſalms*, *Proverbs*, *Eccleſiaſtes*, and *Canticles*, as not having much Relation to this Propofition; and proceed to the Confideration of the Prophecies.

Thefe contain the moft important Precepts, Promifes, Threatenings, and Predictions, *i. e.* Prophecies peculiarly fo called, befides the indirect and incidental Mention of the great Events recorded in the hiftorical Books. And as they are full of the fevereft Reproofs and Denunciations againft all Ranks, King, Governors and great Men fubordinate to him, Priefts, Prophets, and People, one cannot expect, that they fhould be favourably received by any, but thofe of the beft moral Characters ; and thefe muft be the firft to detect and expofe a Forgery, if there was any. So that the Prophecies, if they were Forgeries, could not be able to ftand fo rigorous an Examination as the Importance of the Cafe would prompt all Ranks to. And here all the Arguments before ufed to fhew, that the hiftorical Books could neither be forged at the Time of the Facts, nor fo late as *Ezra*'s Time, nor in any intermediate one, are applicable with the fame, or even greater Force. Befides which, it is to be obferved of the Predictions in particular, that, if they were publifhed before the Events, they could not be Forgeries; if afterwards, there would not be wanting amongft the *Jews* many Perfons of the fame Difpofition with *Porphyry*, and the prefent Objectors to the Genuinenefs

of

of the Prophecies, and the Truth of the Facts related or implied in them, who upon that Suppofition would have met with Succefs, as *Porphyry*, and the antient Objectors would have done long ago, had their Objections been folid. Infidelity is the natural and neceffary Product of human Wickednefs and Weaknefs; we fee it, in all other Things, as well as in Religion, whenfoever the Interefts and Paffions of Men are oppcfite to Truth; and the prefent Objectors to the Truth of revealed Religion may be affured, that the antient ones, the murmuring *Ifraelites* in the Wildernefs, the rebellious *Jews* before Chrift, and both *Jews* and *Gentiles* fince Chrift, have done Juftice to their Caufe.

We come, in the laft Place, to confider the Importance of the Books of the New Teftament. Whoever then received thefe in antient Times as genuine and true, muft not only forfake all finful Pleafures, but expofe himfelf to various Hardfhips and Dangers, and even to Death itfelf. They had indeed a future Glory promifed to them, with which the Sufferings of the prefent Time were not worthy to be compared. But then this Glory, being future, muft be fupported with the moft inconteftable Evidences; elfe it could have no Power againft the oppofite Motives; and both together muft fo roufe the Mind, as to make Men exert themfelves to the uttermoft, till they had received full Satisfaction. Befides which, it is to be obferved, that even Joy, and the Greatnefs of an Expectation, incline Men to difbelieve, and to examine with a fcrupulous Exactnefs, as well as Fear and Diflike.

As to thofe who did not receive the Doctrines of the New Teftament, and the Facts there related and implied, they would have fufficient Motives to detect the Forgery or Falfhood, had there been any fuch. They were all condemned for their Unbelief; many for their grofs Vices; the *Jew* for his darling Partiality to his own Nation, and ceremonial Law; and

the

the *Gentile* for his Idolatry and Polytheifm ; and the
moft dreadful Punifhments threatened to all in a future
State. Now thefe were important Charges, and alarming Confiderations, which, if they did not put Men
upon a fair Examination, would, at leaft, make them
defirous to find Fault, to detect and expofe, and, if
they had difcovered any Fraud, to publifh it with the
utmoft Triumph. The Books of the New Teftament
could not but be of fo much Importance to the Unbelievers of the primitive Times, as to excite them
to Vigilance and Earneftnefs, in endeavouring to difcredit and deftroy them. All which is abundantly
confirmed by the Hiftory of thofe Times. And indeed Cafes of the fame Kind, though not of the fame
Degree, occur now to daily Obfervation, which the
Reader will do well to call to Mind. Thus it comes
to pafs, on one hand, that Frauds and Impoftures
are crufhed in the Birth ; and, on the other, that
wicked Men labour againft the Truth in the moft unreafonable and inconfiftent Ways, and are led on from
one Degree of Obftinacy, Prevarication, and Infatuation, to another, without Limits.

It may be added here, That the Perfons reproved
and condemned in the Gofpels, in the *Acts* of the
Apoftles; by St. *Paul* in his Epiftles, by St. *Peter* in
his fecond Epiftle, by St. *John* and St. *Jude* in their
Epiftles, and by St. *John* in the *Revelation,* viz.
the Five Churches, and the *Nicolaitans,* could not but
endeavour to vindicate themfelves. The Books were
all of a public Nature, and thefe Reproofs particularly
fo, as being intended to guard others.

I have now gone through the feveral Parts of the
Scripture, and fhewn briefly how the Importance of
each would be a Security againft Forgery and Fiction
in that Part. I will now add fome general Evidences
to the fame Purpofe.

Firft, then, It is certain, that both *Jews* and *Chriftians* have undergone the fevereft Perfecutions and Sufferings

ferings on account of their facred Books, and yet never could be prevailed with to deliver them up: Which fhews that they thought them of the higheft Importance, moft genuine and true.

Secondly, The Prefervation of the Law of *Mofes*, which is probably the firft Book that was ever written in any Language, while fo many others more modern have been loft, fhews the great Regard paid to it. The fame holds in a lefs Degree of moft of the other Books of the Old Teftament, fince moft of them are antienter than the oldeft *Greek* Hiftorians. And as the Records of all the neighbouring Nations are loft; we muft fuppofe thofe of the *Jews* to have been preferved, from their Importance, or fome other fuch Caufe, as may be an equal Evidence of their Genuinenefs and Truth.

Thirdly, The great Importance of all the facred Books appears from the many early Tranflations and Paraphrafes of them. The fame Tranflations and Paraphrafes muft be an effectual Means of fecuring their Integrity and Purity, if we could fuppofe any Defign to corrupt them.

Fourthly, The Hefitation and Difficulty with which a few Books of the New Teftament were received into the Canon, fhew the great Care and Concern of the primitive Chriftians about their Canon, *i. e.* the high Importance of the Books received into it; and are therefore a ftrong Evidence, firft, for the Genuinenefs and Truth of the Books which were received without Hefitation; and then for thefe others, fince they were received univerfally at laft.

Fifthly, The great religious Hatred and Animofity which fubfifted between the *Jews* and *Samaritans*, and between feveral of the antient Sects amongft the Chriftians, fhew of what Importance they all thought their facred Books; and would make them watch over one another with a jealous Fye.

PROP.

P R O P. 22.

The Language, Style, and Manner of Writing uſed in the Books of the Old and New Teſtaments, are Arguments of their Genuineneſs.

HERE I obſerve, Firſt, That the *Hebrew* Language, in which the Old Teſtament was written, being the Language of an antient People, and one that had little Intercourſe with their Neighbours, and whoſe Neighbours alſo ſpake a Language that had great Affinity with their own, would not change ſo faſt as modern Languages have done, ſince Nations have been variouſly mixed with one another, and Trade, Arts, and Sciences, greatly extended. Yet ſome Changes there muſt be, in paſſing from the Time of *Moſes* to that of *Malachi.* Now, I apprehend, that the Biblical *Hebrew* correſponds to this Criterion with ſo much Exactneſs, that a conſiderable Argument may be deduced thence in favour of the Genuineneſs of the Books of the Old Teſtament.

Secondly, The Books of the Old Teſtament have too conſiderable a Diverſity of Style to be the Work either of one *Jew* (for a *Jew* he muſt be on account of the Language), or of any Set of cotemporary *Jews.* If therefore they be all Forgeries, there muſt be a Succeſſion of Impoſtors in different Ages, who have concurred to impoſe upon Poſterity, which is inconceiveable. To ſuppoſe Part forged, and Part genuine, is very harſh, neither would this Suppoſition, if admitted, be ſatisfactory.

Thirdly, The *Hebrew* Language ceaſed to be ſpoken, as a living Language, ſoon after the Time of the *Babyloniſh* Captivity : But it would be difficult or impoſſible to forge any thing in it, after it was become a dead Language. For there was no Grammar made for the *Hebrew* till many Ages after ; and, as it

is difficult to write in a dead Language with Exactnefs, even by the Help of a Grammar, fo it feems
impoffible without it. All the Books of the Old Teftament muft therefore be, nearly, as antient as the *Babylonifh* Captivity; and, fince they could not all be
written in the fame Age, fome muft be confiderably
more antient; which would bring us again to a Succeffion of confpiring Impoftors.

Fourthly, This laft Remark may perhaps afford a
new Argument for the Genuinenefs of the Book of
Daniel, if any were wanting. But indeed the Septuagint Tranflation fhews both this, and all the other
Books of the Old Teftament to have been confidered
as antient Books, foon after the Times of *Antiochus
Epiphanes*, at leaft.

Fifthly, There is a Simplicity of Style, and an unaffected Manner of Writing, in all the Books of the
Old Teftament; which is a very ftrong Evidence of
their Genuinenefs, even exclufively of the Suitablenefs
of this Circumftance to the Times of the fuppofed
Authors.

Sixthly, The Style of the New Teftament is alfo
fimple and unaffected, and perfectly fuited to the
Time, Places, and Perfons. Let it be obferved farther, that the Ufe of Words and Phrafes is fuch, alfo
the Ideas, and Method of Reafoning, as that the Books
of the New Teftament could be written by none but
Perfons originally *Jews*; which would bring the Inquiry into a little narrower Compafs, if there was any
Occafion for this.

One may alfo obferve, that the Narrations and Precepts of both Old and New Teftament are delivered
without Hefitation; the Writers teach as having Authority; which Circumftance is peculiar to thofe, who
have both a clear Knowlege of what they deliver, and
a perfect Integrity of Heart.

PROP.

P R O P. 23.

The very great Number of particular Circum-
ſtances of Time, Place, Perſons, &c. mentioned
in the Scriptures, are Arguments both of their
Genuineneſs and Truth.

THAT the Reader may underſtand what I mean
by theſe particular Circumſtances, I will recite
ſome of the principal Heads, under which they may
be claſſed.

There are then mentioned in the Book of *Geneſis,*
the Rivers of Paradiſe, the Generations of the antediluvian Patriarchs, the Deluge with its Circumſtances,
the Place where the Ark reſted, the Building of the
Tower of *Babel,* the Confuſion of Tongues, the Diſperſion of Mankind, or the Diviſion of the Earth
amongſt the Poſterity of *Shem,* *Ham,* and *Japhet,* the
Generations of the poſtdiluvian Patriarchs, with the
gradual Shortening of human Life after the Flood,
the Sojournings of *Abraham,* *Iſaac,* and *Jacob,* with
many Particulars of the State of *Canaan,* and the
neighbouring Countries, in their Times, the Deſtruction of *Sodom* and *Gomorrah,* the State of the
Land of *Edom,* both before and after *Eſau*'s Time,
and the Deſcent of *Jacob* into *Egypt,* with the State of
Egypt before *Moſes*'s Time.

In the Book of *Exodus* are the Plagues of *Egypt,*
the Inſtitution of the Paſſover, the Paſſage through
the *Red Sea,* with the Deſtruction of *Pharaoh* and his
Hoſt there, the Miracle of Manna, the Victory over
the *Amalekites,* the ſolemn Delivery of the Law from
Mount *Sinai,* many particular Laws both moral and
ceremonial, the Worſhip of the golden Calf, and
a very minute Deſcription of the Tabernacle, Prieſts
Garments, Ark, *&c.*

In

In *Leviticus* we have a Collection of ceremonial Laws, with all their Particularities, and an Account of the Deaths of *Nadab* and *Abihu*.

The Book of *Numbers* contains the firft and fecond Numberings of the feveral Tribes with their Genealogies, the peculiar Offices of the three feveral Families of the *Levites*, many ceremonial Laws, the Journeyings and Encampments of the People in the Wildernefs during forty Years, with the Relation of fome remarkable Events which happened in this Period ; as the Searching of the Land, the Rebellion of *Korah*, the Victories over *Arad*, *Sihon*, and *Og*, with the Divifion of the Kingdoms of the two laft among the *Gadites*, *Reubenites*, and *Manaffites*, the Hiftory of *Balak* and *Balaam*, and the Victory over the *Midianites*, all defcribed with the feveral Particularities of Time, Place, and Perfons.

The Book of *Deuteronomy* contains a Recapitulation of many things contained in the three laft Books, with a fecond Delivery of the Law, chiefly the moral one, by *Mofes* upon the Borders of *Canaan*, juft before his Death, with an Account of this.

In the Book of *Jofhua*, we have the Paffage over *Jordan*, the Conqueft of the Land of *Canaan* in Detail, and the Divifion of it among the Tribes, includeing a minute geographical Defcription.

The Book of *Judges* recites a great Variety of public Tranfactions, with the private Origin of fome. In all, the Names of Times, Places, and Perfons, both among the *Ifraelites*, and the neighbouring Nations, are noted with Particularity and Simplicity.

In the Book of *Ruth* is a very particular Account of the Genealogy of *David*, with feveral incidental Circumftances.

The Books of *Samuel*, *Kings*, *Chronicles*, *Ezra*, and *Nehemiah*, contain the Tranfactions of the Kings before the Captivity, and Governors afterwards, all delivered in the fame circumftantial Manner. And
here

here the particular Account of the Regulations ſacred and civil eſtabliſhed by *David,* and of the Building of the Temple by *Solomon,* the Genealogies given in the Beginning of the firſt Book of *Chronicles,* and the Liſts of the Perſons who returned, ſealed, *&c.* after the Captivity, in the Books of *Ezra* and *Nehemiah,* de-ſerve eſpecial Notice, in the Light in which we are now conſidering Things.

The Book of *Eſther* contains a like Account of a very remarkable Event, with the Inſtitution of a Feſtival in Memory of it.

The Book of *Pſalms* mentions many hiſtorical Facts in an incidental Way; and this, with the Books of *Job, Proverbs, Eccleſiaſtes,* and *Canticles,* allude to the Manners and Cuſtoms of antient Times in various Ways.

In the *Prophecies* there are ſome hiſtorical Relations; and in the other Parts the indirect Mention of Facts, Times, Places, and Perſons, is interwoven with the Predictions in the moſt copious and circumſtantial Manner.

If we come to the New Teſtament, the ſame Obſer-vations preſent themſelves at firſt View. We have the Names of Friends and Enemies, *Jews, Greeks,* and *Romans,* obſcure and illuſtrious, the Times, Places, and Circumſtances of Facts, ſpecified directly, and alluded to indirectly, with various References to the Cuſtoms and Manners of thoſe Times.

Now here I obſerve, Firſt, That, in Fact, we do not ever find, that forged or falſe Accounts of Things ſu-perabound thus in Particularities. There is always ſome Truth where there are conſiderable Particularities related, and they always ſeem to bear ſome Propor-tion to one another   Thus there is a great Want of the Particulars of Time, Place, and Perſons, in *Ma-netho's* Account of the *Egyptian* Dynaſties, *Cteſias's* of the *Aſſyrian* Kings, and thoſe which the technical Chronologers have given of the antient Kingdo ns of

Greece;

Greece; and, agreeably thereto, thefe Accounts have much Fiction and Falfhood, with fome Truth: Whereas *Thucydides's* Hiftory of the *Peloponnefian* War, and *Cæfar's* of the War in *Gaul*, in both which the Particulars of Time, Place, and Perfons, are mentioned, are univerfally efteemed true to a great Degree of Exactnefs.

Secondly, A Forger, or a Relater of Falfhoods, would be careful not to mention fo great a Number of Particulars, fince this would be to put into his Reader's Hands Criterions whereby to detect him. Thus we may fee one Reafon of the Fact mentioned in the laft Paragraph, and which in confirming that Fact confirms the Propofition here to be proved.

Thirdly, A Forger, or a Relater of Falfhoods, could fcarce furnifh out fuch Lifts of Particulars. It is eafy to conceive how faithful Records kept from time to time by Perfons concerned in the Tranfactions fhould contain fuch Lifts; nay, it is natural to expect them in this Cafe, from that local Memory which takes ftrong Poffeffion of the Fancy in thofe who have been prefent at Tranfactions; but it would be a Work of the higheft Invention, and greateft Stretch of Genius, to raife from nothing fuch numberlefs Particularities, as are almoft every-where to be met with in the Scriptures. The Account given of Memory, Imagination, and Invention, in the foregoing Part of thefe Obfervations, fets this Matter in a ftrong Light.

There is a Circumftance relating to the Gofpels, which deferves particular Notice in this Place. St. *Matthew* and St. *John* were Apoftles; and therefore, fince they accompanied Chrift, muft have this local Memory of his Journeyings and Miracles.· St. *Mark* was a *Jew* of *Judæa*, and a Friend of St. *Peter's*; and therefore may either have had this local Memory himfelf, or have written chiefly from St. *Peter*, who had. But St. *Luke*, being a Profelyte of *Antioch*, not converted perhaps till feveral Years after Chrift's Refurrection,

tion, and receiving his Accounts from different Eye-witneſſes, as he ſays himſelf, could have no Regard to that Order of Time, which a local Memory would ſuggeſt. Let us ſee how the Goſpels anſwer to theſe Poſitions. St. *Matthew*'s then appears to be in exact Order of Time, and to be a Regulator to St. *Mark*'s, and St *Luke*'s, ſhewing St. *Mark*'s to be nearly ſo, but St. *Luke*'s to have little or no Regard to the Order of Time in his Account of Chriſt's Mi-niſtry. St. *John*'s Goſpel is, like St. *Matthew*'s, in Order of Time; but as he wrote after all the reſt, and with a View only of recording ſome remarkable Par-ticulars, ſuch as Chriſt's Actions before he left *Judæa* to go to preach in *Galilee*, his Diſputes with the *Jews* of *Jeruſalem*, and his Diſcourſes to the Apoſtles at his laſt Supper, there was leſs Opportunity for his local Memory to ſhew itſelf. However, his recording what paſt before Chriſt's going into *Galilee* might be in Part from this Cauſe, as St. *Matthew*,s Omiſſion of it was probably from his Want of this local Memory. For it appears, that St. *Matthew* re-ſided in *Galilee*; and that he was not converted till ſome time after Chriſt's coming thither to preach. Now this Suitableneſs of the Four Goſpels to their reputed Authors, in a Circumſtance of ſo ſubtle and recluſe a Nature, is quite inconſiſtent with the Suppoſition of Fiction or Forgery. This Remark is chiefly taken from Sir *Iſ. Newton*'s Chapter concerning the Times of the Birth and Paſſion of Chriſt, in his Comment on *Daniel.*

Fourthly, If we could ſuppoſe the Perſons who forged the Books of the Old and New Teſtaments, to have furniſhed their Readers with the great Variety of Particulars above-mentioned, notwithſtanding the two Reaſons here alleged againſt it, we cannot, how-ever, conceive, but that the Perſons of thoſe Times when the Books were publiſhed, muſt by the Help of theſe Criterions have detected and expoſed the For-

geries

geries or Falfhoods. For thefe Criterions are fo
attefted by allowed Facts, as at this Time, and
in this remote Corner of the World, to eftablifh the
Truth and Genuinenefs of the Scriptures, as may appear
even from this Chapter, and much more from the
Writings of Commentators, facred Critics, and fuch
other learned Men, as have given the hiftorical Evidences for Revealed Religion in Detail; and by Parity
of Reafon they would fuffice even now to detect the
Fraud, were there any: Whence we may conclude, *a
fortiori*, that they muft have enabled the Perfons who
were upon the Spot, when the Books were publifhed,
to do this; and the Importance of many of thefe
Particulars confidered under *Prop.* 21. would furnifh
them with abundant Motives for this Purpofe. And
upon the Whole I infer, that the very great Number of
Particulars of Time, Place, Perfons, *&c.* mentioned in
the Scriptures, is a Proof of their Genuinenefs and Truth,
even previoufly to the Confideration of the Agreement of
thefe Particulars with Hiftory, Natural and Civil, and
with one another, of which I now proceed to treat.

P R O P. 24.

*The Agreement of the Scriptures with Hiftory,
Natural and Civil, is a Proof of their Genuinenefs and Truth.*

THUS the Hiftory of the Fall agrees in an eminent
manner both with the obvious Facts of Labour,
Sorrow, Pain, and Death, with what we fee and feel
every Day, and with all our philofophical Inquiries into the Frame of the human Mind, the Nature of focial
Life, and the Origin of Evil, as may appear from
thefe Papers amongft other Writings of the fame
kind. The feveral Powers of the little World within
a Man's own Breaft are at Variance with one another,
as well as thofe of the great World; we are utterly
unable

unable to give a complete Solution of the Origin of the Evils which flow from thefe Difcords, and from the jarring of the Elements of the natural World ; and yet there are comfortable Hopes, that all Evil will be overpowered and annihilated at laft, and that it has an intire Subferviency to Good really and ultimately ; *i. e.* tho' the *Serpent bruife our Heel,* yet we fhall *bruife its Head.*

It cannot be denied indeed, but that both the Hiftory of the Creation, and that of the Fall, are attended with great Difficulties. But then they are not of fuch a kind as intimate them to be a Fiction contrived by *Mofes.* It is probable, that he fet down the traditional Account, fuch as he received it from his Anceftors ; and that this Account contains the literal Truth· in fhort, tho' fo concealed in certain Particulars through its Shortnefs, and fome figurative Expreffions made ufe of, that we cannot yet, perhaps never fhall, interpret it fatisfactorily. However, Mr. *Whifton's* Conjectures concerning the fix Days Creation feem to deferve the Attention of future Inquirers ; and there is great Plaufibility in fuppofing with him, that the firft Chapter of *Genefis* contains a Narrative of the Succeffion of vifible Appearances.

One may fuppofe alfo, that there is a typical and prophetic Senfe to be difcovered hereafter, relative perhaps to the fix Millenniums, which are to precede a feventh Sabbatical one ; and that the Words are more accommodated to this Senfe than to the literal one, in fome Places, which I think holds in many of the Prophecies that have double Senfes. However, there is no Appearance of any Motive to a Fraud, either in the Hiftory of the Creation or Fall, nor any Mark of one. And the fame Shortnefs and Obfcurity which prevents our being able to explain, feems alfo to preclude Objections. If we fuppofe thefe Hiftories to have been delivered by traditional Explanations that accompanied hieroglyphical Delineations, this would perhaps account

count for fome of the Difficulties; and help us to conceive how the Hiftories may be exact, and even decy-
pherable hereafter. The Appellations of the Tree
of Life, of the Tree of the Knowlege of Good and
Evil, and of the Serpent, feem to favour this Suppofition. At the utmoft, one can make no Objections
againft thefe Hiftories, but what are confiftent with
the firft and loweft of the Suppofitions above-mentioned
concerning Divine Infpiration.

Natural Hiftory bears a ftrong Teftimony to *Mofes*'s Account of the Deluge; and fhews that it muft
have been univerfal, or nearly fo, however difficult it
may be to us, either to find Sources for fo great a Body of Waters, or Methods of removing them. That
a Comet had fome Share in this Event, feems highly
probable from what Dr. *Halley* and Mr. *Whifton* have
obferved of this Matter: I guefs alfo partly from the
Suppofition, that fome Part of the Tail of a Comet
was then attracted by the Earth, and depofited there,
partly from the great Shortening of human Life after
the Flood, and partly from the fermenting and inebriating Quality of vegetable Juices, which feems firft
to have appeared immediately after the Flood, that
a great Change was made at the Time of the Flood
in the Conftitution of natural Bodies, and particularly
in that of Water. And it feems not improbable to
me, that an Inlargement of the refpective Spheres of
Attraction and Repulfion, and of the Force of thefe,
in the fmall Particles of Water, might greatly contribute to account for fome Circumftances of the Deluge,
mentioned by *Mofes*. For, by the Increafe of the
Sphere, and Force of Attraction, the Waters fufpended
in the Air or Firmament in the Form of a Mift or Vapour
before the Flood, *fee Gen.* ii. 5, 6. might be collected into large Drops, and fall upon the Earth. And
their Fall might give Occafion to rarer watry Vapours,
floating at great Diftances from the Earth in the planetary and intermundane Spaces, to approach it, be in
like

like manner condenſed into large Drops, and fall upon it. This might continue for 40 Days, the Force with which the rare Vapours approached the Earth decreaſing all the latter Part of that Time, and being at the End of it overpowered by the contrary Force of the Vapours raiſed from the Earth, now covered with Water, by the Action of the Sun, and of the Wind, mentioned *Gen.* viii. 1. For it is evident, that the Wind has great Power in raiſing watry Particles, *i. e.* putting them into a State of Repulſion ; and the Wind here conſidered would be far ſtronger than that which now prevails in the *Pacific Ocean*, ſince the whole Globe was one great Ocean during the Height of the Deluge. The Ceſſation of the Rain, and the Increaſe of the Sphere, and Force of Repulſion, above ſuppoſed, would in like manner favour the Aſcent of Vapours from this great Ocean. And thus the precedent Vapours might be driven by the ſubſequent ones into the planetary and intermundane Spaces, beyond the Earth's Attraction. However, ſince the Quantity of the ſubſequent Vapours muſt perpetually decreaſe by the Decreaſe of the Surface of the Ocean, a Limit would be ſet to the Aſcent of the Vapours, as was before to their Deſcent.

According to this Hypotheſis, that State of our Waters, which was ſuperinduced at the Deluge, may both be the Cauſe of the Rainbow, *i. e.* of Drops of a Size proper for this Purpoſe, and exempt us from the Danger of a ſecond Deluge. For a freſh Intermixture of like cometical Particles could not now ſuperinduce a new State. The Rainbow may therefore be a natural Sign and Evidence, *that the Waters ſhall no more become a Flood to deſtroy the Earth.*

As to the breaking up the Fountains of the great Deep, mentioned *Gen.* vii. 11. though no ſatisfactory Account has been given of this hitherto, yet ſurely there is great Plauſibility in ſuppoſing, that the increaſed Attraction of a Comet, conſequent upon its near

Approach

Approach to the Earth, might have fome fuch Effect, and at the fame time contribute to produce fuch Changes in the Earth, as a mere Deluge could not.

Civil Hiftory affords likewife many Evidences, which fupport the *Mofaic* Account of the Deluge. Thus, firft, We find from Pagan Authors, that the Tradition of a Flood was general, or even univerfal. Secondly, The Paucity of Mankind, and the vaft Tracts of uninhabited Land, which are mentioned in the Accounts of the firft Ages, fhew that Mankind are lately fprung from a fmall Stock, and even fuit the Time affigned by *Mofes* for the Flood. Thirdly, The great Number of fmall Kingdoms, and petty States, in the firft Ages, and the late Rife of the great Empires of *Egypt*, *Affyria*, *Babylon*, &c. concur to the fame Purpofe. Fourthly, The Invention and Progrefs of Arts and Sciences concur likewife. And this laft favours the *Mofaic* Hiftory of the Antediluvians. For as he mentions little of their Arts, fo it appears from the late Invention of them after the Flood, that thofe who were preferved from it were poffeffed of few.

It has been objected to the *Mofaic* Hiftory of the Deluge, That the Ark could not contain all the Animals which are now found upon the Earth, with the proper Provifions for them during the Time of the Deluge. But this, upon an accurate Computation, has been proved to be otherwife ; fo that what was thought an Objection is even fome Evidence. For it is extremely improbable, that a Perfon who had feigned the Particular of the Ark, fhould have come fo near the proper Dimenfions. It is to be confidered here, that the feveral Speciefes of both Plants, and brute Animals, which differ from each other by fmall Degrees, feem to be multiplied every Day by the Varieties of Climates, Culture, Diet, Mixture, &c. alfo, that if we fuppofe an univerfal Deluge, the Ark, with the Entrance of the Animals, &c. feem neceffary alfo. For as we can trace up the firft imperfect

perfect Rudiments of the Art of Shipping amongſt the *Greeks*, there could be no Shipping before the Flood; confequently no Animals could be ſaved. Nay, it is highly improbable, that even Men, and domeſtic Animals, could be ſaved, not to mention wild Beaſts, Serpents, &c. tho' we ſhould ſuppoſe, that the Antediluvians had Shipping, unleſs we ſuppoſe alſo, that they had a Divine Intimation and Directions about it, ſuch as *Moſes* relates; which would be to give up the Cauſe of Infidelity at once.

It has been objected likewiſe, That the *Negro* Nations differ ſo much from the *Europeans*, that they do not ſeem to have deſcended from the ſame Anceſtors. But this Objection has no ſolid Foundation. We cannot preſume to ſay what Alterations Climate, Air, Water, Soil, Cuſtoms, &c. can or cannot produce. It is no-ways to be imagined, that all the national Differences in Complexion, Features, Make of the Bones, &c. require ſo many different Originals; on the contrary, we have Reaſon from Experience to aſſert, that various Changes of this Kind are made by the Incidents of Life, juſt as was obſerved, in the laſt Paragraph, of Plants, and brute Animals. And, with reſpect to the different Complexions of different Nations, Dr. *Mitchell* has ſhewn with great Appearance of Truth, *Phil. Tranſ. Numb.* 474. that theſe ariſe from external Influences. It will confirm this, if it be found, that the *Jews*, by reſiding in any Country for ſome Generations, approach to the Complexion of the original Natives. At the ſame time we muſt obſerve from the Hiſtory of Diſtempers, that acquired Diſpoſitions may be tranſmitted to the Deſcendents for ſome Generations; which is perhaps one of the great Truths intimated in the Account of the Fall. And thus the Children of *Negroes* may be black, tho' born and bred up in a Country where the original Natives are not ſo.

A

A Third Objection is, That it is difficult to account for the Original of the *Americans*, and for the wild Beasts and Serpents that are found in that Quarter of the World, according to the *Mosaic* History. But to this one may answer, First, That *America* may be even now contiguous to the North-east Part of *Asia*. Secondly, That it might have been contiguous to other Parts of our great Continent for some Centuries after the Deluge, though that Contiguity be since broken off. Thirdly, That the first Sailors, who ventured out of the Streights, or others, might be driven, by Stress of Weather, and their own Ignorance, first within the Influence of the Trade-Winds, and then to some Part of *America*. One can offer nothing certain on either Side, in respect of these Points. However, it seems to me, that many Customs found amongst the *Negroes* and *Americans* are stronger Evidences, that they are of the same Original with the *Asiatics* and *Europeans*, than any which have yet appeared to the contrary. And, upon the Whole, I conclude certainly, that the *Mosaic* Account of the Deluge is much confirmed by both Natural and Civil History, if we embrace the First and lowest Hypothesis concerning Divine Inspiration; and has very strong Presumptions for it, according to the Second or Third.

If we could suppose the high Mountains in *South America* not to have been immerged in the Deluge, we might the more easily account for the wild Beasts, poisonous Serpents, and curious Birds of *America*. Might not the Ark be driven round the Globe during the Deluge? And might not *Noah* be aware of this, and observe that it had been immerged fifteen Cubits in Water? And may not the *Mosaic* Account be partly a Narrative of what *Noah* saw, partly the Conclusions which he must naturally draw from thence? Thus the Tops of some of the highest Mountains might escape, consistently with the *Mosaic* Account. The future Inquiries of Natural Historians may perhaps determine this Point.

The

The next great Event recorded in *Geneſis* is the Confuſion of Languages. Now the *Moſaic* Account of this appears highly probable, if we firſt allow that of the Deluge. For it ſeems impoſſible to explain how the known Languages ſhould ariſe from one Stock. Let any one try only in *Hebrew, Greek, Latin,* and *Engliſh.* The Changes which have happened in Languages ſince Hiſtory has been certain, do not at all correſpond to a Suppoſition of this kind. There is too much of Method and Art in the *Greek* and *Latin* Tongues for them to have been the Inventions of a rude and barbarous People ; and they differ too much from *Hebrew, Arabic,* &c. to have flowed from them without Deſign. As to the *Chineſe,* it is difficult to make any probable Conjectures about it, partly from its great Heterogeneity in reſpect of other Languages, partly becauſe learned Men have not yet examined it accurately. However, the moſt probable Conjecture ſeems to be, that it is the Language of *Noah*'s Poſt-diluvian Poſterity; the leaſt probable one, that it could have flowed naturally from any known Language, or from the ſame Stock with any ; which it muſt have done, if we admit the Deluge, and yet reject the Confuſion of Languages.

The Diſperſion of the three Sons of *Noah* into different Countries, related in the Tenth Chapter of *Geneſis,* comes next under Conſideration, being a Conſequence, not the Cauſe, of the Diverſity of Languages. Now here Antiquarians, and learned Men, ſeem to be fully agreed, that the *Moſaic* Account is confirmed, as much as can be expected in our preſent Ignorance of the State of antient Nations. And it is to be obſerved of all the Articles treated of under this Propoſition, that we, who live in the North-weſt Corner of *Europe,* lie under great Diſadvantages in ſuch Reſearches. However, ſince thoſe who have ſtudied the Oriental Languages and Hiſtories, or have travelled into the Eaſtern Parts, have made many

Diſcoveries

Difcoveries of late Years, which have furprifingly confirmed the Scripture Accounts, one may hope and prefume, that if either our learned Men be hereafter fuffered to have free Accefs to thofe Parts, or the Natives themfelves become learned, both which are furely probable in the higheft Degree, numberlefs unexpected Evidences for the Truth of the Scripture Hiftory will be brought to Light.

Let us next come to the State of Religion in the antient Poftdiluvian World, according to *Mofes*, and the fucceeding facred Hiftorians. The Poftdiluvian Patriarchs then appear to have worfhiped the One Supreme Being by Sacrifices, but in a fimple Manner, and to have had frequent Divine Communications. By degrees their Pofterity fell off to Idolatry, worfhiped the Sun, Moon, and Stars, deified dead Men, and polluted themfelves with the moft impure and abominable Inftitutions. The *Ifraelites* alone were kept to the Worfhip of the true God, and even they were often infected by their idolatrous Neighbours. Now all this is perfectly agreeable to what we find in Pagan Hiftory. The Idolatries of the Pagans are acknowleged on all hands. It appears alfo from Pagan Hiftory, that they grew up by degrees, as the Scriptures intimate. All the Pagan Religions appear to have had the Worfhip of one God fuperior to the reft, as their common Foundation. They all endeavoured to render him propitious by Sacrifice; which furely cannot be an human Invention, nor a Cuftom, which, if invented in one Nation, would be readily propagated to another. They all joined mediatorial and inferior, alfo local and tutelar Deities to the one God. And they all taught the Frequency of Divine Communications. Hence the Pagan Religions appear to be merely the degenerated Offspring of Patriarchal Revelations, and to infer them as their Caufe. Hence the Pretences of Kings, Lawgivers, Priefts, and great Men, to Infpiration, with the Credulity of the Multitude.

titude. That there had been Divine Communications, was beyond Diſpute; and therefore all that Reluctance to admit them, which appears in the preſent Age, was over-ruled. At firſt there were no Impoſtors. When therefore they did ariſe, it would not be eaſy for the Multitude to diſtinguiſh between thoſe who had really Divine Communications, and thoſe who only pretended to them; till at laſt all real Inſpiration having ceaſed amongſt the Gentile World, their ſeveral Religions kept Poſſeſſion merely by the Force of Education, Fraud in the Prieſts, and Fear in the People; and even theſe Supports began to fail at laſt, about the time of Chriſt's Coming. And thus many Things, which have been thought to weaken the Evidences for the Scripture Accounts, are found to ſtrengthen them, by flowing naturally from that State of Religion in antient Times, and from that only, which the Scripture delivers.

A farther Confirmation of the ſame Scripture Accounts of the Flood, Diſperſion of Mankind, and Patriarchal Revelations, may be had from the following very remarkable Particular: It appears from Hiſtory, that the different Nations of the World have had, *cæteris paribus*, more or leſs Knowlege, Civil and Religious, in proportion as they were nearer to, or had more intimate Communication with, *Egypt, Palæſtine, Chaldæa*, and the other Countries, that were inhabited by the moſt eminent Perſons amongſt the firſt Deſcendents of *Noah*, and by thoſe who are ſaid in Scripture to have had particular Revelations made to them by God; and that the firſt Inhabitants of the extreme Parts of the World, reckoning *Palæſtine* as the Centre, were in general mere Savages. Now all this is utterly inexplicable upon the Footing of Infidelity, of the Excluſion of all Divine Communications. Why ſhould not human Nature be as ſagacious, and make as many Diſcoveries, Civil and Religious, at the Cape of *Good Hope*, or in *America*, as in *Egypt, Palæſtine, Meſopotamia, Greece*, or *Rome?* Nay, why ſhould *Palæſtine* ſo far exceed them all,

as

as it did confeffedly? Allow the Scripture Accounts, and all will be clear and eafy. Mankind, after the Flood, were firft difperfed from the Plains of *Mefopotamia*. Some of the chief Heads of Families fettled there, in *Palæftine*, and in *Egypt*. *Palæftine* had afterwards extraordinary Divine Illuminations beftowed upon its Inhabitants, the *Ifraelites* and *Jews*. Hence its Inhabitants had the pureft Notions of God, and the wifeft Civil Eftablifhment. Next after them come the *Egyptians* and *Chaldæans*, who, not being removed from their firft Habitations, and living in fertile Countries watered by the *Nile*, *Tigris*, and *Euphrates*, may be fuppofed to have preferved more both of the antediluvian and poftdiluvian Revelations, alfo to have had more Leifure for Invention, and a more free Communication with the *Ifraelites* and *Jews*, than any other Nations: Whereas thofe fmall Parties, which were driven farther and farther from each other into the Extremes of Heat and Cold, intirely occupied in providing Neceffaries for themfelves, and alfo cut off by Rivers, Mountains, or Diftance, from all Communication with *Palæftine*, *Egypt*, and *Chaldæa*, would lofe much of their original Stock, and have neither Inclination nor Ability to invent more.

Let us now confider the Hiftory of particular Facts, and inquire what Atteftations we can produce from Pagan Hiftory for the Scripture Accounts of *Abraham*, and his Pofterity the *Ifraelites* and *Jews*. We cannot expect much here, partly becaufe thefe Things are of a private Nature, if compared to the univerfal Deluge, partly becaufe the Pagan Hiftory is either deficient, or grofly corrupted with Fable and Fiction, till we come to the Times of the Declenfion of the Kingdoms of *Ifrael* and *Judah*. However, fome faint Traces there are in antient Times, and many concurring Circumftances in fucceeding ones; and, as foon as the Pagan Records come to be clear and certain, we have numerous and ftrong Confirmations of the

2   Sacred

Sacred Hiſtory. Thus the Hiſtory of *Abraham* ſeems to have tranſpired in ſome meaſure. It is alſo probable, that the antient *Brachmans* were of his Poſterity by *Keturah*, that they derived their Name from him, and worſhiped the true God only. *Moſes* is mentioned by many Heathen Writers, and the Accounts which they give of his conducting the *Iſraelites* from *Egypt* to *Canaan* are ſuch as might be expected. The Authors lived ſo long after *Moſes*, and had ſo little Opportunity or Inclination to know the exact Truth, or to be particular, that their Accounts cannot invalidate the Scripture Hiſtory, though they do a little confirm it. The Expulſion of the *Canaanites* by *Joſhua* ſeems to have laid the Foundation of the Kingdom of the *Shepherds* in the *Lower Egypt* mentioned by *Manetho*, and of the Expulſion of the Natives into the *Upper Egypt*; who, after ſome Centuries, drove the *Shepherds* back again into *Canaan* about the Time of *Saul*. The *Canaanites* mentioned by St. *Auſtin* and others, upon the Coaſt of *Afric*, may be of the ſame Original. *See Newton's Chronol. Page* 198. We may conclude from the Book of *Judges*, that there were many petty Sovereignties in the Neighbourhood of *Canaan*; and it appears from Pagan Hiſtory, as Sir *Iſ. Newton* has rectified it, that the firſt great Empire, that of *Egypt*, was not yet riſen. When *David* ſubdued the *Philiſtines* or *Phœnicians*, *Cadmus* and others ſeem to have fled into *Greece*, and to have carried Letters with them, which the *Philiſtines* had probably learnt, about a Generation before, from the Copy of the Law found in the Ark taken from the *Iſraelites*. After *Solomon's* Temple was built, the Temple of *Vulcan* in *Egypt*, and others in other Places, began to be built in Imitation of it; juſt as the Oracles of the Heathens were Imitations of God's Communications to the *Iſraelites*, and particularly of that by *Urim* and *Thummim*. *Shiſhak*, who came out of *Egypt* in the 5th Year of *Rehoboam*, is the *Seſoſtris* of *Herodotus*; and this

Point,

Point, being fettled, becomes a capital Pin, upon which all the Pagan Chronology depends. Hence *Herodotus*'s Lift of the *Egyptian* Kings is made probable and confiftent. As we advance farther to the *Affyrian* Monarchy, the Scripture Accounts agree with the profane ones rectified ; and when we come ftill farther to the *Æra* of *Nabonaffar*, and to the Kings of *Babylon* and *Perfia*, which are pofterior to this *Æra*, and recorded in *Ptolemy*'s Canon, we find the Agreement of facred and profane Hiftory much more exact, there being certain Criterions in the profane Hiftory for fixing the Facts related in it. And it is remarkable, that not only the direct Relations of the Hiftorical Books, but the indirect, incidental Mention of Things in the Prophecies, tallies with true Chronology; which furely is fuch an Evidence for their Genuinenefs and Truth, as cannot be called in Queftion. And, upon the Whole, it may be obferved, that the facred Hiftory is diftinct, methodical, and confiftent throughout ; the profane utterly deficient in the firft Ages, obfcure, and full of Fictions, in the fucceeding ones ; and that it is but juft clear and precife in the principal Facts about the Time that the facred Hiftory ends. So that this corrects and regulates that, and renders it intelligible in many Inftances, which muft otherwife be given up as utterly inexplicable. How then can we fuppofe the facred Hiftory not to be genuine and true, or a wicked Impofture to rife up, and continue not only undifcovered, but even to increafe to a moft audacious Height, in a Nation which of all others kept the moft exact Accounts of Time ? I will add one Remark more : This fame Nation, who may not have loft fo much as one Year from the Creation of the World to the *Babylonifh* Captivity, as foon as they were deprived of the Affiftance of Prophets, became moft inaccurate in their Methods of keeping Time, there being nothing more erroneous than the Accounts of *Jofephus*, and the

modern

modern *Jews*, from the Time of *Cyrus*, to that of
Alexander the Great; notwithſtanding that all the requiſite Aſſiſtances might eaſily have been borrowed
from the neighbouring Nations, who now kept regular Annals. Hence it appears, that the Exactneſs of
the ſacred Hiſtory was owing to the Divine Aſſiſtance.

It is an Evidence in favour of the Scriptures, allied
to thoſe which I am here conſidering, that the Manners of the Perſons mentioned in the Scriptures have
that Simplicity and Plainneſs, which is alſo aſcribed
to the firſt Ages of the World by Pagan Writers; and
both of them concur, by this, to intimate the Novelty
of the then preſent Race, *i. e.* the Deluge.

Beſides theſe Atteſtations from profane Hiſtory,
we may conſider the *Jews* themſelves as bearing Teſtimony to this Day, in all Countries of the World, to
the Truth of their antient Hiſtory, *i. e.* to that of
the Old and New Teſtaments. Allow this, and it
will be eaſy to ſee how they ſhould ſtill perſiſt in their
Attachment to that Religion, thoſe Laws, and thoſe
Prophecies, which ſo manifeſtly condemn them, both
in paſt times, and in the preſent. Suppoſe any conſiderable Alteration made in their antient Hiſtory, *i. e.*
any ſuch as may anſwer the Purpoſes of Infidelity, and
their preſent State will be inexplicable.

The Books of the New Teſtament are verified by
Hiſtory, in a manner ſtill more illuſtrious; theſe
Books being written, and the Facts mentioned
therein tranſacted, during the Times of *Auguſtus*, *Ti-
berius*, and the ſucceeding *Cæſars*. Here we may
obſerve,

Firſt, That the incidental Mention of the *Roman*
Emperors, Governors of *Judæa*, and the neighbouring Provinces, the *Jewiſh* High-Prieſts, Sects of the
Jews, and their Cuſtoms, of Places, and of Tranſactions, is found to be perfectly agreeable to the Hiſtories of thoſe Times. And as the whole Number of

theſe

thefe Particulars is very great, they may be reckoned a full Proof of the Genuinenefs of the Books of the New Teftament; it being impoffible for a Perfon who had forged them, *i. e.* who was not an Eye and Ear-witnefs, and otherwife concerned with the Tranf-actions as the Books require, but who had invented many Hiftories and Circumftances, *&c.* not to have been deficient, fuperfluous, and erroneous. No Man's Memory or Knowlege is fufficient for fuch an Adapta-tion of feigned Circumftances, and efpecially where the Mention is incidental. Let any one confider how often the beft Poets fail in this, who yet endeavour not to vary from the Manners and Cuftoms of the Age of which they write; at the fame time that Poetry neither requires nor admits fo great a Minute-nefs in the particular Circumftances of Time, Place, and Perfons, as the Writers of the New Teftament have defcended to naturally and incidentally.

Secondly, That Chrift preached in *Judæa* and *Ga-lilee*, made many Difciples, and was crucified under *Pontius Pilate*, at the Inftigation of the chief Men among the *Jews*; alfo that his Difciples preached after his Death, not only in *Judæa*, but all over the *Roman* Empire, that they converted Multitudes, were perfe-cuted, and at laft fuffered Death, for their firm Adhe-rence to their Mafter; and that both *Chrift* and his Difciples pretended to work many Miracles; are Facts attefted by Civil Hiftory in the ampleft manner, and which cannot be called in Queftion. Now thefe Facts are fo connected with the other Facts mentioned in New Teftament, that they muft ftand or fall together. There is no probable Account to be given of thefe Facts, but by allowing the reft. For the Proof of this, I appeal to every Reader who will make the Trial. It may alfo be concluded from the remark-able Unwillingnefs of the prefent Unbelievers to allow even the plaineft Facts in exprefs Terms. For it fhews them to be apprehenfive, that the Connexion between

between the ſeveral principal Facts mentioned in the New Teſtament is inſeparable, and that the Atteſtation given to ſome by Civil Hiſtory may eaſily be extended to all.

It has been objected, That more Mention ought to have been made of the common Facts by the profane Writers of thoſe Times, alſo ſome Acknowlegement of the miraculous ones, had they been true. To this we may anſwer, Firſt, That *Judæa* was but a ſmall and diſtant Province of the *Roman* Empire, and the *Jews* themſelves, with whom the Chriſtians were for a long time confounded, much deſpiſed by the *Romans*. Secondly, That Hiſtorians, Politicians, Generals, &c. have their Imaginations ſo much preoccupied by Affairs of State, that Matters purely religious are little regarded by them. *Gallio cared for none of theſe Things.* Thirdly, That a Perſon who attended in any great Degree to the Chriſtian Affairs, if a good Man, could ſcarce avoid becoming a Chriſtian ; after which his Teſtimony ceaſes to be Pagan, and becomes Chriſtian ; of which I ſhall ſpeak under the next Head. Fourthly, That both thoſe who were Favourers of the Chriſtians, and thoſe averſe to them in a moderate Degree, one of which muſt be the Caſe with great Numbers, would have Motives to be ſilent ; the Half-Chriſtians would be ſilent for fear of being perſecuted ; and the others would affect to take no Notice of what they diſliked, but could not diſprove ; which is a Fact that occurs to daily Obſervation. Laſtly, When theſe things are laid together, the Atteſtations of the profane Writers to the common Facts appear to be ſuch as one might expect, and their Silence as to the miraculous ones is accounted for.

Thirdly, All the Chriſtian Writers, from the Time of the Apoſtles and downwards, bear Teſtimony to the Genuineneſs of the Books of the New Teſtament, and the Truth of the Facts, in a great Variety of Ways, direct and indirect, and in ſuch manner as might be ex-

I 4 pected.

pected. Their Quotations from them are numberlefs, and agree fufficiently with the prefent Copies. They go every-where upon the Suppofition of the Facts, as the Foundation of all their Difcourfes, Writings, Hopes, Fears, &c. They difcover every-where the higheft Regard, and even Veneration, both for the Books and the Authors. In fhort, one cannot fee how this Teftimony in favour of the Books of the New Teftament can be invalidated, unlefs by fuppofing all the Ecclefiaftical Writings of the firft Centuries to be forged alfo; or all the Writers to have concurred to write as if they believed the Genuinenefs and Truth of thefe Books, though they did not; or to have had no Ability or Inclination to diftinguifh Genuinenefs and Truth from Forgery and Falfhood; or by fome other fuch Suppofition, as will fcarce bear to be named.

Here Three Queftions may be afked, that bear fome Relation to this Subject; and the Anfwers to which will, I think, illuftrate and confirm what has been advanced in the laft Paragraph.

Thus, Firft, It may be afked, Why we have not more Accounts of the Life of Chrift tranfmitted to us. To this I anfwer, That it is probable from St. *Luke's* Preface, that there were many fhort and imperfect Accounts handed about very early; the Authors of which, though they had not taken care to inform themfelves accurately, did not, however, endeavour to impofe on others defignedly; and that all thefe grew into Difufe, of courfe, after the Four Gofpels, or perhaps the Three firft, were publifhed, or, at leaft, after the Canon of the New Teftament was formed; alfo that after this the Chriftians were fo perfectly fatisfied, and had the Four Gofpels in fuch Efteem, that no one prefumed to add any other Accounts, and efpecially as all the Apoftles were then dead.

The Second Queftion is, How come we to have fo little Account, in the primitive Writers, of the Lives, Labours, and Sufferings of the Apoftles? I anfwer,

That

That the Apoſtles ſeem to have reſided in *Judæa*, till
Nero's Army invaded it, and afterwards to have travelled into diſtant Parts ; and that neither their Converts in *Judæa*, nor thoſe in the diſtant barbarous
Countries, into which they traveled, could have any probable Motive for writing their Lives : Alſo, that, as to
other Chriſtians, they had neither Opportunities nor
Motives. The Chriſtians looked up to Chriſt, as their
Maſter, not to the Apoſtles. Their great Buſineſs
was to promote Chriſtianity, not to gratify their own
or others fruitleſs Curioſity. They were not learned
Men, who had ſpent their Lives in the Study of Annal-
iſts and Biographers. They did not ſuſpect, that an
Account of the Lives of the Apoſtles would ever be
wanted, or that any one could call their Integrity,
Inſpiration, Miracles, &c. in Queſtion. St. *Luke*
ſeems to have deſigned by his *Acts*, chiefly to ſhew
how the Goſpel firſt got firm Footing amongſt *Jews*,
Proſelytes of the Gate, and idolatrous Gentiles ; in
order to encourage the new Converts to copy the Examples of the Apoſtles, and firſt Preachers, and to
publiſh the Goſpel in all Nations. Laſtly, The primitive Chriſtians had early Diſputes with *Jews*, Heathens, Heretics, and even with one another ; which
took up much of their Attention and Concern.

Thirdly, It may be aſked, Who were the Perſons
that forged the ſpurious Acts and Revelations of ſeveral of the Apoſtles, &c. I anſwer, That, amongſt
the Number of thoſe who joined themſelves to the
Chriſtians, there muſt be many whoſe Hearts were
not truly purified, and who, upon apoſtatizing, would
become more ſelf-intereſted, vain-glorious, and impure, than before. Theſe were Antichriſts, as St. *John*
calls them, who left the Church becauſe they were
not of it. Some of theſe forged Books to ſupport
themſelves, and eſtabliſh their own Tenets. Others
might write partly like Enthuſiaſts, partly like Impoſtors. And, laſtly, There were ſome both weak
and

and wicked Men, though not fo abandoned as the antient Heretics, who in the latter End of the fecond Century, and afterwards, endeavoured to make Converts by Forgeries, and fuch other wicked Arts. However, all thofe who are ufually called Fathers, in the firft Ages, ftand remarkably clear of fuch Charges.

Fourthly, The Propagation of Chriftianity, with the Manner in which it was oppofed by both *Jews* and Gentiles, bears Witnefs to the Truth and Genuinenefs of the Books of the New Teftament. But I forbear entering upon this Argument, as it will come more properly in another Place. Let me only obferve here, that there are many Paffages in the Talmudical Writings, which afford both Light and Confirmation to the New Teftament, notwithftanding that one principal Defign of the Authors was to difcredit it.

P R O P. 25.

The Agreement of the Books of the Old and New Teftaments with themfelves and with each other, is an Argument both of their Genuinenefs and Truth.

THE Truth of this Propofition will be evident, if a fufficient Number of thefe mutual Agreements can be made out. It is never found, that any fingle Perfon, who deviates much from the Truth, can be fo perfectly upon his Guard as to be always confiftent with himfelf. Much lefs therefore can this happen in the Cafe of a Number, living alfo in different Ages. Nothing can make them confiftent, but their copying faithfully after real Facts. The Inftances will make this clearer.

The Laws of the *Ifraelites* are contained in the Pentateuch, and referred to in a great Variety of Ways, direct and indirect, in the hiftorical Books, in the Pfalms, and in the Prophecies. The hiftorical

Facts

Facts also in the preceding Books are often referred to in those that succeed, and in the Psalms and Prophecies. In like manner, the Gospels have the greatest Harmony with each other, and the Epistles of St. *Paul* with the *Acts of the Apostles.* And indeed one may say, that there is scarce any Book of either Old or New Testament, which may not be shewn to refer to many of the rest in some way or other. For it is to be observed, that the Bible has been studied and commented upon far more than any other Book whatsoever; and that it has been the Business of Believers in all Ages to find out the mutual Relations of its Parts, and of Unbelievers to search for Inconsistencies; also that the first meet every Day with more and more Evidences in favour of the Scriptures from the mutual Agreements and Coincidences here considered; and that Unbelievers have never been able to allege any Inconsistencies that could in the least invalidate the Truth of the principal Facts; I think, not even affect the Divine Inspiration of the historical Books, according to the second or third Hypothesis abovementioned.

It will probably illustrate this Proposition, to bring a parallel Instance from the *Roman* Writers. Suppose then that no more remained of these Writers than *Livy, Tully,* and *Horace.* Would they not by their References to the same Facts and Customs, by the Sameness of Style in the same Writer, and Differences in the different ones, and numberless other suchlike Circumstances of critical Consideration, prove themselves and one another to be genuine, and the principal Facts related, or alluded to, to be true?

It is also to be observed, that this mutual Harmony and Self-consistency, in its ultimate Ratio, is the Whole of the Evidence which we have for Facts done in antient Times, or distant Places. Thus, if a Person was so sceptical as to call in question the whole *Roman* History, even the most notorious Facts, as their Conquests quefts firft of *Italy*, and then of the neighbouring Countries, the Death of *Cæfar*, and the Fall of the Weftern Empire by the Invafions of the *Goths* and *Vandals*, with all the Evidences of thefe from Books, Infcriptions, Coins, Cuftoms, *&c.* as being all forged in order to deceive; one could only fhew him, that it is inconfiftent with what he fees of human Nature, to fuppofe that there fhould be fuch a Combination to deceive; or that the Agreement of thefe Evidences with each other is far too great to be the Effect of any fuch fraudulent Defign, of Chance, *&c.* And all thefe Arguments are, in effect, only bringing a Number of concurring Evidences, whofe Sum total foon approaches to the ultimate Limit, *i. e.* to Unity, or abfolute Certainty, nearer than by any diftinguifhable Difference. It does not therefore import, in refpect of real Conviction, after a certain Number are brought, whether we bring any more or no; they can only add this imperceptible Defect, *i. e.* practically nothing. Thus I fuppofe, that the remaining Writings of *Livy*, *Tully*, and *Horace* alone would fatisfy any impartial Man fo much of the general Extenfivenefs of the *Roman* Conquefts, *&c.* that nothing perceptible could be added to his Conviction; no more than any common Event can, or ever does in Fact, appear more credible from the Teftimony of a thoufand than of ten or twenty Witneffes of approved Integrity. And whoever will apply this Reafoning to the prefent Cafe, muft perceive, as it appears to me, that the numberlefs minute, direct, and indirect Agreements and Coincidences, that prefent themfelves to all diligent Readers of the Scriptures, prove their Truth and Genuinenefs beyond all Contradiction, at leaft according to the firft and loweft Hypothefis concerning Divine Infpiration.

As to thofe few and fmall apparent Inconfiftencies, which are fuppofed to confine the Infpiration of the Scriptures to this loweft Senfe; one may obferve, that
they

they decreaſe every Day as learned Men inquire farther ; and that, were the Scriptures perfectly exact in
every Particular, there muſt be ſome apparent Difficulties, ariſing merely from our Ignorance of antient
Languages, Cuſtoms, diſtant Places, &c. and conſequently that if theſe be not more, than our Ignorance
makes it reaſonable to expect, they are no Objection
at all. And of apparent Inconſiſtencies one may remark in particular, that they exclude the Suppoſition
of Forgery. No ſingle Forger, or Combination of
Forgers, would have ſuffered the apparent Inconſiſtencies which occur in a few Places, ſuch as the different
Genealogies of Chriſt in St. *Matthew* and St. *Luke,*
and ſome little Variations in the Narration of the
ſame Fact in different Goſpels. Theſe are too obvious
at firſt Sight not to have been prevented, had there
been any Fraud.

I will here add an Hypotheſis, by which, as it appears to me, one may reconcile the Genealogies of
St. *Matthew* and St. *Luke.* I ſuppoſe then, that St.
Matthew relates the real Progenitors of *Joſeph* ; St.
Luke the Series of thoſe who were Heirs to *David* by
Birthright ; and that both tranſcribed from genealogical Tables, well known to the *Jews* of thoſe Times.
St. *Matthew* after *David* takes *Solomon,* from whom *Joſeph* lineally deſcended. St. *Luke* takes *Nathan,* upon
whom, though younger than ſome others, and even
than *Solomon,* we muſt ſuppoſe the Birthright to be
conferred, as in the Inſtances of *Jacob* and *Joſeph.*
St. *Matthew* proceeds by real Deſcent to *Salathiel,* at
the Time of the Captivity ; St. *Luke* proceeds by the
Heirs according to Birthright, and comes to *Salathiel*
likewiſe. We muſt therefore ſuppoſe, that *Salathiel,*
Solomon's Heir, was now *David's* alſo, by the Extinction of all the Branches of *Nathan's* Family. St.
Matthew then takes *Zorobabel* as *Joſeph's* real Progenitor, St. *Luke* takes him as Heir or eldeſt Son to *Salathiel.* Again, St. *Matthew* takes *Abiud* the real
Progenitor,

Progenitor, St. *Luke Rhefa* the eldeft Son; and thus
St. *Matthew* proceeds by lineal Defcent to *Jofeph*, St.
Luke by Heirs to the fame *Jofeph*; for we are to fuppofe, that *Heli* dying without Heirs Male, *Jofeph*
became his Heir by Birthright, *i. e.* Heir to *Zorobabel*,
i. e. to *David*. If we farther fuppofe, that the Virgin
Mary was Daughter to *Heli*, for which there appears
to be fome Evidence, the Solution will be more complete, and more agreeable to the *Jewifh* Cuftoms. It
confirms this Solution, that St. *Matthew* ufes the
Word ἐγέννησε, which reftrains his Genealogy to lineal
Defcent; whereas St. *Luke* ufes the Article τῦ, which
is very general. It confirms it alfo, that St. *Luke's*
Defcents, reckoning from *David* to *Salathiel*, are but
about twenty-two Years apiece; which is much too
fhort for Defcents from Father to Son, but agrees very
well to Defcents by Birthright. As to St. *Matthew's*
Defcents, they are far too long, after the Captivity,
for Defcents from Father to Son; but then it is eafy to
fuppofe, that fome were left out on account of dying
before their Fathers, or fome other Reafon. Three
of the Kings of *Judah* are left out after *Joram*,
perhaps on account of their being of the immediate
Pofterity of the idolatrous *Abab's* Daughter *Athaliah*.
Others are left out after the Captivity, perhaps for
fome fimilar Reafon.

P R O P. 26.

The Unity of Defign, which appears in the
Difpenfations recorded in the Scriptures, is
an Argument not only of their Truth and
Genuinenefs, but alfo of their Divine Au-
thority.

FOR this Unity is not only fo great as to exclude
Forgery and Fiction, in the fame Way as the
mutual Agreements mentioned in the laft Propofition,
but

but alſo greater than the beſt and ableſt Men could have preſerved, in the Circumſtances of theſe Writers, without the Divine Aſſiſtance. In order to ſee this, let us inquire what this Deſign is, and how it is purſued by the Series of Events, and Divine Interpoſitions, recorded in the Scriptures. The Deſign is that of bringing all Mankind to an exalted, pure, and ſpiritual Happineſs, by teaching, enforcing, and begetting in them Love and Obedience to God. This appears from many Paſſages in the Old Teſtament, and from almoſt every Part of the New. Now we are not here to inquire in what Manner an almighty Being could ſooneſt and moſt effectually accompliſh this. But the Queſtion is, Whether, laying down the State of Things as it has been, is, and probably will be, for our Foundation, there be not a remarkable Fitneſs in the Diſpenſations aſcribed to God in the Scriptures, to produce this glorious Effect; and whether the Perſons who adminiſtred theſe Diſpenſations did not here concur with a ſurpriſing Uniformity, though none of them ſaw God's ultimate Deſign completely, and ſome but very imperfectly; juſt as Brutes by their Inſtincts, and Children by the Workings of their natural Faculties, contribute to their own Preſervation, Improvement, and Happineſs, without at all foreſeeing, that they do this. If we alter any of the Circumſtances of the Microcoſm or Macrocoſm, of the Frame of our own Natures, or of the external World that ſurrounds us, we ſhall have Queſtion riſe up after Queſtion in an endleſs Series, and ſhall never be ſatisfied, unleſs God ſhould be pleaſed to produce Happineſs inſtantaneouſly, *i. e.* without any Means, or ſecondary inſtrumental Cauſes, at all; and, even then, we ſhould only be where we were at our firſt Setting out, if Things be conſidered in the true, ultimate Light. We are therefore to lay down the real State of Things, as our Foundation; *i. e.* we are to ſuppoſe Man to be in a State of Good

mixed

mixed with Evil, born with Appetites, and expofed to Temptations, to which if he yields, Suffering muft follow; which Suffering, however, tends to eradicate the Difpofition from whence it flowed, and to implant a better: We are to fuppofe him to be endued with voluntary Powers, which enable him to model his Affections and Actions according to a Rule; and that the Love of God, his ultimate Happinefs, can never be genuine, but by his firft learning to fear God, by his being mortified to Pleafure, Honour, and Profit, and the moft refined felfifh Defires, and by his loving his Neighbour as himfelf; *i. e.* we muft fuppofe all that which practical Writers mean by a State of Trial, Temptation, moral Exercife and Improvement, and of practical Free-will. Let us fee therefore, how the feveral Difpenfations mentioned in the Scriptures, their being recorded there, and the fubordinate Parts, which the Prophets and Apoftles acted, confpired to bring about this ultimate End of Man, both in each Individual, and in the whole Aggregate, confidered as one great Individual, as making up the myftical Body of Chrift, according to the Language of St. *Paul*; and inquire, whether, if all other Reafons were fet afide, the mere Harmony and Concurrence of fo many Parts, and fo many Perfons removed from each other by long Intervals of Time, in this one great Defign, will not compel us to acknowlege the Genuinenefs, Truth, and Divine Authority, of the Scriptures.

The firft Thing which prefents itfelf to us in the the Scriptures, is the Hiftory of the Creation and Fall. Thefe are not to be accounted for, as was faid above, being the Foundation upon which we go. However, the recording them by *Mofes*, as Tradition began to grow weak and uncertain, has been of great Ufe to all thofe, who have had them communicated by this means perfectly or imperfectly, *i. e.* to a great Part of the World. This Hiftory impreffes an awful and amiable Senfe of the Divine Being, our Creator and

Judge;

Judge; ſhews the Heinouſneſs of Sin; and mortifies us to this World, by declaring that our Paſſage through it muſt be attended with Labour and Sorrow. We find ourſelves in this State: Revealed Religion did not bring us into it: Nor is this State an Objection to Revealed Religion, more than to Natural: However, Revealed Religion goes a Step higher than Natural, and ſhews the immediate ſecondary Cauſe, *viz.* the Sin and wilful Diſobedience of our firſt Parents. And when the Account of Paradiſe, of Man's Expulſion thence, and of the Curſe paſt upon him in the Beginning of *Geneſis*, are compared with the Removal of this Curſe, of Sorrow, Crying, Pain, and Death, with the Renovation of all Things, and with Man's Reſtoration to the Tree of Life and Paradiſe, and his Admiſſion into the new *Jeruſalem* in the laſt Chapters of the Revelation, Hope and Fear quicken each other; and both conſpire to purify the Mind, and to advance the great Deſign conſidered under this Propoſition.

How far the Deluge was neceſſary, *cæteris manentibus*, for the Purification of thoſe who were deſtroyed by it, *i. e.* for accompliſhing this great End in them, we cannot preſume to ſay. It is ſufficient, that there is no contrary Preſumption, that no Methods conſiſtent with the State of Things in the antient World were neglected, as far as we know, and that we are not in the leaſt able to propoſe a better Scheme. We leave theſe rebellious, unhappy People, now tranſlated into another State, to the ſame kind Providence which attended them in this, and all whoſe Puniſhments on this ſide the Grave are for Melioration. However, the evident Footſteps of this in the World, and the clear Tradition of it, which would continue for ſeveral Ages, alſo the Hiſtory of it delivered by *Moſes*, have an unqueſtionable good Tendency. Sinners, who reflect at all, cannot but be alarmed at ſo dreadful an Inſtance of Divine Severity. Farther, if this Hiſtory ſhould open to us a new Relation, *viz.* that which we bear to the Comets, this, compared with other Parts of the Scriptures, may give us hereafter such Intimations concerning the Kind, Degree, and Duration of future Punishment, as will make the most Obdurate tremble, and work in them that Fear which is the Beginning of Wisdom, and of the perfect Love which casteth out Fear. At the same time we may observe, that the Covenant which God made, not only with *Noah* and his Posterity, but with all living Creatures, after the Flood, has a direct and immediate Tendency to beget Love.

The Confusion of Languages, the consequent Dispersion of Mankind, and the Shortening of the Lives of the Postdiluvians, all concurred to check the exorbitant Growth and Infection of Wickedness. And we may judge how necessary these Checks were, *cæteris manentibus*, from the great Idolatry and Corruption which appeared in the World within less than a thousand Years after the Flood. The Patriarchal Revelations mentioned and intimated by *Moses* had the same good Effects, and were the Foundations of those Pagan Religions, and, in great measure, of that moral Sense, which, corrupt and imperfect as they were, could not but be far preferable to an intire want of these. If it be objected, that, according to this, greater Checks, and more Divine Communications, were wanted; I answer, that a greater Dispersion, or Shortening of human Life, might have prevented the destined Increase of Mankind, or the Growth of Knowlege, Civil and Religious, &c. and that more or more evident Divine Interpositions might have restrained the voluntary Powers too much, or have precluded that Faith which is necessary to our ultimate Perfection. These are Conjectures indeed ; but they are upon the Level with the Objection, which is conjectural also.

The next remarkable Particular that occurs, is the Calling of *Abraham,* the Father of the Faithful. Now

in

in this Part of the Scripture History, as it is explained
by the New Testament, we have the strongest Evidences of God's great Design to purify and perfect
Mankind. He is called to forsake his Relations,
Friends, and Country, lest he should be corrupted
by Idolatry ; he receives the Promise of the Land of
Canaan, without seeing any probable Means of obtaining it, besides this Promise, in order to wean him
from the Dependence on external Means ; he waits
for a Son till all natural Expectations ceased, for the
same Purpose ; by obtaining him he learns to trust in
God notwithstanding apparent Impossibilities ; and the
Command to sacrifice *his Son, his only Son Isaac, whom
he loved,* affords him a noble Opportunity of exercising
this Trust, and of shewing, that his Principle of Obedience to God was already superior to the purest of
earthly Affections. Lastly, when God promises him,
as a Reward for all his Faith and Obedience, as the
highest Blessing, that *in him and his Seed all the Nations of the Earth should be blessed,* we must conceive
this to be a Declaration, first, that God himself is infinitely benevolent; and, secondly, that the Happiness
of *Abraham,* of his Seed, and of all Mankind who
were to be blessed in his Seed, must arise from their
Imitation of God in his Benevolence. This whole
Universe is therefore a System of Benevolence, or, as
St. *Paul* expresses it, a Body, which, being *fitly framed
and compacted together, increaseth itself in Love.*

As to the Objection which is sometimes made to
the Sacrifice of *Isaac,* we may observe, that *Abraham* had himself received so many Divine Communications, and had been acquainted with so many
made to his Ancestors, that he had no Doubt about
the Command's coming from God, did not even ask
himself the Question. It is probable, that in that
early Age there had as yet been few or no false Pretences, or Illusions. *Abraham* could as little doubt of
God's Right to *Isaac's* Life, or of his Care of him in

K 2 another

another State.   Thefe Things were Parts of the Patriarchal Religion.   And yet great Faith was required
in *Abraham*, before he could overcome his natural
Affection and Tendernefs for *Ifaac* out of a Principle
of Obedience to God, and truft God for the Accomplifhment of his Promife, though he commanded him
to deftroy the only apparent Means of accomplifhing
it.   Unlefs *Abraham* had been highly advanced in
Faith and Obedience, he could not have ftood fo fevere a Trial ; but this Trial would greatly confirm
thefe.   And thus this Hiftory is fo far from being liable to Objection, that it is peculiarly conformable to
thofe Methods, which mere Reafon and Experience
dictate as the proper ones, for advancing and perfecting true Religion in the Soul.   When the typical
Nature of it is alfo confidered, one cannot furely doubt
of its Divine Authority.   And, in the previous Steps,
through which *Abraham* paffed in order to obtain this
Bleffing, we have an Adumbration and Example
of that Faith, Patience, and gradual Progrefs in the
fpiritual Life, which are neceffary to all thofe who
hope to be *bleffed with faithful Abraham.*

Let us next pafs on to *Mofes*, and the *Ifraelites* under his Conduct.   Here we enter upon the Confideration of that People, who are the Type of Mankind
in general, and of each Individual in particular ; who
were the Keepers of the Oracles of God, and who, under
God, agreeably to his Promife to *Abraham*, have been,
and will hereafter be a Bleffing to all Nations, and the
Means of reftoring Man to his paradifiacal State.   And
firft they are oppreffed with a cruel Slavery in *Egypt*,
left, being delighted with its Fertility, and the prefent
Pleafures of Senfe which it afforded, they fhould forget their true earthly Country, *the Land of Promife.*
They then fee the moft amazing Judgments inflicted
upon their Enemies the *Egyptians* by God, whilft they
themfelves were protected and delivered, that fo they
might learn Confidence in his Power and Favour, and
                                                    be

be thus prepared for their Inſtitution in Religion, and their Trial and Purification in the Wilderneſs. And here the awful Delivery of the Law, their being fed from Day to Day by Miracle, their being kept from all Commerce with other Nations, and from all Cares of this World in Building, Planting, &c. till their old Habits, and *Egyptian* Cuſtoms and Idolatries, were quite effaced, and the Practice of the new Law eſtabliſhed, their having the Hiſtory of the World, and particularly of their Anceſtors, laid before them in one View, their Tabernacle, their numerous Rites and Ceremonies, additional to thoſe of the Patriarchal Religion, and oppoſite to the growing Idolatries of their Neighbours the *Egyptians* and *Canaanites*, and which, beſides their Uſes as Types, were Memorials of their Relation to God, and of his conſtant Preſence and Protection, and, laſtly, the total Extinction of that murmuring Generation, who longed for the Fleſh-pots of *Egypt*, cannot but appear to be intended for the Purification of this choſen People, as being remarkably analogous to the Methods of Purification, which every good Man experiences in himſelf, and ſees in others, *i. e.* cannot but appear highly conducive to the great Deſign conſidered under this Propoſition. At laſt, the Education and Inſtruction of this People being finiſhed, they are admitted to inherit the earthly Promiſe made to their Forefathers, and take Poſſeſſion of the Land of *Canaan* under *Joſhua*. And thus we come to a remarkable Period in God's Diſpenſations to them.

Now therefore they are, in ſome meaſure, left to themſelves, for the ſake of moral Improvement, the Divine Interpoſitions being far leſs frequent and ſolemn, than at the firſt Erection of the Theocracy under *Moſes*'s Adminiſtration. However, there were many ſupernatural Interpoſitions, Appointments, Favours, Corrections, &c. from *Joſhua* to *Malachi*, on account of their yet infant State in reſpect of internal Purity,

K 3 whoſe

whofe Tendency to improve both the Body Politic of the Nation, and each Individual, is fufficiently evident. After *Malachi* they were intirely left to themfelves; their Canon being completed, they were then only to hear and digeft what *Mofes* and the Prophets had delivered unto them; and by this means to prepare themfelves for the laft and completeft Difpenfation.

But, before we enter upon this, let us briefly confider the State of the Gentile World, in the Interval between *Abraham* and Chrift, and what Intimations the Old Teftament gives us of their being alfo under the Care of Providence, and in a State of moral Difcipline. They had then, according to this, Firft, The Traditions of Patriarchal Revelations. Secondly, All the Nations in the Neighbourhood of *Canaan* had frequent Opportunities and Motives to inform themfelves of the true Religion. Thirdly, All thofe who conquered them at any time could not but learn fomething both from their Subjection, and their Deliverance afterwards. Fourthly, The Captivities by *Salmanefer* and *Nebuchadnezzar* carried the Knowlege of the true God to many diftant Nations. Laftly, The Diftractions of the *Jewifh* State during the cotemporary Empires of *Syria* and *Egypt*, the Rife of the *Samaritan* Religion, and the Tranflation of the Old Teftament into *Greek*, conduced eminently to the fame Purpofe. And as it is neceffary in the prefent State of Things, for the Exercife of various Affections, and our moral Improvement, that there fhould be Degrees and Subordinations in common Things, fo it feems equally neceffary, that it fhould be fo in religious Matters: And thus the Gentiles may have had, in the Interval between *Abraham* and Chrift, all that fuited their other Circumftances, all that they could have improved by in internal voluntary Purity, other Things remaining the fame, which is always fuppofed. And it is remarkable in the View of this Propofition, that we learn fo

much

much from the Scriptures concerning the moral Diſcipline which God afforded to the *Gentiles.*

When we come to the New Teſtament, the great Deſign of all God's Diſpenſations appears in a ſtill more conſpicuous Manner. Here we ſee how Chriſt began to erect his ſpiritual Kingdom, and the Apoſtles extended it; we have the ſublimeſt Doctrines, and pureſt Precepts, for effecting it in ourſelves and others, and the ſtrongeſt Aſſurances, that it will be effected at laſt, that this Leaven will continue to operate till the whole Lump be leavened. But, above all, it is remarkable, that the principal Means for effecting this is by Submiſſion and Sufferance, not Reſiſtance, and external Violence. The Preachers are to undergo Shame, Perſecution, and Death, as the Lord of Life and Glory did before them, This is that *Fooliſhneſs of God,* which is *wiſer than Men,* and that *Weakneſs of God,* which is *ſtronger than Men.* Theſe Means ſeem fooliſh and weak to the falſe Wiſdom of this World. But if they be compared with the Frame of our Natures, and with the real Conſtitution of Things, they will appear to be perfectly ſuited to produce in all Mankind that beſt of Ends, the Annihilation of Self, and worldly Deſires, and the pure and perfect Love of God, and of all his Creatures, in and through him.

Setting aſide therefore the Greatneſs of this End, and its Suitableneſs to the Divine Goodneſs, ſetting aſide alſo the Miracles which have concurred in it, I ſay that the Coincidence of the Hiſtories, Precepts, Promiſes, Threatenings, and Prophecies of the Scriptures in this one Point is an Argument not only of their Genuineneſs and Truth, but of their Divine Authority. Had the Writers been guided by their own Spirits, and not by the ſupernatural Influences of the Spirit of Truth, they could neither have opened to us the various Diſpenſations of God tending to this one Point, nor have purſued it themſelves, with ſuch intire Steadineſs

and

and Uniformity, through fo many different Ages of the World.

The gradual Opening of this Defign is an Argument to the fame Purpofe. Man's Wifdom, if it could have formed fuch a Defign, would have ruſhed forward upon it prematurely. At the fame time we may obferve, that this Defign is implied in the Scriptures from the firft, though not expreffed fo as to be then underftood ; which is another Argument of their Divine Original.

Cor. From the Reafoning ufed under this Propofition we may be led to believe, that all the great Events which happen in the World, have the fame Ufe as the Difpenfations recorded in the Scriptures, *viz.* that of being a Courfe of moral Difcipline for Nations and Individuals, and of preparing the World for future Difpenfations. Thus the Irruption of the barbarous Nations into the *Roman* Empire, the *Mahometan* Impofture, the Corruptions of the Chriftian Religion, the Ignorance and Darknefs which reigned for fome Centuries during the groffeft of thefe Corruptions, the Reformation, Reftoration of Letters, and the Invention of Printing, three great cotemporary Events which fucceeded the dark Times, the Rife of the Enthufiaftical Sects fince the Reformation, the vaft Increafe and Diffufion of Learning in the prefent Times, the growing Extenfivenefs of Commerce between various Nations, the great Prevalence of Infidelity amongft both *Jews* and *Chriftians*, the Difperfion of *Jews* and *Jefuits* into all known Parts of the World, *&c. &c.* are all Events, which, however mifchievous fome of them may feem to human Wifdom, are, *cæteris manentibus*, the moft proper and effectual way of haftening the Kingdom of Chrift, and the Renovation of all Things.

PROP.

P R O P. 27.

*Divine Communications, Miracles, and Prophe-
cies, are agreeable to Natural Religion, and
even seem necessary in the Infancy of the
World.*

SINCE God is a Being of infinite Justice, Mercy, and
Bounty, according to Natural Religion, it is rea-
sonable to expect, that if the Deficiences of Natural
Reason, or the Inattention of Mankind to the Footsteps of his Providence, were such at any time, as
that all the World were in Danger of being lost in
Ignorance, Irreligion, and Idolatry, God should inter-
pose by extraordinary Instruction, by alarming Instances of Judgment and Mercy, and by prophetical Declarations of Things to come, in order to teach Men
his Power, his Justice, and his Goodness, by sensible
Proofs and Manifestations. We must not say here,
that God could not suffer this; but inquire from History, whether he has or no. Now I suppose it will
easily be acknowleged, that this was the Case with the
Gentile World in antient Times, and that the *Judaical*
and *Christian* Institutions have greatly checked Irreligion and Idolatry, and advanced true Natural Religion ; which is a remarkable Coincidence in favour
of these Institutions, though all other Evidences for
them were set aside. Neither must we say here, that
since God permits gross Ignorance in some Nations,
the *Hottentots* for Instance, even to this Day, he might
have permitted it in all Mankind. Allow that we
know so little of his unsearchable Judgments, as not
to be able to make any certain Conclusion : Yet
surely it is much more agreeable to the forenamed
Attributes, and to the Analogies of other Things,
that the Bulk of Mankind should have such a Knowlege of God, as suits their intellectual Faculties, and
other

other Circumftances, and carries them forwards in moral Improvement, than that all fhould ftand ftill, or go backwards, or make lefs Improvement in Religion, than tallies with their Improvements in other Things; alfo that there fhould be a Subordination in religious Advantages, rather than a perfect Equality.

Natural Religion alfo teaches us to confider God as our Governor, Judge, and Father. Now all thefe Superiors have two Ways of Adminiftration, Inftruction, and Providence for the Well-being of their Inferiors, ordinary and extraordinary. It is therefore natural to expect upon great Occafions an extraordinary Interpofition by Revelation, Miracle, and Prophecy; and that efpecially in that Infancy of the World after the Deluge, which both Sacred and Profane Hiftory affure us of; inafmuch as both States and Individuals require much more of the extraordinary Interpofition of Governors and Parents in their Infancy, than afterwards: All which has a remarkable Correfpondence with the Hiftory of Revelation, as it is in fact. And the Analogical Prefumptions for Miracles, in this and the laft Paragraph, feem at leaft equal to any Prefumption we have, or can have, in this our State of Ignorance of the Whole of Things, againft them.

But there is another Argument in favour of miraculous Interpofitions, which may be drawn from the foregoing Theory of human Nature. I take it for granted, that Mankind have not been upon this Earth from all Eternity. Eternity neither fuits an imperfect, finite Race of Beings, nor our Habitation the Earth. It cannot have revolved round the Sun, as it does now, from all Eternity; it muft have had fuch Changes made in it from its own Fabric and Principles, from the Shocks of Comets, &c. in infinite Time, as would be inconfiftent with our Survival. There was therefore a Time when Man was firft placed upon

the

the Earth. In what State was he then placed? An
Infant, with his Mind a Blank, void of Ideas, as
Children now are born? He would periſh inſtantly,
without a Series of Miracles to preſerve, educate, and
inſtruct him. Or if he be ſuppoſed an Adult with a
blank Mind, *i. e.* without Ideas, Aſſociations, and
the voluntary Powers of Walking, Handling, Speaking, &c. the Concluſion is the ſame; he muſt periſh
alſo, unleſs conducted by a miraculous Interpoſition
and Guardianſhip. He muſt therefore have ſo much
of Knowlege, and of voluntary and ſecondarily
automatic Powers, amongſt which Speech muſt
be reckoned as a principal one, impreſſed upon
him in the way of Inſtinct, as would be neceſſary
for his own Preſervation, and that of his Offspring;
and this Inſtinct is, to all Intents and Purpoſes, Divine
Revelation, ſince he did not acquire it by natural
Means. It is alſo of the Nature of Prophecy; for it
ſeems impoſſible for Mankind to ſubſiſt upon the Earth,
as it now is, without ſome Foreknowlege, and the
conſequent Methods of providing for Futurity, ſuch,
for Inſtance, as Brutes have, or even greater, ſince
Man, unprovided with manual Arts, is peculiarly expoſed to Dangers, Neceſſities, and Hardſhips.

Let us next conſider, how the firſt Men are to be
provided with the Knowlege of God, and a moral
Senſe: For it ſeems neceſſary, that they ſhould be
poſſeſſed of ſome Degree of theſe; elſe the ſenſual
and ſelfiſh Deſires would be ſo exorbitant, as to be
inconſiſtent both with each Man's own Safety, and
with that of his Neighbour; as may be gathered from
the Accounts of ſavage Nations, who yet are not intirely deſtitute of the Knowlege of God, and the moral Senſe. Now, to deduce the Exiſtence and Attributes of God, even in a very imperfect Manner, from
natural Phænomena, requires, as it ſeems to me,
far more Knowlege and Ratiocination, than Men could
have for many Generations, from their natural Powers;

and

and that efpecially if we fuppofe Language not to be infpired, but attained in a natural Way. And it appears both from the foregoing Account of the moral Senfe, and from common Obfervation, that this requires much Time, Care, and Cultivation, befides the previous Knowlege of God, before it can be a Match for the Impetuofity of natural Defires. We may conclude therefore, that the firft Men could not attain to that Degree of the Knowlege of God, and a moral Senfe, which was neceffary for them, without Divine Infpiration.

There are feveral Particulars in the *Mofaic* Account of the Creation, Fall, and Circumftances of the antient World, which tally remarkably with the Method of Reafoning ufed here. Thus, Man is at firft placed in a Paradife, where there was nothing noxious, and confequently where he would need lefs miraculous Interpofition in order to preferve him. He lives upon the Fruits of the Earth, which want no previous Arts of preparing them, and which would ftrike him by their Smells, and, after an Inftance or two, incite him to pluck and tafte : Whereas Animal Diet, befides its Inconfiftency with a State of pure Innocence and Happinefs, requires Art and Preparation neceffarily. There is only one Man, and one Woman, created, that fo the Occafions for exerting the focial Affections may not offer themfelves in any great Degree, before thefe Affections are generated ; but, on the contrary, the Affections may grow naturally, as it were, out of the Occafions. The Nakednefs, and Want of Shame, in our firft Parents, are concurring Evidences of the Abfence of Art, acquired Affections, Evil, &c. *i. e.* of a paradifiacal State. In this State they learnt to give Names to the Animal World, perhaps from the automatic and femivoluntary Exertions of the Organs of Speech, which the Sight of the Creatures, or the Sound of their feveral Cries, would excite ; having probably a fufficient Stock of Language

for

for Communication with God and for converſing with each other about their daily Food, and other neceſſary Things, given them by immediate Inſtinct or In piration. And thus they would be initiated, by naming the Animals, into the Practice of inventing, learning, and applying Words. For the ſame Reaſons we may ſuppoſe, that they learnt many other Things, and particularly the Habit of Learning, during their Abode in Paradiſe. Nay, it may perhaps be, that this Growth of acquired Knowlege, with the Pleaſantneſs of it, might put them upon learning Evil as well as Good, and excite the forbidden Curioſity. After the Fall, we find God providing them with Cloaths, *Cain* baniſhed from the Preſence of God, an Argument that others were permitted to have recourſe to this Preſence to aſk Counſel, &c. his Poſterity inventing Arts for themſelves, *Enoch* and *Noah* walking with God before the Flood, and *Abraham* afterwards; all the Antediluvian Patriarchs long-lived, the Poſtdiluvian long-lived alſo for ſome Generations; amongſt other Reaſons, that they might inſtruct Poſterity in Religious and other important Truths; and the Divine Interpoſitions continuing through the whole Antediluvian World, and gradually withdrawn in the Poſtdiluvian. And it ſeems to me, to ſay the leaſt, a very difficult Thing for any Man, even at this Day, to invent a more probable Account of the firſt Peopling of this Earth, than that which *Moſes* has given us.

P R O P.

P R O P. 28.

*The Objection made against the Miracles recorded
in the Scriptures, from their being contrary
to the Course of Nature, is of little or no
Force.*

IT is alleged here by the Objectors, That the Course
of Nature is fixed and immutable ; and that this is
evinced by the concurrent Testimony of all Mankind
in all Ages ; and consequently that the Testimony of
a few Persons, who affirm the contrary, cannot be
admitted ; but is, *ipso facto*, invalidated by its op-
posing general, or even universal Experience. Now
to this I answer,

Firft, That we do not, by admitting the Testimony of Mankind concerning the Descent of heavy Bodies upon the Surface of our Earth, the common Effects of Heat and Cold, &c. suppose that this invali-
dates the Testimony of those who declare they have
met with contrary Appearances in certain Cases.
Each Party testifies what they have seen ; and why
may not the Evidence of both be true ? It does not
follow, because a Thing has happened a thousand, or
ten thousand times, that it never has failed, nor ever
can fail. Nothing is more common or constant, than
the Effect of Gravity in making all Bodies upon the
Surface of our Earth tend to its Centre. Yet the
rare extraordinary Influences of Magnetism and Electricity can suspend this Tendency. Now, before
Magnetism and Electricity were discovered, and verified by a Variety of concurrent Facts, there would have
been as much Reason to disallow the Evidence of their
particular Effects attested by Eye-witnesses, as there
is now to disallow the particular Miracles recorded in
the Scriptures ; and yet we see, that such a Disallow-
ance would have been a hasty Conclusion, would
have

have been quite contrary to the true Nature of Things. And, in fact, whatever may be the Cafe of a few Perfons, and particularly of thofe, who think that they have an Intereft in difproving Revealed Religion, the Generality of Mankind, learned and unlearned, philofophical and vulgar, in all Ages, have had no fuch Difpofition to reject a Thing well attefted by Witneffes of Credit, becaufe it was contrary to the general, or even univerfal, Tenor of former Obfervations. Now it is evident to confidering Perfons, efpecially if they reflect upon the foregoing Hiftory of Affociation, that the Difpofitions to affent and diffent are generated in the human Mind from the Sum total of the Influences, which particular Obfervations have had upon it. It follows therefore, fince the Bulk of Mankind, of all Ranks and Orders, have been difpofed to receive Facts the moft furprifing, and contrary to the general Tenor, upon their being attefted in a certain limited Degree, that extraordinary Facts are not, in a certain Way of confidering the Thing, out of the Tenor of Nature, but agreeable to it; that here therefore, as well as in common Facts, the Strefs is to be laid upon the Credibility of the Witneffes; and that to do otherwife is an Argument either of fome great Singularity of Mind, or of an undue Biafs.

Secondly, If it fhould be alleged by the Objectors, That they do not mean, by the Courfe of Nature, that Tenor of common Obfervations which occurred to the firft rude Ages of the World, or even that Tenor which is ufually called fo at prefent; but thofe more general Laws of Matter and Motion, to which all the various Phænomena of the World, even thofe which are apparently moft contrary to one another, may be reduced; and that it is probable, that univerfal Experience would concur to fupport the true Laws of Nature of this Kind, were Mankind fufficiently induftrious and accurate in bringing together

the

the Facts, and drawing the Conclusions from them, in which Case, any Deviations from the Tenor of Nature, thus supported and explained, would be far more improbable, than according to the Supposition of the foregoing Paragraph; we answer, That this Objection is a mere Conjecture. Since we do not yet know what these true Laws of Matter and Motion are, we cannot presume to say whether all Phænomena are reducible to them, or not. Modern Philosophers have indeed made great Advances in Natural Knowlege; however, we are still in our infant State, in respect of it, as much as former Ages, if the Whole of Things be taken into Consideration. And this Objection allows and supposes it to be so. Since therefore it was the proper Method for former Ages, in order to make Advances in real Knowlege, to abide by the Award of credible Testimonies, however contrary these Testimonies might appear to their then Notions and Analogies, so this is also the proper Method for us.

If indeed we put the Course of Nature for that Series of Events, which follow each other in the Order of Cause and Effect by the Divine Appointment, this would be an accurate and philosophical Way of speaking; but then we must at once acknowlege, that we are so ignorant of what may be the Divine Purposes and Appointments, of secret Causes, and of the corresponding Variety of Events, that we can only appeal to the Facts, to credible Relations of what actually has been, in order to know what is agreeable to the Course of Nature thus explained. The Scripture Miracles may not be at all contrary to its Fixedness and Immutability. Nor can any Objection lie against them, if we consider Things in this Light, from the present Notions of philosophical Men; *i. e.* from the Course of Nature, understood in a popular Sense; since this falls so short of the true Course of Nature as here defined; *i. e.* as admitting
the

the Inſtrumentality of Beings ſuperior to us, Men divinely inſpired, good Angels, evil Spirits, and many other Influences, of which our preſent Philoſophy can take no Cognizance. With reſpect to moral Analogy, the Caſe is ſomewhat different. If the moral Attributes of God, and the general Rules of his Providence, be ſuppoſed to be eſtabliſhed upon a ſure Footing, then a Series of Events, which ſhould be contrary to theſe, would have a ſtrong Preſumption againſt them. And yet it becomes us to be very diffident here alſo. God is infinite, and we finite: We may therefore, from ſeeing only a ſmall Portion, judge what we ſee to be different from what it is. However, Revealed Religion has no Occaſion in general for any ſuch Apology. Natural and Revealed Religion, the Word and Works of God, are in all principal Things moſt wonderfully analogous; as has been ſufficiently ſhewn by the Advocates for Revealed Religion, and moſt eſpecially by Biſhop *Butler* in his Analogy. As far therefore as moral Analogy carries Weight, there is poſitive Evidence for the Scripture Miracles. And our Comprehenſion of natural Analogy is ſo imperfect as ſcarce to afford any Preſumption againſt them; but leaves the Evidence in their Favour, of nearly the ſame Strength as it would have had for other Facts.

Thirdly, Let it be obſerved, that the Evidences for the Scripture Miracles are ſo numerous, and, in other reſpects, ſo ſtrong, as to be nearly equal to any Evidences that can be brought for the moſt common Facts. For it is very manifeſt, as has been obſerved before, that a great Number of credible Evidences make a Sum total, that is equal to Unity, or abſolute Certainty, as this has been conſidered in the foregoing Part of this Work, nearer than by any perceptible Difference: And the greateſt Number can never arrive quite to Unity. The Evidence therefore for common Facts cannot exceed that for the Scripture

Miracles by more than an imperceptible Difference, if we estimate Evidences according to the truest and most accurate Manner. Hence the nearly equal Evidences for each must establish each in nearly an equal Degree, unless we suppose either some such Inconsistency between them, as that, common Facts being allowed, the Scripture Miracles must be absolutely rejected, or that there is some Evidence against the Scripture Miracles, which may be put in Competition with that for them; neither of which Things can be said with any Colour of Reason.

Fourthly, This whole Matter may be put in another, and perhaps a more natural, as well as a more philosophical Light; and that especially if the foregoing Account of the Mind be allowed. Association, *i. e.* Analogy, perfect and imperfect, is the only Foundation upon which we in fact do, or can, or ought to assent; and consequently a Dissonance from Analogy, or a Repugnancy thereto, is a necessary Foundation for Dissent. Now it happens sometimes, that the same Thing is supported and impugned by different Analogies; or, if we put Repugnance to Analogy as equivalent to Miracle, that both a Fact and its Non-existence imply a Miracle; or, since this cannot be, that that Side alone, which is repugnant to the most and the most perfect Analogies, is miraculous, and therefore incredible. Let us weigh the Scripture Miracles in this Scale. Now the Progress of the human Mind, as may be seen by all the Inquiries into it, and particularly by the History of Association, is a Thing of a determinate Nature; a Man's Thoughts, Words, and Actions, are all generated by something previous; there is an established Course for these Things, an Analogy, of which every Man is a Judge from what he feels in himself, and sees in others; and to suppose any Number of Men in determinate Circumstances to vary from this general Tenor of human Nature in like Circumstances, is a Miracle,

and

and may be made a Miracle of any Magnitude, *i. e.*
incredible to any Degree, by increaſing the Number
and Magnitude of the Deviations. It is therefore a
Miracle in the human Mind, as great as any can be
conceived in the human Body, to ſuppoſe that infinite
Multitudes of Chriſtians, *Jews,* and Heathens in the
primitive Times, ſhould have borne ſuch unqueſtionable Teſtimony, ſome expreſly, others by indirect
Circumſtances, as Hiſtory informs us they did, to
the Miracles ſaid to be performed by Chriſt, and his
Apoſtles, upon the human Body, unleſs they were
really performed. In like manner, the Reception
which the Miracles recorded in the Old Teſtament
met with, is a Miracle, unleſs thoſe Miracles were true.
Thus alſo the very Exiſtence of the Books of the Old
and New Teſtaments,- of the *Jewiſh* and Chriſtian
Religions, *&c. &c.* are Miracles, as is abundantly
ſhewn by the Advocates for Chriſtianity, unleſs we
allow the Scripture Miracles. Here then a Man muſt
either deny all Analogy and Aſſociation, and become
an abſolute Sceptic, or acknowlege that very ſtrong
Analogies may ſometimes be violated; *i. e.* he muſt
have recourſe to ſomething miraculous, to ſomething
ſupernatural, according to his narrow Views. The
next Queſtion then will be, Which of the two oppoſite Miracles will agree beſt with all his other Notions;
whether it be more analogous to the Nature of God,
Providence, the allowed Hiſtory of the World, the
known Progreſs of Man in this Life, *&c. &c.* to ſuppoſe that God imparted to certain ſelect Perſons, of
eminent Piety, the Power of working Miracles; or to
ſuppoſe that he confounded the Underſtandings, Affections, and whole Train of Aſſociations, of intire
Nations, ſo as that Men, who, in all other Things,
ſeem to have been conducted in a manner like all
other Men, ſhould, in reſpect of the Hiſtory of Chriſt,
the Prophets and Apoſtles, act in a manner repugnant to all our Ideas and Experiences. Now, as this

laſt

laft Suppofition cannot be maintained at all upon the Footing of Deifm, fo it would be but juft as probable as the firft, even though the Objeĉtor fhould deny the Poffibility of the Being of a God. For the leaft Prefumption; that there may be a Being of immenfe or infinite Power, Knowlege, and Goodnefs, immediately turns the Scale in favour of the firft Suppofition.

Fifthly, It is to be confidered, That the Evidences for the Scripture Miracles are many, and moft of them independent upon one another, whereas the Difpenfation itfelf is a conneĉted Thing, and the Miracles remarkably related to each other. If therefore only fo much as one Miracle could be proved to have been really wrought in Confirmation of the *Jewifh* or Chriftian Revelations, there would be lefs Objeĉtion to the Suppofition of a Second ; and, if this be proved, ftill lefs to that of a Third, *&c.* till at laft the Reluĉtance to receive them would quite vanifh (Which indeed appears to have been the Cafe in the latter Part of the primitive Times, when the inconteftable Evidences for the Chriftian Miracles had been fo much examined and confidered, as quite to overcome this Reluĉtance ; and it feems difficult to account for the Credulity in receiving falfe Miracles, which then appeared, but upon Suppofition, that many true ones had been wrought). But it is not fo with the Evidences. The greateft Part of thefe have fo little Dependence on the reft, as may be feen even from this Chapter, that they muft be fet afide feparately by the Objeĉtor. Here it ought to be added, that the Objeĉtors have fcarce ever attempted to fet afide any Part of the Evidence, and never fucceeded in fuch an Attempt ; which is of itfelf a ftrong Argument in favour of the Scriptures, fince this is plainly the moft natural and eafy way of difproving a Thing that is falfe. It ought alfo to be obferved here, that the Accomplifhment of Prophecy, by implying a Miracle, does in like manner overbear the Reluĉtance to receive Miracles.

Miracles. So that if any confiderable Events, which have already happened in the World, can be proved to have been foretold in Scripture in a manner exceeding Chance, and human Forefight, the Objection to Miracles, confidered in this Propofition, falls to the Ground at once.

Sixthly, If any one fhould affirm or think, as fome Perfons feem to do, that a Miracle is impoffible, let him confider, that this is denying God's Omnipotence, and even maintaining, that Man is the fupreme Agent in the Univerfe.

P R O P. 29.

The historical Evidences for the Genuinenefs, Truth, and Divine Authority of the Scriptures do not grow lefs from Age to Age ; but, on the contrary, it may rather be prefumed, that they increafe.

IT is fometimes alleged as an indirect Objection to the Chriftian Religion, that the Evidence for Facts done in former Times, and at remote Places, decreafes with the Diftance of Time and Place ; and confequently that a Time may come hereafter, when the Evidence for the Chriftian Religion will be fo inconfiderable as not to claim our Affent, even allowing that it does fo now. To this I anfwer,

Firft, That Printing has fo far fecured all confiderable Monuments of Antiquity, as that no ordinary Calamities of Wars, Diffolutions of Governments, &c. can deftroy any material Evidence now in being, or render it lefs probable, in any difcernible Degree, to thofe who fhall live five hundred or a thoufand Years hence.

Secondly, That fo many new Evidences and Coincidences have been difcovered in favour of the *Jewifh* and *Chriftian* Hiftories, fince the three great concur-

ring

ring Events of Printing, the Reformation of Religion
in thefe Weftern Parts, and the Reftoration of Letters,
as, in fome meafure, to make up for the Evidences
loft in the preceding Times ; and, fince this Improvement of the hiftorical Evidences is likely to continue,
there is great Reafon to hope, that they will grow
every Day more and more, irrefiftible to all candid,
ferious Inquirers.

One might alfo allege, if it were needful, that *our*
proper Bufinefs is to weigh carefully the Evidence
which appears at prefent, leaving the Care of future
Ages to Providence ; that the prophetical Evidences
are manifeftly of an increafing Nature, and fo may
compenfate for a Decreafe in the hiftorical ones ; and
that though, in a grofs way of fpeaking, the Evidences for Facts diftant in Time and Place are weakened by this Diftance, yet they are not weakened in
an exact Proportion in any Cafe, nor in any Proportion in all Cafes.   No one can think a Fact relating
to the *Turkifh* Empire lefs probable at *London* than at
Paris, or at 50 Years Diftance than at 40.

PROP. 30.

*The Prophecies delivered in the Scriptures prove
the Divine Authority of the Scriptures, even
previoufly to the Confideration of the Genuinenefs of thefe Prophecies; but much more, if
that be allowed.*

IN order to evince this Propofition,   I will diftinguifh the Prophecies into four Kinds,   and fhew
in what manner it holds in refpect of each Kind.

There are then contained in the Scriptures,

Firft, Prophecies that relate to the State of the
Nations which bordered upon the Land of *Canaan.*

Secondly, Thofe that relate to the political State
of the *Ifraelites* and *Jews* in all Ages.

Thirdly,

Thirdly, The Types and Prophecies that relate to the Office, Time of Appearance, Birth, Life, Death, Refurrection, and Afcenfion of the promifed *Meffiah*, or Chrift.

Fourthly, The Prophecies that relate to the State of the Chriftian Church, efpecially in the latter Times, and to the fecond Coming of Chrift.

I begin with the Prophecies of the firft Kind, or thofe which relate to the State of *Amalek*, *Edom*, *Moab*, *Ammon*, *Tyre*, *Syria*, *Egypt*, *Nineveh*, *Babylon*, and the four great fucceffive Empires of the *Babylonians*, *Perfians*, *Greeks*, and *Romans*. Now here I obferve, Firft, That if we admit both the Genuinenefs of thefe Prophecies and the Truth of the common Hiftory of the Scriptures, the very remarkable Coincidence of the Facts with the Prophecies will put their Divine Authority out of all Doubt; as I fuppofe every Reader will acknowlege, upon recollecting the many particular Prophecies of this Kind, with their Accomplifhments, which occur in the Old Teftament. Secondly, If we allow only the Genuinenefs of thefe Prophecies, fo great a Part of them may be verified by the Remains of antient Pagan Hiftory, as to eftablifh the Divine Authority of that Part. Thus, if *Daniel's* Prophecies of the Image, and four Beafts, were written by him in the time of the *Babylonian* Empire, if the Prophecies concerning the Fall of *Nineveh*, *Babylon*, *Tyre*, &c. be genuine, &c. even profane Hiftory will fhew, that more than human Forefight was concerned in the Delivery of them. Thirdly, That fuch of thefe prophetic Events as remain to this Day, or were evidently pofterior to the Delivery of the Prophecies, prove their Divine Authority even antecedently to the Confideration of their Genuinenefs, as is affirmed in the former Part of the Propofition. Of this Kind are the perpetual Slavery of *Egypt*; the perpetual Defolation of *Tyre* and *Babylon*; the wild, unconquered State of the

L 4 *Ifhmaelites*;

Ishmaelites; the great Power and Strength of the
Roman Empire beyond thofe of the three foregoing
Empires ; its Divifion into ten Kingdoms ; its not
being fubdued by any other, as the three foregoing
were; the Rife of the *Mahometan* Religion, and
Saracenic Empire ; the limited Continuance of this
Empire ; and the Rife and Progrefs of the Empire of
the *Turks.* To thefe we may add the Tranfactions
that paffed between the cotemporary Kingdoms of
Syria and *Egypt,* prophefied of in the eleventh Chapter of *Daniel.* For, fince thefe Prophecies reach
down to the Times of *Antiochus Epiphanes,* and the
beginning Subjection of thefe Kingdoms to the *Roman* Power, they cannot but have been delivered prior
to the Events, as may appear both from the Confideration of the Septuagint Tranflation of the Book of
Daniel, and the Extinction of the Biblical *Hebrew* as
a living Language before that Time, even though the
Book of *Daniel* fhould not be confidered as a genuine
Book ; for which Sufpicion there is, however, no
Foundation. Laftly, we may remark, That thefe,
and indeed all the other Prophecies, have the fame
Marks of Genuinenefs as the reft of the Scriptures,
or as any other Books ; that they cannot be feparated
from the Context without the utmoft Violence, fo
that, if this be allowed to be genuine, thofe muft alfo;
that Hiftory and Chronology were in fo uncertain a
State in antient Times, that the Prophecies concerning foreign Countries could not have been adapted to
the Facts, even after they had happened, with fo
much Exactnefs as modern Inquirers have fhewn the
Scripture Prophecies to be, by a learned Nation, and
much lefs by the *Jews,* who were remarkably ignorant of what paffed in foreign Countries ; and that
thofe Prophecies, which are delivered in the Manner
of Dream and Vifion, have a very ftrong internal
Evidence for their Genuinenefs, taken from the Nature

ture of Dreams, as this is explained in the foregoing Part of this Work.

I proceed, in the Second place, to ſhew how the Prophecies, that relate to the political State of the *Jews*, prove the Divine Authority of the Scriptures. And here, paſſing by many Prophecies of inferior Note, and of a ſubordinate Nature, we may confine ourſelves to the Promiſe, or Prophecy, of the Land of *Canaan*, given to *Abraham, Iſaac,* and *Jacob* ; to the Prophecies concerning the Captivity of the ten Tribes, and the *Babyloniſh* Captivity of the two Tribes, with their Return after ſeventy Years ; and to thoſe concerning the much greater Captivity and Deſolation predicted to fall upon this choſen People in the xxviiith Chapter of *Deuteronomy*, in various Places of the Prophecies, and by Chriſt and his Apoſtles in the New Teſtament. There was no natural Probability, at the time when theſe Prophecies were delivered, that any of theſe Events ſhould happen in the manner in which they were predicted, and have accordingly happened ; but, in ſome, the utmoſt Improbability : So that it muſt appear to every candid intelligent Inquirer, that nothing leſs than ſupernatural Knowlege could have enabled thoſe who delivered theſe Predictions, to make them. The Divine Authority, therefore, of the Books which contain theſe Predictions, is unqueſtionable, provided we allow them to be genuine.

Now, beſides the forementioned Evidences of this, theſe Prophecies have ſome peculiar ones attending them. Thus the mere Departure of the *Iſraelites* out of *Egypt*, in order to go to the Land of *Canaan*, their burying *Jacob* in *Canaan*, and carrying *Joſeph*'s Bones with them, plainly imply that the Promiſe of this Land had been given to their Anceſtors. Thus alſo the Prophecies relating to the Captivities of *Iſrael* and *Judah*, and to their Reſtorations, make ſo large a Part of the Old Prophets, that, if they be not genuine,

nuine, the whole Books muſt be forged ; and the
Genuineneſs of thoſe in the New Teſtament cannot
but be allowed by all.

I come now, in the Third place, to ſpeak of the
Types and Prophecies that relate to Chriſt, the Time
of his Appearance, his Offices, Birth, Life, Death,
Reſurrection, and Aſcenſion. Many of theſe are applied to him by ·himſelf, and by the Authors of the
Books of the New Teſtament; but there are alſo
many others, whoſe Diſcovery and Application are
left to the Sagacity and Induſtry of Chriſtians in all
Ages. This ſeems to be a Field of great Extent,
and the Evidence ariſing from it of an increaſing Nature. It is probable, that the Chriſtians of the firſt
Ages were acquainted with ſo many more Circumſtances relating to the Life, Death, &c. of Chriſt, as
on this account to be able to apply a larger Number
of Types and Prophecies to him than we can. But
then this may perhaps be compenſated to us by the
daily Opening of the Scriptures, and our growing
Knowlege in the typical and prophetical Nature of
them. What is already diſcovered of this Kind,
ſeems no·ways poſſible to be accounted for, but from
the Suppoſition, that God, by his Power and Foreknowlege, ſo ordered the Actions, Hiſtory, Ceremonies, &c. of the *Patriarchs* and *Jews*, and the
Language of the Prophets, as to make them correſpond with Chriſt, his Offices, Actions, and Sufferings.
If any one doubts of this, let him attempt to apply
the Types and Prophecies to any other Perſon. I
will juſt mention Four·Claſſes, into which theſe Types
and Prophecies may be diſtinguiſhed, and under each
of them a few remarkable Inſtances. There are
then,

Firſt, Prophecies which evidently relate to Chriſt,
and either to him alone, or to others in an inferior
Degree only. Such are that of *Jacob* concerning
Shiloh, of *Moſes* concerning a great Prophet and Law-
giver

giver that should come after him, . of *Isaiah* in his
liid and liiid Chapters, of *Daniel* concerning the
Messiah, many in almost all the Prophets concerning
a great Prince, a Prince of, the House of. *David*, &c.
who should make a new Covenant with his People,
&c. &c.

Secondly, Typical Circumstances in the Lives of
eminent Persons, as of *Isaac*, *Joseph*, *Joshua*, *David*,
Solomon, *Jonah*; and in the common History of the
Jewish People, as its being called out of *Egypt*.

Thirdly, Typical Ceremonies in the *Jewish* Wor-
ship, as their Sacrifices in general, those of the Pass-
over and Day of Expiation in particular, *&c.* To
this Head we may also refer the typical Nature of
the High-Priesthood, and of the Offices of King,
Priest, and Prophet, amongst the *Jews*, &c.

Fourthly, The apparently incidental Mention of
many Circumstances in these Things, which yet agree
so exactly, and in a way so much above Chance,
with Christ, as to make it evident, that they were
originally intended to be applied to him. The not
breaking a Bone of the Paschal Lamb ; the Mention
of renting the Garment, and casting Lots upon the
Vesture, by *David*; of offering Gall and Vinegar, of
looking on him whom they had pierced, of the Third
Day upon numerous Occasions, *&c.* are Circumstances
of this Kind.

Now, these Types and Prophecies afford nearly
the same Evidence, whether we consider the Books
of the Old Testament as genuine, or no. For no
one calls.in Question their being extant as we now
have them, small immaterial Variations excepted,
before. the time of Christ's Appearance. Many of
them do indeed require the common History of the
New Testament to be allowed as true. But there
are some, those, for Instance, which relate to the Humi-
liation and Death of Christ, and the Spirituality of his
Office, the Proofs of whose Accomplishment are
sufficiently

sufficiently evident to the whole World, even independently of this.

The Fourth Branch of the prophetical Evidences are those which relate to the Christian Church. Here the Three following Particulars deserve attentive Consideration.

First, The Predictions concerning a new and pure Religion, which was to be set up by the Coming of the promised *Messiah*.

Secondly, A great and general Corruption of this Religion, which was to follow in After-times.

Thirdly, The Recovery of the Christian Church from this Corruption, by great Tribulations; and the final Establishment of true and pure Religion, called *the Kingdom of Righteousness, of the Saints, the New Jerusalem,* &c.

The Predictions of the First and Third Kinds abound every-where in the Old Prophets, in the Discourses of Christ, and in the Writings of the Apostles. Those of the second Kind are chiefly remarkable in *Daniel,* the *Revelation,* and the Epistles of St. *Paul,* St. *Peter,* St. *John,* and St. *Jude.* In how surprising a manner the Events of the First and Second Kind have answered to the Predictions, cannot be unknown to any inquisitive serious Person, in any Christian Country. At the same time it is evident, that the Predictions of these Things could have no Foundation in probable Conjectures when they were given. The Events of the Third Class have not yet received their Accomplishment; but there have been for some Centuries past, and are still, perpetual Advances and Preparations made for them; and it now seems unreasonable to doubt of the natural Probability of their Accomplishment, unless we doubt at the same time of the Truth of the Religion itself. If it be true, it must, upon more diligent and impartial Examination, both purify itself, and overcome all Opposition.

And

And it is remarkably agreeable to the Tenor of Providence in other Things, that that Accompliſhment of Prophecy, which will hereafter evidence the Truth of the Chriſtian Religion in the moſt illuſtrious manner, ſhould be effected by preſent Evidences of a leſs illuſtrious Nature.

Let me add here, that many of the Pſalms are peculiarly applicable to the Reſtoration and Converſion of the *Jews,* and to the final Prevalence and Eſtabliſhment of the Chriſtian Church; *i. e.* to the Events of the Third Claſs.

PROP. 31.

The Degree of Obſcurity which is found in the Prophecies of the Scriptures, is not ſo great as to invalidate the foregoing Evidences for their Divine Authority; but, on the contrary, is itſelf an indirect Teſtimony in their Favour.

IN order to prove this Propoſition, I obſerve,

Firſt, That there are a ſufficient Number of Prophecies, whoſe Interpretation is certain, clear, and preciſe, to ſhew that their Agreement with the Events predicted is far above the Powers of Chance, or human Foreſight. But for the Proof of this Point, which takes in a great Compaſs of Literature, I muſt refer to the Authors who have treated it in Detail. And as thoſe who have examined this Point with Accuracy and Impartiality, do, as I preſume, univerſally agree to the Poſition here laid down, ſo thoſe who have not done ſo, can have no Pretence for aſſerting the contrary; this being an hiſtorical Matter, which is to be determined as others of a like Kind, *viz.* by the hiſtorical Evidences. The Reader may, however, form ſome Judgment, in the groſs, even from the few Inſtances, which are alleged under the laſt Propoſition.

Secondly,

Secondly, That, even in the Types and Prophecies where Interpreters differ from each other, the Differences are often so inconsiderable, and the Agreements so general, or else the Prophecy so suited to the several Events, to which it is applied by different Interpreters, as to exclude both Chance, and human Foresight, *i. e.* to infer a Divine Communication. This Point requires also a careful and candid Examination, and then, I think, cannot but be determined in the affirmative; especially when the very great Number of Types and Prophecies is taken into Confideration. Fitnefs in numerous Inftances is always an Evidence of Defign; this is a Method of Reafoning allowed, explicitly or implicitly, by all. And though the Fitnefs may not be perfectly evident or precife in all, yet, if it be general, and the Inftances very numerous, the Evidence of Defign, arifing from it, may amount to any Degree, and fall fhort of Certainty by an imperceptible Difference only. And indeed it is upon thefe Principles alone, that we prove the Divine Power, Knowlege, and Goodnefs, from the Harmonies, and mutual Fitneffes, of vifible Things, and from final Caufes, inafmuch as thefe Harmonies and Fitneffes are precifely made out only in a few Inftances, if compared to thofe in which we fee no more than general Harmonies, with particular fubordinate Difficulties, and apparent Incongruities.

That the Reader may fee in a ftronger Light, how fully the Fitneffes, confidered in the two foregoing Paragraphs, exclude Chance, and infer Defign, let him try to apply the Types and Prophecies of the Four Claffes before-mentioned to other Perfons and Events befides thofe, to which Chriftian Interpreters have applied them ; and efpecially let him confider the Types and Prophecies relating to Chrift. If Defign be excluded, thefe ought to be equally, or nearly fo, applicable to other Perfons and Events ; which yet, I think, no ferious confiderate Perfon can affirm. Now, if

Chance

Chance be once excluded, and the Neceffity of having recourfe to Defign admitted, we fhall be inftantly compelled to acknowlege a Contrivance greater than human, from the long Diftances of Time intervening between the Prophecy and the Event, with other fuch-like Reafons.

Thirdly, I obferve that thofe Types and Prophecies, whofe Interpretation is fo obfcure, that Interpreters have not been able to difcover any probable Application, cannot any-ways invalidate the Evidence arifing from the reft. They are analogous to thofe Parts of the Works of Nature, whofe Ufes, and Subferviency to the reft, are not yet underftood. And as no one calls in Queftion the Evidences of Defign, which appear in many Parts of the human Body, becaufe the Ufes of others are not yet known; fo the Interpretations of Prophecy, which are clearly or probably made out, remain the fame Evidence of Defign, notwithftanding that unfurmountable Difficulties may hitherto attend many other Parts of the prophetic Writings.

Fourthly, It is predicted in the Prophecies, that in the latter Times great Multitudes will be converted to the Chriftian Faith; whereas thofe who preach or prophefy, during the great Apoftafy, fhall be able to do this only in an obfcure, imperfect manner, and convert but few. Now the paft and prefent Obfcurity of Prophecy agrees remarkably with this Prediction; and the Opening, which is already made, fince the Revival of Letters, in applying the Prophecies to the Events, feems to prefage, that the latter Times are now approaching; and that by the more full Difcovery of the true Meaning of the prophetic Writings, and of their Aptnefs to fignify the Events predicted, there will be fuch an Acceffion of Evidence to the Divine Authority of the Scriptures, as none but the wilfully Ignorant, the Profligate, and the Obdurate, can withftand. It is therefore a Confirmation of the

prophetic

prophetic Writings, that, by the Obſcurity of one Part of them, a Way ſhould be prepared for effecting that glorious Converſion of all Nations, which is predicted in others, in the Time and Manner in which it is predicted.

P R O P. 32.

It is no Objection to the foregoing Evidences taken from the Types and Prophecies, that they have double, or even manifold, Uſes and Applications; but rather a Confirmation of them.

FOR the foregoing Evidences all reſt upon this Foundation, *viz.* that there is an Aptneſs in the Types and Prophecies to prefigure the Events, greater than can be ſuppoſed to reſult from Chance, or human Foreſight. When this is evidently made out from the great Number of the Types and Prophecies, and the Degree of Clearneſs and Preciſeneſs of each, the ſhewing afterwards, that theſe have other Uſes and Applications, will rather prove the Divine Interpoſition, than exclude it. All the Works of God, the Parts of a human Body, Syſtems of Minerals, Plants, and Animals, elementary Bodies, Planets, fixed Stars, &c. have various Uſes and Subſerviencies, in reſpect of each other; and, if the Scriptures be the Word of God, Analogy would lead one to expect ſomething correſponding hereto in them. When Men form Deſigns, they are indeed obliged to have one Thing principally in View, and to ſacrifice ſubordinate Matters to principal ones; but we muſt not carry this Prejudice, taken from the narrow Limits of our Power and Knowlege, to him who is infinite in them. All his Ends centre in the ſame Point, and are carried to their utmoſt Perfection by one and the ſame Means. Thoſe Laws, Ceremonies, and Incidents,

which

which beft fuited the *Jewish* State, and the feveral Individuals of it, were alfo moft apt to prefigure the promifed Meffiah, and the State of the Chriftian Church, according to the perfect Plan of thefe Things, which, in our way of fpeaking, exifted in the Divine Mind from all Eternity ; juft as that Magnitude, Situation, *&c.* of our Earth, which beft fuits its prefent Inhabitants, is alfo beft fuited to all the Changes which it muft hereafter undergo, and to all the Inhabitants of other Planets, if there be any fuch, to whom its Influence extends.

The following Inftance may perhaps make this Matter more clearly underftood. Suppofe a Perfon to have ten Numbers, and as many Lines, prefented to his View; and to find by Menfuration, that the ten Numbers expreffed the Lengths of the ten Lines refpectively. This would make it evident, that they were intended to do fo. Nor would it alter the Cafe, and prove that the Agreement between the Numbers and Lines arofe, without Defign, and by Chance, as we exprefs it, to allege that thefe Numbers had fome other Relations ; that, for Inftance, they proceeded in Arithmetical or Geometrical Progreffion, were the Squares or Cubes of other Numbers, *&c.* On the contrary, any fuch remarkable Property would rather increafe than diminifh the Evidence of Defign in the Agreement between the Numbers and Lines. However, the chief Thing to be inquired into would plainly be, whether the Agreement be too great to be accounted for by Chance. If it be, Defign muft be admitted.

P R O P. 33.

The Application of the Types and Prophecies of the Old Teſtament by the Writers of the New does not weaken the Authority of theſe Writers, but rather confirm it.

FOR the Objections, which have been made to the Writers of the New Teſtament on this Head, have been grounded principally upon a Suppoſition, that when an obvious literal Senſe of a Paſſage, or a maniſeſt Uſe of a Ceremony, ſuited to the then preſent Times, are diſcovered, all others are excluded. ſo as to become Miſapplications. But this has been ſhewn in the laſt Propoſition to be a Prejudice ariſing from the Narrowneſs of our Faculties and Abilities. Whence it follows, that, if the Scripture Types and Prophecies be remarkably ſuited to different Things, which is a Point that is abundantly proved by learned Men, they cannot but, in their original Deſign, have various Senſes and Uſes. And it is ſome Confirmation of the Divine Authority of the Writers of the New Teſtament, that they write agreeably to this original Deſign of God.

It may perhaps afford ſome Satisfaction to the Reader to make ſome Conjectures concerning the Light in which the Types and Prophecies, which have double Senſes, would appear firſt to the antient *Jews*, and then to thoſe who lived in the Time of our Saviour From hence we may judge in what Light it is reaſonable they ſhould be taken by us.

Let our Inſtance be the Second Pſalm, which we are to ſuppoſe written by *David* himſelf, or, at leaſt, in the time of his Reign. It is evident, that there are ſo many Things in this Pſalm peculiarly applicable to *David*'s Aſcent to the Throne by God's ſpecial Appointment, to the Oppoſition which he met with both in his own Nation, and from the neighbouring

ones,

ones, and to his Victories over all his Oppoſers through
the Favour of God, that the *Jews* of that Time
could not but conſider this Pſalm as relating to *David*.
Nay, one can ſcarce doubt, but the Pſalmiſt himſelf,
whether he ſeemed to himſelf to compoſe it from his
own proper Fund, or to have it dictated immediately
by the Spirit of God, would have *David* principally
in View. At the ſame time it is evident, that there
are ſome Paſſages, particularly the laſt, *Bleſſed are all
they that put their Truſt in him,* i. e. in the Son,
which it would be impious, eſpecially for an *Iſraelite,*
to apply to *David,* and which therefore no Allowance
for the Sublimity of the Eaſtern Poetry could make
applicable. It may be ſuppoſed therefore, that many,
or moſt, conſidered ſuch Paſſages as having an Obſcurity in them, into which they could no-ways penetrate; whereas a few perhaps, who were peculiarly
enlightened by God, and who meditated Day and
Night upon the Promiſes made to their Anceſtors,
particularly upon thoſe to *Abraham,* would preſume
or conjecture, that a future Perſon, of a much higher
Rank than *David,* was prefigured thereby And the
Caſe would be the ſame in regard to many other
Pſalms: They would appear to the Perſons of the
then preſent Times both to reſpect the then preſent
Occurrences, and alſo to intimate ſome future more
glorious ones; and would mutually ſupport this latter
Interpretation in each other.

When the Prophets appeared in the Declenſion and
Captivities of the Kingdoms of *Iſrael* and *Judah,* the
ſame Interpretation would be ſtrengthened, and the
Expectations grounded thereon increaſed, by the
plainer and more frequent Declarations of the Prophets concerning ſuch a future Perſon, and the Happineſs which would attend his Coming. The great
and various Sufferings of this choſen People, their
Return and Deliverance, their having their Scriptures collected into one View by *Ezra,* and read in

M 2 *their*

their Synagogues during the Interval from *Ezra* to Chrift, the figurative Senfes put upon Dreams, Vifions, and Parables, in their Scriptures, &c. would all concur to the fame Purpofe, till at laft it is reafonable to expect, that the *Jews* in our Saviour's Time would confider many of the Inftitutions and Ceremonies of their Law, of the hiftorical Events, of the Pfalms appointed for the Temple-worfhip, and of the infpired Declarations of the Prophets, as refpecting the future Times of the *Meffiah*; and this, in fome Cafes, to the Exclufion of the more obvious Senfes and Ufes, which had already taken place; being led thereto by the fame Narrow-mindednefs, which makes fome in thefe Days reject the typical and more remote Senfe, as foon as they fee the literal and more immediate one. Now, that this was, in fact, the Cafe of the *Jews* in the Time of Chrift, and for fome time afterwards, appears from the New Teftament, from the Chriftian Writers of the firft Ages, and from the Talmudical ones.

A great Part, however, of the Scripture Types and Prophecies appeared to the *Jews* to have no Relation to their promifed *Meffiah*, till they were interpreted by the Event. They expected a Perfon that fhould correfpond to *David* and *Solomon*, two glorious Princes; but they did not fee how *Ifaac*, or the Pafchal Lamb, fhould typify him; or that the Circumftance of being called out of *Egypt*, the Appellation of *Nazarene*, or the parting Garments, and cafting Lots upon a Vefture, fhould contribute to afcertain him. However, it is certain, that to Perfons who had for fome time confidered their Scriptures in the typical, prophetical View mentioned in the laft Paragraph, every remarkable Circumftance and Coincidence of this Kind, verified by the Event, would be a new Acceffion of Evidence, provided we fuppofe a good Foundation from Miracles, or Prophecies of undoubted Import, to have been laid previoufly.

Nay,

Nay, such Coincidences may be considered not only as Arguments to the *Jews* of Christ's Time, but as solid Arguments in themselves, and that exclusively of the Context. For though each of these Coincidences, singly taken, affords only a low Degree of Evidence, and some of them scarce any ; yet it is a Thing not to be accounted for from Chance, that separate Passages of the Old Testament should be applicable to the Circumstances of Christ's Life, by an Allusion either of Words or Sense, in ten or an hundred times a greater Number, than to any other Persons, from mere Accident. And this holds in a much higher Degree, if the separate Passages or Circumstances be subordinate Parts of a general Type. Thus the parting the Garments, the offering Vinegar and Gall, and the not breaking a Bone, have much more Weight, when it is considered, that *David*, and the Paschal Lamb, are Types of the *Messiah.* And when the whole Evidence of th Kind, which the Industry of pious Christians has brought to Light in the first Ages of Christianity, and again since the Revival of Letters, is laid together, it appears to me to be both a full Proof of the Truth of the Christian Religion, and a Vindication of the Method of arguing from typical and double Senses.

It may be added in favour of typical Reasoning, that it corresponds to the Method of Reasoning by Analogy, which is found to be of such extensive Use in Philosophy. A Type is indeed nothing but an Analogy, and the Scripture Types are not only a Key to the Scriptures, but seem also to have contributed to put into our Hands the Key of Nature, Analogy. And this shews us a new Correspondence or Analogy between the Word and Works of God. However, since certain well-meaning Persons seem to be prejudiced against typical and double Senses, I will add some Arguments, whereby the Writers of the New Testament may be defended upon this Footing also.

First,

Firſt, then, Since the *Jews* in the Times of the Writers of the New Teſtament, and conſequently theſe Writers themſelves, were much given to typical Reaſonings, and the Application of Paſſages of the Old Teſtament in a ſecondary Senſe to the Times of the *Meſſiah*, this would be a common Foundation for theſe Writers, and thoſe to whom they wrote, to proceed upon, derived from Aſſociation, and the acquired Nature of their Minds. And it is as eaſy to conceive, that God ſhould permit them to proceed upon this Foundation for the then preſent Time, though it would not extend to the World in general, to diſtant Ages, and to Perſons of different Educations, as that they ſhould be left to the Workings of their own acquired Natures in many other reſpects, notwithſtanding the ſupernatural Gifts beſtowed upon them in ſome; or as it is to conceive, that God ſhould confer any thing, Exiſtence, Happineſs, *&c.* in any particular Manner or Degree.

Secondly, There are ſome Paſſages in the New Teſtament quoted from the Old in the way of mere Alluſion. This cannot, I think, be true of many, where the Paſſage is ſaid to be *fulfilled*, without doing Violence to the natural Senſe of the Words, and of the Context, in the New Teſtament: However, where it is, it intirely removes the Objection here conſidered.

Thirdly, If we ſhould allow, that the Writers of the New Teſtament were ſometimes guilty of erroneous Reaſonings in theſe or other Matters, ſtill this does not affect their moral Characters at all; nor their intellectual ones, which are ſo manifeſt from the general Soundneſs and Strength of their other Reaſonings, in any ſuch manner as to be of Importance in reſpect of the Evidence for the general Truth of the Scriptures, or for their Divine Authority in the firſt and loweſt Senſe above conſidered.

P R O P.

PROP. 34.

The moral Charaƈters of Chriſt, the Prophets and Apoſtles, prove the Truth and Divine Authority of the Scriptures.

LET us begin with the Conſideration of the Character of Chriſt. This, as it may be colleƈted from the plain Narrations of the Goſpels, is manifeſtly ſuperior to all other Charaƈters, fiƈtitious or real, whether drawn by Hiſtorians, Orators, or Poets. We ſee in it the moſt intire Devotion and Reſignation to God, and the moſt ardent and univerſal Love to Mankind, joined with the greateſt Humility, Self-denial, Meekneſs, Patience, Prudence, and every other Virtue, divine and human. To which we are to add, That, according to the New Teſtament, Chriſt, being the Lord and Creator of all, took upon himſelf the Form of a Servant, in order to ſave all; that, with this View, he ſubmitted to the Helpleſſneſs and Infirmities of Infancy, to the Narrowneſs of human Underſtanding, and the Perturbations of human Affeƈtions, to Hunger, Thirſt, Labour, Wearineſs, Poverty, and Hardſhips of various Kinds, to lead a ſorrowful, friendleſs Life, to be miſunderſtood, betrayed, inſulted, and mocked, and at laſt to be put to a painful and ignominious Death; alſo (which deſerves our moſt ſerious Conſideration, however incongruous to our narrow Apprehenſions it may appear at firſt Sight) to undergo the moſt bitter mental Agony previouſly. Here then we may make the following Obſervations.

Firſt, That, laying down the preſent Diſorders of the moral World, and the Neceſſity of the Love of God and our Neighbour, and of Self-annihilation, in order to the pure and ultimate Happineſs of Man, there ſeems to be a Neceſſity alſo for a ſuffering Saviour. At leaſt, one may affirm, that the Conde-

ſcenſion

scenfion of Chrift, in leaving the Glory which he had
with the Father before the Foundation of the World,
and in fhewing himfelf a perfect Pattern of Obedience
to the Will of God, both in doing and fuffering, has
a moft peculiar Tendency to rectify the prefent
moral Depravity of our Natures, and to exalt us
thereby to pure fpiritual Happinefs. Now it is remarkable, that the Evangelifts and Apoftles fhould
have thus hit upon a Thing, which all the great Men
amongft the antient Heathens miffed, and which,
however clear it does and ought now to appear to us,
was a great Stumbling-block to them, as well as to the
Jews; the firft feeking after Wifdom, *i. e.* human
Philofophy and Eloquence; and the laft requiring a
Sign, or a glorious temporal Saviour. Nor can this
be accounted for, as it feems to me, but by admitting
the Reality of the Character, *i. e.* the Divine Miffion
of hrift, and the confequent Divine Infpiration of thofe
who drew it, *i. e.* the Truth and Divine Authority
of the New Teftament.

Secondly, If we allow only the Truth of the common Hiftory of the New Teftament, or even, without having recourfe to it, only fuch a Part of the Character of Chrift, as neither antient nor modern *Jews*,
Heathens, or Unbelievers, feem to conteft, it will be
difficult to reconcile fo great a Character, claiming
Divine Authority, either with the moral Attributes of
God, or indeed with itfelf, upon the Suppofition of
the Falfhood of that Claim. One can fcarce fuppofe,
that God would permit a Perfon apparently fo innocent and excellent, fo qualified to impofe upon Mankind, to make fo impious and audacious a Claim without having fome evident Mark of Impofture fet upon
him; nor can it be conceived, how a Perfon could be
apparently fo innocent and excellent, and yet really
otherwife.

Thirdly, The Manner in which the Evangelifts
fpeak of Chrift, fhews that they drew after a real

Copy;

Copy; *i. e.* ſhews the Genuineneſs and ruth of the Goſpel-Hiſtory. There are no direct Encomiums upon him, no laboured Defences or Recommendations. His Character ariſes from a careful impartial Examination of all that he ſaid and did, and the Evangeliſts appear to have drawn this greateſt of all Characters without any direct Deſign to do it. Nay, they have recorded ſome Things, ſuch as his being moved with the Paſſions of human Nature, as well as being affected by its Infirmities, which the Wiſdom of this World would rather have concealed. But their View was to ſhew him to the Perſons to whom they preached as the promiſed *Meſſiah* of the *Jews*, and the Saviour of Mankind; and as they had been convinced of this themſelves from his Diſcourſes, Actions, Sufferings, and Reſurrection, they thought nothing more was wanting to convince ſuch others as were ſerious and impartial, but a ſimple Narrative of what Jeſus ſaid and did. And if we compare the tranſcendent Greatneſs of this Character with the indirect Manner in which it is delivered, and the Illiterateneſs and low Condition of the Evangeliſts, it will appear impoſſible, that they ſhould have forged it, that they ſhould not have had a real Original before them, ſo that nothing was wanting but to record ſimply and faithfully. How could mean and illiterate Perſons excel the greateſt Geniuſes, antient and modern, in drawing a Character? How came they to draw it an indirect Manner? This is indeed a ſtrong Evidence of Genuineneſs and Truth; but then it is of ſo recluſe and ſubtle a Nature, and, agreeably to this, has been ſo little taken notice of by the Defenders of the Chriſtian Religion, that one cannot conceive the Evangeliſts were at all aware, that it was an Evidence. The Character of Chriſt, as drawn by them, is therefore genuine and true; and conſequently proves his Divine Miſſion both by its tranſcendent Excellence, and by his laying Claim to ſuch a Miſſion.

Here

Here it ought to be particularly remarked, that our Saviour's intire Devotion to God, and Sufferings for the sake of Men in Compliance with his Will, is a Pitch of Perfection, which was never propofed, or thought of, before his Coming (much lefs attempted or attained); unlefs as far as this is virtually·included in the Precepts for loving God above all, and our Neighbour as ourfelves, and other equivalent Paffages in the Old Teftament.

We come, in the next place, to confider the Characters of the Prophets, Apoftles, and other eminent Perfons mentioned in the Old and New Teftaments. Here then we may obferve,

Firft, That the Characters of the Perfons who are faid in the Scriptures to have had Divine Communications, and a Divine Miffion, are fo much fuperior to the Characters which occur in common Life, that we can fcarce account for the more eminent fingle ones, and therefore much lefs for fo large a Succeffion of them, continued through fo many Ages, without allowing the Divine Communications and Affiftance, which they allege. It is true indeed, that many of thefe eminent Perfons had confiderable Imperfections, and fome of them were guilty of great Sins occafionally, though not habitually. However, I fpeak here of the Balance, after proper Deductions are made, on account of thefe Sins and Imperfections; and leave it to the impartial Reader to confider, whether the Prophets, Apoftles, &c. were not fo much fuperior, not only to Mankind at an Average, but even to the beft Men amongft the *Greeks* and *Romans*, as is not fairly to be accounted for by the mere Powers of human Nature.

Secondly, If this fhould be doubted, their Characters are, however, far too good to allow the Suppofition of an impious Fraud and Impofture; which muft be the Cafe, if they had not Divine Authority. We have therefore this double Argument for the
Divine

Divine Authority of the Scriptures, if we only allow the Genuineneſs and Truth of its common Hiſtory.

Thirdly, The Characters of the eminent Perſons mentioned in the Scriptures ariſe ſo much, in an indirect Way, from the plain Narrations of Facts, their Sins and Imperfections are ſo fully ſet forth by themſelves, or their Friends, with their Condemnation and Puniſhment, and the Vices of wicked Men, and the Oppoſers of God and themſelves, related in ſo candid a Way, with all fit Allowances, that we have in this a remarkable additional Evidence for the Truth of this Part of the Scripture Hiſtory, beſides the common ones before given, which extend to the Whole.

Fourthly, The eminent Perſons here conſidered are ſometimes charged by Unbelievers with Crimes, where, all Circumſtances being duly weighed, they did nothing unjuſtifiable, nothing more than it was their indiſpenſable Duty to God to do; as *Abraham* in preparing to ſacrifice *Iſaac*, *Joſhua* in deſtroying the *Canaanites*, &c. We cannot determine an Action to be ſinful from a mere, abſtracted, general Definition of it, as that it is the taking away the Life of a Man, &c. but muſt carefully weigh all Circumſtances. And indeed there are no Maxims in Morality that are quite univerſal; they can be no more than general; and it is ſufficient for human Purpoſes, that they are ſo much, notwithſtanding that the Addition of peculiar Circumſtances makes the Action vary from the general Rule. Now the certain Command of God may ſurely be ſuch a Circumſtance.

Laſtly, The Perfection of Virtue being of an ever-growing infinite Nature, it is reaſonable to expect, that Mankind in its infant State, ſoon after the Flood, and ſo onwards for ſome time, ſhould be more imperfect, and have leſs of the pure and ſublime Precepts concerning Indifference to this World, and all preſent Things, univerſal unlimited Charity, Mortification, Abſtinence, Chaſtity, &c. delivered to them, than

we

we Chriftians have, and lefs expected from them. And yet, upon the Whole, the Patriarchs and eminent Perfons among the *Jews* were *burning and fhining Lights* in their refpective Generations. However, it is alfo to be obferved here, that the moft fublime Precepts of the Gofpel do appear from the firft in the Old Teftament, though under a Veil; and that they were gradually opened more and more under the later Prophets.

P R O P. 35.

The Excellence of the Doctrine contained in the Scriptures is an Evidence of their Divine Authority.

THIS is an Argument which has great Force, independently of other Confiderations. Thus let us fuppofe, that the Author of the Gofpel which goes under St. *Matthew*'s Name, was not known; and that it was unfupported by the Writers of the primitive Times; yet fuch is the unaffected Simplicity of the Narrations, the Purity of the Doctrines, and the fincere Piety and Goodnefs of the Sentiments, that it carries its own Authority with it. And the fame Thing may be faid in general of all the Books of the Old and New Teftaments: So that it feems evident to me, that, if there was no other Book in the World befides the Bible, a Man could not reafonably doubt of the Truth of Revealed Religion. *The Mouth fpeaks from the Abundance of the Heart.* Mens Writings and Difcourfes muft receive a Tincture from their real Thoughts, Defires, and Defigns. It is impoffible to play the Hypocrite in every Word and Expreffion. This is a Matter of common daily Obfervation, that cannot be called in queftion; and the more any one thinks upon it, or attends to what paffes in himfelf or others, to the Hiftory of the human Thoughts,

Words,

Words, and Actions, and their neceſſary mutual Connexions, *i. e.* to the Hiſtory of Aſſociation, the more clearly will he ſee it. We may conclude therefore, even if all other Arguments were ſet aſide, that the Authors of the Books of the Old and New Teſtaments, whoever they were, cannot have made a falſe Claim to Divine Authority.

But there is alſo another Method of inferring the Divine Authority of the Scriptures from the Excellence of the Doctrine contained therein. For the Scriptures contain Doctrines concerning God, Providence, a future State, the Duty of Man, *&c.* far more pure and ſublime than can any-ways be accounted for from the natural Powers of Men, ſo circumſtanced as the ſacred Writers were. That the Reader may ſee this in a clearer Light, let him compare the ſeveral Books of the Old and New Teſtaments with the cotemporary Writers amongſt the *Greeks* and *Romans*, who could not have leſs than the natural Powers of the human Mind ; but might have, over and above, ſome traditional Hints derived ultimately from Revelation. Let him conſider whether it be poſſible to ſuppoſe, that *Jewiſh* Shepherds, Fiſhermen, *&c.* ſhould, both before and after the Riſe of the Heathen Philoſophy, ſo far exceed the Men of the greateſt Abilities and Accompliſhments in other Nations, by any other means, than Divine Communications. Nay, we may ſay, that no Writers, from the Invention of Letters to the preſent Times, are equal to the Penmen of the Books of the Old and New Teſtaments, in true Excellence, Utility, and Dignity; which is ſurely ſuch an internal Criterion of their Divine Authority, as ought not to be reſiſted. And perhaps it never is reſiſted by any, who have duly conſidered theſe Books, and formed their Affections and Actions according to the Precepts therein delivered.

An Objection is ſometimes made againſt the Excellence of the Doctrines of the Scriptures, by charging

upon

upon them erroneous Doctrines, established by the Authority of Creeds, Councils, and particular Churches. But this is a Manner of proceeding highly unreasonable. The Unbeliever, who pays so little Regard to the Opinions of others, as to reject what all Churches receive, the Divine Mission of Christ, and the Evidences for the Truth of the Scriptures, ought not at other times to suppose the Churches, much less any particular one, better able to judge of the Doctrine ; but should in the latter Case, as well as the first, examine for himself.; or, if he will take the Doctrine upon Trust, he ought much rather to take the Evidence so.

If it can be shewn, either that the true Doctrine of the Scriptures differs from that which is commonly received, or that Reason teaches something different from what is commonly supposed, or lastly that we are insufficient Judges what are the real Doctrines of Scripture, or Reason, or both, and consequently that we ought to wait with Patience for farther Light, all Objections of this Kind fall to the Ground. One may also add, that the same Arguments which prove a Doctrine to be very absurd, prove also, for the most part, that it is not the Sense of the Passage ; and that this is a Method of Reasoning always allowed in interpreting profane Authors.

PROP. 36.

The many and great Advantages which have accrued to the World from the Patriarchal, Judaical, *and* Christian *Revelations, prove the Divine Authority of the Scriptures.*

THESE Advantages are of two Sorts, relating respectively to the Knowlege and Practice of Religion. I begin with the First.

Now

Now it is very evident, that the Chriſtian Revelation has diffuſed a much more pure and perfect Knowlege of what is called Natural Religion, over a great Part of the World, *viz.* where-ever the Profeſſion either of Chriſtianity or Mahometiſm prevails. And the ſame thing will appear, in reſpect of the *Judaical* and *Patriarchal* Revelations, to thoſe who are acquainted with antient Hiſtory. It will be found very difficult by ſuch Perſons, to account even for the Pagan Religions without recurring to ſuch Patriarchal Communications with God, as are mentioned in the Pentateuch, and to the more full Revelations made to the *Jews.* So that one is led to believe, that all that is good in any pagan or falſe Religion, is of Divine Original; all that is erroneous and corrupt, the Offspring of the Vanity, Weakneſs, and Wickedneſs of Men; and that properly ſpeaking, we have no Reaſon from Hiſtory to ſuppoſe, that there ever was any ſuch thing as mere Natural Religion, *i. e.* any true Religion, which Men diſcovered to themſelves by the mere Light of Nature. Theſe Poſitions ſeem to follow from Inquiries into the Antiquities of the Heathen World, and of their Religions. The Heathen Religions all appear to be of a derivative Nature; each Circumſtance in the Inquiry confirms the Scriptural Accounts of Things, and ſends us to the Revelations expreſſly mentioned, or indirectly implied, in the Old Teſtament, for the real Original of the Pagan Religions in their ſimple State. This Opinion receives great Light and Confirmation from Sir *Iſaac Newton's* Chronology.

It appears alſo very probable to me, that a careful Examination of the Powers of human Underſtanding would confirm the ſame Poſition; and that, admitting the Novelty of the preſent World, there is no way of accounting for the Riſe and Progreſs of religious Knowlege, as it has taken place in fact, without having recourſe to Divine Revelation. If we admit
the

the *Patriarchal*, *Judaical*, and *Christian* Revelations, the Progress of Natural Religion, and of all the false Pretences to Revelation, will fairly arise (at least, appear possible in all Cases, and probable in most) from the Circumstances of Things, and the Powers of human Nature; and the foregoing Doctrine of Association will cast some Light upon the Subject. If we deny the Truth of these Revelations, and suppose the Scriptures to be false, we shall cast utter Confusion upon the Inquiry, and human Faculties will be found far unequal to the Task assigned to them.

Secondly, If we consider the Practice of true Religion, the good Effects of Revelation are still more evident. Every Man who believes, must find himself either excited to Good, or deterred from Evil, in many Instances, by that Belief; notwithstanding that there may be many other Instances, in which religious Motives are too weak to restrain violent and corrupt Inclinations. The same Observations occur daily with regard to others, in various Ways and Degrees. And it is by no means conclusive against this obvious Argument for the good Effects of Revelation upon the Morals of Mankind, to allege, that the World is not better now, than before the Coming of Christ. This is a Point which cannot be determined by any kind of Estimation, in our Power to make; and, if it could, we do not know what Circumstances would have made the World much worse than it is, had not Christianity interposed. However, it does appear to me very *probable*, to say the least, that *Jews* and *Christians*, notwithstanding all their Vices and Corruptions, have, upon the Whole, been always better than Heathens and Unbelievers. It seems to me also, that as the Knowlege of true, pure, and perfect Religion is advanced and diffused more and more every Day, so the Practice of it corresponds thereto: But then this, from the Nature of the Thing, is a Fact of a less obvious Kind; however, if it be true, it
will

will become manifeſt in due time.   Let us ſuppoſe a
Perſon to maintain, that Civil Government, the Arts
of Life, Medicines, &c. have never been of Uſe to
Mankind, becauſe it does not appear from any certain
Calculation, that the Sum total of Health and Happineſs is greater among the polite Nations, than among
the barbarous ones.   Would it not be thought a ſufficient Anſwer to this, to appeal to the obvious good
Effects of theſe Things in innumerable Inſtances, without entering into a Calculation impoſſible to be made ?
However, it does here alſo appear, that, as far as we
are able to judge, civilized Countries are, upon the
Whole, in a more happy State than barbarous ones,
ın all theſe reſpects.

Now, as the Divine Original of Revelation may be
directly concluded from its being the ſole Fountain of
all religious Knowlege, if that can be proved ; ſo it
will follow in an indirect Way, if we ſuppoſe, that
Revelation has only promoted the Knowlege and Practice of true Religion.   It is not likely, that Folly or
Deceit of any Kind ſhould be eminently ſerviceable in
the Advancement of Wiſdom and Virtue.   Every
Tree muſt produce its proper Fruit.   Enthuſiaſm and
Impoſture cannot contribute to make Men prudent,
peaceable and moderate, diſintereſted and ſincere.

P R O P. 37.

The wonderful Nature, and ſuperior Excellence,
of the Attempt made by Chriſt, and his Apo-
ſtles, are Evidences of their Divine Autho-
rity.

THIS Attempt was that of reforming all Mankind, and making them happy in a future State.
And, when we conſider firſt the Attempt itſelf, and
then the Aſſurance of Succeſs in it, which appears in
all their Words and Actions, by Ways both direct

and indirect, there arises from thence alone, a strong
Presumption in their Favour, as well as in Favour of
the Authors of the Books of the Old Testament, who
have concurred in the same Attempt, though less informed of the true Nature and full Extent of it. For
Ideas and Purposes of this Kind could scarce enter into
the Hearts of weak or wicked Men ; much less could
such Persons enter upon and prosecute so great an Un-
dertaking with such Prudence, Integrity, and Constan-
cy, or form such right Judgments both of the Opposition they should meet with, and of the Prevalence of
their own Endeavours, and those of their Successors,
over this Opposition.   Nay, one may say, that nothing less than supernatural Assistance could qualify
them for these Purposes.   No Design of this Kind
was ever formed, or thought of, till the Coming of
Christ ; and the Pretences of Enthusiasts and Impostors
to the same Commission since, have all been copied
from Christ, as being necessary to their succeeding in
any measure, since his Coming.   If it be supposed to
be the true Interpretation and Meaning of the Scriptures, to publish final Redemption, Conversion, and
Salvation to all Mankind, even the most Wicked,
in some distant future State, this will add great Force
to the present Argument.

P R O P. 38.

*The Manner in which the Love of God, and of
our Neighbour, is taught and inculcated in
the Scriptures, is an Evidence of their Divine
Authority.*

FOR it appears, that the Scriptures do virtually include, or even expresly assert, all that the modern
Philosophy has discovered or verified concerning these
important Subjects ; which Degree of Illumination, as
it can with no Plausibility be accounted for in illiterate
4   Men

Men in the Time of *Auguſtus* from natural Cauſes, ſo much leſs can it in the preceding Times from Chriſt up to *Moſes.* This Propoſition is included in the 35th; however, the Subject of it is of ſo much Importance, as to deſerve a ſeparate Place.

Here then, Firſt, We may obſerve, that *Moſes* commands the *Iſraelites* to love God with all the Heart, and Soul, and Might, whereas they are to love their Neighbours only as themſelves. Now, though this infinite Superiority of the Love due to God over that due to our Neighbour be perfectly agreeable to that infinite Majeſty and Goodneſs of God, and Nothingneſs of the Creatures, which every new Diſcovery in Philoſophy now opens to View; yet it was ſo little known, many Ages after *Moſes,* amongſt the wiſeſt of the *Greeks* and *Romans,* that we cannot aſcribe it to his mere natural Sagacity. The natural Equality of all Men, and the Self-annihilation, implied in the Precept of loving *all* our Brethren as well as ourſelves, are alſo the genuine Dictates of true Philoſophy.

Secondly, In order to ſhew the Divine Authority of the Scriptures, from the Manner in which the Love of God is taught in them, we muſt conſider not only the direct Precepts concerning this Love, but alſo all thoſe concerning Hope, Truſt, Fear, Thankfulneſs, Delight, *&c.* for all theſe concur to inculcate and beget in us the Love of God. The ſame may be ſaid of all the Scriptural Deſcriptions of God, and his Attributes, and of the Addreſſes of good Men to him, which are there recorded. God is declared in the Scriptures to be Light, Love, Goodneſs, the Source of all Happineſs and Perfection, the Father and Protector of all, *&c.* And the eminent Perſons who compoſed the Pſalms, and other ſuch like Addreſſes to God, appear to have devoted themſelves intirely to him. Now, when we reflect, that there is ſcarce any thing of this kind in the Writings of the Philoſophers who preceded Chriſt, and nothing comparable

parable

parable to the Scripture Expreſſions even in thoſe who came after him ; when we farther reflect, that the Writings of the ableſt and beſt Men of the preſent Times contain nothing excellent of the devotional Kind, but what may be found in the Scriptures, and even in the Old Teſtament ; there ſeems to be a Neceſſity for having recourſe to Divine Inſpiration, as the original Source of this great Degree of Illumination in the Patriarchs, Prophets, and Apoſtles.

Thirdly, Good Perſons are, in the Scriptures, ſtyled *Children of God* ; *Members of Chriſt* ; *Partakers of the divine Nature* ; *one with God and Chriſt, as Chriſt is with God* ; *Members of each other* ; *Heirs of God, and Coheirs with Chriſt* ; *Heirs of all Things*, &c. Expreſſions which have the ſtrongeſt Tendency to raiſe in us an unbounded Love to God, and an equal one to our Neighbour, and which include and convey the moſt exalted, and at the ſame time the moſt ſolid, Conceptions of this great Syſtem of Things. And if we ſuppoſe, that theſe high Titles and Privileges are, according to the Scriptures, to be hereafter extended to all Mankind, the Divine Original of the Scriptures will receive a new Acceſſion of Evidence on this Account.

PROP. 39.

The Doctrine of the neceſſary Subſerviency of Pain to Pleaſure, unfolded in the Scriptures, is an Evidence of their Divine Authority.

THE Scriptures give frequent and ſtrong Intimations, that the ultimate Happineſs which they promiſe, is not to be obtained in this our degenerate State, but by a previous Paſſage through Pain. *Bleſſed are they that mourn. We muſt rejoice in Tribulation. The Palm-bearing Multitude comes out of great Tribulation. The Captain of our Salvation*, and therefore

fore all his Soldiers, muſt be *made perfect through Suffer-ings. Without ſhedding of Blood there is no Remiſ-ſion of Sins. It is good for us to be afflicted, that we may learn to keep the Commandments of God.* The *Jews* muſt be captivated, and undergo the ſevereſt Afflictions, before they can be made happy finally, as the People of God. *Man muſt eat his Bread in the Sweat of his Brow* all his Life, *and return to Duſt* at laſt ; and yet ſtill *the Seed of the Woman ſhall bruiſe the Serpent's Head,* and gain Re-admiſſion to *the Tree of Life, whoſe Leaves ſhall heal the Nations,* &c. &c. Now there is a ſurpriſing Correſpondence between ſuch Expreſſions as theſe, and many modern Diſcove-ries, which ſhew that Pain is, in general, intro-ductory and ſubſervient to Pleaſure ; and particularly, that ſuch is the preſent Frame of our Natures, and Conſtitution of the external World, which affects our Organs, that we cannot be delivered from the Senſua-lity and Selfiſhneſs, that ſeize upon us at our firſt En-trance into Life, and advanced to Spirituality and Diſintereſtedneſs, to the Love of God and our Neigh-bour, we cannot have our, Wills broken, and our Faculties exalted and purified, ſo as to reliſh Happi-neſs where-ever we ſee it, but by the perpetual Cor-rection and Reformation of our Judgments and Deſires from painful Impreſſions and Aſſociations. And all philoſophical Inquiries of this Kind ſeem to caſt a peculiar Light and Evidence upon the Scripture Ex-preſſions before-mentioned, and to make their Accu-racy, and Congruity with Experience and Obſervation, be much more plainly ſeen and felt.

PROP.

P R O P. 40.

The mutual Inſtrumentality of Beings to each others Happineſs and Miſery, unfolded in the Scriptures, is an Argument of their Divine Authority.

TO this Head is to be referred all that the Scriptures deliver concerning good and evil Angels ; Chriſt, the Lord of all, becoming the Redeemer of all ; *Adam*'s injuring all his Poſterity through his Frailty ; *Abraham*'s becoming the Father of the Faithful, and all Nations being bleſſed through him ; the *Jews* being the Keepers of the Oracles of God, and of the true Religion ; Tyrants being Scourges in the Hand of God ; the Fulneſs of the Gentiles being the Occaſion of the final Reſtoration of the *Jews* ; and, in general, the Doctrine that God prepares and diſpoſes of every thing ſo, as that nothing is for itſelf alone, but every Perſon and Nation has various Relations to others, co-operates with them through Chriſt, who is *the Head*, and through whom the *whole Body being fitly joined together, and compacted by that which every Joint ſupplieth, increaſeth and edifieth itſelf in Love*, till *all Things, both in Heaven and Earth*, arrive, in their ſeveral Orders, to the *Meaſure of the Stature of the Fulneſs of Chriſt*. Now whoever compares theſe Scripture Expreſſions and Doctrines with the various mutual Relations, Subſerviences, and Uſes of the Parts of the external World, heavenly Bodies, Meteors, Elements, Animals, Plants, and Minerals, to each other, cannot help ſeeing a wonderful Analogy between the Works of God and the Scriptures, ſo wonderful as juſtly to intitle the laſt to the Appellation of the Word of God.

And thus we may perceive, that the Scripture Account of the Fall of Man, his Redemption by Chriſt,

and the Influences exerted upon him by good and
evil Angels, is ſo far from affording an Objection
againſt the Chriſtian Religion, that it is a conſiderable
Evidence for it, when viewed in a truly philoſophical
Light. God works in every thing by Means, by thoſe
which, according to our preſent Language and Short-
ſightedneſs, are termed bad and unfit, as well as by
the good and evidently fit ones; and all theſe Means
require a definite Time, before they can accompliſh
their reſpective Ends. This occurs to daily Obſervation in the Courſe and Conſtitution of Nature. And
the Scripture Doctrines concerning the Fall, the Redemption by Chriſt, and the Influences of good and
evil Angels, are only ſuch Intimations concerning
the principal inviſible Means that lead Man to his ultimate End, Happineſs in being united to God, as
accelerate him in his Progreſs thither. According to
the Scriptures, *Adam* hurts all, through Frailty; Chriſt
ſaves all, from his Love and Compaſſion to all; evil
Angels tempt, through Malice; and good ones aſſiſt
and defend, in Obedience to the Will of God, and
his original and ultimate Deſign of making all happy.
Theſe Things are indeed cloathed in a conſiderable
Variety of Expreſſions, ſuited to our preſent Ways of
acting, conceiving, and ſpeaking (which Ways are,
however, all of Divine Original, God having taught
Mankind, in the Patriarchal Times, the Language, as
one may ſay, in which he ſpake to them then and
afterwards); but theſe Expreſſions can have no greater
real Import, than that of ſignifying to us the Means
made uſe of by God; he being, according to the
Scriptures, as well as Reaſon, the one only real Agent
in all the Tranſactions that relate to Man, to Angels,
&c. And to object to the Method of producing
Happineſs by this or that Means, becauſe of the
Time required to accompliſh the End, of the Mixture
of Evil, *&c.* is to require, that all God's Creatures
ſhould at once be created infinitely happy, or rather

have

have exifted fo from all Eternity, *i. e.* fhould be *Gods,* and not *Creatures.*

PROP. 41.

The Divine Authority of the Scriptures may be inferred from the fuperior Wifdom of the Jew-ifh Laws, confidered in a political Light; and from the exquifite Workmanfhip fhewn in the Tabernacle and Temple.

ALL thefe were Originals amongft the *Jews,* and fome of them were copied partially and imperfectly by antient Heathen Nations. They feem alfo to imply a Knowlege fuperior to the refpective Times. And I believe, that profane Hiftory gives fufficient Atteftation to thefe Pofitions. However, it is certain from Scripture, that *Mofes* received the whole Body of his Laws, alfo the Pattern of the Tabernacle, and *David* the Pattern of the Temple, from God; and that *Bezaleel* was infpired by God for the Workmanfhip of the Tabernacle. Which Things, being laid down as a fure Foundation, may encourage learned Men to inquire into the Evidences from profane Hiftory, that the Knowlege and Skill to be found amongft the *Jews* were fuperior to thofe of other Nations at the fame Period of Time, *i. e.* were fupernatural.

PROP. 42.

The Want of Univerfality in the Publication of Revealed Religion is no Objection to it; but, on the contrary, the Time and Manner, in which the Scriptures were written, and delivered to the World, are Arguments for their Divine Authority.

HERE I obferve,
    Firft, That Objections of this Kind ought never to be admitted againft hiftorical Evidence.;
and,

and, in fact, are not, upon other Subjects. It is evident, as was obſerved in the Beginning of this Chapter, that to allow the Truth of the Scripture Hiſtory, is to allow the Truth of the Chriſtian Religion. Now it is very foreign to the Purpoſe of an Inquiry into the Truth of the Scripture Hiſtory, to allege that it has not been made known to all Mankind, in all Ages, and under all Circumſtances of each Individual. It muſt require much abſtracted and ſubtle Reaſoning, and ſuch as can never be put in Competition with plain hiſtorical Evidence, to connect this Objection with the Propoſition objected to. This is therefore, at leaſt, a ſtrong Preſumption againſt the Validity of ſuch an Objection.

Secondly, This Objection ſeems to derive its whole Force from ſuch Poſitions relating to the moral Attributes of God, as make it neceſſary for us to ſuppoſe, either that he deals with all his Creatures at preſent in an equally favourable Manner, or, at leaſt, that nothing ſhall be ultimately wanting to their Happineſs. Now the firſt Suppoſition appears, upon the moſt tranſient View which we take of Things, to be utterly falſe. There are Differences of all Degrees at preſent, in reſpect of all the good Things which God has given us to enjoy; and therefore may be in the beſt of all good Things, Revealed Religion. And indeed, if it was otherwiſe in reſpect of Revealed Religion, one ſtrong Argument in its Favour would be wanting, *viz.* its Analogy with the Courſe of Nature. The moral Attributes of God are to be deduced from Obſervations made upon the Courſe of Nature. If therefore the Tenor of Revelation be agreeable to that of Nature, it muſt be ſo to the moral Attributes of God. But if any one ſuppoſes, in the Second place, that, notwithſtanding preſent and apparent Differences in the Circumſtances of God's Creatures, there are no real and ultimate ones; at leaſt, that the Balance will ultimately be in favour of each Individual finitely, or

perphaps

perhaps infinitely ; I anfwer, That this Suppofition is
as agreeable to Revelation as to natural Reafon ; that
there are as probable Evidences for it in the Word of
God, as in his Works, there being *no Acceptance of Perfons with God, no Difference between the Jew and the
Gentile*, according to the Scriptures; and that we
may infer as ftrongly from the Scriptures, that Chrift
will fave all, as it can be inferred from Philofophy,
that all will be made happy in any way ; both which
Pofitions I fhall endeavour to eftablifh hereafter, with
the mutual Illuftrations and Confirmations, which
thefe glorious Doctrines of Natural and Revealed
Religion afford to each other. And the gradual Diffufion of the *Patriarchal*, *Judaical*, and *Chriftian* Revelations, compared with the Prophecies relating to
the future Kingdom of Chrift, and with the prefent
Circumftances of Things, will afford great Satisfaction
and Joy to every pious, benevolent Perfon, who in-
quires into this Subject. Thefe Confiderations will
incline him to believe, that the Gofpel will, fooner or
later, be preached to *every Creature in Heaven, in
Earth, under the Earth*, &c. and not only preached,
but received, obeyed, and made the Means of un-
fpeakable Happinefs to them. And thus this Objection will be removed not only in Speculation, and
according to Reafon, but in Fact, from the prefent
unhappy Objectors; and *they will look on him whom
they have pierced.*

 Thirdly, Having fhewn that a gradual and partial
Promulgation is not inconfiftent with the Suppofition
of a true Revelation, we may farther affirm, that the
particular Time and Manner, in which the feveral
Patriarchal, *Judaical*, and *Chriftian* Revelations have
been publifhed to the World, are even Arguments in
their Favour. This Subject has been well handled by
various learned Men, particularly by Mr. *Arch. Law*,
in his Confiderations on the State of the World, *&c.*
Thefe Gentlemen have fhewn, that, *cæteris manentibus*,
which

which is in theſe Things always to be previouſly
allowed, the Diſpenſations recorded in the Scriptures
have been, as far as we can judge, perfectly ſuited to
the States of the World at the Times when theſe Diſpenſations were made reſpectively ; *i. e.* to the Improvement of Mankind in Knowlege ſpeculative and
practical, to their Wants, and to their Ability to profit in moral Accompliſhments ; ſo that if we ſuppoſe
either much more, or much leſs, Light to have been
afforded to Mankind in a ſupernatural Way *(cæteris
manentibus*; and particularly their voluntary Powers
over their Affections and Actions, or Free-will in the
practical Senſe, remaining the ſame), their Advancement in moral Perfection, in voluntary Obedience to,
and pure Love of God, would probably have been
leſs: Which Suitableneſs of each Revelation to the
Time when it was made, and to the Production of
the *Maximum* of moral Perfection, is an Argument
for the Syſtem of Revelation, of the ſame Kind with
thoſe for the Goodneſs of God, which are drawn from
the mutual Fitneſſes of the finite and imperfect Parts
of the natural World to each other, and to the Production of the *Maximum*, or greateſt poſſible Quantity, of Happineſs.

P R O P. 43.

*The Excluſion of all great Degrees of Enthu-
ſiaſm and Impoſture from the Characters of
Chriſt, the Prophets and Apoſtles, proves their
Divine Authority.*

THAT Chriſt, the Prophets and Apoſtles, cannot
be charged with any great Degrees of Enthuſiaſm
or Impoſture, ſeems allowed by many Unbelievers; and
is evident from the firſt View of their Diſcourſes and
Writings, and of Hiſtory ſacred and profane. We
might ſay, that much more is evident. However,
for

for the prefent, let us only fuppofe all great Degrees of Enthufiafm and Impofture excluded, and inquire how far their Divine Miffion may be inferred from that Suppofition.

Firft, then, If all great Degrees, of Enthufiafm be excluded, Chrift, the Prophets and Apoftles, muft know whether or no they were under the Influence of the Divine Spirit, fo as to prophefy, fpeak, and interpret Languages, which they had never learnt, and work Miracles. Indeed to fuppofe them not capable of diftinguifhing thefe Powers in themfelves and each other, is to charge them with downright Madnefs.

Secondly, Since then they claimed thefe Powers every-where, as the Seal of their Commiffion from God; if they had them not, *i. e.* if they had not Divine Authority, they muft be Impoftors, and endeavour to deceive the World knowingly and deliberately. And this Impofture, whether we confider the Affront offered to God, or the Injury done to Mankind, or its Duration, its Audacioufnefs, *&c.* would be the deepeft and blackeft that has ever appeared in the World. It is therefore excluded by Suppofition; and confequently, fince a lefs Degree will not account for a falfe Claim to Divine Authority, we muft allow, that Chrift, the Prophets and Apoftles, made a true one.

Thirdly, Let it be obferved, that though cautious Unbelievers do not venture to charge Chrift, the Prophets and Apoftles, either with grofs Enthufiafm, or abandoned Impofture, in exprefs Terms; yet they find themfelves obliged to infinuate both in all their Attacks upon Revealed Religion: Which is, in effect, to acknowlege the Truth of the prefent Propofition; for it is the fame Thing, as to acknowlege, that both the Charge of grofs Enthufiafm, and that of abandoned Impofture, are neceffary to fupport the Objections againft Revealed Religion. Now, as neither Charge, fingly taken, can be maintained; fo both
together

together are inconſiſtent. Groſs Enthuſiaſm does not admit that conſtant Caution, and cool diſpaſſionate Cunning, which abandoned Impoſture ſuppoſes and requires in order to ſucceed.

PROP. 44.

The Reception which Chriſt, his Forerunners and Followers, with their Doctrines, have met with in all Ages, is an Argument of their Divine Authority.

THIS Evidence does, as it were, embrace all the others, and give a particular Force to them. For it will be a ſtrong Confirmation of all the Evidences for the *Jewiſh* and Chriſtian Religions, if we can ſhew, that the Perſons to whom they have been offered, have been influenced by them as much as there was Reaſon to expect, admitting them to be true; and far more than could be expected, on Suppoſition that they were falſe. The moſt illuſtrious Inſtance of this, is the Victory which the Chriſtian Miracles and Doctrines, with the Sufferings of our Saviour, and his Followers, gained over the whole Powers, firſt, of the *Jewiſh* State, and then of the *Roman* Empire, in the primitive Times. For here all Ranks and Kinds of Men, Princes, Prieſts, *Jewiſh* and Heathen, Philoſophers, Populace, with all their aſſociated Prejudices from Cuſtom and Education, with all their corrupt Paſſions and Luſts, with all the external Advantages of Learning, Power, Riches, Honour, and, in ſhort, with every thing but Truth, endeavoured to ſuppreſs the Progreſs that Chriſt's Religion made every Day in the World; but were unable to do it. Yet ſtill the Evidence was but of a limited Nature; it required to be ſet forth, atteſted, and explained, by the Preacher, and to be attended to, and reflected upon, with ſome Degree of Impartiality,

tiality, by the Hearer: And therefore, though the Progress of it was quick, and the Effect general, yet they were not instantaneous and universal. However, it is very evident, that any Fraud, or false Pretence, must soon have yielded to so great an Opposition so circumstanced.

The Efficacy which the Christian Doctrine then had in reforming the Lives of many Thousands, is here to be considered as a principal Branch of this Argument, it being evidently the most difficult of all Things, to convert Men from vicious Habits to virtuous ones, as every one may judge from what he feels in himself, as well as from what he sees in others; and whatever does this, cannot, as it seems to me, but come from God. The false Religions, and various Corruptions of the true, which have from time to time appeared in the World, have been enabled to do this in the imperfect Manner in which they have done it, merely, as it seems to me, from that Mixture of important Truths, and good Motives, which they have borrowed from real Revelations, *Patriarchal*, *Judaical*, and *Christian*.

In like manner, as the Propagation of Christianity, upon its first Appearance in the World, evinces its Divine Original, so does the Progress it has since made, and the Reception which it meets with at present, amongst the several Ranks and Orders of Men. The Detail of this would run out to a great Length. It may, however, be of some Use, just to observe, that, notwithstanding the great Prevalence of Infidelity in the present Times, it is seldom found to consist with an accurate Knowlege of antient History, sacred and profane, and never with an exalted Piety and Devotion to God.

And it is as peculiarly for the Credit of Christianity, that it should now be supported by the Learned, as that it was first propagated by the Unlearned; and an incontestable Evidence for it, as appears to me, that
it

it has been univerfally embraced by all eminently pious Perfons, to whom it has been made known in a proper Manner.

The analogous Obfervations may be made upon the Reception which the *Jewifh* Religion met with both from the *Jews* themfelves, and from the neighbouring Nations. It feems impoffible for *Mofes* to have delivered the *Jews* from their Oppreffion in *Egypt*, and afterwards to have fubjected them to his Laws, for *Jofhua* to have conquered *Canaan*, for the Religion to have fubfifted in the fucceeding Times of the Judges and Kings, for the Priefts and Prophets to have maintained their Authority, for the People to have returned, after their Captivity, with their Religion in an uncorrupted State, and to have fupported it and themfelves againft the Kings of *Syria* and *Egypt*, and the Power of the *Romans*, and to remain at this Day a feparate People difperfed all over the World, according to the Prophecies, unlefs the miraculous Part of the Hiftory of the Old Teftament be allowed to be true, as well as the other.

PROP. 45.

The Reception which falfe Religions have met with in the World, are Arguments of the Truth of the Chriftian.

I Will here make a few fhort Remarks,

Firft, Upon the Polytheiftical, Idolatrous Religions of the antient World.

Secondly, Upon the religious Inftitutions of *Zoroafter.*

Thirdly, Upon the Impofture of *Mahomet.*

Fourthly, Upon the Enthufiaftical Sects, which have appeared from time to time amongft Chriftians.

All thefe feem to have met with fuch Succefs, as might be expected from the Mixture of Truth and
Falfhood

Falſhood in them, compared with the then Circumſtances of Things. They are therefore indirect Evidences for the Truth of the Chriſtian Religion, ſince
this has met with ſuch Succeſs, as cannot be reconciled
to the Circumſtances of Things, unleſs we ſuppoſe it
true.

And, Firſt, The antient Pagan Religions ſeem evidently to be the degenerated Offspring of the Patriarchal Revelations; and ſo far to have been true, as
they taught a God, a Providence, a future State, ſupernatural Communications made to particular Perſons,
eſpecially in the Infancy of the World, the preſent
Corruption of Man, and his Deviation from a pure
and perfect Way, the Hopes of a Pardon, a mediatorial Power, the Duties of Sacrifice, Prayer, and
Praiſe, and the Virtues of Prudence, Temperance,
Juſtice, and Fortitude. They were falſe, as they
mixed and polluted theſe important Truths with numberleſs Fables, Superſtitions, and Impieties. That
Degree of Truth, and moral Excellence, which remained in them, was a principal Cauſe of their Succeſs, and eaſy Propagation, among the People; for
their moral Senſe would direct them to approve and
receive what was fit and uſeful. And, had the People of thoſe Times penetrated ſufficiently into the
Powers of the human Mind, they might have concluded, that religious Truths could not be of human Invention. However, as the Impreſſions, which the
hiſtorical and prophetical Evidences for the Patriarchal
Revelations had made upon Mankind, were not yet
obliterated; they believed, upon the Authority of
Tradition, that all important Knowlege, eſpecially in
ſacred Matters, was of Divine Original.

As to the Miracles ſaid to be wrought upon certain
Occaſions in Pagan Nations, we may make theſe two
Remarks: Firſt, That the Evidence for theſe is far
inferior to that for the *Jewiſh* and Chriſtian Miracles;
ſo that theſe may be true, though thoſe be falſe. Se-

I

condly, that we are not ſufficiently informed of the
Ways of Providence, to infer that God did not per-
mit, or cauſe, ſome Miracles to be wrought, even in
Times and Places, where great Corruption prevailed.
Divine Communications and Miracles were probably
moſt common ſoon after the Flood, in the Infancy of
Mankind: Afterwards, as they advanced towards
adult Age, theſe ſupernatural Interpoſitions grew
more rare (unleſs upon ſingular Occaſions, as upon
the Publication of the Law by *Moſes*, and of the
Goſpel by Chriſt; at which times, many and great
Miracles ſucceeded each other at ſhort Intervals, in
order to command Awe, Attention, and Belief);
and it may be, that they ceaſed in the Pagan World
for ſome Ages before Chriſt: Or it may be otherwiſe; and that, in rare and extraordinary Caſes, the
Hand of God appeared in a miraculous Manner.
Analogy favours the laſt Opinion, as it ſeems to me;
which alſo appears to be more countenanced by Hiſtory, than the contrary one; and yet the Pretences to
Miracles amongſt the Pagans were undoubtedly falſe,
in the general.

I come, in the Second place, to conſider the religious Inſtitutions of *Zoroaſter*. We have not ſo full
and authentic an Hiſtory of theſe, as to compare them
properly with the *Jewiſh* or Chriſtian Revelations. If
we ſuppoſe, that *Zoroaſter* and *Hyſtaſpes* ſet up the
Worſhip of One God, in a ſimple Manner, teaching
and inculcating the Practice of Virtue at the ſame
time, this Religion may be ſaid to have conſiderable
moral Evidence in its Favour. If, farther, we ſuppoſe it to be in part derived, either from the Deſcendents of *Abraham* by *Keturah*, called *Brachmans* from
him, or from that Knowlege of the true God, which
the Ten Tribes, and the *Jews*, had then communicated to that Part of the World, it will become an Evidence for the *Jewiſh* Religion.

Thirdly, The Religion of *Mahomet* allows and pre-
suppofes the Truth of the *Jewifh* and Chriftian.   Its
rapid Propagation was owing chiefly to the Mixture
of political Interefts.   That Part of its Doctrines,
which is good, is manifeftly taken from the Scriptures; and this contributed to its Succefs.   However,
a Comparifon of Mahometifm with Chriftianity, in
the feveral Particulars of each, feems to fhew, that
whenever a ftrict Examination is made into the Hiftory of Mahometifm by its Profeffors, the Falfhood
of it will quickly be made evident to them.   It could
not ftand fuch a Trial, as Chriftianity has, fince the
Revival of Learning in thefe Weftern Parts.

It feems eafy to apply what has been delivered in
the three laft Paragraphs to the analogous Particulars
of the Religion of *Confucius,* and of other Religions
found in the *Eaft* and *Weft-Indies,* as far as their Hiftories are fufficiently full and authentic for that Purpofe.

Laftly, One may make the following Remarks,
with refpect to the feveral enthufiaftic Sects, that arife
from time to time amongft Chriftians.

Firft, That their Pretences to Miracles and Prophecies have, in general, been detected and expofed, after
fome Examination and Inquiry; unlefs the Sect has
begun to decline from other Caufes, before a ftrict
Examination became neceffary.

Secondly, That their pretended Miracles were not
of that evident Kind, nor done in the fame open
Manner, *&c.* as the *Jewifh* and Chriftian Miracles.

Thirdly, That thefe pretended Miracles have not
produced lafting Effects upon the Minds of Men, like
the *Jewifh* and *Chriftian.*   Now, though a Religion
may fucceed for a time without true Miracles, yet it
feems hard to believe, that any fhould fail with
them

Fourthly, The Succefs of Sects has, in general,
been owing to their making greater Pretences to Purity, and Gofpel Perfection, than eftablifhed Churches,
and

and to their both teaching and practiſing ſome neceſſary Duties, which eſtabliſhed Churches have too
much neglected in the corrupted State of Chriſtianity.
And in this Light they have been true in part, and
have done the moſt important Service to the World.
Every Sect of Chriſtians has magnified ſome great
Truth, not above its real Value, but above the Value
which other Sects have ſet upon it; and by this means
each important religious Truth has had the Advantage
of being ſet in a full Light by ſome Party or other,
though too much neglected by the reſt. And the
true Catholic Church and Communion of Saints unites
all theſe Sects, by taking what is right from each, and
leaving the Errors, Falſhoods, and Corruptions of
each to combat and deſtroy one another.

And it may be, that Mankind will be able in future
Generations to ſee, how every other Sect, and Pretence to Revelation, beſides thoſe of enthuſiaſtic Chriſtians, in whatever Age or Country it has appeared,
has been, all other Things remaining the ſame, ſuited
in the beſt poſſible Manner, both to particular and
general Purpoſes; and that each has prepared the
Way, in its proper Place, for that more complete
State predicted in the Scriptures under the Titles of
the Kingdom of Heaven, and *of Righteouſneſs, of the
New Jeruſalem,* &c. Even Infidelity, Atheiſm, and
Scepticiſm, have their Uſe. The Veſſels of Wrath
are ſtill Veſſels belonging to the Maker and Lord of
all Things, and anſwering his infinitely beneficent
Purpoſes. *Offences muſt come,* though *Wo be to thoſe,
by whom they come!* Each Sect, and Pretence, and
Objection, has given, or will give, way in its Time.
The true and pure Religion of Chriſt alone grows
more evident and powerful from every Attack that is
made upon it, and converts the Bitterneſs and Poiſon
of its Adverſaries into Nouriſhment for itſelf, and an
univerſal Remedy for the Pains and Sorrows of a miſerable, degenerate World.

O 2 C H A P,

CHAP. III.

Of the RULE *of* LIFE.

HAVING delivered, in the Two foregoing Chapters, the refpective Evidences for Natural and Revealed Religion, I proceed now to inquire into the Rule of Life injoined by them. This, it is evident, muft be Compliance with the Will of God. Both Natural and Revealed Religion teach this at firft View; which is alfo the immediate Dictate of rational Self-intereft. It is farther evident, that the Love of God, and of our Neighbour, with Moderation in all felfifh Enjoyments, muft be the Will of him, who is infinitely benevolent, *i. e.* in the popular Phrafe, infinitely holy, merciful, juft, and true, who has fent us into this World to make ourfelves and others happy. This we may learn from Natural Religion, and the Scriptures abound every-where with the fame Precepts. I propofe therefore, in this Chapter, to enter into the Detail of thefe Precepts, and to apply them to the feveral particular Circumftances of human Life, digefting what I have to offer, under the Heads of the feven Kinds of Pleafure and Pain, whofe Hiftory I have given in the foregoing Part of this Work. But firft I will, in the Four Propofitions that follow next, premife an Argument in favour of Virtue, which ought to have fome Weight, as it feems to me, even with an Atheift or Sceptic.

SECT. I.

Of the Rule of Life, as deducible from the Practice and Opinions of Mankind.

PROP. 46.

The Practice of Mankind affords a Direction, which, though an imperfect one, may, however, be of some Use in our Inquiry after the Rule of Life.

THIS follows, First, Becaufe, in all the fubordinate Arts of Life, we always pay great Regard to the common Judgment, Practice, and Experience of Mankind, taken at an Average, as one may fay. And this is thought to be more particularly requifite for thofe Perfons to do, who are ignorant and Novices in refpect of thefe Arts. Now what is reafonable in the inferior Arts, muft alfo be reafonable in the Art of Arts, that of living happily, of attaining our *Summum Bonum*, or greateft poffible Happinefs, here and hereafter, if there be an Hereafter; which there may be, even confiftently with Atheifm and Scepticifm. There feems therefore a peculiar Obligation, from Self-intereft at leaft, upon Atheifts and Sceptics, fince they muft live here upon the fame Terms as other Men, and ftand the fame Chance for an Hereafter, to pay fome Deference to the Practice of others, confidered as an Hint and Caution how to fecure their own Intereft.

Secondly, Mankind are evidently endued with a Defire of attaining Happinefs, and avoiding Mifery; and arrive at a competent Knowlege of the Means, which lead to this End. I have, in the foregoing

O 3   Part

Part of this Work, endeavoured to ſhew how this Deſire and Knowlege are generated. But the Fact is certain and obvious, whether that Account be ſatiſfactory or no.

Thirdly, Thoſe who admit a benevolent Author of Nature, in any Senſe of theſe Words, will be inclined to believe, that Mankind muſt in ſome Degree be fitted to attain Happineſs; and alſo, in conſequence thereof, attain it in fact. And even atheiſtical and ſceptical Perſons, when they ſee how blind Fate, or Nature, or whatever Term elſe they think fit to uſe, gives to all Animals Appetites, Inſtincts, and Objects, in general, ſuited to their Well-being, ought, from an Argument of Induction, to expect ſomething analogous to this in Mankind, previouſly to their Inquiry into the Fact.

It appears therefore, that the Practice of Mankind, taken at an Average, may be of ſome Uſe to us in our Inveſtigation of the Rule of Life ; and yet theſe ſame Conſiderations ſhew, that the Light thereby afforded can be no more than a very imperfect one. The Error, Irregularity, and Miſery, which are every-where conſpicuous, prove at once, that the Practice of Mankind is no infallible Guide.

P R O P. 47.

The Opinions of Mankind afford an imperfect Direction in reſpect of the Rule of Life, which is preferable to that drawn from their Practice.

THAT the Opinions of Mankind, concerning the Means of obtaining Happineſs, are both of real Uſe, and yet an imperfect Rule in many reſpects, will appear, if we apply the Reaſoning uſed in the foregoing Propoſition to them.

That

That this imperfect Rule is, however, preferable
to that drawn from the mere Practice, follows, inafmuch as the Opinions of Mankind are, in general,
formed after Experience, and often upon mature Deliberation, when they are free from the violent Im-
pulfes of their Appetites and Paffions, and at a more
proper and equal Diftance from the Objects under
Confideration, than can well be at the time of
Action.

P R O P. 48.

*The Rule of Life drawn from the Practice and
Opinions of Mankind, taken at an Average, is
favourable to the Caufe of Virtue.*

I Will firft confider the Rule fuppofed to be taken
from the mere Practice of Mankind.

Now it appears at firft Sight, that this Rule would
exclude all eminent Degrees both of Virtue and Vice.
A Perfon who fhould be fimilar to the whole Aggregate of Mankind, confidered as one great Individual,
would have fome Seeds and Shoots of every Virtue,
and every Vice, and yet none in an eminent Degree :
His Virtues and Vices would only exert themfelves,
when called forth by ftrong Motives and Occafions :
In which Cafes, however, this fictitious Perfon, this
Type and Reprefentative of the whole Species, would
not fail to fhew, that he had all Kinds of good and
bad Difpofitions, all balancing and reftraining one
another, unlefs where extraordinary Incidents turn the
Scale in favour of each Particular refpectively : So
that, if the mere Practice of Mankind fhould be
thought fufficient to ground a Rule upon, we fhould
be directed by this to avoid all great Degrees both of
Virtue and Vice, and to keep our Appetites and Paffions in Subjection to one another, fo as that none
fhould prevail over the reft, unlefs upon particular

O 4 extraordinary

extraordinary Occasions. And a Person, formed according to this Model, would be reckoned a neutral, moderate, prudent Man, not much loved or hated by those with whom he conversed; however, respected and regarded, rather than otherwise. We may also suppose, that his Life would be much chequered with Happiness and Misery; and yet, for the most part, be void of all high Degrees of either; upon the Whole, probably rather happy, than miserable. And thus the Practice of Mankind would, as it appears to me, lead to a low Degree both of Virtue and Happiness, and exclude all that Violence and Exorbitancy of Passion and Appetite, which is one chief Source and Occasion of Vice. For almost all Kinds of Vice are the Excesses, and monstrous Offsprings, of natural Appetites; whereas the Virtues are, in general, of a moderate Nature, and lie between the two Extremes. That Moderation therefore, which the Practice of Mankind, taken so as to make the opposite Extremes balance each other, directs us to, must, upon the Whole, be more favourable to Virtue than to Vice.

Let us next inquire to what Rule of Life the Opinions of Mankind would lead us, or how far the several Virtues or Vices are generally esteemed to conduce to Happiness or Misery. Now, as the general Practice of Mankind excludes all gross Vices, so does the general Opinion, but in a stronger manner. It does also exclude all eminent Virtues; but then it does this in a weaker manner than the general Practice; and, upon the Whole, it turns the Scale greatly in favour of Virtue, and against Vice, as Means of private Happiness; as will immediately appear, if we consider the particular Virtues and Vices of Temperance and Intemperance, Meekness and Anger, Beneficence and Avarice, Gratitude and Ingratitude, &c. as opposed to, and put in Competition with, each other, in the Judgement of Mankind. And yet it does not seem by any means, that, according to the general

Opinion

Opinion of Mankind, the greateſt Degree of Virtue has the faireſt Proſpect for Happineſs in this World.

But then, with reſpect to that other World, for which there is at leaſt this Preſumption of general Opinion, we have almoſt an univerſal Conſent of all Ages and Nations, that all Degrees of Virtue and Vice will there meet with their proper and proportional Reward and Puniſhment. Now an impartial Sceptic muſt either enter the Liſts, and fairly conſider what Arguments there are for or againſt a future State, and reaſon upon the Subject, *i. e.* ceaſe to be a Sceptic ; or elſe this general Opinion of Mankind in favour of a future State muſt, for the mechanical Reaſons alleged in the Firſt Part of this Work, give ſome Degree of Determination to him here, as in other Caſes, where the Mind is perfectly *in æquilibrio.* For the ſame Reaſons, the almoſt univerſal Conſent of Mankind in the ſuperior Advantages of Virtue in a future State, by them ſuppoſed, ought to have ſome Weight with ſuch a Perſon, even though he ſhould ſtill remain *in æquilibrio*, as to the Opinion of a future State, becauſe then it would be as probable as the other Side of the Queſtion.

And, upon the Whole, we may make the following Concluſions.

1. That a Perſon who ſhould form his Life partly upon the Practice of Mankind, and partly upon their Opinions, would incline conſiderably to the Side of Virtue.

2. That, if he thought the Rule drawn from the Opinions of Mankind preferable to that drawn from their Practice, according to the laſt Propoſition, he muſt incline more to the Side of Virtue.

3. That, if the future State, which commences at the Expiration of this Life, be ſuppoſed of indefinitely more Value than it, and certain, he ought to adhere ſtrictly to Virtue, and renounce all Vice. And the Concluſion will be the ſame, though there be only a
ſtrong,

ftrong, or a moderate Probability, or even an equal
Chance, nay, I might almoft fay, a bare Poffibility,
of the Reality, and great Importance, of a future
Life ; fince what he would forfeit in this Life by a
ftrict Adherence to Virtue, is confeffedly of fmall
Importance in common Cafes.

4. That all great Degrees of Vice are contrary to
the common Senfe, Practice, and Experience of
Mankind.

5. And therefore, laftly, If a Man gives himfelf up
to vicious Courfes, pretending cool rational Scepticifm
and Uncertainty in religious Matters, he muft either
deceive himfelf, or endeavour to impofe upon others.
A Perfon who lay intirely aftoat, would from the
Sufceptibility of Infection, allowed by all, and above
explained from our Frame, fuffer himfelf to be formed by the Practices and Opinions of Mankind at an
Average ; *i. e.* would incline to the Side of Virtue :
And therefore a Perfon who inclines the contrary Way,
muft be drawn afide from the neutral Point of Scepticifm by fecret Prejudices and Paffions.

It may be objected to the Reafoning ufed in the
former Part of this Propofition, that whatever be the
Opinions of Mankind, their Practice at an Average is
by no means at an equal Diftance from perfect Virtue,
and grofs Vice ; but approaches much nearer to the
latter Extreme : And that this appears both from the
Obfervation of the Facts, and from the Declarations
of the Scriptures.

Firft, then, Let us confider the Obfervation of
the Facts. And here the Objectors will be ready to
heap together the many Inftances of Violence, Revenge, Cruelty, Injuftice, Ingratitude, Treachery,
want of natural Affection, brutal Senfuality, Anger,
Envy, Morofenefs, Ambition, Avarice, and Selfifhnefs, which Hiftory and Experience, public and private, are able to furnifh ; and will urge, that a Perfon who fhould copy after Mankind taken at a

2   Medium,

Medium, would be a very fenfual, felfifh, malevolent, and every way vicious Creature. And it muft be confeffed, nay, I am fo far from denying, that I every-where fuppofe, and lay down as a Principle, that there is much Corruption and Wickednefs all over the World. But that the moral Evil in the World exceeds the moral Good, would be very difficult to prove.

For, Firft, How fhall we make the Computation? Who fhall fum up for us all the Inftances of the foregoing and other Vices, and weigh them in a juft Balance againft the contrary Inftances of Love to Relations, Friends, Neighbours, Strangers, Enemies, and the brute Creation; of Temperance and Chaftity, Generofity, Gratitude, Compaffion, Courage, Humility, Piety, Refignation, &c.? The Cafe between the Virtues and the Vices, *i. e.* between Moral Good and Evil, feems to refemble that between Pleafure and Pain, or Natural Good and Evil. The Inftances of Pleafure are, in general, more numerous, but lefs in Quantity, than thofe of Pain; and though it is impoffible to fpeak with Certainty, becaufe no Man can be qualified to make the Eftimate, yet Pleafure feems to prevail upon the Whole. In like manner, the Inftances of Benevolence of fome Kind or other, though mixed with many Imperfeftions, of a partial Self-government, of a fuperftitious, enthufiaftic, idolatrous, or lukewarm Piety, one or other, occur in almoft all the moft familiar Circumftances of human Life, and intermix themfelves with the moft common, ordinary Thoughts, Words, and Aftions: Whereas the Inftances of Senfuality, Malevolence, and Profanenefs, are rarer, as it feems, though often of a more glaring Nature.

Secondly, The Imperfeftion of Virtue, which I allow, and even lay down in Mankind in general, makes them, in general, apt to magnify the Vices of others. Perfeft Virtue may be fuppofed to be but

juft

juſt perfectly candid and equitable; and therefore imperfect Virtue is moſt probably too cenſorious, eſpecially ſince Men, by blaming others, hope to exculpate or exalt themſelves. And, agreeably to this, common Experience ſhews, that bodily Infirmities, Diſappointments, Pride, Self-indulgence, and Vice of all Kinds, diſpoſe Men to look upon the dark Side of every Proſpect, and to magnify the Evils natural and moral, that àre in the World, both in their own Thoughts, and in their Diſcourſes to others. It is alſo to be added here, that as our Opinions are more in favour of Virtue than our Practice, ſo our Rule of judging muſt of conſequence much condemn the general Practice. This Circumſtance is very neceſſary for the moral Improvement of the World; but, if overlooked, it may miſlead in the preſent Inquiry.

Thirdly, The greater Intenſeneſs of the particular Pains above the correſponding Pleaſures in general, and of the particular Vices above the oppoſite Virtues, as juſt now mentioned, tends, for moſt eminent and beneficent final Cauſes in both Caſes, to affect the Imagination and Memory with ſtronger and more laſting Impreſſions, ſo as to occur more readily to the Invention in all Inquiries and Speculations of this Kind.

Fourthly, If we ſuppoſe, that natural Good prevails, upon the Whole, in the World, Analogy ſeems to require, that moral Good (which is, in general, its Cauſe) ſhould alſo prevail in like manner. Farther, as we judge, that natural Good prevails from the general Deſire of Life, the Pleaſure of recollecting Perſons and Places, and renewing our Acquaintance with them, &c. ſo the ſame Things ſeem to determine, that Mankind is, upon the Whole, rather amiable and reſpectable, than hateful and contemptible, *i. e.* rather virtuous than vicious.

Laſtly, It is to be obſerved, That, in an accurate way of ſpeaking, Virtue and Vice, are mere relative

Terms,

Terms, like Great and Little. Whence the Average of Mankind may be confidered as a middle Point between the pofitive and negative Quantities of Virtue and Vice, as a neutral Situation. And, upon this Suppofition, we might firft fhew, that it is Man's greateft Intereft, his *Summum Bonum*, at leaft, to be neutral ; and afterwards, that he ought to prefs forward with all poffible Earneftnefs towards the infinite Perfection of God, though ever at an infinite Diftance. For, as every finite Length is infinitely nearer to nothing, than to a metaphyfically infinite one (to make this Suppofition for Argument's fake) ; fo all finite Virtue is infinitely more diftant from the infinite Perfection of God, than from nothing. And thus indeed all our Righteoufnefs is *filthy Rags*, and all our Virtue infinite Vice. But this Method of confidering the prefent Subject is far from oppofing the Purport of this Section.

If we fhould call all mere Self-regards Vice, and all Regards to God, and our Neighbour, Virtue ; which is a very proper Language, and one that would render the Terms of this Inquiry precife ; it feems probable to me, that Virtue abounds more, upon the Whole, than Vice. A View to the Good of others, at leaft near Relations, is a general Motive to Action ; and a Defign to pleafe God, at leaft not to offend him, is very common in the Bulk of Mankind, or even the worft. The moft ordinary and trivial Actions are performed without any explicit View at all, at leaft any that we remember a few Moments after the Action, *i. e.* are automatic fecondarily ; and fo cannot be confidered as either virtuous or vicious; or, if they be, we muft judge of their Complexion by that of the more eminent ones.

Secondly, It may be objected, That, according to the Scriptures, Mankind are in a loft fallen State; *that they are all gone out of the Way, and become corrupt and abominable* ; *that there is none that doth Good,* &c.

I

I anfwer, That thefe and fuch-like Expreffions feem to refer to a former State of Innocence in Paradife, to a future Kingdom of Righteoufnefs, promifed in both the Old and New Teftament, and to the Rule of Life laid down there, with the Conditions requifite to our Admittance into this happy State : And that, in this View of Things, the Virtue of Mankind in general is as deficient, as their Happinefs falls fhort of the Joys of the Bleffed ; agreeably to which, the prefent Life is, in the Scripture, reprefented as a Scene of Vanity, Labour, and Sorrow. And it is a moft important and alarming Confideration, that the common Virtue of Mankind will not intitle us to a future Reward after Death ; *that few fhall find the ftreight Gate ; and that, unlefs our Righteoufnefs exceed that of the Scribes and Pharifees, we can in no-wife enter into the Kingdom of Heaven,* here or hereafter. But then, as, notwithftanding the Curfe paffed upon Man, and upon the Ground, God is reprefented in Scripture *as opening his Hand, and filling all Things living with Plenteoufnefs,* as being kind to all, and manifefting his infinite and invifible Goodnefs by vifible Things, *i. e.* as making natural Good to prevail upon the Whole, that fo we may, on this account, be thankful to him, and love him with all our Hearts, as he commands ; fo the correfponding Precept of loving our Neighbour as ourfelves, feems to infer, that our Neighbour is amiable upon the Whole. And we may fuppofe, that moral Good prevails in general, in a Degree proportional to the Prevalence of natural Good : Or, however we underftand the Scripture Language on this Head, it cannot be contrary to the foregoing Reafoning. It muft appear from thence, that we ought to be, at leaft, as good as Mankind at a *Medium,* in order to obtain the *Medium* of Happinefs ; and that, if we have higher Views, our Road lies towards the infinite Perfection of Virtue, towards Spirituality. Benevolence,

lence, and Piety, and not towards Senfuality, Selfifhnefs, or Malevolence.

P R O P. 49.

*The Rule of Life, drawn from the Practice and
Opinions of Mankind, corrects and improves
itfelf perpetually, till at laft it determines intirely for Virtue, and excludes all Kinds and
Degrees of Vice.*

FOR, fince the imperfect Rule, drawn in the laft
Propofition, is, at leaft, fo favourable to Virtue,
as to exclude all great Vices, we may conclude, that
all grofly vicious Perfons ought to be left out in col-
lecting the Rule of Life from the Practice and Opinions of Mankind; and that our Rule will approach
nearer to a perfect one thereby. And as this our Second Rule, taken from the virtuous and fuperior Orders of the Vicious, determines more in favour of Virtue, than our Firft, taken indifferently from all the
Orders both of the Virtuous and Vicious, fo it will
engage us to exclude more of the Vicious from our
future Eftimate; and fo on, till at laft we determine
intirely in favour of Virtue. At leaft, this is a Prefumption, which rifes up to View, when we confider
the Subject in the Method here propofed. Since it
appears from the firft general Confideration of the
Practice and Opinions of Mankind, that grofly vicious
Perfons muft be unhappy, it is not reafonable to allow
them any Weight in determining what is the proper
Method for attaining the greateft poffible Happinefs.
And as the fame Obfervation recurs perpetually, with
refpect to all the Orders of the Vicious, we fhall at
laft be led to take the moft Virtuous only, as the proper Guides of Life.

Grofly vicious Perfons may alfo be excluded, from
the manifeft Blindnefs and Infatuation in common

Affairs,

Affairs, which attends them; and as this extends to the Vice of Senfuality in particular, fo this Vice may be farther excluded from that Tendency of our Natures to Spirituality, in our Progrefs through Life, which is allowed by all, and explained in the foregoing Part of this Work upon the Principle of Affociation. Malevolence is alfo excluded, becaufe it is itfelf Mifery; and, by Parity of Reafon, Benevolence muft be a proper Recommendation for thofe, whofe Example and Judgment we would follow in our Endeavours after Happinefs. And it does not appear in this Way of propofing thefe Matters, that the ultimate Ratio of Things admits of any Limit to our Spirituality or Benevolence, provided we fuppofe, that, at the Expiration of this Life, a progreffive Scene of the fame Kind commences.

The Method of Reafoning here ufed bears fome Refemblance to, and is fomewhat illuftrated by, the Method of Approximation practifed by Mathematicians, in order to determine the Roots of Equations to any propofed Degree of Exactnefs. Farther, as it is common in infinite Seriefes for the three or four Firft Terms either to fhew what the whole Series is, or, at leaft, that it is infinite; fo here the ever-growing and fuperior Excellence of Spirituality and Benevolence, which the foregoing Confiderations open to View, by recurring perpetually, and correcting the immediately precedent Determination in every Step, may incline one to think, in Correfpondence to that Method of Reafoning in Seriefes, that Spirituality and Benevolence ought to be made infinite in the ultimate Ratio which they bear to Senfuality and Selfifhnefs.

But this Method of Reafoning may alfo be illuftrated, in a more popular way, by applying it to more obvious Inquiries. I will give Two Inftances of this, the Firft in the Health of the Body Natural, the Second in the Welfare of the Body Politic.

Suppofe

Suppofe then that a Perfon intirely ignorant of Phyfic, theoretical and practical, and difpofed to treat it as mere Guefs-work and Uncertainty, fhould, however, be defirous to know, fince he muft eat, what Diet is moft conducive to Health. The firft and moft obvious Anfwer will be, The general Diet of Mankind ; becaufe this is the Refult of general Experience, and of the natural Appetites, which are in fo many other Inftances fitted to the Objects themfelves, and to the Ufes and Pleafures, public and private, of human Life. And thus the Inquirer would be reftrained from all grofs Exceffes in the Quantity or Qualities of his Diet. But if he farther obferves, that the Opinions of Mankind tend more to Moderation in Diet, than their Practice; and that both the Practice and Opinions of thofe who appear by other Criterions to be the beft Judges, tend more to Moderation than thofe of Mankind at an Average ; and, laftly, that the Senfual and Intemperate ought intirely to be excluded from having any Share in determining this Inquiry ; this will lead him to great Moderation in Diet, or even to Abftemioufnefs.

In like manner let it be afked, What Principles of Government are moft conducive to the public Welfare ? Are private Virtues, or private Vices, moft to be encouraged ? Here indeed the Anfwer drawn from the Average of States will not be an exact Medium between both, fo as to difcourage all the Virtues, and all the Degrees of them, as much as the Vices, and their Degrees; and, *vice verfa*, to encourage both equally ; but will, upon the Whole, be greatly favourable to Virtue. However, fince Avarice, Vainglory, Refentment, Luxury, &c. are, in certain refpects, even promoted, and the greateft Virtues fometimes perfecuted, the Practice of Legiflators and Magiftrates, in enacting and enforcing Laws, will not be intirely favourable to Virtue. But then, if we take their Opinions, efpecially thofe of the Legiflators the moft celebrated for Wifdom, and leave out barbarous

Nations, infant States as yet unfettled, and fuch as approach near to their Diffolution, the Average from the Remainder will give the Advantage to Virtue more and more perpetually. And it may be remarked of both thefe Inftances, that they prove in part the Thing to be illuftrated by them, being not mere Emblems only, but in part the Reality itfelf. For Moderation in Diet is one principal Virtue, and extremely requifite to preferve Benevolence in Perfection; and Health a great Ingredient towards Happinefs. And the public Happinefs, which arifes from the Cultivation of private Virtues, includes private Happinefs within itfelf.

Perhaps it may not difpleafe the Reader juft to hint, that the fame Method of Reafoning may be made ufe of in favour of the Chriftian Religion.— All Ages and Nations have in general believed fome Revelation. There muft therefore be fome true one. But the Chriftian is plainly the Religion of the moft learned and knowing Part of Mankind, and is, in general, more earneftly believed, in proportion as Men are wifer and better. If we except the *Mahometans*, the reft of the World are mere Savages. But Mahometifm bears Teftimony to both the Old and New Teftament. If the Unbeliever will not be determined by this himfelf, let him at leaft allow, that the more Ignorant and Unlearned may be directed by it to the true Religion. But then they are not to be fuppofed capable of making Objections. Whoever has a Capacity for this, has alfo a Capacity to receive the proper Anfwers.

It is evident, however, that Obfervations of this Kind, drawn from the common Senfe and Judgment of Mankind, cannot carry us to great Lengths with Precifion and Certainty. They are very convincing and ftriking, in refpect of the firft Principles and Rudiments; but, if we would defcend to minute Particulars with Accuracy, Recourfe muft be had to the feveral practical Theories of each Art.

S E C T.

S E C T. II.

Of the Regard due to the Pleasures and Pains of Sensation in forming the Rule of Life.

P R O P. 50.

The Pleasures of Sensation ought not to be made a primary Pursuit.

IN order to shew this, let us put the extreme Case of the primary Pursuit of sensible Pleasure; and suppose, that a Person endeavours to gratify every Impulse of his bodily Appetites, however contrary such Gratification may be to the Virtues of Temperance and Chastity. Now it is evident, that such a one would soon destroy the bodily Faculties themselves, thereby rendering the Objects of sensible Pleasure useless, and also precipitate himself into Pain, Diseases, and Death, those greatest of Evils in the Opinion of the Voluptuous. This is a plain Matter of Observation, verified every Day by the sad Examples of loathsome, tortured Wretches, that occur which way soever we turn our Eyes, in the Streets, in private Families, in Hospitals, in Palaces. Whether the Scriptures give a true Account how all this Sin and Misery were first introduced into the World; also whether our Reason be able to reconcile it with the moral Attributes of God, or no; still, that positive Misery, and the Loss even of sensual Happiness, are thus inseparably connected with Intemperance and Lewdness, is an evident Fact, that no Unbeliever, no Atheist, no Sceptic, that will open his Eyes, can dispute. And it is to be observed, that the real In-

stances

stances do not, cannot, come up to the Case here put of a Man's yielding to every sensual Inclination. The most Gross and Debauched have had some Restraints from some other Desires or Fears, from the Quarters of Imagination, Ambition, &c. It is evident therefore, *a fortiori*, that the mere Gratification of our sensual Appetites cannot be our primary Pursuit, our *summum Bonum*, or the Rule and End of Life. They must be regulated by, and made subservient to, some other Part of our Natures ; else we shall miss even the sensible Pleasure, that we might have enjoyed, and shall fall into the opposite Pains ; which, as has been observed before, are, in general, far greater, and more exquisite, than the sensible Pleasures.

That Indulgence in sensual Gratifications will not afford us our *summum Bonum*, may also be inferred from the following Arguments ; *viz.* That it destroys the mental Faculties, the Apprehension, Memory, Imagination, Invention ; That it exposes Men to Censure and Contempt ; That it brings them to Penury ; That it, is absolutely inconsistent with the Duties and Pleasures of Benevolence and Piety ; and that it is all along attended with the secret Reproaches of the moral Sense, and the Horrors of a guilty Mind. Now it is impossible, as will appear from the foregoing History of Association, how much soever a Man may be devoted to sensual Indulgences, intirely to prevent the Generation of the several mental Affections ; but it is in our Power, by an inordinate Pursuit of the sensible Pleasures, to convert the mental Affections into Sources of Pain, and to impair and cut off many of the intellectual Pleasures, so as that the Balance shall be against us upon the Whole. It follows therefore from this utter Inconsistency of the sensible Pleasures, when made a primary Pursuit, with the intellectual ones, that they ought not to be so ; but must be subjected to, and regulated by, some more impartial Law, than that of mere sensual Desire.   The

The fame thing may be concluded, in a more direct Way, from the Hiftory of Affociation. For the fenfible Pleafures are the firft Pleafures of which we are capable, and are the Foundation of the intellectual ones, which are formed from them in Succeffion, according to the Law of Affociation, as before explained. Now which Way foever we turn our View, that which is prior in the Order of Nature is always lefs perfect and principal, than that which is pofterior, the laft of two contiguous States being the End, the firft the Means fubfervient to that End, tho' itfelf be an End in refpect of fome foregoing State. The fenfible Pleafures therefore cannot be fuppofed of equal Value and Dignity with the intellectual, to the Generation of which they are made fubfervient. And we might be led to infer this from the mere Analogy of Nature, from the numberlefs parallel Inftances which daily Obfervation fuggefts, and without taking into Confideration the infinite Beneficence of the Supreme Caufe, which yet makes this Argument much more fatisfactory and convincing.

Nay, one may go farther, and obferve, that as many Perfons are evidently forced from the inordinate Purfuit of fenfible Pleafure by its Inconfiftency with itfelf, and with the other Parts of our Frame, fo it feems, that, if human Life was continued to an indefinite Length, and yet nothing abated from the Rigour of thofe wholfome Severities, and penal Sufferings, which Senfuality brings upon us, more and more Individuals would perpetually be advanced thereby to a State of Spirituality; and that it would be impoffible for any Man to perfift for ever in facrificing all to his fenfual Appetites, in *making his Belly his God*, upon fuch difadvantageous and painful Terms. Intellectual Defires (*i. e.* Defires in which no particular fenfible Pleafure is confpicuous, though they arife from a multiform Aggregate of the Traces of fuch) muft be formed, as we fee they are in fact, in the moft

Luxurious

Luxurious and Debauched ; and thefe would at laft become fufficient to ftruggle with and overpower the fenfual Defires, which would at the fame time be weakened by Affociations with intenfe Pains and Sufferings. And this affords us a pleafing Glimpfe not only of a future State, but alfo of what may be done there by ftill greater Severities, for thofe whom the Miferies of this Life conld not free from the Slavery to their bodily Appetites ; at the fame time that it is the ftrongeft Incentive to us all, to apply ourfelves with Earneftnefs and Affiduity to the great Bufinefs and Purport of the prefent Life, the Transformation of Senfuality into Spirituality, by affociating the fenfible Pleafures, and their Traces, with proper foreign Objects, and fo forming Motives to beneficent Actions, and diffufing them over the whole general Courfe of our Exiftence.

Laftly, The inferior Value of the fenfible Pleafures may be deduced from their being of a confined local Nature, and injuring or deftroying prematurely, *i. e.* before the Body in general comes to its Period, the particular Organs of each, when indulged to Excefs ; whereas the intellectual Pleafures affect the whole nervous Syftem, *i. e.* all the fenfible Parts, and that nearly in an equal manner, on account of the Varieties and Combinations of fenfible local, and of nafcent intellectual Pleafures, which concur in the Formation of the mature intellectual ones ; fo that though fome of them fhould be indulged to Excefs, and out of due Proportion to the reft, this will be more confiftent with the gentle, gradual Decay of the mortal Body.

We may add, that the Duration of mere fenfual Pleafure is neceffarily fhort ; and that, even when free from Guilt, it cannot, however, afford any pleafing Reflections ; whereas one of the principal Tendencies of our Natures is, and muft be, from the Power of Affociation in forming them, to the Pleafures

of

of Reflection and Confcioufnefs. In like manner, the evident Ufe and Reftriction thereto of one of the principal fenfible Pleafures to preferve Life and Health, with all the confequent mental Faculties, and executive bodily Powers ; of the other to continue the Species, and to generate and inlarge Benevolence ; make the fubordinate Nature of both manifeft in an obvious Way, and without entering minutely into the Hiftory of Affociation : At the fame time that thefe Remarks, when further purfued, unite with that Hiftory, and are eminent Parts of the foregoing Argument, taken directly from thence.

Thus it appears, that the Pleafures of Senfation ought not to be made the primary Purfuit of Life ; but require to be reftrained and directed by fome foreign regulating Power. What that Power is, I now come to fhew in the next Propofition.

PROP. 51.

The Purfuit of fenfible Pleafure ought to be regulated by the Precepts of Benevolence, Piety, and the Moral Senfe.

THIS may be proved by fhewing, that the Regulation of our fenfible Pleafures, here propofed, will contribute both to their own Improvement, and to that of the other Parts of our Natures.

Now Benevolence requires, that the Pleafures of Senfe fhould be made intirely fubfervient to the Health of the Body and Mind, that fo each Perfon may beft fill his Place in Life, beft perform the feveral relative Duties of it, and prolong his Days to their utmoft Period, free from great Difeafes and Infirmities ; Inftances of which have much Authority, and a very beneficial Influence, in the World. All Gratifications therefore, which tend to produce Difeafes in the Body, and Difturbances in the Mind, are forbidden by Bene-

volence,

volence, and the moſt wholſome Diet as to Quantity
and Quality injoined by it. The Rules of Piety are
to the ſame Purpoſe, whether they be deduced from
our Relation to God, as our common Father and Be-
nefactor, who wills that all his Children ſhould uſe
his Bleſſings ſo as to promote the common Good thereby; or from the natural Signatures of his Will in the
immediate Pleaſures and Advantages ariſing from moderate Refreſhment, and the manifeſt Inconveniences
and Injuries cauſed by Exceſs in Quantity or Quality;
or from his revealed Will, by which Temperance is
commanded, and all Intemperance ſeverely threatened.
In like manner, the Moral Senſe directs us implicitly to the ſame Moderation, and Government of our
Appetites, whether it be derived explicitly from the
foregoing Rules of Piety and Benevolence, or from
Ideas of Decency, rational Self-intereſt, the Practice
of wiſe and good Men, the Loathſomeneſs of Diſeaſes,
the Odiouſneſs and Miſchiefs of violent Paſſions, &c.
It is evident therefore, that all theſe three Guides of
Life lead to the ſame End, *viz.* great Moderation in
ſenſual Enjoyments, though they differ ſomewhat in
their Motives, and the Commodiouſneſs of their Application as a Rule in the particular Occurrences of
Life.

It is evident at the ſame time, that we are no
Loſers, in reſpect of the ſenſible Pleaſures, by this
ſteady Adherence to Moderation. Our Senſes, and
bodily Faculties, are by this means preſerved in their
Perfection; ſo as to afford the natural exquiſite Gratification, and to enable us to perform the ſeveral
animal Functions with Eaſe and Pleaſure, and to carry us on to old Age with all the Integrity of theſe
Senſes and Faculties, that is conſiſtent with the neceſſary Decay and Diſſolution of our earthly Body. The
ſame Moderation, and Health ariſing from it, inſpire
Men with perpetual Serenity, Chearfulneſs, and
Good-will, and with Gratitude towards God, who
gives

gives us all Things richly to enjoy, and the fenfible
Pleafures in particular, as the Means and Earneft of
of far greater, both here and hereafter. Now it is obfervable in the common Intercourfes of Life, that affociated Circumftances add greatly to our Pleafures.
Thus the Pleafure of receiving a Thing from a
Friend, of making a Friend Partaker of it, of Sociality
and Mirth at the time of Enjoyment, *&c.* greatly
enhance the Gratificatiöns of Tafte, as in Feafts, and
public Entertainments. Much more then may the
pure and exalted Pleafures of Benevolence and Piety,
the Eating and Drinking to the Glory of God, improve
thefe Pleafures.

And as we are no Lofers, but great Gainers, upon
the Whole, by religious Abftemioufnefs, in refpeĉt
of the fenfible Pleafure ; fo are we much more ob-
vioufly fo, in refpeĉt of the fenfible Pains and Sufferings, which the Intemperate bring upon themfelves.
Thefe are of the moft exquifite Kind, and often of
long Duration, efpecially when they give Intervals of
Refpite, . thus exceeding the Inventions of the moft
cruel Tyrants. They impair the bodily and mental
Faculties, fo as to render moft other Enjoyments im-
perfeĉt· and infipid, difpofe to Peevifhnefs, Paffion,
and Murmuring againft Providence, and are attended
with the Horrors of a guilty Mind. It follows therefore, that he who would obtain the *Maximum* of the
fenfible Pleafures, even thofe of Tafte, muft not give
himfelf up to them ; but reftrain them, and make
them fubjeĉt to Benevolence, Piety, and the Moral
Senfe.

Cor. Befides the fenfible Pains, which Exceffes
bring upon Men, there are fome which occur in the
daily Difcharge of the Functions of Life, from Fatigue, Labour, Hardfhips, *&c.* Now it follows
from the fame Method of Reafoning, as that ufed in
the two foregoing Propofitions, that the proper Method
of avoiding thefe Pains is not to aim at it direĉtly,

but

but in every thing to be guided by the Precepts of Benevolence, Piety, and the Moral Senfe; and that delicate and effeminate Perfons endure more from this Head of Sufferings, than the Charitable and Devout, who *go about doing Good*, at the apparent Expence of their Eafe and Quiet.

PROP. 52.
To deduce practical Rules concerning Diet.

WHAT that Moderation in Diet is, which would moft contribute to the Health of the Body and Mind, and confequently which Duty requires, is difficult to determine in particular Cafes. The following fubordinate Rules may, however, afford fome Affiftance in this Matter.

Firft, then, It is neceffary to abftain from all fuch Things as the common Experience of Mankind determines to be unwholfome, either in general, or to the particular Perfons who make the Inquiry. There are indeed fome vulgar Errors of this Kind, that are generally received, and which, by being obferved, may a little abridge one's Liberty, without Ufe or Neceffity. However, this is of fmall Moment, in Comparifon of the Dangers arifing from the free Ufe of Meats and Drinks found by the repeated Obfervation of thofe who have made the Trial, to be hurtful, generally or particularly. There ftill remains, after all thefe are fet afide, a fufficient Variety of Things approved as wholfome by the fame common Experience, to anfwer all the Purpofes of Life, Health, and even fenfible Pleafure. This Rule will be farther explained by thofe that follow.

Secondly, We ought either totally to abftain from, or, however, to ufe with great Caution and Moderation, all Foods of high Relifh, whofe Taftes and Smells are pungent and acrid; all which, though made

made grateful by Cuſtom, are at firſt diſagreeable; all which bear a great Affinity in Taſte, Smell, and generical or ſpecific Characteriſtics, to ſuch as are known to be hurtful; which are poiſonous during a particular State, previous to Coction, or other Preparation; which are uncommon, or which have very particular Effects upon the Functions and Secretions. For all theſe Things are Signs of active Properties in the Foods to which they belong, and ſhew them to be rather proper for Medicines, than for common Diet; to be Bodies which by an extraordinary Efficacy may reduce the Solids and Fluids back to their natural State, when they have deviated from it; and therefore which are very unſuitable to the natural State.

We may conſider farther, that ſtrong Taſtes, Smells, &c. are, according to the modern Philoſophy, Marks of great Powers of Attraction and Coheſion in the ſmall component Particles of natural Bodies. Since therefore it is the manifeſt Deſign of the deſcending Serieſes of Arteries in Animals to ſeparate the Particles of their Aliment from each other, alſo the Particles of theſe Particles, &c. that ſo the ſmalleſt Particles, or the *minima diviſibilia*, meeting in the Veins, may unite according to their reſpective Sizes, and mutual Actions, *i. e.* to ſeparate what is heterogeneous, and congregate what is homogeneous, a great Difficulty and Burden muſt be laid upon the Circulation, and upon what is called Nature in the Body, by all highly agreeable Flavours; and, unleſs a proportional Degree of muſcular Action impels the Blood forward, Particles of an undue Size muſt remain undivided, and form Obſtructions, which may either never be removed, or not till the obſtructing Particles become putrid; and thus, being diſſolved, and mixed with the animal Juices, infect them with Putreſcence.

Still farther, it may be remarked, that the ſame active Particles in Foods are probably the Sources and Recruits of that nervous Power, or of ſome requiſite

to

to it, by which animal Senfation and Motion, and, by confequence, intellectual Apprehenfion and Affection, and their Effects upon the Body, are carried on. Now it is evident, that Affection raifed to a certain Height, and executive Powers ready to anfwer the firft Call, are a mental Difeafe of the moft pernicious Tendency. High-relifhed Aliments, which generate it, are therefore carefully to be avoided; on one hand; as a very infipid Diet, on the other, feems infufficient to qualify us for performing the requifite Functions of Life. But there is little Danger of erring on this hand, our Appetites being but too fenfibly gratified with the high Relifhes. We may add, as nearly allied to thefe Confiderations, that by ftoring our Blood, and the Solids thence formed, with active Properties, we lay up Matter for future Pains, both bodily and mental, whenever either Body or Mind become difordered, at the fame time that a high Diet has, as we fee, an evident Tendency to diforder both.

This Second Rule coincides, for the moft part, with the Firft; and may be made ufe of to extend and confirm it. Thofe Meats and Drinks, which are found by Experience to be hurtful, have, for the moft part, high Relifhes. We may therefore determine againft an Aliment of a high Flavour from a narrower Experience, than againft one of a common moderate Flavour. And it is very neceffary to attend to this Criterion, fince the beft Obfervations upon Diet are much perplexed by foreign Circumftances.

Thirdly, All Liquors, which have undergone vinous Fermentation, fince they obtain thereby an inflammable, inebriating Spirit, have from this inebriating Quality, which impairs Reafon, and adds Force to the Paffions, a Mark fet upon them, as dangerous not only on this Account, but on others, to bodily Health, &c. and as either totally to be avoided, or not to be ufed, except in fmall Quantities, and rarely.

The

The general Agreeablenefs of Wines and fermented Liquors to the Tafte, their immediate good Effects in Languors, Dejections, and Indigeftion, and their exhilarating Quality, when taken fparingly, are indeed Arguments to fhew, that there may be a proper Ufe of them. But this feems rather to be that of Medicines, or Refrefhments upon fingular Occafions, than of daily Food.

It may perhaps be, that the Changes produced in the Earth at the Deluge did fo alter the Nature of vegetable Juices, as to render them then firft capable of producing an inflammable inebriating Spirit by Fermentation; and that this Alteration in the Juices of Vegetables had a principal Share in fhortening the Life of Man; perhaps of other Animals, which laft might farther contribute to the firft. So great an Event as the Deluge may well be fuppofed to make a great Alteration in all the Three Kingdoms, Mineral, Vegetable, and Animal. We are fure of the firft from Natural Hiftory, and of the laft from the Scriptures, which relate the gradual Shortening of Man's Life after the Flood. And the Account of *Noah*'s Drunkennefs feems to intimate, that it was fomething new and unexpected. The Connexion of the Three Kingdoms with each other is alfo fo great, that we may reafonably infer a Change in any one, either as a Caufe, or as an Effect, from finding it in the other Two. However, the Sin of our common Parent *Noah*, and his expofing his Nakednefs, which alfo bears fome Refemblance to the immediate Confequence of *Adam*'s Tranfgreffion, ought to make us particularly upon our Guard. At the fame time feveral other Paffages of Scripture feem fairly to intimate, that there is an allowable Ufe of Wine in the Intercourfes of human Life, as where *Wine* is faid *to make glad the Heart of Man*, and therefore to be Matter of Praife; our Saviour's turning Water into Wine; his bleffing it at his laft Supper, and making it the Reprefentative

of

of his Blood; and St. *Paul's* Advice to *Timothy.*
But very great Caution ought to be ufed in this Point.
The inebriating Quality of fermented Liquors, by
difordering the Mind, is a ftrong Evidence, that they
are alfo hurtful to the Body, both becaufe of the intimate Connexion between Body and Mind, and becaufe all the beneficent Ends of Providence are an-
fwered always by one and the fame Means, and centre in one and the fame Point. Whenever therefore
we deviate in one refpect, we muft deviate in all.
The Abftinence from Wine injoined upon the *Naza-
rites* at all times, and upon the Priefts during their
Miniftration, appears to be a ftrong Intimation of the
Unfuitablenefs of Wine to thofe who aim at Perfection; who would deviate as little as poffible from the
Divine Life.

This Third Rule coincides remarkably with both the
Firft and Second. The ill Effects of fermented Liquors, when indulged in, are evident from Experience;
and their high Flavours are a principal Temptation
to an immoderate Ufe of them.

Fourthly, With refpect to animal Diet, let it be
confidered, that taking away the Lives of Animals, in
order to convert them into Food, does great Violence
to the Principles of Benevolence and Compaffion.
This appears from the frequent Hard-heartednefs and
Cruelty found amongft thofe Perfons, whofe Occupations engage them in deftroying animal Life, as well
as from the Uneafinefs which others feel in beholding
the Butchery of Animals. It is moft evident, in refpect of the larger Animals, and thofe with whom
Mankind have a familiar Intercourfe, fuch as Oxen,
Sheep, domeftic Fowls, &c. fo as to diftinguifh,
love, and compaffionate Individuals. Thefe Creatures
refemble us greatly in the Make of the Body in general, and in that of the particular Organs of Circulation, Refpiration, Digeftion, &c. alfo in the Formation of their Intellects, Memories, and Paffions,
and

and in the Signs of Diftrefs, Fear, Pain, and Death. They often likewife win our Affections by the Marks of peculiar Sagacity, by their Inftincts, Helpleffnefs, Innocence, nafcent Benevolence, &c. And if there be any Glimmering of the Hope of an Hereafter for them, if they fhould prove to be our Brethren and Sifters in this higher Senfe, in Immortality as well as Mortality, in the permanent Principle of our Minds, as well as the frail Duft of our Bodies, if they fhould be Parta- kers of the fame Redemption as well as of our Fall, and be Members of the fame myftical Body, this would have a particular Tendency to increafe our Tendernefs for them. At the fame time the prefent Circumftances of Things feem to require, that no very great Alteration fhould be made in this Matter : We ourfelves are under the fame Law of Death, and of becoming Food to our Fellow-Animals ; and Philofophy has of late difcovered fuch numberlefs Or- ders of fmall Animals in Parts of Diet formerly efteemed to be void of Life, and fuch an Extenfion of Life into the Vegetable Kingdom, that we feem un- der the perpetual Neceffity, either of deftroying the Lives of fome of the Creatures, or of perifhing our- felves, and fuffering many others to perifh. This therefore feems to be no more than an Argument to ftop us in our Career, to make us fparing and tender in this Article, and put us upon confulting Experience more faithfully and impartially, in order to determine what is moft fuitable to the Purpofes of Life and Health, our Compaffion being made by the forego- ing Confiderations, in fome meafure, a Balance to our impetuous bodily Appetites. At leaft, Abftinence from Flefh-meats feems left to each Perfon's Choice, and not neceffary, unlefs in peculiar Circumftances.

The Doctrine of the Scriptures on this Head ap- pears very agreeable to thefe Dictates of Sympathy. For *Noah*, and we in him, received a Permiffion from God to eat Flefh ; and that this was no more
than

I

than a Permiſſion, may be concluded from its not being given to *Adam*, from the Shortening of human Life after the Flood, from the ſtrict Command concerning Blood, from the *Iſraelites* being reſtrained from animal Food for 40 Years during their Purification and Inſtitution in Religion in the Wilderneſs, from the Diſtinction of Animals into clean and unclean, from the Burning of Part in Sacrifice, and ſometimes the Whole, from the Practice of many *Jews* and *Chriſtians* particularly eminent for Piety, *&c.* All theſe may be conſidered as Hints and Admonitions to us, as Checks and Reſtraints upon unbridled carnal Appetites and Luſts : At the ſame time that our Saviour's partaking in Meats with all Kinds of Men, and many expreſs Inſtances and Teſtimonies both in the Old and New Teſtament, as particularly the Command to eat the Paſchal Lamb, and other Sacrifices, remove all Scruple from thoſe Perſons who eat with Moderation, and in Conformity to the Rules of Piety, Benevolence, and the Moral Senſe.

The Coincidence of this Fourth Rule with the Firſt and Second appears in the ſame manner as that of the Third with them.

Fifthly, Having laid down theſe Four Rules concerning the Quality of our Aliments, I come next to obſerve, that the Quantity ought ſcarce ever to be ſo much as our Appetites prompt us to, but, in general, to fall a little ſhort of this. The Goodneſs of this Rule is verified by common Obſervation ; nay, one may affirm, that ſmall Errors in the Quality of our Diet may be quite rectified by a proper Moderation in reſpect of Quantity ; whereas a Tranſgreſſion in regard to Qantity cannot be compenſated by the Innocence of the Aliment. Such a Tranſgreſſion is, however, more rare, where the Quality of the Aliment is not improper.

Here

Here it may be afked how it comes to pafs, that the Appetites fhould, in fome Inftances, be the beft Guides to us both in refpect of Quality and Quantity, and in moft fo to the brute Creation ; and yet, in other Inftances, be fo greatly apt to miflead us, to hurry us on to Pain, Difeafes, and Death, and thefe not rare and fingular ones, but the moft frequent and ordinary that occur. Almoft every Man is tempted by Fruits, by Wines, natural and artificial Savours, and high Relifhes, &c. to tranfgrefs either in Quantity or Quality. Now to this we may anfwer, That in young Children the Appetites deviate very feldom, and very little, from what is moft conducive to the Body ; and that they would probably deviate lefs, were Children conducted better, were not their Taftes and Appetites perverted and corrupted by Cuftoms and Practices derived from our Corruptions, or our Ignorance. This may, at firft Sight, feem harfh, in refpect of them ; but it is at the fame time a ftrong Inftance and Argument, amongft many others, of the intimate Connexion and Sympathy, that unite us all to each other, of our being Members of the fame myftical Body, and of the great Syftem of the World's being a Syftem of Benevolence ; and thus it concurs to eftablifh the fundamental Pofition of thefe Papers. However, thefe Perverfions and Corruptions, from whatever Caufe they arife, feldom grow to a great Height, till fuch time as Children arrive at Years of Difcretion in a certain Degree, till they get fome Ideas of Fitnefs, Decency, Obedience to Superiors, and to God, Confcience, &c. Now, at firft indeed, the Child is mere Body, as it were ; and therefore it is not at all incongruous to fuppofe, that he may be directed by mere bodily Appetites and Inftincts. But, when the mental Faculties are generated, he then becomes a Compound of Body and Mind ; and confequently it would be incongruous to fuppofe him directed in any thing that affects both

Body

Body and Mind, as Diet plainly does, by mere bodily Appetites. On the contrary, his Rule ought now to be a Compound of bodily and mental Inftincts, Inclinations, Admonitions, &c. directing, influencing, and affifting one another. Let this be fo, and the Child or Man will very feldom deviate from what is moft conducive to Health and Happinefs of all Kinds. And it is to be obferved, that the bodily Pains and Sufferings, which follow from yielding to mere bodily Appetites, in Oppofition to mental Conviction, are one principal Means, by which the Authority and Influence of Confcience are eftablifhed with refpect to other Branches of Defire. And when a Perfon, from thefe or other Motives, reverfes his own Steps in refpect of the Pleafures of Tafte, the Irregularity and Inordinatenefs of the bodily Appetites decline by the fame Degrees, as they grew exceffive through unlawful Gratification. So that, after a Perfon has governed himfelf, for a confiderable time, with Strictnefs, from a Senfe of Duty, he will find little Difficulty afterwards. The natural Appetites will themfelves become the proper Subftitutes of Benevolence, Piety, and the Moral Senfe, and direct a Man what and how much is requifite.

All this Reafoning is confirmed by the Obfervation before made on Brutes. They continue mere Body, as it were, to the laft; and therefore their bodily Appetites fcarce ever miflead them. And the evil Influences which our corrupt Practices and Cuftoms have upon them, is a farther Argument for the Relation we all bear to each other. In like manner, all the evil mutual Influences in Animals, with all their original Deviations, are Marks and Evidences of a fallen and degenerate State, however difficult this may be to be accounted for. They are therefore Evidences alfo of the Truth of the Scriptures, which not only declare this our Degeneracy, and give a general Idea of the Means by which it

was

was introduced, but alſo publiſh the glorious Tidings of our Redemption from it.

Sixthly, Since the Circumſtances of the World are ſuch, as that it is almoſt impoſſible for thoſe who do not retire from it, to avoid Errors both in the Quantity and Quality of their Diet, there ſeems a Neceſſity for Faſting upon certain Occaſions. This is a compendious Method of reverſing our own wrong Steps, of preventing the ill Effects of Exceſs upon the Body and Mind, breaking ill Habits of this ſort at once, and bringing us back, by haſty Motions, to the higheſt Degrees of Self-government, to which imperfect Creatures in this World of Temptations can attain. It is therefore a Duty, which implies and preſuppoſes the preſent Imperfection and Degeneracy of our Natures. And yet this Duty, harſh as it ſeems, is probably productive even of ſenſible Pleaſure in moſt Inſtances; ſince, under due Reſtrictions, it appears to be extremely conducive to Health and long Life, as well as to the Regulation of our Paſſions. It may be true indeed, that conſtant Abſtemiouſneſs would be preferable, in theſe reſpects, to what is called common Moderation, practiſed upon ordinary Occaſions, and rectified by Faſting upon particular ones. But the due Degree of Abſtemiouſneſs is ſcarce practicable for a Conſtancy, as I obſerved juſt now, to thoſe whoſe Duty engages them to converſe freely with the World. Let me add here, that Faſting will have much more Efficacy towards reducing us to a right Courſe of Action, when it is accompanied with ſuch religious Exerciſes, as the Practice of good Men has joined with it, Prayer, Self-examination, and Works of Charity.

Seventhly, Where a Perſon has been ſo happily educated, as ſcarce to have tranſgreſſed the Bounds of ſtrict Moderation, either in Eating or Drinking, and with reſpect both to Quantity and Quality, or where he has corrected and brought back himſelf by due Se-

verity,

verity, fufficiently continued, it is better to pay a Regard to the foregoing and fuch-like Precepts, only to a certain Degree, upon Occafions of Importance, and without Scrupulofity and Rigour; and, in the fmall inftantaneous Occurrences of Life, to be directed by the natural Appetites, agreeably to the original Intention of the Author of Nature. For Anxiety, Solicitude, and Scrupulofity, are greatly prejudicial to the Health both of the Body and Mind, turn us from our natural and equitable Judgment of Things, augment Selfifhnefs, and difqualify for the Practice of the higheft Duties, Good-will to Men, and Complacence and Delight in God. The Scripture Precept is *to eat and drink to the Glory of God,* not with a Solicitude about ourfelves.

PROP. 53.

To deduce practical Rules concerning the Commerce between the Sexes.

THAT Benevolence, Love, Efteem, and the other fympathetic Affections, give the chief Value, and higheft Perfection, to the fenfible Pleafures between the Sexes, is fufficiently evident to ferious and confiderate Perfons. It appears alfo, that thefe Pleafures were intended by Providence, as a principal Means, whereby we might be enabled to transfer our Affection and Concern from ourfelves to others, and learn firft in the fingle Inftance of the beloved Perfon, afterwards in thofe of the common Offspring, to fympathize in the Pleafures and Pains of our Neighbours, and to love them as ourfelves. It follows therefore, that if this great Source of Benevolence be corrupted, or perverted to other Purpofes, the focial Affections thereon depending will be perverted likewife, and degenerate into Selfifhnefs or Malevolence. Let us inquire in what manner the ftrong Inclinations of the

Sexes

Sexes to each other may be beſt conducted, ſo as moſt to contribute to public and private Happineſs, ſo as to obtain the *Maximum* of it, both from this Quarter, and from the other Parts of our Nature, which are neceſſarily connected with it.

Firſt, then, It is evident, that unreſtrained promiſcuous Concubinage would produce the greateſt Evils, public and private. By being unreſtrained, it would deſtroy the Health and the Propagation of Mankind; by being promiſcuous, become ineffectual to promote Love, and the tender Affections, either between the Perſons themſelves, or towards their Offspring, and alſo raiſe endleſs Jealouſies and Quarrels amongſt Mankind. There has never perhaps been any Nation in the World, where this intire Licentiouſneſs has been allowed; the Miſchiefs which evidently follow from all great Degrees of it, having always laid Mankind under ſome Reſtraints, and produced ſome imperfect Regulations at leaſt, and ſome Approaches towards Marriage. However, the Miſery and Deſolation of the barbarous Nations of *Africa* and *America*, in whom the Violence of Paſſion, and the Degeneracy of Nature, have almoſt obliterated the faint Traces of the Patriarchal Religion; and the many Evils, public and private, which attend all unlawful Commerce between the Sexes in the more civilized Countries; are abundantly ſufficient to evince what is affirmed. The ſhameful, loathſome, and often fatal Diſeaſe, which peculiarly attends the Vice of Lewdneſs, may be conſidered as a moſt unqueſtionable Evidence of the Divine Will. This Diſeaſe, with all its Conſequences, would ſoon ceaſe amongſt Mankind, could they be brought under the Reſtraints of lawful Marriage; but muſt ever continue, whilſt Licentiouſneſs continues. And it is perhaps to this Diſeaſe that we owe the preſent tolerable State of Things. It may be, that, without this Check, the Licentiouſneſs, which has always been obſerved to follow Improvements in Arts

and

and Politenefs, and to attend upon Bodies Politic in
their Declenfion, and which the Corruption of the
Chriftian Religion in fome, and the Difbelief of it in
others, have, in a manner, authorized, would have
brought on utter Diffolutenefs in this Weftern Part of
the World, fuch as would have been inconfiftent with
the very Exiftence of regular Government. Nay, it
may be, that this will ftill be the Cafe, and that we
are haftening to our Period, through the great
Wickednefs of the World in this refpect particularly,
though our Lives, as a Body Politic, be fomewhat
prolonged, by this Correction.

Secondly, Promifcuous Concubinage being thus
evidently excluded, it comes next to be inquired,
whether the Gofpel Rule of confining One Man to
One Woman during Life, except in the Cafe of the
Woman's Adultery, be calculated to produce the
greateft poffible Good, public and private. And here
we muft own ourfelves utterly unable to form any
exact Judgment. It is impoffible to dermine by any
Computation, which of all the Ways, in which Marriage has been or may be regulated, is moft conducive
to Happinefs upon the Whole: This would be too
wide a Field, and where alfo we could have no fixed
Points to guide us: Juft as, in the Matter of Civil
Government, it is impoffible for us to determine,
what particular Form, Monarchy, Ariftocracy, &c.
or what Mixture of thefe, is moft accommodated to
human Nature, and the Circumftances of Things.
Here therefore we feem particularly to want a Revelation to direct us; and therefore are under a particular Obligation to abide by its Award. Now Revealed
Religion commands us, in the Cafe of Government,
to obey thofe Powers that are actually eftablifhed, of
whatever Kind they be, leaving that to the Children
of this World to difpute; and, in refpect of Marriage, gives a Permiffion to enter into this State to
thofe who find it requifite, and alfo a farther Permiffion

fion to divorce an Adultrefs, and marry another Woman; but at the fame time injoins the ftricteft Purity
in our Thoughts, Words, and Actions; and that not
only in all fuch as refpect other Perfons befides the
Hufband and Wife, but in every thing that has a
Tendency to heighten carnal Defire. Now, though
it does not appear, that Mankind ever did, or ever
would, make fo ftrict a Rule for themfelves; yet this
Rule, when made, approves itfelf to our Judgments.
The ftricteft Purity and Watchfulnefs over ourfelves
are neceffary, in order to make Marriage of any Kind
(which we fee by the laft Article to be itfelf neceffary)
happy, and productive of private Pleafure and Comfort, and of public Good, by the united Labours of
the married Pair for themfelves, their Offspring, and
their Relatives. In the prefent imperfect State of
Things, the forbidding to divorce an Adultrefs might
feem a harfh Commandment, above the Frailty of
our Natures, as requiring the moft intire Love and
Affection, where there are Returns of the greateft
Contempt and Averfion, and the greateft Violation of
what are called juft Rights and Properties. Now,
though the Gofpel requires Perfection of us ultimately,
i. e. the moft intire Love in Return for the moft bitter
Hatred, and an abfolute Difregard of all Property
both for ourfelves, and for thofe whom we make our
Subftitutes after Death; yet it makes Allowance for
human Frailty in this eminent Inftance; leaving it,
however, to every Man, who is arrived at a fufficient
Degree of Perfection, to walk thereby.

That a greater Liberty of Divorcing would be lefs
fuited to produce Good, public and private, upon
the Whole, appears probable, becaufe no definite
Rule could be given in refpect of other Offences, they
all admitting of various Degrees; and becaufe the Profpect of divorcing, or being divorced, would often
increafe Breaches, at the fame time that frequent Di-
vorces would have the worft Confequences in refpect of

Children,

Children, and even approach to promiscuous Concubinage; whereas the Indissolubility of the Marriage Bond, with the Affection to the common Offspring, often produce in both Parties the Christian Virtues of Forbearance, and Forgiveness to each other. It is not at all improbable, that wicked Casuists, who have explained away so many express Gospel Precepts, would, by the Influence of Princes and Great Men, have rendered Marriage almost of no Effect, by increasing the Liberty of Divorcing.

Thirdly, The great Sinfulness of Adultery, Fornication, and Impurity of every Kind, appears not only from the manifest and great Evils and Miseries of various Sorts attending them, the Shame, Intemperance, Jealousies, Murders, &c. and from the Strictness of the Gospel Precepts, and the Practices of the first Christians in this respect; but also because the great Sin of Idolatry is represented by Adultery and Fornication in the prophetic Writings; and because the most heavy Judgments are denounced against these last Sins in those Writings, when understood both in figurative and literal Senses. And indeed, as the idolatrous Rites of the Heathens were generally accompanied with abominable Lewdness, so these vicious Pleasures may be considered as one of the grossest Kinds of Idolatry, as withdrawing our Affections from the true Object, and fixing them on a mere animal Pleasure, on one from the first and lowest Class, and as worshiping the heathen Deities of *Bacchus* and *Venus*. It is true indeed, that the Pursuits of this Kind are seldom from the alone View of bodily Pleasure, the very Nature of our Bodies not suffering this, since the Law of the Body must transfer bodily Pleasures upon foreign Objects, so as to form intellectual Pleasures. But then the intellectual Pleasure accompanying these Pursuits is always a vicious one, generally that of a vain mischievous Ambition, which occasions

the

the greateſt Confuſion, Havock, and Diſtreſs, in Families, and indeed in the whole Race of Mankind.

Fourthly, It follows from the Shame attending theſe Pleaſures, the Organs, their Functions, &c. in all Ages and Nations, the Account of the Origin of this Shame in the Third Chapter of *Geneſis,* the Directions concerning the Uncleanneſs of Men and Women given in the *Jewiſh* Law, the Rite of Circumciſion, the Pains of Childbirth, with the Account of their Origin in the Third Chapter of *Geneſis,* the Strictneſs required in the *Jewiſh* Prieſts, the Abſtinence required in others upon ſacred Occaſions, the miraculous Conception of Chriſt, his Expreſſions concerning marrying, and giving in Marriage, at the Times of the Flood, and laſt Judgment, his and St. *Paul*'s Recommendation of Celibacy, the honourable Mention of Virginity in the *Revelation,* &c. that theſe Pleaſures are to be conſidered, as one of the Marks of our preſent fallen degenerate State. The Mortality of the preſent Body, introduced by *Adam*'s Sin, would of courſe require ſome ſuch Method of Propagation as now ſubſiſts, though nothing of this Kind had taken place before the Fall ; and therefore it may be, that nothing did, or ſomething greatly different from the preſent Method. And one may deduce from hence, as well as from the parallel Obſervations concerning Abſtinence in Diet, and Faſting (for the ſimilar Nature, and reciprocal Influence, of the ſenſible Pleaſures juſtifies our Inferences here, made either way), alſo from the Sickneſſes and Infirmities of human Life, and particularly from thoſe of Women, that great Moderation, and frequent Abſtinence, are requiſite. Nay, it even appears, that in many Circumſtances Marriage itſelf is not to be approved ; but rather that Men and Women, who are advanced to or paſt the Meridian of Life, who have a Call to Offices of Religion, Charity, &c. who labour under certain hereditary Diſtempers, have Relations

and

and Dependents that are neceffitous, *&c.* fhould endeavour to fubdue the Body by Prayer and Fafting. However, great Care ought here to be taken not to lay a Snare before any one.

If we admit the Doctrine of this laft Páragraph, *viz.* that thefe Pleafures are only permitted, and that they are Marks of our fallen State, we may perhaps be enabled thereby to caft fome Light upon the Scripture Hiftory of the *Patriarchs* and *Jews.* We Chriftians, who live in the more adult Ages of Mankind, have ftricter Precepts, and are obliged to higher Degrees of Spirituality, as we approach nearer to the fpiritual Kingdom of Chrift; and yet fome Permiffions are fuitable to our State. No Wonder then, that larger Permiffions were requifite in the grofs, corporeal, infant State of Mankind, confidered as one Individual tending ever from Carnality to Spirituality, in a manner analogous to that of each Perfon. However, thefe were only Permiffions to the *Jews* and *Patriarchs*, not Commands. It may perhaps be, that, while Polygamy fubfifted according to Permiffion, the Number of Women might be greater than that of Men. This is indeed mere Hypothefis; but fuch Things deferve to be examined, as foon as proper Principles are difcovered, upon which to proceed. The proportional Number of Men deftroyed by Wars in antient Times, appears to be much greater than it is now.

Here it may be afked, If it be requifite in certain Perfons not to marry at all, and in every one to be abftinent, how can it be faid, that this Rule of Life gives the *Maximum* of thofe Pleafures? Now, with refpect to thofe who never marry, at the fame time devoting themfelves really and earneftly to God, to attend upon him without Diftraction, it may be obferved, that they enjoy the peculiar Privilege of being exempted from many of the great Cares and Sorrows of this Life; and that the prophetical Bleffing of the

Barren's

Barren's having more Children than fhe which hath an Hufband, is eminently applicable to them. They that marry, muft have Sorrow in the Flefh ; and if thofe who are under the Neceffity of marrying, becaufe they burn, humble themfelves agreeably to this Experierice of their own Weaknefs, they will find Marriage to be a proper Clue to lead them through the Difficulties and Miferies of this Life to a better State. But if a Perfon, who is likewife humble, can humbly hope, upon a fair Examination, that he is not under this Neceffity, there is no Occafion, that he fhould take this Burden upon him. The benevolent and devout Affections, though wanting one Source, will, upon the Whole, grow fafter from other Caufes ; and if he makes all with whom he has any Intercourfes, all to whom his Defires, Prayers, and Endeavours, can extend, his fpiritual Children, ftill with all Humility, and Diffidence o himfelf, their fpiritual ultimate Happinefs, through the infinite Mercy of God, will be a Fund of Joy far fuperior to any that is, and muft be, tinctured with the Defilements of this World, as that of natural Parents cannot but be. As to thefe, *i. e.* the Perfons that marry, it is probable, that they approach to the *Maximum* of the fenfible Pleafures much more than the Diffolute ; and if, in any Cafe, they do, for the fake of Religion, forego any Part of what is permitted, it cannot be doubted, but this will be repaid with ample Intereft by fpiritual Pleafures. But this Subject is of too nice and difficult a Nature to be farther purfued. Let thofe who need particular Information, apply to God for it ; and efpecially let them pray, that they may join Chriftian Prudence with Chriftian Purity and Holinefs.

It may alfo be afked here, If Marriage be only permitted, and Celibacy preferable in the Chriftian Senfe of Things, what becomes of the Propagation and Increafe of Mankind, which feem to have a neceffary Connexion with the greateft public Good? I anfwer,

That

That this Kind of Cares is far above us, and therefore foreign to our proper Bufinefs ; whereas the Precept, or Admonition rather, to thofe who can receive it, is plain, and ftands upon the Authority of the Chriftian Revelation itfelf, and of the other natural Signatures of the Divine Will before-mentioned. I anfwer alfo, That this World is a ruined World ; that it muft be deftroyed by Fire, as *Sodom* was, perhaps on account of our great Corruption in this refpect ; fo that its Perfection in this State of Things is impoffible, and therefore no End for us, though its Correction and Melioration be, as far as we have Opportunity ; that this Admonition cannot be received by all ; and therefore that the few, by whom alone it can be received, may contribute more to the Increafe of Mankind by their promoting Virtue, and reftraining Vice, than any Pofterity of theirs could do ; and laftly, That, if it could be obferved by all, we fhould all be near to Chriftian Perfection, *i. e.* to the glorious Kingdom of Chrift, and the new State of Things. Obfervations of the fame Kind may be made upon all the other Gofpel Precepts. If thefe be kept in their utmoft Purity by a few only, they feem to promote even temporal Happinefs upon the Whole ; and this appears to be the Truth of the Cafe, the real Fact, fince no Directions or Exhortations can extend to, and prevail with, more than a few, in Comparifon of the Bulk of Mankind, however good and earneft they may be. If all could be influenced at once, it would be ftill infinitely preferable, becaufe this would be *Life from the Dead,* and *the Kingdom of Righteoufnefs.* But this feems impoffible. We need not therefore fear any intermediate Degree. The more Chriftian Purity and Perfection prevail, the better muft it be on all real accounts, whatever becomes of Trade, Arts, Grandeur, *&c.*

Laftly, I cannot difmifs this Subject without making fome Remarks upon Education. The Defires

fires between the Sexes are far more violent than any others; the final Caufe of which is by Writers very juftly faid to be, that Men and Women may be compelled, as it were, to undertake the neceffary Cares and Labours, that attend the married Pair, in providing for themfelves, and their Offspring. But there is Reafon to believe from other parallel Cafes, that thefe Defires are not originally much difproportionate to the End ; and that, if due Care was taken, they would not arife in Youth much before the proper Time to fet about this End, before the Bodies of the Sexes were mature, able to endure Labour and Fatigue, and the Woman to undergo Childbirth, with its Confequences, of nurfing the Infant, *&c.* and their Minds ripe for the Cares and Forefight required in Family Affairs. Something of this Kind would probably happen, whatever Care the Parents took of the Bodies and Minds of their Children, on account of our fallen degenerate State, our State of Trial, which appears in all our other bodily Appetites, and intellectual Defires. But the Violence and Unfeafonablenefs of thefe Paffions are fo manifeft in the Generality of young Perfons, that one cannot but conclude the general Education of Youth to be grofly erroneous and perverted. And this will appear very evident in fact upon Examination. The Diet of Children, and young Perfons, is not fufficiently plain and fparing; which would at the fame time lay a better Foundation for Health, and Freedom from Difeafes, and put fome Check upon thefe Paffions. They are brought up in Effeminacy, and Neglect of bodily Labour, which would prepare both Body and Mind for Care and Sorrow, and keep down carnal Defire. The due Culture of the Mind, efpecially in refpect of Religion, is almoft univerfally neglected; fo that they are unfit for Bufinefs, left expofed to Temptations through Idlenefs, and Want of Employment, and are deftitute of the chief Armour, that of religious Motives, whereby to oppofe Temptation.

Laftly,

Laftly, The Converfation which they hear, and the Books which they read, lewd heathen Poets, modern Plays, Romances, &c. are fo corrupt in this refpect, that it is matter of Aftonifhment, how a Parent, who has any Degree of Serioufnefs (I will not fay Religion) himfelf, or Concern for his Child, can avoid feeing the immediate deftructive Confequences, or think that any Confiderations, relating to this World, can be a Balance to thefe.

PROP. 54.

To deduce practical Rules concerning the Hardfhips, Pains, and Uneafineffes, that occur in the daily Intercourfes of Life.

I Have already obferved in general, *Prop.* 51. *Cor.* that a Regard to the Precepts of Benevolence, Piety, and the Moral Senfe, affords us the beft Profpect for avoiding and leffening thefe. I will now exemplify and apply this Doctrine more particularly.

Firft, then, It is evident, that Luxury, Self-indulgence, and an indolent Averfion to perform the Duties of a Man's Station, do not only bring on grofs bodily Difeafes; but alfo, previoufly to this, are often apt to lead Men into fuch a Degree of Solicitude, Anxiety, and Fearfulnefs, in minute Affairs, as to make them inflict upon themfelves greater Torments, than the moft cruel Tyrant could invent. The Complaints, which are ufually ftyled nervous, are peculiarly apt to infeft this Clafs of Perfons; and I need not fay to thofe, who either have themfelves experienced them, or attended to them in others, of how grievous a Nature they are. Now, though fomething is to be allowed here to natural Conftitution, and hereditary Tendencies, alfo to the great Injuries fometimes done to the nervous Syftem by profufe Evacuations, and violent Diftempers, in confequence whereof

of it may be proper and neceffary in certain Cafes to adminifter fuch Medicines, as are fuitable to the particular Symptoms, and temporary Exigences; yet there feems to be no way fo probable of getting out of this felf-tormenting State, this Labyrinth of Error and Anxiety, as by Prayer and Refignation to God, by Charity, and taking upon one's felf the Cares and Fears of others according to our Rank and Station in Life, eafing our own Burden thereby, and by conftant, laborious, bodily Exercife, fuch particularly as occurs in the faithful Difcharge of Duty, with great Moderation in the fenfible Pleafures. Could the unhappy Perfons of this Sort be prevailed upon to enter on fuch a Courfe with Courage and Steadinefs, notwithftanding the Pains, Difficulties, and Uneafineffes, which would attend it at firft, all would generally begin to clear up even in refpeft of this World, fo as that they would regain fome tolerable Degrees of Health, Serenity, and even Chearfulnefs.

Secondly, Human Life is in fo imperfeft and diforderly a State, on account of the Fall, that it is impoffible to avoid all Exceffes, and Hardfhips from Heat, Cold, Hunger, Accidents, &c. But then thefe may be rendered harmlefs and eafy to a great Degree, by accuftoming the Body to them; which the conftant and faithful Difcharge of Duty by each Perfon, in particular, does, in refpeft of thofe Exceffes and Hardfhips, that are moft likely to befal *him.*

Thirdly, External Injuries fall much to the Share of the Imprudent. Now Prudence is a Virtue, *i. e.* a Diftate of the Moral Senfe, and a Command from God; and Imprudence, agreeably hereto, the manifeft Offspring of fome vicious Paffion or other, for the moft part.

Fourthly, Bodily Pains are often inflifted by Men, either in the way of public Authority, or of private Refentment and Malice. But it is very evident, that

3   the

the Benevolent muſt fare better in this reſpect, than the Malevolent and Miſchievous.

Fifthly, Whatever Evils befal a Man, Religion, and the Belief of a happy Futurity, enable him to ſupport himſelf under them much better than he could otherwiſe do. The true Chriſtian not only ought, but is alſo able, for the moſt part, to *rejoice in Tribulation.* And this is the genuine, ultimate, and indeed only perfect Solution of all Difficulties relating to the Pleaſures and Pains, both ſenſible and intellectual. For, though it be certain, that a benevolent and pious Man has the faireſt Proſpect for obtaining ſenſible Pleaſure, and avoiding ſenſible Pain, in general, and upon a fair Balance; alſo that the more wicked any one is, the leſs Pleaſure, and more Pain, muſt he expect; yet ſtill it will often happen, that a Perſon is obliged from a Senſe of Duty, from Benevolence, Adherence to true Religion, the Dictates of Conſcience, or a Goſpel Precept, to forego Pleaſures, or endure Pains, where there is no Probability, that a Recompence will be made during this Life; and ſometimes it is required of a Man even to ſeal his Teſtimony with his Blood. Now, in theſe Caſes, rational Self-intereſt has nothing left, which can ſatisfy its Demands, beſides the Hope and Expectation of a happy Futurity; but the preſent Pleaſure, which theſe afford, is ſome Earneſt of the Thing hoped and expected; it is alſo, in certain Caſes, ſo great, as to overpower, and almoſt annihilate, the oppoſite Pains.

Here let it be obſerved, That as this frail corruptible Body muſt at laſt return to its original Duſt, and loſe its Power of conveying Pleaſure to us, which it does gradually for a long time before Death from mere old Age; ſo it is natural to expect, that the *Maximum* of its Pleaſures ſhould not always be attained, even by that which is the genuine Rule of Life. For Death is a Mark of our preſent fallen State; and

therefore

therefore we may have this farther Mark alfo, that the true Rule, which, in a Paradifiacal State, would have carried every thing in its Order to Perfection, will now do it only in the general; fhewing us, firft, by its being very general, that it is the true Rule; and fecondly, by its not being univerfal, that we have deviated from our original Make.

It may not be amifs to add a few Words here concerning Sleep. The Analogy taken from the foregoing Rules teaches, that we ought not to indulge in this to the utmoft, but to break it off a little before the natural Inclination thereto totally expires. And this Pofition is remarkably confirmed both by the many Advantages to Body and Mind, which refult from rifing early; and by the Scripture Precepts concerning *Watching*; which, as appears to me, ought to be taken as well in their ftrictly literal Senfe upon proper Occafions, as in their more diftant and figurative one.

S E C T.   III.

*Of the Regard due to the Pleasures and
Pains of Imagination in forming the
Rule of Life.*

P R O P.   55.

*The Pleasures of Imagination ought not to be
made a primary Pursuit.*

FOR, First, It does not appear, that those who
devote themselves to the Study of the polite Arts,
or of Science, or to any other Pleasure of mere Imagination, as their chief End and Pursuit, attain to a
greater Degree of Happiness than the rest of the World.
The frequent Repetition of these Pleasures cloys, as in
other Cases: And though the whole Circle of them is
so extensive, as that it might, in some measure, obviate this Objection ; yet the human Fancy is too
narrow to take in this whole Circle, and the greatest
Virtuosos do, in fact, seldom apply themselves to
more than one or two considerable Branches.— The
Ways in which the Pleasures of Beauty are usually
generated, and transferred upon the several Objects,
are often opposite to, and inconsistent with, one another ; so as to mix Deformity with Beauty, and to
occasion an unpleasing Discordancy of Opinion, not
only in different Persons, but even in the same.   This
is evident from the foregoing History of these Pleasures, and of their Derivation from arbitrary and accidental Associations, as well as from the Observation
of the Fact in real Life.   And it is not uncommon to
see Men, after a long and immoderate Pursuit of one
Class of Beauty, natural or artificial, deviate into such
By-paths

By-paths and Singularities, as that the Objects excite
Pain rather than Pleasure ; their Limits for Excellence
and Perfection being narrow, and their Rules abfurd;
and all that falls fhort of thefe, being condemned by
them, as deformed and monftrous.— Eminent Votaries of this Kind are generally remarkable for Ignorance and Imprudence in common neceffary Affairs;
and thus they are expofed to much Ridicule and Contempt, as well as to other great Inconveniences.— The
fame Perfons are peculiarly liable to Vanity, Self-conceit,
Cenforioufnefs, Morofenefs, Jealoufy, and Envy; which
furely are very uneafy Companions in a Man's own
Breaft, as well as the Occafions of many Infults and
Harms from abroad.— And I think I may add, that
Scepticifm in religious Matters is alfo a frequent At-
tendant here; which, if it could be fuppofed free
from Danger as to Futurity, is at leaft very uncom-
fortable as to the prefent. For as the extravagant
Encomiums beftowed upon Works of Tafte and Genius beget a more than ordinary Degree of Self-conceit in the Virtuofo, fo this Self-conceit, this Superiority which he fanfies he has over the reft of the World
in one Branch of Knowlege, is by himfelf often fuppofed to extend to the reft, in which yet it is probable
that he is uncommonly ignorant through want of
Application : And thus he becomes either dogmatical
or fceptical; the firft of which Qualities, though feem-
ingly oppofite to the laft, is, in Reality, nearly related to it. And, as the fympathetic and theopathetic Affections are peculiarly neceffary for underftanding
Matters of a religious Nature aright, no Kind or Degree of Learning being fufficient for this Purpofe
without thefe, if the Purfuit of Literature, or
Science, be fo ftrong, as to ftifle and fupprefs the
Growth of thefe, or to diftort them, Religion, which
cannot be reconciled to fuch a Temper, will probably
be treated as incomprehenfible, abfurd, uncertain, or
incredible.—— However, it is difficult to reprefent

juftly,

juftly, in any of the refpects here mentioned, what is
the genuine Confequence of the mere Purfuit of the
Pleafures of Imagination, their Votaries being alfo,
for the moft part, extremely over-run with the grofs
Vice of Ambition, as was juft now obferved. But
then this does not invalidate any of the foregoing Objections, as will be feen when we come to confider that
Vice in the next Section.

Secondly, It is evident, that the Pleafures of Imagination were not intended for our primary Purfuit,
becaufe they are, in general, the firft of our intellectual Pleafures, which are generated from the fenfible ones by Affociation, come to their Height early
in Life, and decline in old Age. There are indeed
fome few Perfons, who continue devoted to them
during Life; but there are alfo fome, who remain
Senfualifts to the laft; which Singularities are, however, in neither Cafe, Arguments of the Defign of
Providence, that it fhould be fo. And, in general,
we may reafon here, as we did above, in deducing
the inferior Value of the fenfible Pleafures from their
being the loweft Clafs. The Pleafures of Imagination
are the next Remove above the fenfible ones, and
have, in their proper Place and Degree, a great Efficacy in improving and perfecting our Natures. They
are to Men in the early Part of their adult Age, what
Playthings are to Children; they teach them a Love
for Regularity, Exactnefs, Truth, Simplicity; they
lead them to the Knowlege of many important Truths
relating to themfelves, the external World, and its
Author; they habituate to invent, and reafon by
Analogy and Induction; and when the focial, moral,
and religious Affections begin to be generated in us,
we may make a much quicker Progrefs towards the
Perfection of our Natures by having a due Stock, and
no more than a due Stock, of Knowlege in natural
and artificial Things, of a Relifh for natural and artificial Beauty. It deferves particular Notice here, that
the

the Language uſed in reſpect of the Ideas, Pleaſures, and Pains of Imagination, is applicable to thoſe of the Moral Senſe with a peculiar Fitneſs and Significancy ; as, *vice verſa,* the proper Language of the Moral Senſe does, in many Caſes, add great Beauty to Poetry, Oratory, *&c.* when uſed catachreſtically. And we may obſerve in general, that as the Pleaſures of Imagination are manifeſtly intended to generate and augment the higher Orders, particularly thoſe of Sympathy, Theopathy, and the Moral Senſe ; ſo theſe laſt may be made to improve and perfect thoſe, as I ſhall now endeavour to ſhew under the Propoſition that follows.

PROP. 56.

The Purſuit of the Pleaſures of Imagination ought to be regulated by the Precepts of Benevolence, Piety, and the Moral Senſe.

FOR, Firſt, Thoſe Parts of the Arts and Sciences which bring Glory to God, and Advantage to Mankind, which inſpire Devotion, and inſtruct us how to be uſeful to others, abound with more and greater Beauties, than ſuch as are profane, miſchievous, unprofitable, or minute. Thus the Study of the Scriptures, of Natural Hiſtory, and Natural Philoſophy, of the Frame of the human Mind, *&c.* when undertaken and purſued with benevolent and pious Intentions, lead to more elegant Problems, and ſurpriſing Diſcoveries, than any Study intended for mere private Amuſement.

Secondly, It may be conſidered as a Reaſon for this, that ſince this World is a Syſtem of Benevolence, and conſequently its Author the Object of unbounded Love and Adoration, Benevolence and Piety are the only true Guides in our Inquiries into it, the only Keys which will unlock the Myſteries of Nature, and Clues which lead through her Labyrinths. Of this

R 3 all

all Branches of Natural Hiftory, and Natural Philofophy, afford abundant Inftances; and the fame
Thing may be faid of Civil Hiftory, when illuftrated
and cleared by the Scriptures, fo as to open to View
the fucceffive Difpenfations of God to Mankind; but
it has been more particularly taken notice of in the
Frame of the human Body, and in the Symptoms
and Tendencies of Diftempers. In all thefe Matters
let the Inquirer take it for granted previoufly, that
every thing is right, and the beft that it can be,
cæteris manentibus; i. e. let him, with a pious Confidence, feek for benevolent Purpofes; and he will
be always directed to the right Road, and, after a
due Continuance in it, attain to fome new and valuable Truth; whereas every other Principle and Motive of Examination, being foreign to the great Plan,
upon which the Univerfe is conftructed, muft lead into endlefs Mazes, Errors, and Perplexities.

Thirdly, It may be confidered as a farther Reafon of the fame thing, that Benevolence and Piety,
and, by confequence, their Offspring, the Moral
Senfe, are the only Things which can give a genuine and permanent Luftre to the Truths that are
difcovered. A Man with the moft perfect Comprehenfion, that his Faculties will allow, of that infinite
Profufion of Good which overflows the whole Creation, and of all the Fountains and Conduits of it,
and yet having no Share of the original Source from
whence all thefe were derived, having no Pittance or
Ray of the inexhauftible Benevolence of the great
Creator, no Love for that boundlefs Ocean of Love,
or Senfe of Duty to Him, would be no more happy, than an Accomptant is rich by reckoning up
Millions, or a Mifer by poffeffing them.

Fourthly, It may be remarked, that the Pleafures
of Imagination point to Devotion in a particular
manner by their unlimited Nature. For all Beauty,
both natural and artificial, begins to fade and languifh

guifh after a fhort Acquaintance with it: Novelty is
a never-failing Requifite: We look down, with Indifference and Contempt, upon what we comprehend
eafily ; and are ever aiming at, and purfuing, fuch
Objeats as are but juft within the Compafs of our
prefent Faculties. What is it now, that we ought to
learn from this Diffatisfaɛtion to look behind us, and
Tendency to prefs forward ; from this endlefs Grafp-
ing after Infinity ? Is it not, that the infinite Author
of all Things has fo formed our Faculties, that nothing lefs than himfelf can be an adequate Objeɛt for
them ? That it is in vain to hope for full and lafting
Satisfaɛtion from any thing finite, however great and
glorious, fince it will itfelf teach us to conceive and
defire fomething ftill more fo ? That, as nothing can
give us more than a tranfitory Delight, if its Relation
to God be excluded ; fo every thing, when confidered as the Produɛtion of his infinite Wifdom and
Goodnefs, will gratify our utmoft Expeɛtations, fince
we may, in this View, fee that every thing has infinite Ufes and Excellencies ? There is not an Atom
perhaps in the whole Univerfe, which does not
abound with Millions of Worlds ; and, converfly,
this great Syftem of the Sun, Planets, and fixed Stars,
may be no more than a fingle conftituent Particle of
fome Body of an immenfe relative Magnitude, *&c.*
In like manner, there is not a Moment of Time fo
fmall, but it may include Millions of Ages in the
Eftimation of fome Beings ; and, converfly, the lar-
geft Cycle which human Art is able to invent, may
be no more than the Twinkling of an Eye in that of
others, *&c.* The infinite Divifibility and Extent of
Space and Time admit of fuch Infinities upon Infinities, afcending and defcending, as make the Imagination giddy, when it attempts to furvey them. But,
however this be, we may be fure, that the true Syftem of Things is infinitely more tranfcendent in
Greatnefs and Goodnefs, than any Defcription or Con-

ception

ception of ours can make it ; and that the Voice of Nature is an univerfal Chorus of Joy and Tranfport, in which the leaft and vileft, according to common Eftimation, bear a proper Part, as well as thofe whofe prefent Superiority over them appears indefinitely great, and may bear an equal one in the true and ultimate Ratio of Things. And thus the Confideration of God gives a Relifh and Luftre to Speculations, which are otherwife dry and unfatisfactory, or which perhaps would confound and terrify. Thus we may learn to rejoice in every thing we fee, in the Bleffings paft, prefent, and future ; which we receive either in our own Perfons, or in thofe of others; to become Partakers of the Divine Nature, loving and lovely, holy and happy.

P R O P. 57.

To deduce practical Rules concerning the Elegancies and Amufements of Life.

BY the Elegancies of Life I mean the artificial Beauties of Houfes, Gardens, Furniture, Drefs, &c. which are fo much ftudied in high Life. There is in thefe, as in all other Things, a certain middle Point, which coincides with our Duty, and our Happinefs ; whilft all great Deviations from it incur the Cenfure of Vicioufnefs, or, at leaft, of Unfuitablenefs and Abfurdity. But it is not eafy to determine this Point exactly, in the feveral Circumftances of each particular Perfon. I will here fet down the principal Reafons againft an Excefs on each hand, leaving it to every Perfon to judge for himfelf how far they hold in his own particular Circumftances.

We may then urge againft the immoderate Purfuit of the Elegancies of Life ;

Firft, That Vanity, Oftentation, and the unlawful Pleafures of Property, of calling Things our own, are

are almoſt inſeparable from the Purſuit of theſe Elegancies, and often engroſs all to themſelves.

Secondly, That the Profuſion of Expence requiſite
here is inconſiſtent with the Charity due to thoſe, that
are afflicted in Mind, Body, and Eſtate.

Thirdly, That the Beauties of Nature are far ſuperior to all artificial ones, *Solomon in all his Glory
not being arrayed like a Lily of the Field* ; that they
are open to every one, and therefore rather reſtrain
than feed the Deſire of Property ; and that they lead
to Humility, Devotion, and the Study of the
Ways of Providence. We ought therefore much
rather to apply ourſelves to the Contemplation of natural than of artificial Beauty.

Fourthly, Even the Beauties of *Nature* are much
chequered with Irregularities and Deformities, this
World being only the Ruins of a Paradiſiacal one.
We muſt not therefore expect intire Order and Perfection in it, till we have paſſed through the Gate of
Death, and are arrived at our Second Paradiſiacal
State, till the Heavens and Earth, and all Things in
them, be made anew. How much leſs then can we
hope for Perfection in the Works of human Art !
And yet, if we ſeriouſly apply ourſelves to theſe, we
ſhall be very apt to flatter ourſelves with ſuch falſe
Hopes, and to forget *that* heavenly Country, the Deſire and Expectation of whoſe Glories and Beauties
can alone carry us through the preſent Wilderneſs
with any Degree of Comfort and Joy.

But then, on the contrary, that ſome Attention
may lawfully, and even ought to be paid to artificial
Beauty, will appear from the following Reaſons.

Firſt, Convenience and Utility are certainly lawful
Ends; nay, we are even ſent hither to promote theſe
publicly and privately. But theſe coincide, for the
moſt part, with, and are promoted by, Simplicity,
Neatneſs, Regularity, and Juſtneſs of Proportion, *i. e.*
with ſome of the Sources of artificial Beauty ; though
not

not with all ; fuch as Grandeur, profufe Variety, Accumulation of natural Beauties and Luftres, and Sumptuoufnefs.

Secondly, The Study of artificial Beauty draws us off from the grofs fenfual Pleafures ; refines and fpiritualizes our Defires ; and, when duly limited, teaches us to transfer and apply our Ideas of Simplicity, Uniformity, and Juftnefs of Proportion, to the Heart and Affections.

Thirdly, It is neceffary for us in this degenerate State, and World of Temptations, to be occupied in innocent Purfuits, left we fall into fuch as are mifchievous and finful. It is therefore, in its proper Place and Degree, as great Charity to Mankind to employ the Poor in improving and ornamenting external Things, rewarding them generoufly and prudently for their Labours, as to give Alms ; and as ufeful to the Rich to be employed in contriving and conducting fuch Defigns at certain times, as to read, meditate, or pray, at others. Our Natures are too feeble to be always ftrained to the Pitch of an active Devotion or Charity, fo that we muft be content at fome Intervals to take up with Engagements that are merely innocent, fitting loofe to them, and purfuing them without Eagernefs and Intention of Mind. However, let it be well obferved, that there are very few upon whom this Third Reafon for the Purfuit of artificial Beauty need be inculcated ; and that I prefume not at all to interfere with thofe holy Perfons, who find themfelves able to devote all their Talents, their whole Time, Fortunes, bodily and mental Abilities, &c. to the great Author of all, in a direct and immediate Manner.

Now thefe and fuch-like Reafons, for and againft the Purfuit of the Elegancies of Life, hold in various Degrees according to the feveral Circumftances of particular Perfons ; and it will not be difficult for thofe who fit loofe to the World, and its Vanities,

to

to balance them againſt one another in each Caſe, ſo
as to approach nearly to that *Medium*, wherein our
Duty and Happineſs coincide.

The Practice of playing at Games of Chance and
Skill is one of the principal Amuſements of Life;
and it may be thought hard to condemn it as abſolutely unlawful, ſince there are particular Caſes of Perſons infirm in Body or Mind, where it ſeems requiſite
to draw them out of themſelves, by a Variety of
Ideas and Ends in View, which gently engage the
Attention. But this Reaſon takes place in very few
Inſtances. The general Motives to Play are Avarice,
joined with a fraudulent Intention, explicit or implicit, Oſtentation of Skill, and Spleen through the
Want of ſome ſerious, uſeful Occupation. And as
this Practice ariſes from ſuch corrupt Sources, ſo it
has a Tendency to increaſe them; and indeed may be
conſidered as an expreſs Method of begetting and inculcating Self-intereſt, Ill-will, Envy, *&c.* For by
Gaming a Man learns to purſue his own Intereſt
ſolely and explicitly, and to rejoice at the Loſs of
others, as his own Gain; grieve at their Gain, as his
own Loſs; thus intirely reverſing the Order eſtabliſhed by Providence for ſocial Creatures, in which the
Advantage of one meets in the ſame Point as the
Advantage of another, and their Diſadvantage likewiſe. Let the Loſs of Time, Health, Fortune, Reputation, Serenity of Temper, *&c.* be conſidered
alſo.

PROP. 58.

*To deduce practical Rules concerning Mirth,
Wit, and Humour.*

HERE it is neceſſary,
Firſt, To avoid all ſuch Mirth, Wit, and Humour, as has any Mixture of Profaneneſs in it; *i. e.*
all ſuch as leſſens our Reverence to God, and religious
Subjects;

Subjects; aggrieves our Neighbour; or excites corrupt and impure Inclinations in ourselves. Since then it appears from the History of Wit and Humour, given in the foregoing Part of this Work, that the greatest Part of what passes under these Names, and that which strikes us most, has a sinful Tendency, it is necessary to be extremely moderate and cautious in our Mirth, and in our Attention to, and Endeavours after, Wit and Humour.

Secondly, Let us suppose the Mirth to be innocent, and kept within due Bounds; still the frequent Returns of it beget a Levity and Dissipation of Mind, that are by no means consistent with that Seriousness and Watchfulness which are required in Christians, surrounded with Temptations, and yet aiming at Purity and Perfection; in Strangers and Pilgrims, who ought to have the uncertain Time of their Departure hence always in View. We may add, that Wit and Humour, by arising, for the most part, from fictitious Contrasts and Coincidences, disqualify the Mind for the Pursuit after Truth, and attending to the useful, practical Relations of Things, as has already been observed in the History of them; and that the State of the Brain which accompanies Mirth cannot subsist long, or return frequently, without injuring it; but must, from the very Frame of our Natures, end at last in the opposite State of Sorrow, Dejection, and Horror.

Thirdly, There is, for the most part, great Vainglory and Ostentation in all Attempts after Wit and Humour. Men of Wit seek to be admired and caressed by others for the Poignancy, Delicacy, Brilliancy, of their Sayings, Hints, and Repartees; and are perpetually racking their Inventions from this Desire of Applause. Now, as so sinful a Motive must defile all that proceeds from it, so the straining our Faculties to an unnatural Pitch is inconsistent with that Ease and Equality in Conversation, which our social Nature, and a mutual Desire to please, and be pleased, require.   Fourthly,

Fourthly, A due Attention being previoufly paid
to the foregoing and fuch-like Cautions, it feems not
only allowable, but even requifite, to endeavour at a
State of perpetual Chearfulnefs, and to allow ourfelves
to be amufed and diverted by the modeft, innocent
Pleafantries of our Friends and Acquaintance, con-
tributing alfo ourfelves thereto, as far as is eafy and
natural to us. This Temper of Mind flows from Benevolence and Sociality, and in its Turn begets them;
it relieves the Mind, and qualifies us for the Difcharge
of ferious and afflicting Duties, when the Order of
Providence lays them upon us ; is a Mark of Upright-
nefs and Indifference to the World, this infantine
Gayety of Heart being moft obfervable in thofe who
look upon all that the World offers as mere Toys and
Amufements ; and it helps to correct, in ourfelves
and others, many little Follies and Abfurdities, which,
though they fcarce deferve a feverer Chaftifement,
yet ought not to be overlooked intirely.

PROP. 59.

*To deduce practical Rules concerning the Purfuit
of the polite Arts; and particularly of Mufic,
Painting, and Poetry.*

I Will here enumerate the principal Ways in which
the Three Sifter Arts of Mufic, Painting, and Poetry, contribute either to corrupt or improve our
Minds ; as it will thence appear in what Manner, and
to what Degree, they are allowable, or even com-
mendable, and in what Cafes to be condemned as the
Vanities and finful Pleafures of the World, abjured
by all fincere Chriftians.

Firft, then, It is evident, that moft Kinds of Mufic, Painting, and Poetry, have clofe Connexions
with Vice, particularly with the Vices of Intemperance
and Lewdnefs ; that they reprefent them in gay, pleafing

ing Colours, or, at leaſt, take off from the Abhorrence due to them ; that they cannot be enjoyed without *evil Communications*, and Concurrence in the Pagan Shew and Pomp of the World ; and that they introduce a Frame of Mind, quite oppoſite to that of Devotion, and earneſt Concern for our own and others future Welfare. This is evident of public Diverſions, Collections of Pictures, Academies for Painting, Statuary, &c. antient heathen Poetry, modern Poetry of moſt Kinds, Plays, Romances, &c. If there be any who doubt of this, it muſt be from the Want of a duly ſerious Frame of Mind.

Secondly, A Perſon cannot acquire any great Skill in theſe Arts, either as a Critic, or a Maſter of them, without a great Conſumption of Time : They are very apt to excite Vanity, Self-conceit, and mutual Flatteries, in their Votaries ; and, in many Caſes, the Expence of Fortunes is too conſiderable to be reconciled to the Charity and Beneficence due to the Indigent.

Thirdly, All theſe Arts are capable of being devoted to the immediate Service of God and Religion in an eminent manner ; and, when ſo devoted, they not only improve and exalt the Mind, but are themſelves improved and exalted to a much higher Degree, than when employed upon profane Subjects ; the Dignity and Importance of the Ideas and Scenes drawn from Religion adding a peculiar Force and Luſtre thereto. And, upon the Whole, it will follow, that the polite Arts are ſcarce to be allowed, except when conſecrated to religious Purpoſes ; but that here their Cultivation may be made an excellent Means of awakening and alarming our Affections, and transferring them upon their true Objects.

P R O P.

P R O P. 60.

*To deduce practical Rules concerning the Pursuit
of Science.*

BY the Pursuit of Science I here mean the Investi-
gation of such Truths, as offer themselves in the
Study of the several Branches of Knowlege enume-
rated in the first Part of this Work ; Philology, Mathematics, Logic, History Civil and Natural, Natural Philosophy, and Theology, or Divine Philosophy.
Now here we may observe,

Firft, That though the Pursuit of Truth be an
Entertainment and Employment suitable to our rational Natures, and a Duty to him who is the *Fountain
of all Knowlege and Truth*, yet we must make frequent Intervals and Interruptions ; else the Study of
Science, without a View to God and our Duty, and
from a vain Desire of Applause, will get Possession of
our Hearts, engross them wholly, and, by taking
deeper Root than the Pursuit of vain Amusements,
become in the End a much more dangerous and obsti-
nate Evil than that. Nothing can easily exceed the
Vain-glory, Self-conceit, Arrogance, Emulation, and
Envy, that are found in the eminent Professors of the
Sciences, Mathematics, Natural Philosophy, and even
Divinity itself. Temperance in these Studies is there-
fore evidently required, both in order to check the
Rise of such ill Passions, and to give room for the
Cultivation of other essential Parts of our Natures.
It is with these Pleasures as with the sensible ones ;
our Appetites must not be made the Measure of our
Indulgences ; but we ought to refer all to an higher
Rule.

Secondly, When the Pursuit of Truth is directed
by this higher Rule, and entered upon with a View
to the Glory of God, and the Good of Mankind,

2   there

there is no Employment more worthy of our Natures, or more conducive to their Purification and Perfection. Thefe are the *Wife*, who in the *Time of the End fhall underftand*, and make an *Increafe of Knowlege*; who, by ftudying, and comparing together, the Word and Works of God, fhall be enabled to illuftrate and explain both; and who, *by turning many to Righteoufnefs, fhall* themfelves *fhine as the Stars for ever and ever.*

But we are not to confine this Bleffing to thofe who are called *learned* Men, in the ufual Senfe of this Word. Devotion, Charity, Prayer, have a wonderful Influence upon thofe who read the Scriptures, and contemplate the Works of Creation, with a practical Intention; and enable Perfons, otherwife illiterate, not only to fee and feel the important Truths therein manifefted, for their own private Purpofes, but to preach and inculcate them upon others with fingular Efficacy and Succefs.

PROP. 61.

To deduce practical Rules concerning the Ignorance, Difficulties, and Perplexities, in which we find ourfelves involved.

THESE are Pains, which ought to be referred to the Head of Imagination, as above noted; and which therefore require to be confidered here. But it muft alfo be obferved, that Self intereft has no fmall Share in increafing thefe Pains; our Ignorance and Perplexity occafioning the moft exquifite Uneafinefs to us in thofe Inftances, where our future Happinefs and Mifery are at ftake. Thus, in the Difficulties which attend our Inquiries into the Origin of Evil, Free-will, the Nature of our future Exiftence, the Degree and Duration of future Punifhment, and the moral Attributes of God, our Uneafinefs arifes not
only

only from the Darkneſs which ſurrounds theſe Subjects, and the Jarring of our Concluſions, but from the great Importance of theſe Concluſions. The following practical Rules deſerve our Attention.

Firſt, To avoid all Wrangling and Contention, all Bitterneſs and Cenſoriouſneſs, in ſpeaking or writing upon theſe Subjects. This is a Rule which ought to extend to all Debates and Inquiries upon every Subject; but it is more peculiarly requiſite to be attended to in difficult ones of a religious Nature; inaſmuch as theſe ill Diſpoſitions of Mind are moſt unſuitable to Religion, and yet moſt apt to ariſe in abſtruſe and high Speculations; alſo as they increaſe the Pains conſidered in this Propoſition by being of a Nature nearly related to them; *i. e.* by being attended with a nearly related State of the Brain.

Secondly, We ought to lay it down as certain, that this Perplexity and Uneaſineſs commenced with the Fall, with the Eating of the Fruit of the Tree of the Knowlege of Good and Evil; and that it can never be intirely removed till our Readmiſſion to Paradiſe, and to the Tree whoſe Leaves are for *the Healing of the Nations*. We muſt expect therefore, that, though humble and pious Inquiries will always be attended with ſome Succeſs and Illumination, ſtill much Darkneſs and Ignorance will remain. And the Expectation of this will contribute to make us eaſy under it.

Thirdly, The Scriptures give us Reaſon to hope, that this, as well as the reſt of our Evils, will be removed in a future State. We may therefore, if we labour to ſecure our Happineſs in a future State, enjoy, as it were by Anticipation, this important Part of it, that we ſhall then *ſee God and live, ſee him, though he be inviſible, ſee him as he is, and know as we are known.*

Laſtly, Of whatever Kind or Degree our Perplexity be, an implicit Confidence in the infinite Power, Knowlege, and Goodneſs of God, which are

manifeſted,

manifested, both in his Word and Works, in so great a Variety of Ways, is a certain Refuge. If our Ideas of the Divine Attributes be sufficiently strong and practical, their Greatness and Gloriousness, and the Joy arising from them, will overpower any Gloominess or Dissatisfaction, which a narrow and partial View of Things may excite in us.

SECT.

SECT. IV.

Of the Regard due to the Pleafures of Honour, and the Pains of Shame, in forming the Rule of Life.

PROP. 62.

The Pleafures of Honour ought not to be made a primary Purfuit.

THIS may appear from the following Confiderations.

Firft, Becaufe an eager Defire of, and Endeavour after, the Pleafures of Honour, has a manifeft Tendency to difappoint itfelf. The Merit of Actions, *i. e.* that Property of them for which they are extolled, and the Agents loved and efteemed, is, that they proceed from Benevolence, or fome religious or moral Confideration; whereas, if the Defire of Praife be only in part the Motive, we rather cenfure than commend. But, if Praife be fuppofed the greateft Good, the Defire of it will prevail above the other Defires, and the Perfon will by degrees be led on to Vanity, Self-conceit, and Pride, Vices that are moft contemptible in the Sight of all. *For whofoever exalteth himfelf, fhall be abafed; and he that humbleth himfelf, fhall be exalted.*

Secondly, What fhall be the Matter of the Encomiums, if Praife be the fupreme Good of the Species? What is there, to which all can attain, and which all fhall agree to commend and value? Not external Advantages, fuch as Riches, Beauty, Strength, *&c.* Thefe are neither in the Power of all, nor univerfally commended. Not great Talents, Wit, Sa-

gacity,

gacity, Memory, Invention. Thefe, though more
the Subject of Encomiums, yet fall to the Lot of
very few only. In fhort, Virtue alone is both univerfally efteemed, and in the Power of all, who are fufficiently defirous to attain it. But Virtue cannot
confift with the Purfuit of Praife, much lefs with
its being made a primary Purfuit. It follows
therefore, that it ought not to be made fuch.

Thirdly, If it be faid, That thofe who enjoy great
external Advantages, or are bleft with happy Talents,
may perhaps purfue Praife with Succefs; I anfwer,
That the numberlefs Competitions and Superiorities of
others, Follies and Infirmities of a Man's felf, Miftakes and Jealoufies of thofe from whom he expects
Praife, make this quite impoffible in general. Nay, it
is evident from the very Nature of Praife, which fuppofes fomething extraordinary in the Thing praifed,
that it cannot be the Lot of many. So that he who
purfues it, muft either have a very good Opinion
of himfelf, which is a dangerous Circumftance in a
Seeker of Praife, or allow that there are many Chances againft him.

Fourthly, If we recollect the Hiftory of thefe Pleafures delivered above, we fhall fee, that though Children are pleafed with Encomiums upon any advanta-
geous Circumftances that relate to them, yet this
wears off by degrees; and, as we advance in Life,
we learn more and more to confine our Pleafures of
this Kind to Things in our Power (according to the
common Acceptation of thefe Words), and to Virtue.
In like manner, the judicious Part of Mankind, *i. e.*
thofe whofe Praife is moft valued, give it not except
to Virtue. Here then, again, is a moft manifeft Subferviency of thefe Pleafures to Virtue. They not only tell
us, that they are not our primary Purfuit, or ultimate
End, but alfo fhew us what is.

Fifthly,

Fifthly, The early Rife of thefe Pleafures, and their Declenfion in old Age, for the moft part, are Arguments to the fame Purpofe, and may be illuftrated by the fimilar Obfervations made on the Pleafures of Senfation and Imagination, being not fo obvious here as there.

Sixthly, There is fomething extremely abfurd and ridiculous in fuppofing a Perfon to be perpetually feafting his own Mind with, and dwelling upon, the Praifes that already are, or which he hopes will hereafter be, given to him. And yet, unlefs a Man does this, which befides would evidently incapacitate him for deferving or obtaining Praife, how can he fill up a thoufandth Part of his Time with the Pleafures of Ambition?

Seventhly, Men that are much commended, prefently think themfelves above the Level of the reft of the World; and it is evident, that Praife from Inferiors wants much of that high Relifh, which ambitious Men expect, or even that it difgufts. It is even uneafy and painful to a Man to hear himfelf commended, though he may think it his Due, by a Perfon that is not qualified to judge. And, in this View of Things, a truly philofophic and religious Mind fees prefently, that all the Praifes of all Mankind are very trivial and infipid.

Eighthly, As the Defire of Praife carries us perpetually from lefs to larger Circles of Applauders, at greater Diftances of Time and Place, fo it neceffarily infpires us with an eager Hope of a future Life; and this Hope alone is a confiderable Prefumption in favour of the Thing hoped for. Now it will appear from numberlefs Arguments, fome of which are mentioned in thefe Papers, that every Evidence for a future Life is alfo an Evidence in favour of Virtue, and of its fuperior Excellence as the End of Life; and *vice verfa.* The Pleafures of Ambition lead therefore, in this way alfo, from themfelves, fince they lead to

S 3 thofe

thofe of Virtue. Let it be confidered farther, that all Reflections upon a future Life, the new Scenes which will be unfolded there, and the Difcovery which will then be made of *the Secrets of all Hearts*, muft caft a great Damp upon every Ambition, but a virtuous one; and beget great Diffidence even in thofe, who have the beft Teftimony from their Confciences.

PROP. 63.

The Pleafures of Honour may be obtained in their greateft Degree, and higheft Perfection, by paying a ftrict Regard to the Precepts of Benevolence, Piety, and the Moral Senfe.

THIS appears, in part, from what has been delivered under the laft Propofition; but it may be farther confirmed by the following Remarks.

First, Benevolence, Piety, and the Moral Senfe, engage Men to obtain all fuch Qualifications, and to perform all fuch Actions, as are truly honourable. They preferve them alfo from that Oftentation in refpect both of thefe and other Things, which would render them ridiculous and contemptible. Indeed Honour is affixed by the Bulk of Mankind, after fome Experience of Men and Things, chiefly to Acts of Generofity, Compaffion, public Spirit, &c. i. e. to Acts of Benevolence; and the Encomiums beftowed upon fuch Acts are one of the principal Sources of the Moral Senfe. The *Maximum* of Honour muft therefore coincide with Benevolence, and the Moral Senfe, and confequently with Piety alfo, which is clofely connected with them.

It may be objected here, That Acts of direct Piety are not, in general, honourable in this profane World; but, on the contrary, that they expofe to the Charges

of

of Enthuſiaſm, Superſtition, and Folly; and this not
only from the groſly vicious, but, in ſome Caſes, even
from the Bulk of Mankind. And it muſt be allowed,
that ſome Deductions ought to be made on this Account. But then let it be conſidered, that it is impoſſible to obtain the Applauſes both of the Good
and the Bad; that, as thoſe of the laſt ſcarce afford
Pleaſure to any, ſo their Cenſure need not be feared;
and that ſuch Perſons as are truly devout, as regard
God in all their Actions, and Men only in Subordina-
tion to him, are not affected by the Contempt and
Reproaches of the World; but, on the contrary,
*rejoice when Men revile them, and ſpeak all manner of
Evil againſt them falſly, for the ſake of Chriſt.* Let
it be obſerved farther, that Humility is the principal
of all the Qualifications which recommend Men to
World; and that it is difficult, or even impoſſible, to
attain this great Virtue without Piety, without a high
Veneration for the infinite Majeſty of God, and a
deep Senſe of our own Nothingneſs and Vileneſs in his
Sight; ſo that, in an indirect way, Piety may be ſaid
to contribute eminently to obtain the good Opinion of
the World.

Secondly, It is plain from the above-delivered Hiſtory of Honour, as paid to external Advantages, to
bodily, intellectual, and moral Accompliſhments,
that Happineſs of ſome Kind or other, accruing to a
Man's ſelf, or to the World by his means, is the
Source of all Honour, immediately or mediately. He
therefore who is moſt happy in himſelf, and moſt the
Cauſe of Happineſs to others, muſt in the End, from
the very Law of our Natures, have the greateſt Quantity of honourable Aſſociations transferred upon him.
But we have already ſhewn in part, and ſhall ſhew
completely in the Progreſs of this Chapter, that Benevolence, Piety, and the Moral Senſe, are the only
true, laſting Foundations of private Happineſs; and
that the public Happineſs ariſes from them, cannot be

S 4 doubted

doubted by any one. The benevolent, pious, and
confcientious Perfon muft therefore, when duly
known, and rightly underftood, obtain all the Honour
which Men good or bad can beftow ; and, as the Honour from the firft is alone valuable, fo he may expect to receive it early, as an immediate Reward
and Support to his prefent Virtues, and an Incitement
to a daily Improvement in them.

Thirdly, For the fame Reafon that we defire Honour, Efteem, and Approbation, from Men, and
particularly from the Wife and Good ; we muft defire
them from fuperior good Beings, and, above all,
from God, the higheft and beft.   Or, if we do not
defire this, it muft arife from fuch an Inattention to
the moft real and important of all Relations, as cannot confift with true Happinefs.   Now a Regard to
Benevolence, Piety, and the Moral Senfe, is, by the
Confeffion of all, the fole Foundation for obtaining
this greateft of Honours, the Approbation of God.
We cannot indeed enjoy this in Perfection, whilft feparated from the invifible World by this flefhly Tabernacle ; but the Teftimony of a good Confcience
gives us fome Foretafte and Anticipation of it.   How
vain and infipid, in refpect of this *eternal Weight of
Glory*, are all the Encomiums, which all Mankind
could beftow!

P R O P. 64.

*To deduce practical Obfervations on the Nature
of Humility, and the Methods of attaining it.*

HERE we may obferve,
    Firft, That Humility cannot require any Man
to think worfe of himfelf than according to Truth and
Impartiality : This would be to fet the Virtues at
Variance with each other, and to found one of the

moft

2

moſt excellent of them, Humility, in the baſe Vice of Falſhood.

Secondly, True Humility conſiſts therefore in having right and juſt Notions of our own Accompliſhments and Defects, of our own Virtues and Vices. For we ought not to deſcend lower than this by the foregoing Paragraph; and to aſcend higher, would evidently be Pride, as well as Falſhood.

Thirdly, It follows, notwithſtanding this Definition of Humility, and even from it, that humble Men, eſpecially in the Beginning of a religious Courſe, ought to be much occupied in conſidering and impreſſing upon themſelves their own Miſery, Imperfection, and Sinfulneſs, excluding, as much as poſſible, all Thoughts, and Trains of Thought, of a contrary Nature; alſo in attending to the Perfections of others, and rejecting the Conſideration of their Imperfections. For, ſince all Thoughts which pleaſe are apt to recur frequently, and their Contraries to be kept out of Sight, from the very Frame of the Mind, as appears from *Prop.* 22. *Cor.* 3. and other Places of the Firſt Part of this Work, it cannot but be, that all Men, in their natural State, muſt be proud; they muſt, by dwelling upon their own Perfections, and the Imperfections of others, magnify theſe; by keeping out of View the Contraries, diminiſh them; *i. e.* they muſt form too high Opinions of themſelves, and too low ones of others, which is Pride: And they cannot arrive at juſt and true Opinions of themſelves and others, which is Humility, but by reverſing the former Steps, and impreſſing upon themſelves their own Imperfection and Vileneſs, and the Perfections of others, by expreſs Acts of Volition.

Fourthly, A truly humble Man will avoid comparing himſelf with others; and when ſuch Compariſons do ariſe in the Mind, or are forced upon it, he will not think himſelf better than others. I do not mean, that thoſe who are eminent for Knowlege or Virtue,

ſhould

should not see and own their Superiority, in these re-spects, over Persons evidently ignorant and illiterate, or avowedly vicious. This cannot be avoided; but then this Superiority does not minister any Food to Pride, and a vain Complacence in a Man's own Ex-cellencies. Nor do I mean, that good Men may not both humbly hope, that they themselves are within the Terms of Salvation; and also fear, that the Bulk of Mankind are not; the first being a Support to their Infant Virtue, and a Comfort allowed by God in their Passage through this Wilderness; the last a great Security against Infection from a wicked World. I only affirm, that every Person, who is duly aware of his own Ignorance, as to the secret Causes of Merit and Demerit in himself and others, will first find him-self incapable of judging between Individuals; and then, if he has duly studied his own Imperfections, according to the last Paragraph, he will not be apt to presume in his own Favour.

Fifthly, It is an inseparable Property of Humility, not to seek the Applauses of the World; but to ac-quiesce in the Respect paid by it, however disproportionate this may be to the Merit of the Action under Consideration. For the contrary Behaviour must produce endless Inquietude, Resentment, Envy, and Self-conceit.

Sixthly, It is, in like manner, inseparable from true Humility, to take Shame to ourselves where we have deserved it, to acquiesce under it where we think we have not, and always to suspect our own Judg-ment in the last Case. There is no way so short and efficacious as this to mortify that Pride, and over-weening Opinion of ourselves, which is the Result of our Frame in this degenerate State. Nay, we ought even to rejoice when we are meanly esteemed, and de-spised, as having then an Opportunity offered of imitating him who was *meek and lowly in Heart*, and of *finding Rest to our Souls* thereby.

Seventhly,

Seventhly, It may conduce to eradicate that Tendency which every Man has to think himfelf a Nonpareil, in fome refpect or other, to confider natural Productions, Flowers, Fruits, Gems, &c. It would be very abfurd to affirm of one of thefe, that it was a Nonpareil in its Kind, becaufe it is endued with great Beauty and Luftre; much lefs therefore ought we to fanfy this of that Degree of Beauty, Parts, Virtue, which happen to be our Lot, and which is certainly magnified beyond the Truth in own Eyes, from the Intereft which we have in ourfelves.

Eighthly, There is fcarce a more effectual Method of curbing Oftentation and Self-conceit, than frequently to impofe upon one's felf a voluntary Silence, and not to attempt to fpeak, unlefs where a plain Reafon requires it. Voluntary Silence is, in refpect of Oftentation and Self-conceit, what Fafting is, in refpect of Luxury and Self-indulgence. All Perfons, who fpeak much, and with Pleafure, intend to engage the Attention, and gain the Applaufe, of the Audience; and have an high Opinion of their own Talents. And if this daily, I may fay hourly, Source and Effect of Vain-glory was cut off, we might with much greater Facility get the Victory over the reft. When a Perfon has, by this means, reduced himfelf to a proper Indifference to the Opinions of the World, he may by degrees abate of the Rigour of his Silence, and fpeak naturally and eafily, as Occafion offers, without any explicit Motive; juft as when Fafting, and other Severities, have brought our Appetites within due Bounds, we may be directed by them in the Choice and Quantity of common wholfome Foods.

Ninthly, The Doctrine of philofophical Free-will is the Caufe and Support of much Pride and Self-conceit; and this fo much the more, as it is a Doctrine not only allowed, but even infifted upon and required, and made effential to the Diftinction between Virtue

and

and Vice. Hence Men are commanded, as it were, to fet a Value upon their own Actions, by efteeming them their own in the higheft Senfe of the Words, and taking the Merit of them to themfelves. For philofophical Free-will fuppofes, that God has given to each Man a Sphere of Action, in which he does not interpofe; but leaves Man to act intirely from himfelf, independently of his Creator; and as, upon this Foundation, the Affertors of philofophical Free-will afcribe all the Demerit of Actions to Men fo they are obliged to allow Men to take the Merit of good Actions to themfelves, *i. e.* to be proud and felf-conceited. This is the plain Confequence of the Doctrine of philofophical Free-will. How far this Objection againft it overbalances the Objections brought againft the oppofite Doctrine of Mechanifm, I do not here confider. But it was neceffary, in treating of the Methods of attaining true Humility, to fhew in what Relation the Doctrine of Free-will ftood to this Subject.

But we are not to fuppofe, that every Man, who maintains philofophical Free-will, does alfo claim the Merit of his good Actions to himfelf. The Scriptures are fo full and explicit in afcribing all that is good to God, and the Heart of a good Man concurs fo readily with them, that he will rather expofe himfelf to any Perplexity of Underftanding, than to the Charge of fo great an Impiety. Hence it is, that we fee, in the Writings of many good Men, philofophical Free-will afferted, on one hand; and Merit difclaimed, on the other; in both Cafes, with a View to avoid Confequences apparently impious; though it be impoffible to reconcile thefe Doctrines to each other. However, this Subjection of the Underftanding to the moral Principle is a noble Inftance of Humility, and Rectitude of Heart.

As the Affertors of philofophical Free-will are not neceffarily proud, fo the Affertors of the Doctrine of Mechanifm

Mechanifm are much lefs neceffarily humble. For, however they may, in Theory, afcribe all to God; yet the Affociations of Life beget the Idea and Opinion of *Self* again and again, refer Actions to this Self, and connect a Variety of Applaufes and Complacencies with thefe Actions. Nay, Men may be proud of thofe Actions, which they directly and explicitly afcribe to God, *i. e.* proud, that they are Inftruments in the Hand of God for the performing fuch Actions. Thus the Pharifee, in our Saviour's Parable, though he thanked God, that he was no Extortioner, *&c.* yet boafted of this, and made it a Foundation for defpifing the Publican. However, the frequent Recollection, that all our Actions proceed from God; that we have nothing which we did not receive from him; that there can be no Reafon in ourfelves, why he fhould felect one, rather than another, for an Inftrument of his Glory in this World, *&c.* and the Application of thefe important Truths to the various real Circumftances of our Lives; muft greatly accelerate our Progrefs to Humility and Self-annihilation. And, when Men are far advanced in this State, they may enjoy Quiet and Comfort, notwithftanding their paft Sins and Frailties; for they approach to the Paradifiacal State, in which our firft Parents, though naked, were not afhamed. But the greateft Caution is requifite here, left by a frefh Difobedience we come to know Evil as well as Good again, and, by defiring to be Gods, to be independent, make the Return of Shame, Punifhment, and myftical Death, neceffary for our Readmiffion to the Tree of Life.

Tenthly, It will greatly recommend Humility to us, to confider how much Mifery a Difpofition to glory in our Superiority over others may hereafter occafion. Let it be obferved therefore, that every finite Perfection, how great foever, is at an infinitely greater Diftance from the infinite Perfection of God, than from nothing; fo that every finite Being may

have,

have, and probably has, infinitely more Superiors than Inferiors. But the fame Difpofition, which makes him glory over his Inferiors, muft make him envy his Superiors : He will therefore have, from this his Difpofition, infinitely more Caufe to grieve, than to rejoice. And it appears from this Way of confidering Things, that nothing could enable us to bear the Luftre of the invifible World, were it opened to our View, but Humility, Self-annihilation, and the Love of God, and of his Creatures, in and through him.

Eleventhly, If we may be allowed to fuppofe all God's Creatures ultimately and indefinitely happy, according to the Third Suppofition made above for explaining the infinite Goodnefs of God, this would unite the profoundeft Humility with the higheft Gratification of our Defires after Honour. For this makes all God's Creatures equal in the Eye of their Creator ; and therefore, as it obliges us to call the vileft Worm our Sifter, fo it transfers upon us the Glory of the brighteft Archangel ; we are all equally made *to inherit all Things*, are all equally *Heirs of God, and Coheirs with Chrift.*

S E C T.

SECT. V.

Of the Regard due to the Pleasures and Pains of Self-interest in forming the Rule of Life.

PROP. 65.

The Pleasures of Self-interest ought not to be made a primary Pursuit.

SELF-INTEREST is of Three Kinds, as has been already explained ; *viz.*

First, Gross Self-interest, or the Pursuit of the Means for obtaining the Pleasures of Sensation, Imagination, and Ambition.

Secondly, Refined Self-interest, or the Pursuit of the Means for obtaining the Pleasures of Sympathy, Theopathy, and the Moral Sense.

Thirdly, Rational Self-interest, or the Pursuit of such Things, as are believed to be the Means for obtaining our greatest possible Happiness, at the same time that we are ignorant, or do not consider, from what particular Species of Pleasure this our greatest possible Happiness will arise.

Now it is my Design, under this Proposition, to shew, that none of these Three Kinds of Self-interest ought to be cherished and indulged as the Law of our Natures, and the End of Life ; and that even rational Self-interest is allowable, only when it tends to re-strain other Pursuits, that are more erroneous, and destructive of our true Happiness.

I begin with the Arguments against gross Self-interest.

Firſt,

Firſt, then, We ought not to purſue the Means for obtaining the Pleaſures of Senſation, Imagination, and Ambition, primarily, becauſe theſe Pleaſures themſelves ought not to be made primary Purſuits, as has been ſhewn in the Three laſt Sections. The Means borrow all their Luſtre from the Ends by Aſſociation ; and, if the original Luſtre of the Ends be not ſufficient to juſtify our making them a primary Purſuit, the borrowed one of the Means cannot. In like manner, if the original Luſtre be a falſe Light, an *Ignis fatuus*, that miſleads and ſeduces us, the borrowed one muſt miſlead and ſeduce alſo. And indeed, though we ſometimes reſt in the Means for obtaining the Pleaſures of Senſation, Imagination, and Ambition, and deſire Riches, Poſſeſſions of other Kinds, Power, Privileges, Accompliſhments bodily and mental, for their own ſakes, as it were ; yet, for the moſt part, they introduce an explicit Regard to theſe exploded Pleaſures ; and conſequently muſt increaſe the Corruption, and falſe Cravings, of our Minds ; and, if they did not, their borrowed Luſtre would gradually languiſh, and die away, ſo that they would ceaſe to excite Deſire. It is to be added, that, if they be conſidered and purſued as Means, they will be uſed as ſuch, *i. e.* will actually involve us in the Enjoyment of unlawful Pleaſures.

Secondly, The treaſuring up the Means of Happineſs bears a very near Relation to Ambition. Thoſe who deſire great Degrees of Riches, Power, Learning, &c. deſire alſo that their Acquiſitions ſhould be known to the World. Men have a great Ambition to be thought happy, and to have it in their Power to gratify themſelves at Pleaſure ; and this oſtentatious Deſign is one principal Motive for acquiring all the ſuppoſed Means of Happineſs. The Reaſons therefore, which exclude Ambition, muſt contribute to exclude Self-intereſt alſo.

Thirdly,

Thirdly, Grofs Self-intereft has a manifeft Tendency to deprive us of the Pleafures of Sympathy, and to expofe us to its Pains. Rapacioufnefs extinguifhes all Sparks of Good-will and Generofity, and begets endlefs Refentments, Jealoufies, and Envies. And indeed a great Part of the Contentions, and mutual Injuries, which we fee in the World, arife, becaufe either one or both of the contending Parties defire more than an equitable Share of the Means of Happinefs. It is to be added, that grofs Self-intereft has a peculiar Tendency to increafe itfelf from the conftant Recurrency, and confequent Augmentation, of the Ideas and Defires that relate to *Self*, and the Exclufion of thofe that relate to others.

Now this Inconfiftency of grofs Self intereft with Sympathy would be fome Argument againft it, barely upon Suppofition, that Sympathy was one neceffary Part of our Natures, and which ought to have an equal Share with Senfation, Imagination, and Ambition; but as it now begins to appear from the Exclufion of thefe, and other Arguments, that more than an equal Share is due to Sympathy, the Oppofition between them becomes a ftill ftronger Argument againft Self-intereft.

Fourthly, There is, in like manner, an evident Oppofition between grofs Self-intereft, and the Pleafures of Theopathy, and of the Moral Senfe, and, by confequence, an infuperable Objection to its being made our primary Purfuit, deducible from thefe effential Parts of our Nature.

Fifthly, Grofs Self-intereft, when indulged, devours many of the Pleafures of Senfation, and moft of thofe of Imagination and Ambition, *i. e.* many of the Pleafures from which it takes its Rife. This is peculiarly true and evident in the Love of Money; but it holds alfo, in a certain Degree, with refpect to the other felfifh Purfuits. It muft therefore deftroy itfelf in part, as well as the Pleafures of Sympathy,

Theopathy, and the Moral Senfe, with the refined Self-intereft grounded thereon. And thus it happens, that in very avaricious Perfons nothing remains but Senfuality, fenfual Selfifhnefs, and an uneafy Hankering after Money, which is a more imperfect State, than that in which they were at their firft fetting off in Infancy. Some of the ftronger and more ordinary fenfible Pleafures and Pains, with the Defires after them, muft remain in the moft fordid, as long as they carry their Bodies about with them, and are fubjected to the Cravings of the natural Appetites, and to the Impreffions of external Objects. But a violent Paffion for Money gets the better of all Relifh for the Elegancies and Amufements of Life, of the Defire of Honour, Love, and Efteem, and even of many of the fenfual Gratifications. Now it cannot be, that a Purfuit which is fo oppofite to all the Parts of our Nature, fhould be intended by the Author of it for our primary one.

Sixthly, Men, in treafuring up the Means of Happinefs without Limits, feem to go upon the Suppofition, that their Capacity of enjoying Happinefs is infinite; and confequently that the Stock of Happinefs, laid up for them to enjoy hereafter, is proportional to the Stock of Means, which they have amaffed together. But our Capacity for enjoying Happinefs is narrow and fluctuating; and there are many Periods, during which no Objects, however grateful to others, can afford us Pleafure, on account of the Diforder of our Bodies or Minds. If the Theory of thefe Papers be admitted, it furnifhes us with an eafy Explanation of this Matter, by fhewing that our Capacity for receiving Pleafure depends upon our Affociations, and upon the State of the medullary Subftance of the Brain; and confequently that it muft fail often, and correfpond very imperfectly to the Objects, which are ufually called pleafurable ones.

3

Seventhly,

Seventhly, It is very evident in fact, that self-interested Men are not more happy than their Neighbours, whatever Means of Happiness they may possess. I presume indeed, that Experience supports the Reasoning already alleged; but, however that be, it certainly supports the Conclusion. Nay, one ought to say, that covetous Men are, in general, remarkably miserable. The Hardships, Cares, Fears, Ridicule, and Contempt, to which they subject themselves, appear to be greater Evils, than what fall to the Share of Mankind at an Average.

Eighthly, One may put this whole Matter in a short and obvious Light, thus: The Pursuit of the Means of Happiness cannot be the primary one, because, if all be Means, what becomes of the End? Means, as Means, can only be pleasant in a derivative way from the End. If the End be seldom or never obtained, the Pleasure of the Means must languish. The intellectual Pleasures, that are become Ends by the intire Coalescence of the associated Particulars, fade from being diluted with the Mixture of neutral Circumstances, unless they be perpetually recruited. A selfish Expectation therefore, which is never gratified, must gradually languish.

I come now, in the Second place, to shew that refined Self-interest, or the Pursuit of the Means for obtaining the Pleasures of Sympathy, Theopathy, and the Moral Sense, ought not to be made a primary Pursuit.

A Person who is arrived at this refined Self-interest, must indeed be advanced some Steps higher in the Scale of Perfection, than those who are immersed in gross Self-interest; inasmuch as this Person must have overcome, in some measure, the gross Pleasures of Sensation, Imagination, and Ambition, with the gross Self-interest thereon depending, and have made some considerable Progress in Sympathy, Theopathy, and the Moral Sense, before he can make it a Question whether the Pursuit of refined Self-interest ought to be his primary Purfuit or no. However, that it ought not, that this would detain him, and even bring him lower in the Scale of Perfection, will appear from the following Reafons.

Firft, Many of the Objections which have been brought againft grofs Self-intereft, retain their Force againft the refined, though in a lefs Degree. Thus refined Self-intereft puts us upon treafuring up the fame Means as the Grofs; for the Perfons, who are influenced by it, confider Riches, Power, Learning, &c. as Means of doing good to Men, bringing Glory to God, and enjoying comfortable Reflections in their own Minds in confequence thereof. But the Defire of Riches, Power, Learning, muft introduce Ambition, and other Defilements, from the many corrupt Affociations that adhere to them. In like manner, refined Self-intereft has, like the grofs, a Tendency to deftroy the very Pleafures from which it took its Rife, *i. e.* the Pleafures of Sympathy, Theopathy, and the Moral Senfe; it cannot afford Happinefs, unlefs the Mind and Body be properly difpofed; it does not, in fact, make Men happy; but is the Parent of Diffatisfaction, Murmurings, and Aridity; and, being profeffedly the Purfuit of a bare Means, involves the Abfurdity of having no real End in View. It may not be improper here for the Reader juft to review the Objections made above to grofs Self-intereft.

Secondly, Refined Self-intereft, when indulged, is a much deeper and more dangerous Error than the grofs, becaufe it fhelters itfelf under Sympathy, Theopathy, and the Moral Senfe, fo as to grow through their Protection; whereas the grofs Self-intereft, being avowedly contrary to them, is often ftifled by the Increafe of Benevolence and Compaffion, of the Love and Fear of God, and of the Senfe of Duty to him.

Thirdly, It is allied to, and, as it were, Part of the foregoing Objection, which yet deferves a particular

cular

cular Confideration, that the Pride attending on refined Self-intereft, when carried to a certain Height,
is of an incorrigible, and, as it were, diabolical Nature. And, upon the Whole, we may obferve,
that as grofs Self-intereft, when it gets Poffeffion of a
Man, puts him into a lower Condition than the mere
fenfual brutal one, in which he was born; fo refined
Self-intereft, when that gets Poffeffion, depreffes him ftill
farther, even to the very Confines of Hell. However,
it is ftill to be remembred, that fome Degree muft arife
in the Beginning of a religious Courfe; and that this,
if it be watched and refifted, is an Argument of our
Advancement in Piety and Virtue. But the beft Things,
when corrupted, often become the worft.

I come now, in the laft place, to confider what
Objections lie againft rational Self-intereft, as our
primary Purfuit.

Now here it may be alleged, Firft, That as we
cannot but defire any particular Pleafure propofed to
us, as long as the Affociations, which formed it,
fubfift in due Strength; fo, when any thing is believed to be the Means of attaining our greateft poffible Happinefs, the whole Frame of our acquired
Nature puts us upon purfuing it. Rational Self-
intereft muft therefore always have a neceffary Influence over us.

Secondly, It may be alleged, That I have my-
felf made rational Self-intereft the Bafis of the prefent Inquiry after the Rule of Life, having fuppofed
all along, that our greateft poffible Happinefs is the
Object of this Rule.

And it certainly follows hence, that rational Self-
intereft is to be put upon a very different Footing
from that of the grofs and refined; agreeably to
which the Scriptures propofe general and indefinite
Hopes and Fears, and efpecially thofe of a future
State, and inculcate them as good and proper Motives of Action. But then, on the other hand, the

Scriptures inculcate many other Motives, diftinct from Hope and Fear; fuch as the Love of God and our Neighbour, the Law of our Minds, &c. *i. e.* the Motives of Sympathy, Theopathy, and the Moral Senfe, as explained in this Work. And we may fee from the Reafoning ufed in refpect of grofs and refined Self-intereft, that a conftant Attention to that which is the moft pure and rational, to the moft general Hopes and Fears, would extinguifh our Love of God and our Neighbour, as well as the other particular Defires, and augment the Ideas and Defires, which centre immediately and directly in *Self*, to a monftrous Height. Rational Self-intereft may therefore be faid to lie between the impure Motives of Senfation, Imagination, Ambition, grofs Self-intereft, and refined Self-intereft, on the one hand, and the pure ones of Sympathy, Theopathy, and the Moral Senfe, on the other; fo that when it reftrains the impure ones, or cherifhes the pure, it may be reckoned a Virtue; when it cherifhes the impure, or damps the pure, a Vice. Now there are Inftances of both Kinds, of the firft in grofly vicious Perfons, of the laft in thofe that have made confiderable Advancement in Piety and Virtue. In like manner, the impure Motives of Senfation, Imagination, &c. differ in Degree of Impurity from each other; and therefore may be either Virtues or Vices, in a relative way of fpeaking. It feems, however, moft convenient, upon the Whole, to make rational Self-intereft the middle Point; and this, with all the other Reafoning of this Paragraph, may ferve to fhew, that it ought not to be cultivated primarily. But I fhall have occafion to confider this Matter farther under the next Propofition but one, when I come to deduce practical Obfervations on Self-intereft and Self-annihilation.

It may be reckoned a Part of the grofs and refined Self-interefts, to fecure ourfelves againft the Hazards
of

of falling into the Pains of the other fix Claffes, and a Part of rational Self-intereft, to provide againft our greateft Danger; and it might be fhewn in like manner, that neither ought thefe to be primary Purfuits.

PROP. 66.

A ftrict Regard to the Precepts of Benevolence, Piety, and the Moral Senfe, favours even grofs Self-intereft; and is the only Method, by which the refined and rational can be fecured.

HERE we may obferve,
Firft, That fince the Regard to Benevolence, Piety, and the Moral Senfe, procures the Pleafures of Senfation, Imagination, and Ambition, in their greateft Perfection for the moft part; it muft favour grofs Self-intereft, or the Purfuit of the Means of thefe.

Secondly, This Regard has, in many Cafes, an immediate Tendency to procure thefe Means, *i. e.* to procure Riches, Power, Learning, *&c.* And though it happens fometimes, that a Man muft forego both the Means for obtaining Pleafure, and Pleafure itfelf, from a Regard to Duty; and happens often, that the beft Men have not the greateft Share of the Means; yet it feems that the beft Men have, in general, the faireft Profpect for that Competency, which is moft fuitable to real Enjoyment. Thus, in Trades and Profeffions, though it feldom is obferved, that Men eminent for Piety and Charity amafs great Wealth (which indeed could not well confift with thefe Virtues); yet they are generally in affluent or eafy Circumftances, from the faithful Difcharge of Duty, their Prudence, Moderation in Expences, *&c.* and fcarce ever in indigent ones. A Senfe of Duty begets a Defire to difcharge it; this recommends to the World, to the bad as well as to the good; and,

where

where there are Inftances apparently to the contrary, farther Information will, for the moft part, difcover fome fecret Pride, Negligence, or Imprudence, *i. e.* fomething contrary to Duty, to which the Perfon's ill Succefs in refpect of this World may be afcribed.

Thirdly, A Regard to Duty plainly gives the greateft Capacity for Enjoyment; as it fecures us againft thofe Diforders of Body and Mind, which render the natural Objects of Pleafure infipid or ungrateful.

Fourthly, As to refined Self-intereft, or the Purfuit of the Means for obtaining the Pleafures of Sympathy, Theopathy, and the Moral Senfe, it appears at firft Sight, that a due Regard to thefe muft procure for us both the End, and the Means.

Fifthly, However the grofs or refined Self-intereft may, upon certain Occafions, be difappointed, the rational one never can, whilft we act upon a Principle of Duty. Our future Happinefs muft be fecured thereby. This the Profane and Profligate, as far as they have any Belief of God, Providence, or a future State (and I prefume, that no one could ever arrive at more than Scepticifm and Uncertainty in thefe things), allow, as well as the devout and pious Chriftian. And, when the rational Self-intereft is thus fecured, the Difappointments of the other two become far lefs grievous, make far lefs Impreffion upon the Mind. He that has a certain Reverfion of an infinite and eternal Inheritance, may be very indifferent about prefent Poffeffions.

PROP. 67.

To deduce practical Obfervations on Self-intereft and Self-annihilation.

SElf-intereft being reckoned by fome Writers the only ftable Point upon which a Syftem of Morality can be erected, and Self-annihilation by others

the

the only one in which Man can reft, I will here endeavour to reconcile thefe two Opinions, giving at
the fame time both a general Defcription of what
paffes in our Progrefs from Self-intereft to Self-annihilation, and fome fhort Hints of what is to be approved or condemned in this Practice.

Firft, then, The vicious Pleafures of Senfation, Imagination, and Ambition, being often very expenfive,
are checked by the groffeft of all the Self-interefts,
the mere Love of Money ; and the Principle upon
which Men act in this Cafe is efteemed one Species
of Prudence. This may be tolerated in others,
where it is not in our Power to infufe a better Motive ; but, in a Man's Self, it is very abfurd to have
Recourfe to one, which muft leave fo great a Defilement, when others that are purer and ftronger, rational Self-intereft particularly, are at hand.

Secondly, The Defire of bodily and mental Accomplifhments, Learning particularly, confidered as
Means of Happinefs, often checks both the forementioned vicious Pleafures, and the Love of Money.
Now this kind of Self-intereft is preferable to the laft
indeed ; but it cannot be approved by any that are
truly folicitous about their own Reformation and Purification.

Thirdly, Grofs Self-intereft fometimes excites Perfons to external Acts of Benevolence, and even of Piety ;
and though there is much Hypocrify always in thefe
Cafes, yet an imperfect Benevolence or Piety is fometimes generated in this Way. However, one cannot
but condemn this Procedure in the higheft Degree.

Fourthly, As refined Self-intereft arifes from Benevolence, Piety, and the Moral Senfe ; fo, converfly,
it promotes them in various Ways. But, then, as it
likewife checks their Growth in various other Ways,
it cannot be allowed in many Cafes, and is, upon the
Whole, rather to be condemned than approved.
More Favour may be fhewn to it, where it reftrains
the

the vicious Pleasures of Senfation, Imagination, and Ambition.

Fifthly, Rational Self-intereft puts us upon all the proper Methods of checking the laft-named vicious Pleafures with grofs and refined Self-intereft, and begetting in ourfelves the virtuous Difpofitions of Benevolence, Piety, and the Moral Senfe. This Part of our Progrefs is extremely to be approved, and efpecially the laft Branch of it.

Sixthly, The virtuous Difpofitions of Benevolence, Piety, and the Moral Senfe, and particularly that of the Love of God, check all the foregoing ones, and feem fufficient utterly to extinguifh them at laft. This would be perfect Self-annihilation, and Refting in God as our Centre. And, upon the Whole, we may conclude, that though it be impoffible to begin without Senfuality, and fenfual Selfifhnefs, or to proceed without the other intermediate Principles, and particularly that of rational Self-intereft ; yet we ought never to be fatisfied with ourfelves, till we arrive at perfect Self-annihilation, and the pure Love of God.

We may obferve alfo, that the Method of deftroying *Self*, by perpetually fubftituting a lefs and purer Self-intereft for a larger and groffer, correfponds to fome mathematical Methods of obtaining Quantities to any required Degree of Exactnefs, by leaving a lefs and lefs Error *fine limite*. And though abfolute Exactitude may not be poffible in the firft Cafe, any more than in the laft ; yet a Degree fufficient for future Happinefs is certainly attainable by a proper Ufe of the Events of this Life.

SECT.

S E C T. VI.

Of the Regard due to the Pleasures and Pains of Sympathy in forming the Rule of Life.

P R O P. 68.

The Pleasures of Sympathy improve those of Sensation, Imagination, Ambition, and Self-interest ; and unite with those of Theopathy, and the Moral Sense ; they are self-consistent, and admit of an unlimited Extent : They may therefore be our primary Pursuit.

THAT the Pleasures of Sympathy improve those of Sensation, Imagination, Ambition, and Self-interest, by limiting and regulating them, appears from the Four last Sections.

Their Union and intire Coincidence with those of Theopathy are evident, inasmuch as we are led by the Love of good Men to that of God, and back again by the Love of God to that of all his Creatures in and through him ; also as it must be the Will of an infinitely benevolent Being, that we should cultivate universal unlimited Benevolence.

In like manner, they may be proved to unite and coincide with the Pleasures of the Moral Sense, both because they are one principal Source of the Moral Sense, and because this, in its turn, approves of and enforces them intirely.

In order to prove their unlimited Extent, let us suppose, as we did before of Sensation, that a Person took all Opportunities of gratifying his benevolent Desires ; that he made it his Study, Pleasure, Ambition,

bition, and conftant Employment, either to promote Happinefs, or leffen Mifery, to *go about doing good.*

Firft, then, It is very plain, that fuch a Perfon would have a very large Field of Employment. The Relations of Life, conjugal, parental, filial, to Friends, Strangers, Enemies, to Superiors, Equals, Inferiors, and even to Brutes, and the Neceffities of each, are fo numerous, that, if we were not greatly wanting in benevolent Affections, we fhould have no Want of fit Objects for them.

Secondly, As the Occafions are fufficient to engage our Time, fo we may, in general, expect Succefs. Not only the Perfons themfelves, to whom we intend to do Service, may be expected to concur, but others alfo, in general; inafmuch as Benevolence gains the Love and Efteem of the Beholders, has a Perfuafivenefs and Prevalence over them, and engages them to co-operate towards its Succefs. It is very neceffary indeed, that all benevolent Perfons fhould guard againft the Sallies of Pride, Self-will, and Paffion, in themfelves, *i. e.* take care that their Benevolence be pure; alfo that it be improved by Piety, and the Moral Senfe; elfe it is probable, that they will meet with many Difappointments. But this is no Argument againft the unlimited Nature of Benevolence: It only tends to exclude the Mixture and Defilement of ill Difpofitions; and to fhew the neceffary Connexion of the Love of our Neighbour with that of God, and with the divine Signature of Confcience, which I all along contend for. When our Benevolence is thus pure, and thus directed, it will feldom fail of gaining its Purpofe. And yet Difappointments muft fometimes happen to the pureft Benevolence; elfe our Love of God, and Refignation to his Will, which is the higheft Principle of all, could not be brought to Perfection. But then this will happen fo rarely as to make no Alteration in our

Reafonings, with refpeſt to the general State of Things; which kind of Reafoning and Certainty is all that we are qualified for in our prefent Condition.

Thirdly, As the benevolent Perfon may expeſt both fufficient Employment and Succefs, in general; fo it does not appear from the Experience of thofe who make the Trial, that the Relifh for thefe Pleafures languifhes, as in other Cafes; but, on the contrary, that it gathers Strength from Gratification. We hear Men complaining frequently of the Vanity and Deceitfulnefs of the other Pleafures after Poffeffion and Gratification, but never of thofe of Benevolence, when improved by Religion, and the Moral Senfe. On the contrary, thefe Pleafures are greater in Enjoyment than Expeſtation; and continue to pleafe in Refleſtion, and after Enjoyment. And the foregoing Hiftory of Affociation may enable us to difcover how this comes to pafs. Since the Pleafures of Benevolence are, in general, attended with Succefs, and are confiftent with, and productive of, the feveral inferior Pleafures in their due Degree, as I have already fhewn, and alfo are farther illuminated by the moral and religious Pleafures, it is plain, that they muft receive frefh Recruits upon every Gratification, and therefore increafe perpetually, when cultivated as they ought to be.

The Self-confiftency of Benevolence appears from the peculiar Harmony, Love, Efteem, and mutual Co-operation, that prevail amongft benevolent Perfons; alfo from the Tendency that Aſts of Benevolence, proceeding from *A* to *B*, have to excite correfpondent ones reciprocally from *B* to *A*, and fo on indefinitely. We may obferve farther, that, when Benevolence is arrived at a due Height, all our Defires and Fears, all our Senfibilities for ourfelves, are more or lefs transferred upon others by our Love and Compaffion for them; and, in like manner, that

when

when our Moral Senfe is fufficiently eftablifhed and improved, when we become influenced by what is fit and right, our imperfect Senfibility for others leffens our exorbitant Concern for ourfelves by being compared with it, at the fame time that Compaffion takes off our Thoughts from ourfelves. And thus Benevolence to a fingle Perfon may ultimately become equal to Self-intereft, by this. Tendency of Self-intereft to increafe Benevolence, and reciprocally of Benevolence to leffen Self-intereft ; though Self-intereft was at firft infinitely greater than Benevolence ; *i. e.* we, who come into the World intirely felfifh, earthly, and *Children of Wrath,* may at laft be exalted to *the glorious Liberty of the Sons of God,* by learning to love our Neighbours as ourfelves : We may learn to be as much concerned for others as for ourfelves, and as little concerned for ourfelves, as for others ; both which Things tend to make Benevolence and Self-intereft equal, however unequal they were at firft.

And now a new Scene begins to open itfelf to our View. Let us fuppofe, that the Benevolence of *A* is very imperfect ; however, that it confiderably exceeds his Malevolence ; fo that he receives Pleafure, upon the Whole, from the Happinefs of *B, C, D,* &c. *i. e.* from that of the fmall Circle of thofe, whom he has already learnt to call his Neighbours. Let us fuppofe alfo, that *B, C, D,* &c. though affected with a Variety of Pains, as well as Pleafures, are yet happy, upon the Whole ; and that *A,* though he does not fee this Balance of Happinefs clearly, yet has fome comfortable general Knowlege of it. This then is the Happinefs of good Men in this prefent imperfect State ; and it is evident, that they are great Gainers, upon the Whole, from their Benevolence. At the fame time it gives us a faint Conception of *A*'s unbounded Happinefs, on Suppofition that he confidered every Man as his Friend, his Son, his Neighbour, his fecond Self, and loved him as himfelf ; and

and that his Neighbour was exalted to the fame unbounded Happinefs as himfelf by the fame unlimited
Benevolence. Thus *A*, *B*, *C*, *D*, &c. would all become, as it were, new Sets of Senfes, and perceptive
Powers, to each other, fo as to increafe each other's
Happinefs without Limits; they would all become
Members of the myftical Body of Chrift; all have an
equal Care for each other; all increafe in Love, and
come to their *full Stature*, to perfect Manhood, *by
that which every Joint fupplieth:* Happinefs would
circulate through this myftical Body without End, fo
as that each Particle of it would, in due time, arrive
at each individual Point, or fentient Being, of the
great Whole, that each would *inherit all Things*.

To ftrengthen our Prefumptions in favour of Benevolence, as the primary Purfuit of Life, ftill more;
let it be confidered, that its Pleafures lie open to all
Kinds and Degrees of Men, fince every Man has it in
his Power to benefit others, however fuperior or inferior, and fince we all ftand in need of each other.
And the Difference which Nature has put between us
and the Brutes, in making us fo much more dependent
upon, and neceffary to, each other from the Cradle
to the Grave, for Life, Health, Convenience, Pleafure, Education, and intellectual Accomplifhments,
fo much lefs able to fubfift fingly, or even in fmall
Bodies, than the Brutes, may be confidered as one
Mark of the fuperior Excellence of the focial Pleafures
to Man. All the Tendencies of the Events of Life,
ordinary and extraordinary, of the Relations of Life,
of the foregoing Pleafures and Pains, to connect us to
each other, to convert accidental, natural, inftituted
Affociations into permanent Coalefcences (for all this
is effected by the Power of Affociation fo much
fpoken of in thefe Papers), fo that two ill Men can
fcarce become known to each other familiarly, without conceiving fome Love, Tendernefs, Compaffion,
Complacence for each other, are Arguments to the
fame

fame Purpofe. And our Love to Relations and Friends, that have particular Failings, teaches us to be more candid towards others, who have the like Failings. At the fame time it fhews the Confiftency of Benevolence with itfelf, and its Tendency to improve itfelf; that we love, efteem, affift, and encourage the Benevolent more than others; fo that a benevolent Action not only excites the Receiver to a grateful Return, but alfo the By-ftander to approve and reward; and the benevolent Man receives an hundredfold even in this World. But it would be endlefs to purfue this. Benevolence is indeed the grand Defign and Purport of human Life, of the prefent probationary State; and therefore every Circumftance of human Life muft point to it, directly or indirectly, when duly confidered.

Cor. 1. Since Benevolence now appears to be a primary Purfuit, it follows, that all the Pleafures of Malevolence are forbidden, as being fo many direct Hindrances and Bars to our Happinefs. The Pleafures of Senfation, Imagination, Ambition, and Self-intereft, may all be made confiftent with Benevolence, when limited by, and made fubject to it, at leaft in this imperfect State; but thofe of Malevolence are quite incompatible with it. As far as Malevolence is allowed, Benevolence muft be deftroyed; they are Heat and Cold, Light and Darknefs, to each other. There is, however, this Exception; that where wifhing Evil to fome difpofes us to be more benevolent upon the Whole, as in the Cafe of what is called a juft Indignation againft Vice, it may perhaps be tolerable in the more imperfect Kinds of Men, who have need of this Direction and Incitement to keep them from wandering out of the proper Road, and to help them forward in it. But it is extremely dangerous to encourage fuch a Difpofition of Mind by Satire, Invective, Difpute, however unworthy the Opponent may be, as thefe Practices generally end in rank Malevolence

levolence at laft. *The Wrath of Man worketh not the Righteoufnefs of God.*

Cor. 2. As we muft forego the Pleafures of Male-volence, fo we muft patiently and refolutely endure the Pains of Benevolence, particularly thofe of Com-paffion. But we fhall not be Lofers upon either of thefe Accounts. The Pleafures of the Moral Senfe, which refult from thefe Virtues, will in the firft Cafe compenfate for what we forego, and in the laft over-balance what we endure. Befides which, Mercy and Forgivenefs are themfelves Pleafures, and productive of many others in the Event; and Compaffion gene-rally puts us upon fuch Methods, as both make the afflicted to rejoice, and beget in ourfelves a ftronger Difpofition to rejoice with them. However, we may learn from thefe Two Corollaries, that as our Paffage through the Four inferior, and, as it were, forbidden, Claffes of Pleafure and Pain, is not intire Self-denial and Sufferance, fo fome Degrees of thefe are neceffary in refpect of the Three fuperior Claffes. We muft *weep with thofe that weep,* as well as *rejoice with thofe that rejoice.* In like manner, Theopathy, and the Moral Senfe, are the Occafions of fome Pain, as well as of great and lafting Pleafure; as will appear hereafter.. Now all this Mixture of Pain with Plea-fure in each Clafs, as alfo the Difficulty which we find in bringing the inferior Claffes into a due Subordina-tion to the fuperior, are Confequences and Marks of our fallen and degenerate State.

Cor. 3. As Benevolence is thus fupported by many direct Arguments, fo there are fimilar and op pofite Arguments, which fhew that Malevolence is the Bane of human Happinefs; that it occafions Mi-fery to the Doer, as well as to the Sufferer; that it is infinitely inconfiftent with itfelf, and with the Courfe of Nature; and that it is impoffible, that it fhould fubfift for ever. Now thefe become fo many indirect ones for Benevolence, and for our making it the fu-

preme

preme Pleafure and End of our Lives. In order to
make this appear more fully, let us take a Survey of
human Life on the reverfe Side to that which we
have before confidered. We fhall there fee, that Injuries are increafed in various ways by Reciprocation,
till at laft mutual Sufferings oblige both Parties to
defift; that the Courfe and Conftitution of Nature
give us numberlefs Admonitions to forbear; and that
the Hand of every Man, and the Power of every
Thing, is againft the Malevolent: So that, if we
fhould fuppofe the Beings *A*, *B*, *C*, *D*, &c. to be
purely malevolent, to have each of them an indefinite
Number of Enemies, they would firft ceafe from their
Enmity on account of their mutual Sufferings, and
become purely felfifh, each being his own fole Friend
and Protector; and afterwards, by mutual good Offices, endear themfelves to each other; fo that at laft
each would have an indefinite Number of Friends, *i. e.*
be indefinitely happy. This is indeed a kind of Suppofition; but its obvious Correfpondence with what
we fee and feel in real Life, is a ftrong Argument
both of the infinite Goodnefs of God, and of the confequent Doctrine of the Tendency of all Beings to
unlimited Happinefs through Benevolence. For the
Beings *A*, *B*, *C*, *D*, &c. could no more ftop at pure
Selfifhnefs, or any other intermediate Point, than
they could reft in pure Malevolence. And thus the
Arguments, which exclude pure Malevolence, neceffarily infer pure unlimited Benevolence.

P R O P.

P R O P. 69.

To deduce practical Rules for augmenting the benevolent Affections, and suppressing the malevolent ones.

FOR this Purpose we ought, First, Diligently to practise all such Acts of Friendship, Generosity, and Compassion, as our Abilities of any Kind extend to; and rigorously to refrain from all Sallies of Anger, Resentment, Envy, Jealousy, &c. For though our Affections are not directly and immediately subject to the voluntary Power, yet our Actions are; and consequently our Affections also mediately. He that at first practises Acts of Benevolence by Constraint, and continues to practise them, will at last have associated such a Variety of Pleasures with them, as to transfer a great instantaneous Pleasure upon them, and beget in himself the Affections from which they naturally flow. In like manner, if we abstain from malevolent Actions, we shall dry up the ill Passions, which are their Sources.

Secondly, It will be of great Use frequently to reflect upon the great Pleasures and Rewards attending on Benevolence, also upon the many Evils present and future, to which the contrary Temper exposes us. For thus we shall likewise transfer Pleasure and Pain by Association upon these Tempers respectively; and rational Self-interest will be made to beget pure Benevolence, and to extinguish all Kinds and Degrees of Malevolence.

Thirdly, It is necessary to pray frequently and fervently (*i. e.* as far as we can excite Fervour by our voluntary Powers) for others, Friends, Benefactors, Strangers, Enemies. All Exertions of our Affections cherish them; and those made under the more immediate Sense of the Divine Attributes have an extraordinary

dinary

dinary Efficacy this Way, by mixing the Love, Awe, and other exalted Emotions of Mind attending our Addresses to God, with our Affections towards Men, so as to improve and purify them thereby.   Petitions for the Increase of our Benevolence, and Suppression of our Malevolence, have the same Tendency.

Fourthly, All Meditations upon the Attributes of God, and particularly upon his infinite Benevolence to all his Creatures, have a strong Tendency to refine and augment our benevolent Affections.

Fifthly, The frequent Consideration of our own Misery, Helplessness, Sinfulness, intire Dependence upon God, &c. raises in us Compassion for others, as well as Concern, and earnest Desires and Prayers, for ourselves   And Compassion is, in this imperfect probationary State, a most principal Part of our benevolent Affections.

PROP. 70.

To deduce practical Rules for the Conduct of Men towards each other in Society.

SINCE Benevolence is now proved to be a primary Pursuit, it follows, that we are to direct every Action so as to produce the greatest Happiness, and the least Misery, in our Power.   This is that Rule of social Behaviour, which universal unlimited Benevolence inculcates.

But the Application of this Rule in real Life is attended with considerable Difficulties and Perplexities. It is impossible for the most sagacious and experienced Persons to make any accurate Estimate of the future Consequences of particular Actions, so as, in all the Variety of Circumstances which occur, to determine justly, which Action would contribute most to augment Happiness, and lessen Misery.   We must therefore, instead of this most general Rule, substitute others less general, and subordinate to it, and which
admit

admit of a more commodious practical Application. Of this Kind are the Ten Rules that follow. Where they coincide, we may suppose them to add Strength to each other; where they are opposite, or seemingly so, to moderate and restrain one another; so as that the Sum total shall always be the best Direction in our Power for promoting the Happiness, and lessening the Misery, of others.

The First Rule is Obedience to the Scripture Precepts in the natural, obvious, and popular Meaning of them. That this must, in general, contribute to public Good, needs no Proof: Piety and Benevolence evidently coincide here, as in other Cases. The Scripture Precepts are indeed themselves, *The Rule of Life.* But then there is the same Sort of Difficulty in applying them accurately to particular Cases, as in applying the above-mentioned most general Rule, by means of an Estimate of the Consequences of Actions. It is impossible, in many particular Cases, from the Nature of Language, to determine whether the Action under Consideration come precisely under this or that Scripture Precept, interpreted literally, as may appear from the endless Subtleties and Intricacies of Casuistical Divinity. However, it cannot but be, that the common and popular Application must, for the most part, direct us to their true Intention and Meaning. Let every Man therefore, in the particular Circumstances of real Life, recollect the Scripture Precepts, and follow them in their first and most obvious Sense, unless where this is strongly opposite to some of the following Rules; which yet will seldom happen.

Secondly, Great Regard must be had both to our own Moral Sense, and to that of others. This Rule coincides remarkably with the foregoing. They are together the chief Supports of all that is good, even in the most Refined and Philosophical, as well as in the Vulgar; and therefore must not be weakened, or explained away.

U 3　　　　　　　Thirdly,

Thirdly, It is very proper in all deliberate Actions to weigh, as well as we can, the probable Confequences on each Side, and to fuffer the Balance to have fome Influence in all Cafes, and the chief where the other Rules do not interfere much, or explicitly. But to be determined by our own Judgments as to Confequences, in Oppofition to the two foregoing Rules, or to thofe that follow, favours much of Pride, and is often only a Cloak for Self-intereft and Malicioufnefs.

Fourthly, The natural Motions of Good-will, Compaffion, &c. muft have great Regard paid to them, left we contract a philofophical Hardnefs of Heart, by endeavouring or pretending to act upon higher and more extenfively beneficial Views, than vulgar Minds, the fofter Sex, &c. Some Perfons carry this much too far on the other Side, and encourage many public Mifchiefs, through a falfe, mifguided Tendernefs to Criminals, Perfons in Diftrefs through prefent grofs Vices, &c. For the mere inftantaneous Motions of Good-will and Compaffion, which are generated in fo many different Ways in different Perfons, cannot be in all more than a good general Direction for promoting the greateft Good.

Fifthly, The Rule of placing ourfelves in the feveral Situations of all the Perfons concerned, and inquiring what we fhould then expect, is of excellent Ufe for directing, enforcing, and reftraining our Actions, and for begetting in us a ready, conftant Senfe of what is fit and equitable.

Sixthly, Perfons in the near Relations of Life, Benefactors, Dependents, and Enemies, feem to have, in moft Cafes, a prior Claim to Strangers. For the general Benevolence arifes from our Cultivation of thefe particular Sources of it. The Root muft therefore be cherifhed, that the Branches may flourifh, and the Fruit arrive to its Perfection.

I

Seventhly,

Seventhly, Benevolent and religious Perſons have, all other Circumſtances being equal, a prior Claim to the reſt of Mankind. Natural Benevolence itſelf teaches this, as well as the Moral Senſe. But it is likewiſe of great Importance to the Public, thus to encourage Virtue. Not to mention, that all Opportunities and Powers become more extenſively beneficial, by being entruſted with deſerving Perſons.

Eighthly, Since the Concerns of Religion, and a future State, are of infinitely more Importance than thoſe which relate to this World, we ought to be principally ſolicitous about the Eſtabliſhment and Promotion of true and pure Religion, and to make all our Endeavours concerning temporal Things ſubſervient to the Precepts for teaching all Nations, and for carrying the everlaſting Goſpel to the Ends of the Earth.

Ninthly, We ought to pay the ſtricteſt Regard to Truth, both with reſpect to Affirmations and Promiſes. There are very few Inſtances, where Veracity of both kinds is not evidently conducive to public Good, and Falſhood in every Degree pernicious. It follows therefore, that, in Caſes where Appearances are otherwiſe, the general Regard to Truth, which is of ſo much Conſequence to the World, ought to make us adhere inviolably to it ; and that it is a moſt dangerous Practice to falſify, as is often done, from falſe Delicacy, pretended or even real Officiouſneſs, falſe Shame, and other ſuch diſingenuous Motives, or even from thoſe, that border upon Virtue. The Harm which theſe things do, by creating a mutual Diffidence, and Diſpoſition to deceive, in Mankind, is exceedingly great; and cannot be counterbalanced by the preſent good Effects, aſſigned as the Reaſons for this Practice. Yet ſtill the Degrees are here, as in other Caſes, ſo inſenſible, and the Boundaries ſo nice, that it is difficult, or even impoſſible, to give any exact Rule. A direct Falſhood ſeems ſcarce to

U 4   admit

admit a Toleration, whatever be thrown into the oppofite Scale ; unlefs in Cafes of Madnefs, Murder to be prevented, &c. Equivocations, Concealments, Pretences, are in general unjuftifiable ; but may perhaps be fometimes allowed. The Wifdom of the Serpent joined to the Innocence of the Dove, or Chriftian Prudence to Chriftian Simplicity and Charity, will generally enable Men to avoid all Difficulties. There is fcarce any thing which does greater Violence to the Moral Senfe in well educated Perfons, than Difingenuity of any Kind, which is a ftrong Argument againft it. Lyes and Lyars are particularly noted in the prophetical Writings, and the great Sin of Idolatry is reprefented under this Image. As to falfe Oaths, affirmative or promiffory, there feems to be no poffible Reafon fufficient to juftify the Violation of them. The Third Commandment, and the Reverence due to the divine Majefty, lay an abfolute Reftraint here.

Tenthly, Obedience to the Civil Magiftrate is a fubordinate general Rule of the utmoft Importance. It is evidently for the public Good, that every Member of a State fhould fubmit to the governing Power, whatever that be. Peace, Order, and Harmony, refult from this in the general ; Confufion and Mifchief of all Kinds from the contrary. So that though it may and muft be fuppofed, that Difobedience, in certain particular Cafes, will, as far as the fingle Act, and its immediate Confequences, are confidered, contribute more to public Good, than Obedience ; yet, as it is a dangerous Example to others, and will probably lead the Perfon himfelf into other Inftances of Difobedience afterwards, &c. Difobedience in every Cafe becomes deftructive of public Happinefs upon the Whole. To this we may add, that as Part of our Notions of, and Regards to, the Deity, are taken from the Civil Magiftrate ; fo, converfly, the Magiftrate is to be confidered as God's Vicegerent

on

on Earth; and all Oppofition to him weakens the Force of religious Obligations, as well as of civil ones; and if there be an Oath of Fidelity and Submiffion, or even a bare Promife, this will give a farther Sanction. Laftly, The Precepts of the New Teftament given under very wicked Governors, and the whole Tenor of it, which fuppofes Chriftians to have higher Views, and not to intermeddle with the Kingdoms of this World, injoin an implicit Submiffion.

We ought therefore, in Confequence of this Tenth Rule, to reverence all Perfons in Authority ; not to pafs hafty Cenfures upon their Actions; to make candid Allowances on accouut of the Difficulties of Government, the bad Education of Princes, and Perfons of high Birth, and the Flatteries, and extraordinary Temptations, with which they are furrounded; to obferve the Laws ourfelves, and promote the Obfervance of them, where the Penalties may be evaded, or are found infufficient; to look upon Property as a Thing abfolutely determined by the Laws; fo that though a Man may and ought to recede from what the Law would give him, out of Compaffion, Generofity, Love of Peace, View of the greater Good to the Whole, &c. yet he muft never evade, ftrain, or in any way do Violence to the Laws, in order to obtain what he may think his own according to Equity ; and where-ever he has offended, or is judged by lawful Authority to have offended, he muft fubmit to the Punifhment, whatever it be.

Here two Things may be objected in refpect of this Tenth Rule: Firft, That the Duty to Magiftrates ought to be deduced from the Origin of Civil Government.   Secondly, That it is lawful to refift the fupreme Magiftrate openly, in thofe Cafes, where the good Confequences of open Refiftance appear in the ultimate Refult to overbalance the ill Confequences.

To

To the Firſt I anſwer, That we here ſuppoſe Benevolence to be the Rule of Duty, public Good the End of Benevolence, and Submiſſion to Magiſtrates the Means of promoting the public Good. Unleſs therefore ſomething can be objected to one of theſe three Poſitions, the Concluſion, That Submiſſion to Magiſtrates is a Duty, muſt ſtand. It appears to me alſo, that this Method of deducing Obedience to Magiſtrates is much more ſimple and direct, than that from the Origin of Civil Government. For the real Origin of Civil Government having been either the gradual Tranſition and Degeneration of parental Patriarchal Authority (which being originally directed by pure Love, and ſupported by abſolute Authority, can never be paralleled now) into ſmall Monarchies in the antient World, of which we know nothing accurately ; or the uſurped Power of Conquerors and Tyrants ; or the delegated Power of thoſe, who in difficult and factious Times have gained over the Minds of the Populace to themſelves, and balanced the Intereſts and Ambition of Particulars againſt one another ; it ſeems that little of Uſe to public Happineſs can be drawn from theſe Patterns, where the Perſons concerned were either very little ſolicitous about public Happineſs, or very little qualified to make a proper Eſtimate of the beſt Methods of attaining it, or, laſtly, were obliged to comply with the Prejudices, and eſtabliſhed Cuſtoms, of an ignorant headſtrong Multitude. The only Pattern of great Uſe and Authority appears to be the *Jewiſh* Theocracy. As to the fictitious Suppoſition, that a Set of Philoſophers, with all their natural Rights about them, agree to give up certain of theſe, in order to preſerve the reſt, and promote the Good of the Whole, this is too large a Field. Beſides, Public Good muſt either be made the Criterion of natural Rights, and of the Obligation to give them up, &c. which would bring this Hypotheſis to coincide

with

with the direct obvious Confiderations above-mentioned ; or, if any other Criterion be affumed, the Determinations will be falfe. This Method of Reafoning has been adopted too fervilely, by the Force which Affociation has over the human Mind, from the technical Methods of extending human Laws to Cafes not provided for explicitly, and particularly from the Reafonings made ufe of in the Civil Law. However, the Writers of this Clafs have delivered many excellent particular Precepts, in relation to the Duties both of public and of private Life ; and therefore have deferved well of the World, notwithftanding that their Foundation for the Laws of Nature and Nations be liable to the foregoing Objections.

Secondly, It is faid, that there are certain Cafes, in which open Refiftance is lawful. And it muft be owned, that where there is no Oath of Allegiance, or where that Oath is plainly conditional, Cafes may be put, where Refiftance with all its Confequences feems more likely to produce public Good, than Non-refiftance. If therefore a Man can lay his Hand upon his Heart, and fairly declare, that he is not influenced by Ambition, Self-intereft, Envy, Refentment, &c. but merely by Tendernefs and Good-will to the Public, I cannot prefume to fay, that he is to be reftrained, or that Chriftianity, that *perfect Law of Liberty*, whofe End is *Peace* and *Good-will to Men*, fhould be made an Obftruction to any truly benevolent Endeavours, where Chriftian *Liberty* is not made ufe of as *a Cloak for Malicioufnefs*. But thefe Cafes are fo rare, that it is needlefs to give any Rules about them. In public Difturbances, when Mens Paffions are up, there are fo many Violences on all hands, that it is impoffible to fay, which Side one would wifh to have uppermoft ; only there is always a Prejudice in favour of the laft Eftablifhment, becaufe the Minds of the Multitude may be quieted fooner by getting into the former Road. Rules of this kind

can

can only be fuppofed to relate to thofe that are difpofed to obey them, which are very few in Comparifon. If one could fuppofe, that all would obey implicitly, no Difturbance could arife ; if all difobey, it is infinite Anarchy. Therefore, of all the intermediate Suppofitions, thofe feem to be the beft, in which moft obey. In fhort, it appears to be the Duty of a good Chriftian to fit ftill, and fuffer the Children of this World to difpute and fight about it ; only fubmitting himfelf to the Powers in being, whatever they are (they cannot be intitled to lefs Regard than the Heathen Emperors, to whom the Apoftles injoined Obedience) for the fake of Peace and Quietnefs to himfelf and others ; and, as much as in him lies, moderating the Heats and Animofities of Parties againft each other. However, I do not mean, that thofe who, according to the Conftitution of a Government, have an executive or legiflative Power lodged with them, fhould not exert it with Authority. As to the Cafe of Oaths, no View of public Good can be fufficient to fuperfede fo facred an Obligation. And thus it is not only allowed to, but even required of, a good Chriftian, to be active in the Defence of an Eftablifhment, to which he has given an Oath to that Purpofe.

Other Rules, befides the Ten foregoing, might be affigned, or thefe expreffed in a different Way. I have put down thofe which appear to me to be, in fact, the chief Principles of focial Conduct to wife and good Men. They muft all be fuppofed to influence and interpret each other. Let a Man only diveft himfelf of all Self-regards, as much as poffible, and love his Neighbour as himfelf, and God above all, and he will generally find fome Point, and that without much Difficulty or Perplexity, in which all thefe Rules unite to produce the greateft Good, upon the Whole, to all the Perfons concerned.

I

I proceed next to confider briefly the feveral principal Relations of Life, and the Duties arifing from them, according to the foregoing or fuch-like Rules.

The Firft of thefe is that of Husband and Wife. The loving our Neighbour as ourfelves begins here. This is the firft Inftance of it ; and, where this Love is mutual and perfect, there an intire Equality of the two Sexes takes place. The Authority of the Man is only a Mark of our prefent degenerate State, by reafon of which Dominion muft be placed fomewhere, and therefore in the Man, as being of greater bodily Strength and Firmnefs of Mind. But this is that kind of Right or Property, which Men are obliged to give up, though Women are alfo obliged to acknowlege it. Suppofe the Sexes to fhare all their Joys and Griefs perfectly, to have an intire Concern for each other, and efpecially for each other's eternal Welfare, and they are, as it were, reinftated in Paradife ; and the Dominion of the Man over the Woman, with her Subjection, and confequent Reluctance, can only take place again upon their mutual Tranfgreffion. And though in this imperfect State it feems impoffible, from the Theory above given, for any one to love another, in every Branch of Defire and Happinefs, intirely as himfelf ; yet there appear to be fuch near Approaches to it in benevolent, devout, married Perfons, united upon right Motives, as to annihilate all confiderable, or even perceptible Diftinction. It is of the utmoft Importance, that this grand Foundation of all Benevolence be duly laid, on account both of public and private Happinefs. The chief or only Means of doing this is Religion. Where both Parties have it in a high Degree, they cannot fail of mutual Happinefs ; fcarce, if one have it : Where both are greatly defective in this principal Article, it is almoft impoffible but Diffenfions, Uneafinefs, and mutual Offences, fhould arif .

The

The Second great Relation of Life is that of Parents to Children ; the principal Duty of which is the giving a right Education, or the imprinting ſuch Aſſociations upon the Minds of Children, as may conduct them ſafe through the Labyrinths of this World to a happy Futurity. Religion therefore here again appears to be the one only neceſſary Thing. It is the Deſign of the preſent Chapter to ſhew, that it contributes as certainly to give us the *Maximum* of Happineſs in this World, at leaſt the faireſt Proſpect of it, as to ſecure it in the next. So that a Parent muſt be led to the inculcating Virtue in every View. The chief Errors in Education are owing to the Want of this Perſuaſion in a practical Way ; or to a falſe Tenderneſs and Opinion of the Parent, whereby he is led to believe, or flatter himſelf, that his Child's Nature is not ſo degenerate and corrupt, as to require frequent Corrections and Reſtraints, with perpetual Encouragements and Incentives to Virtue by Reward, Example, Advice, Books, Converſation, &c. Otherwiſe it would appear from the Hiſtory of the Mind, its Affections and Paſſions, before given, that few Children would miſcarry. Where due Care is taken from the firſt, little Severity would ordinarily be neceſſary ; but, in proportion as this Care is neglected in the firſt Years, a much greater Degree of Care, with high Degrees of Severity both bodily and mental, become abſolutely requiſite to preſerve from Miſery here and hereafter. We ſee that Men of the ordinary Standard in Virtue are ſeldom brought to a State of Repentance and Salvation, without great Sufferings, both bodily and mental, from Diſeaſes, ſad external Accidents, Deaths of Friends, Loſs of Fortunes, &c. How then can it be ſuppoſed, that Children can be brought into the right Way, without analogous Methods, both bodily and mental, though gentler indeed, in proportion as the Child's Age is more tender? And this ought to

make

make all affectionate Parents labour from the earlieft
Dawnings of Underftanding and Defire, to check the
growing Obftinacy of the Will; curb all Sallies of
Paffion; imprefs the deepeft, moft amiable, reverential, and awful Apprehenfions of God, a future State,
and all facred Things; reftrain Anger, Jealoufy,
Selfifhnefs; encourage Love, Compaffion, Generofity,
Forgivenefs, Gratitude; excite, and even compel to,
fuch Induftry as the tender Age will properly admit.
For one principal End and Difficulty of Life is to
generate fuch moderate, varying, and perpetually ac-
tuating Motives, by means of the natural fenfible
Defires being affociated with, and parcelled out upon
foreign Objects, as may keep up a State of moderate
Chearfulnefs, and ufeful Employment, during the
whole Courfe of our Lives: Whereas fenfual, blind,
and uninformed Defire preffes violently for immediate
Gratification, is injurious to others, and deftroys its
own Aims, or, at the beft, gives way only to Spleen
and Diffatisfaction.

As to the other Duties towards Children, fuch as
Care of their prefent and future Health of Body, Pro-
vifion of external Neceffaries and Conveniencies for
them, &c. they are fufficiently obvious, and can
fcarce be neglected by thofe, who are truly folicitous
about the principal Point, a religious Education.

The Duties of Children to Parents are Submiffion,
Obedience, Gratitude even to the Worft. For it can
fcarce be fuppofed, that Children have not great Obligations to their Parents, upon the Whole. And as
the Love of Parents to Children may ferve to give
Parents a feeling Conviction of the infinite Benevolence
of God our heavenly Father, fo the Submiffion of
Children to Parents is the Pattern of, and Introduction to,
true Religion; and therefore is of infinite Importance
to be duly paid. Which may ferve as an Admonition
both to Parents, to fhew themfelves fit Vicegerents

of

of God, and to Children to give them the Respect
due to them as such.

As the reciprocal Duties between Parents and Children are Patterns of the reciprocal Duties between Superiors and Inferiors of all Kinds ; so the Duties and
Affections between Brethren and Sisters are our Guides
and Monitors in respect of Equals: Both which Things
are intimated in these and such-like Scripture Phrases ;
*Intreat an Elder as a Father, the younger Men as Bre-
thren* ; *love as Brethren*, &c. The several Events of
Childhood, the Conjunction of Interests, the Examples
of others, *&c.* imprefs upon us a greater Concern,
Love, Compassion, *&c.* for all Persons nearly related
to us in Blood, than for others in like Circumstances.
And though the ultimate Ratio of Duty is to love
every Man equally, because we are to love every Man
as ourselves ; yet since our Condition here keeps us in
some Degree the necessary Slaves of Self-love, it follows that neither ought we to love all Persons equally,
but our Relations, Friends, and Enemies, preferably
to utter Strangers ; left, in endeavouring to love all
equally, we come not to love others more, but our
Brethren less, than we did before.

The cleaving of our Affections to all with whom
we have frequent pleasing Intercourses, with mutual
Obligations, is the Foundation of Friendship ; which
yet cannot subsist long, but amongst the truly Religious. And great Care ought to be taken here, not
to have Mens Persons in Admiration, not to esteem
our Friend a Nonpareil. There is great Pride and
Vanity in this, just as in the like Opinions concerning
ourselves, our Children, Possessions, *&c.* Such Intimacies, by exalting one above measure in our Love
and Esteem, must depress others ; and they generally
end in Jealousies and Quarrels, even between the
two Intimates. All Men are frail and imperfect, and
it is a great Injury to any Man, to think more highly
of him than he deserves, and to treat him so. Our
Regards

Regards cannot continue long ſtrained up to an unnatural Pitch. And if we conſider, that we all have
a proper Buſineſs in Life, which engages us in a Variety of Chriſtian Actions, and conſequently of Friend-
ſhips and Intimacies, this peculiar Attachment of one
Perſon to another of the ſame Sex will appear inconſiſtent with the Duties of Life. Where the Sexes are
different, ſuch an Attachment is either with a View
to Marriage, or elſe it becomes liable to ſtill greater
Objections.

As to Enemies, the forgiving them, praying for
them, doing them good Offices, Compaſſion to them
as expoſing themſelves to Sufferings by a wrong Behaviour, the Senſe of our having injured them,
which is generally the Caſe more or leſs, &c. have in
generous and religious Men a peculiar Tendency to
excite Love and Compaſſion for them.

The laſt Relation which I ſhall conſider is that
of Magiſtrates, *i. e.* the Perſons who in each Society
have the legiſlative or executive Powers, or both,
committed to them. The Duty ariſing from this Relation may be diſtinguiſhed into Two Branches. Firſt,
That towards the Perſons over whom the Magiſtrate
preſides; Secondly, That towards other States.

In reſpect of the Firſt, we may at once affirm,
that the principal Care of a Magiſtrate, of the Father
of a People, is to encourage and enforce Benevolence
and Piety, the Belief and Practice of Natural and
Revealed Religion; and to diſcourage and reſtrain
Infidelity, Profaneneſs, and Immorality, as much as
poſſible. And this,

Firſt, Becauſe the Concerns of another World are
of infinitely greater Importance than any relating to
this; ſo that he who wiſhes well to a People, and
preſides over them for their Good, cannot but be
chiefly ſolicitous and induſtrious in this Particular.

Secondly, Becauſe even the preſent Well-being of
States depends intirely upon the private Virtues of the

Vol. II. X ſeveral

feveral Ranks and Orders of Men. For the public Happinefs is compounded of the Happinefs of the feveral Individuals compofing the Body Politic; and the Virtues of Induftry, Temperance, Chaftity, Meeknefs, Juftice, Generofity, Devotion, Refignation, &c. have a Tendency to promote the Happinefs both of the Perfons that poffefs them, and of others.

It will therefore be the Duty of the Magiftrate, in making and executing Laws, to inquire which Method appears to be moft conducive to Virtue in the People, to purfue this fimply and fteadily, and not to dcubt but that all the fubordinate Ends of Government, as thofe of increafing the Riches and Power of the State, promoting Arts and Sciences, &c. will be obtained in fuch Degrees as they ought, as are productive of real Happinefs to the People, by the fame means. But where it is doubtful what Method is moft conducive to Virtue, there the fubordinate Ends are to be taken into Confideration, each according to its Value : Juft as in the Cafe of Self-intereft in Individuals; where Benevolence, Piety, and the Moral Senfe, are intirely filent, there cool, rational Self-intereft may, and, as it appears, ought to be admitted as a Principle of Action.

As to foreign States, they, and confequently the Magiftrates which prefide over them, are under the fame Obligations, as private Perfons are in refpect of each other. Thus, fince a private Perfon, in order to obtain his own greateft Happinefs, even in this World, muft obey the Precepts of Benevolence, Piety, and the Moral Senfe, with an abfolute and implicit Confidence in them; fo States, *i. e.* their Governors or Reprefentatives, ought to deal with each other according to Juftice, Generofity, Charity, &c. even from the mere Principle of Intereft. For the Reafon is the fame in both Cafes. If Individuals be all Members of the fame myftical Body, much more are

are States, *i. e.* large Collections of Individuals. They ought therefore to have the same Care for each other, as for themselves ; and whoever is an Aggreſſor, or injurious, muſt expect to ſuffer, as in private Life. *They that take the Sword ſhall periſh by the Sword. He that leadeth into Captivity muſt go into Captivity. Babylon muſt receive double for all her Inſults upon other Nations,* &c. All which is verified by Obſervation, both in regard to private Perſons, and to States, as far as it is reaſonable for us to expect to ſee it verified, in this our Ignorance of the real Quantities of Virtue and Vice, and of Happineſs and Miſery. But in all Obſervations of this Kind we ought conſtantly to bear in mind, that God's *Judgments are unſearchable, and his Ways paſt finding out,* in particular Caſes, though ſufficiently manifeſt in the general Courſe and Tenor of Things. By the laſt he ſhews us his moral Attributes, his Providence, and his Relation to us as our Governor ; by the firſt he humbles the Pride, Raſhneſs, and Self-conceit, of human Underſtanding.

It may not perhaps be improper here to ſay ſomething concerning the Lawfulneſs of War. Now this regards either the Magiſtrate, or the Subject. Firſt, then, it is very evident, that as private Perſons are, in general, prohibited by the Law of Chriſt to revenge themſelves, reſiſt Evil, *&c.* ſo are States, and conſequently, Magiſtrates. But then as private Perſons have, under Chriſtianity, that *perfect Law of Liberty,* a Power to puniſh Injuries done to themſelves, oppoſe Violence offered to themſelves, *&c.* when their View in this is a ſincere Regard to others, as affected by theſe Injuries and Violences, ſo Magiſtrates have a Power, and by conſequence lie under an Obligation, of the like Kind, where the real Motive is Tenderneſs to their own People in a juſt Cauſe, or a Regard to the general Welfare of their own State, and the neighbouring

X 2 ones.

ones. Secondly, Though it feems intirely unjuftifiable for private Perfons to enter upon the Profeffion of War wantonly, and with a View to Riches, Honours, &c. efpecially fince fo much Violence and Cruelty, and fo many Temptations, attend this Profeffion; yet where a Perfon is already engaged, and has very urgent Reafons reftraining him from withdrawing, or receives a particular Command from a lawful Magiftrate, it feems to be allowable, or even his Duty.

SECT.

S E C T. VII.

Of the Regard due to the Pleasures and Pains of Theopathy in forming the Rule of Life.

P R O P. 71.

The Love of God regulates, improves, and per-fects all the other Parts of our Nature; and affords a Pleasure superior in Kind and Degree to all the rest: It is therefore our primary Pursuit, and ultimate End.

IN what manner the Precepts of Piety regulate, improve, and perfect the Four inferior Classes of Pleasure, *viz.* those of Sensation, Imagination, Ambition, and Self-interest, has been shewn already in this Chapter. But the Precepts of Piety are those which teach us, what Homage of our Affections, and external Actions, ought to be addressed to the Deity in a direct and immediate manner; and it will appear under the Two next Propositions, in which the Affections and Actions injoined by Piety are particularly considered, that all these terminate ultimately in the Love of God, and are absorbed by it: The Love of God does therefore regulate, improve, and perfect all the Four inferior Classes of Pleasure.

The same thing is evident with respect to the Whole of our Natures, in a shorter Manner, and according to the usual Sense, in which the Phrase of the *Love of God* is taken. For the perpetual Exertion of a pleasing Affection towards a Being infinite in Power, Knowlege, and Goodness, and who is also our Friend and Father, cannot but enhance all our Joys, and alleviate all our Sorrows; the Sense of his

X 3 Presence

Prefence and Protection will reftrain all Actions, that are exceffive, irregular, or hurtful; fupport and encourage us in all fuch as are of a contrary Nature; and infufe fuch Peace and Tranquillity of Mind, as will enable us to fee clearly, and act uniformly. The Perfection therefore of every Part of our Natures muft depend upon the Love of God, and the conftant comfortable Senfe of his Prefence.

With refpect to Benevolence, or the Love of our Neighbour, it may be obferved, that this can never be free from Partiality and Selfifhnefs, till we take our Station in the Divine Nature, and view every thing from thence, and in the Relation which it bears to God. If the Relation to ourfelves be made the Point of View, our Profpect muft be narrow, and the Appearance of what we do fee diftorted. When we confider the Scenes of Folly, Vanity, and Mifery, which muft prefent themfelves to our Sight in this Point; when we are difappointed in the Happinefs of our Friends, or feel the Refentment of our Enemies; our Benevolence will begin to languifh, and our Hearts to fail us; we fhall complain of the Corruption and Wickednefs of that World, which we have hitherto loved with a Benevolence merely human; and fhew by our Complaints, that we are ftill deeply tinctured with the fame Corruption and Wickednefs. This is generally the Cafe with young and unexperienced Perfons, in the Beginning of a virtuous Courfe, and before they have made a due Advancement in the Ways of Piety. Human Benevolence, though *fweet in the Mouth*, is *bitter in the Belly*; and the Difappointments which it meets with, are fometimes apt to incline us to call the Divine Goodnefs in queftion. But he who is poffeffed of a full Affurance of this, who loves God with his whole Powers, as an inexhauftible Fountain of Love and Beneficence to all his Creatures, at all times, and in all Places, as much when he chaftifes, as when he rewards, will

learn

learn thereby to love Enemies, as well as Friends; the finful and miferable, as well as the holy and happy ; to rejoice, and give Thanks, for every thing which he fees and feels, however irreconcileable to his prefent Suggeftions ; and to labour, as an Inftrument under God, for the Promotion of Virtue and Happinefs, with real Courage and Conftancy, *knowing that his Labour fhall not be in vain in the Lord.*

In like manner, the Moral Senfe requires a perpetual Direction and Support from the Love of God, in order to keep it fteady and pure. When Men ceafe to regard God in a due meafure, and to make him their ultimate End, having fome other End, beyond which they do not look, they are very apt to relapfe into Negligence and Callofity, and to act without any virtuous Principle ; and, on the other hand, if they often look up to him, but not with a filial Love and Confidence, thofe *weighty Matters of the Law,* they *tithe Mint, Anife, and Cumin,* and fill themfelves with endlefs Scruples and Anxieties about the Lawfulnefs and Unlawfulnefs of trivial Actions : Whereas he who loves God with all his Heart, cannot but have a conftant Care not to offend him, at the fame time that his amiable Notions of God, and the Confcioufnefs of his Love and Sincerity towards him, are fuch a Fund of Hope and Joy, as precludes all Scruples that are unworthy of the Divine Goodnefs, or unfuitable to our prefent State of Frailty and Ignorance.

We are next to fhew, that the Love of God affords a Pleafure which is fuperior in Kind and Degree to all the reft, of which our Natures are capable. Now this will appear.

Firft, Becaufe *God is Light, and in him there is no Darknefs at all*; becaufe he is *Love* itfelf, fuch Love as quite *cafts out all Fear.* The Love and Contemplation of his Perfection and Happinefs will transform us into his Likenefs, into that Image of him in which we were firſt made ; will make us *Partakers of the Divine Nature*, and conſequently of the Perfection and Happineſs of it. Our Wills may thus be united to his Will, and therefore rendered free from Diſappointments ; we ſhall, by degrees, ſee every thing as God ſees it, *i. e.* ſee every thing that he has made to be good, to be an Object of Pleaſure. It is true, that all this, in its perfect Senſe, in its ultimate Ratio, can only be ſaid by way of Anticipation : Whilſt we carry theſe fleſhly Tabernacles about with us, we muſt have Croſſes to bear, Frailties, and Thorns in the Fleſh, to ſtruggle with. But ſtill our Strength will at laſt be made perfect thro' Weakneſs ; and ſome devout Perſons appear to have been ſo far transformed, in this Life, as to acquieſce, and even rejoice, in the Events of it, however afflicting apparently, to be freed from Fear and Solicitude, and to receive their daily Bread with conſtant Thankfulneſs, *with Joy unſpeakable, and full of Glory.* And though the Number of theſe happy Perſons has probably been very ſmall comparatively, though the Path be not frequented and beaten ; yet we may aſſure ourſelves, that it is in the Power of all to arrive at the ſame State, if their Love and Devotion be ſufficiently earneſt. All other Loves, with all their Defilements and Idolatries, will die away in due Order and Proportion, in the Heart, which yields itſelf to God : For they are all impure and idolatrous, except when conſidered as the Methods appointed by God to beget in us the Love of himſelf : They all leave Stains ; have a Mixture of Evil, as well as of Good ; they muſt all be tried and purified by the Fire of his Love, and paſs thereby from Human to Divine.

Secondly, God is our Centre, and the Love of Him a Pleaſure ſuperior to all the reſt, not only on account of the Mixture of Pain in all the reſt, as ſhewn in the laſt Paragraph, but alſo becauſe they all point to it, like ſo many Lines terminating in the ſame Centre.

When

When Men have entered sufficiently into the Ways of Piety, God appears more and more to them in the whole Course and Tenor of their Lives; and by uniting himself with all their Senfations, and intellectual Perceptions, overpowers all the Pains; augments, and attracts to himself, all the Pleasures. Every thing sweet, beautiful, or glorious, brings in the Idea of God, mixes with it, and vanishes into it. For all is God's; he is the only Cause and Reality; and the Existence of every thing else is only the Effect, Pledge, and Proof, of his Existence and Glory. Let the Mind be once duly seasoned with this Truth, and its practical Applications, and every the most indifferent Thing will become Food for religious Meditation, a Book of Devotion, and a Psalm of Praise. And when the Purity and Perfection of the Pleasures of Theopathy, set forth in the last Article, are added to their unlimited Extent, as it appears in this, it is easy to see, that they must be far superior to all the rest both in Kind and Degree. We may see also, that the Frame of our Nature, and particularly its Subjection to the Power of Affociation, has an obvious and neceffary Tendency to make the Love of God, in fact, superior to our other Affections. If we suppose Creatures subject to the Law of Affociation to be placed in the midst of a Variety of Pleasures and Pains, the Sum total of the first being greater than that of the last, and to connect God with each as its sole Cause, Pain will be overpowered by Pleasure, and the indefinite Number of compound Pleasures resulting from Affociation be at last united intirely with the Idea of God. And this our ultimate Happinefs will be accelerated or retarded, according as we apply ourselves more or less to the Cultivation of the devout Affections, to Reading, and Meditation upon divine Subjects, to Prayer and Praise. Thus we shall the sooner learn to join with the Angels, and *Spirits of just Men made perfect*, in ascribing *Power, and Riches, and Wisdom,*

Wifdom, and Strength, and Honour, and Glory, and Bleſſing, and every affociated Luſtre, to their true Fountain, *to God and the Lamb.*

Thirdly, As all the other Pleaſures have a Mixture of Pain and Impurity in them, and are all evidently Means, not Ends, ſo are the Objects of them frequently taken from us ; whereas no Time, Place, or Circumſtance of Life, can deprive us of, no Height, Depth, or Creature of any Kind, can ſeparate us from, the Love of God. Our Hearts may be turned to him in the greateſt external Confuſion, as well as in the deepeſt Silence and Retirement. All the Duties of Life, when directed to God, become Pleaſures ; and by the ſame means, every the ſmalleſt Action becomes the Diſcharge of the proper Duty of the Time and Place. Thus we may redeem our Time, and turn it to the beſt Advantage ; thus we may convert every Situation and Event of Life into preſent Comfort, and future Felicity.

Fourthly, When the Love of God is made thus to ariſe from every Object, and to exert itſelf in every Action, it becomes of a permanent Nature, ſuitable to our preſent Frame ; and will not paſs into Deadneſs and Diſguſt, as our other Pleaſures do from repeated Gratification.

It is true indeed, that Novices in the Ways of Piety and Devotion are frequently, and more experienced Perſons ſometimes, affected with ſpiritual Aridity and Dejection ; but then this ſeems to be either from Pride, or ſpiritual Selfiſhneſs, *i. e.* from the Impurity of their Love to God. They give themſelves up perhaps to Raptures, and ecſtatic Tranſports, from the preſent Pleaſures which they afford, to the Neglect of the great Duties of Life, of Charity, Friendſhip, Induſtry ; or they think themſelves the peculiar Favourites of Heaven on account of theſe Raptures ; and deſpiſe and cenſure others, as of inferior Claſſes in the School of Piety. Now theſe violent Agitations of

3   the

the Brain cannot recur often without paffing out of the Limits of Pleafure into thofe of Pain ; and particularly into the mental Pains of Morofenefs, Jealoufy, Fear, Dejection, and Melancholy. Both the Greatnefs and the Samenefs of the Pleafures concur, as in other Cafes, to convert them into Pains. But it does not appear, that thofe who feek God in all his Works, and receive all the Pleafures and Pains which the Order of his Providence offers, with Thankfulnefs, and Fidelity in their Duty, as coming from his Hand, would either want that Variety, or that Temperature, which in our prefent State is neceffary to make the Love of God a perpetual Fund of Joy. And it feems peculiarly proper to remark here, that if the primitive Chriftians, inftead of retiring into Deferts, Caves, and Cells, for the Cultivation of fpeculative Devotion, had continued to fhew forth and practife the Love of God by expofing themfelves to all fuch Difficulties and Dangers, as had arifen in the inceffant Propagation of the everlafting Gofpel to *every Nation, and Kindred, and Tongue, and People,* they would perhaps have rejoiced evermore, even in the greateft Tribulations, as the Apoftles, and their immediate Followers, who *kept* their *firft Love,* feem to have done ; alfo that the prefent and future Generations of Chriftians can never be delivered from fuperftitious Fears and Anxieties, from Drynefs, Scrupulofity, and Dejection, till they *go into all the World, and preach the Gofpel to every Creature,* according to our Saviour's laft Command. However, till this happy Time comes, the Alloy of the Pleafures of Theopathy with Pain ferves to remind us of our fallen State, and of the Greatnefs of our Fall, fince our primary and pureft Pleafures are fubject to fuch an Alloy ; and thus, learning Compaffion, Humility, and Submiffion to God, we fhall be exalted thereby, and, after we have *fuffered a while, be perfected, ftablifhed, ftrengthened, fettled.*

PROP.

P R O P. 72.

To deduce practical Rules concerning the Theo-
pathetic Affections, Faith, Fear, Gratitude,
Hope, Trust, Resignation, and Love.

Of Faith in God.

THE First of the Theopathetic Affections is Faith.
He that cometh to God must believe that he is; and
that he is a Rewarder of them that diligently seek him.
But this Faith is of very different Degrees, even in those
who equally acknowlege their Belief of the Exiftence of
God, and agree in their Expreffions concerning his
Nature and Attributes, according as their Ideas of
this Kind are more or lefs vivid and perfect, and
recur more or lefs frequently in the Events of Life.
It is probable indeed, that no Man, efpecially in a
Chriftian Country, can be utterly devoid of Faith.
The Impreffion made upon us in Infancy, our
Converfation afterwards, the Books that we read,
and the Wonders of the vifible World, all concur
to generate Ideas of the Power and Knowlege of God
at leaft, and to excite fuch Degrees of Fear, as give
a Reality to the Ideas, and extort fo much of Affent,
that the moft profeffed Atheifts, did they reflect upon
what paffes in their Thoughts, and declare it fincerely, could not but acknowlege, that at certain
times they are like *the Devils*, who *believe and tremble.*
After thefe come the Perfons who dare not but own
God in Words, who have few or no Objections to
his Nature and Attributes, or who can even produce
many Arguments and Demonftrations in favour of
them; and yet put away the Thoughts of God as
much as they are able.   The next Degree is of fuch
as try to *ferve God and Mammon* together, in various
Proportions; till at laft we come to thofe, whofe *Heart*
is perfect before God, who love him with all their Powers,
and

and *walk in his Presence* continually. Now this laft State of Faith is that which the Scripture puts as equivalent to our whole Duty: For in this laft State it comprehends, and coincides with, all the other Theopathetic Affections, when they are likewife carried to their ultimate Perfection. In their firft Rife they all differ from one another; in their laft State they all unite together, and may be expreffed by the Name of any fingle one, when fuppofed perfect; though the moft ufual, proper, and emphatic Appellation feems to be the Phrafe of *the Love of God*, as before noted. Let us now inquire by what Methods Men may be moft accelerated in their Progrefs from the firft Dawnings of Faith in Infancy to its ultimate Perfection.

Firft, then, An early Acquaintance with the Scriptures, and the conftant Study of them, is the principal Means whereby this Faith is firft to be generated, and afterwards improved and perfected. God taught Mankind before the Flood, and for fome Ages afterwards, his Exiftence, Nature, and Attributes, by exprefs Revelation; and therefore it cannot but be the proper Method for begetting Faith in Children, who are more ignorant, and unqualified for rational Deductions, than Adults in the rudeft Ages of the World, to initiate them early in the Records of Religion. And though afterwards *the invifible Things of God* may be known by the vifible Creation, yet the Miracles delivered in the Scriptures have a peculiar Tendency to awaken the Attention, and to add that Force, Luftre, and Veneration, to our Ideas of God, and his Attributes, which are the Caufes and Concomitants of Affent or Faith, according to the Theory of thefe Papers. The fame thing holds of the Prophecies, Precepts, Promifes, and Threatenings, of the Scriptures, in their refpective Degrees; and it feems, in a manner, impoffible for any one to be perpetually converfant in them, without this happy Influence. All thofe Perfons therefore, who are fo

far

far advanced in Faith, as to cry out with the Father
of the Lunatic in the Gofpel, *Lord, I believe* ; *help
thou my Unbelief*; ought, in confequence of this Prayer,
to apply themfelves to the daily Study of, and Meditation upon, the Scriptures. To which it is to be added,
that as Faith in Chrift is alfo neceffary, as well as Faith
in the one God and Father of all, and can be learnt no
other way than from the Scriptures, we ought upon
this account alfo, to efteem them as the principal
Means, which God has put in our Power, for the
Generation and Improvement of our Faith: *Faith cometh by Hearing, and Hearing by the Word of God.*

Secondly, To the Study of the Word of God muft
be joined that of his Works. They are in all Things
analogous to each other, and are perpetual Comments
upon each other. I do not mean, that a Man muft
be a deep Philofopher, in order to have Faith in God;
for, on the contrary, philofophical Refearches, when
purfued from Curiofity or Ambition, are *vain Deceit,*
and lead People to *make Shipwreck of Faith.* I would
only recommend to every Perfon, according to his
Knowlege and Abilities, to confider the Works of
God as his Works ; to refer all the Power, Wifdom,
and Goodnefs in them, to Him, as the fole Fountain
of thefe ; and to dwell upon the Vaftnefs, the Luftre,
the Beauty, the Beneficence, which are obvious to
vulgar as well as philofophic Eyes, till fuch time as
they have raifed Devotion in the Heart. Such Exercifes would greatly affift to overcome that Gloominefs
and Scepticifm, which fometimes hang about our
Conceptions of the invifible World, and by their re-
iterated Impreffions generate the Caufes of Affent.
We have Examples of this in the Old Teftament, particularly in the *Pfalms*; and the Writers do not feem
to have been eminent for any peculiar Depth in curious Inquiries. Men of the ordinary Ranks in Life
in thefe Times have as much probably of the Myfteries of Nature unfolded to them, as great Saints in
antient

antient Times ; fo that they want nothing to enable them to draw the fame Faith and Devotion from the Works of Creation, but the fame earneft Defire to do it.

Thirdly, An upright Heart, and a fincere Endeavour to do our whole Duty, are neceffary to fupport our Faith, after it is generated. While any Sin remains unconquered, while there are any fecret Mifgivings, the Idea of God will be fo uneafy to the Mind, as not to recur frequently ; Men will feek for Refuge in vain Amufements ; and the falfe Hopes of this World will exclude the real ones of another, and make Religion appear like a Dream. This is the Cafe with far the greateft Part of Mankind ; they *live rather by Sight than Faith* ; and are not fufficiently aware, that a *little Leaven leavens the whole Lump*, and that one favourite Purfuit of this World totally eclipfes thofe Glories of the other, that Sight of *the invifible God*, which the *Pure in Heart*, like *Mofes*, are favoured with. The fame Partiality of our Obedience and Devotion is the Caufe, that the Writings of the Old and New Teftaments do not at once convince all, who perufe them, of their Divine Authority, and of the confequent Truth of Revealed Religion. We judge of the Frame of Mens Minds by that of our own, as appears from the Theory of Affociation ; and whatever differs in a great Degree from our own, puts on the Appearance of fomething romantic and incredible. This is evident in the daily Intercourfes of human Life. Corrupt and defigning Men put the falfeft and moft unnatural Conftructions upon the Actions of the Bulk of Mankind, and often deceive themfelves thereby ; and the Bulk of Mankind are quite at a Lofs to conceive and believe the Poffibility of very heroical, generous, pious Actions. And thus profane Men turn into Ridicule Paffages in the Scriptures, which demand the higheft Admiration and Applaufe ; and Men of inferior Degrees of Goodnefs, though they

do

do not affent to this, are a little ftaggered at it. But they who *will do the Will* of God, will foon perceive the *Doctrine* of the Scriptures to be *from him* ; they who will prefs forward to the Perfection of *Mofes, David,* St. *Peter,* or St. *Paul,* will not only acquit them readily of the Charge of Enthufiafm and Impofture, but will alfo fee and feel experimentally fuch unqueftionable Criterions of Truth, fuch a Reality, in their Words and Actions, as will difpel all the Mifts of Scepticifm and Infidelity, with regard either to Natural or Revealed Religion.

It is much to be wifhed, that thefe things were feriouſly weighed, and laid to Heart, by thofe half-pious Perfons, who abſtain from grofs Sins, and *feek, tho' they do not ſtrive, to enter in at the ſtreight Gate, who are not far from the Kingdom of God.* Thefe Perfons might, by a little more Attention to the Word and Works of God in a practical Way, and *caſting away the Sin that does moſt eaſily beſet them,* not only arrive at that *full Aſſurance of Faith,* which is our greateſt Happineſs in this World, and the Earneſt of an eternal Crown hereafter, but alfo *let their Light fo ſhine before Men, as that they, feeing their good Works, would glorify their Father, which is in Heaven.*

Of the Fear of God.

The immediate Confequence of Faith in God, in its imperfect State, is Fear. And though Love does arife alfo, yet it is faint and tranſient for a long time, whereas the Fear is ſtrong and vivid, and recurs generally with every Recollection of the Divine Attributes. The Cauſe of all this is unfolded in thefe Papers. For, Fear being the Offspring of bodily Pain, and this being much more acute than bodily Pleaſure, the Parent of Love, it follows that Fear muſt, in general, be ſtronger than Love in their naſcent State. The auguſt Ideas of infinite Time and Space, of the Glories of Heaven, and the Torments of Hell,

of

of the great Works of the Creation, &c. which accompany the Idea of God, farther contribute to agitate the Mind, and to carry it within the Limits of Pain or Fear. At the same time we see, that these terrifying Ideas, when mixed with those which generate Love, and moderated by frequent Recurrency, and other means, so as to fall back within the Limits of Pleasure, must greatly increase our Love, and other pleasing Affections, exerted towards the Deity. We are to inquire therefore, both how the Fear of God may most effectually be generated, and how it may be converted most speedily into Love and Delight in God. And the Answer will be, that we must make use of the Means before recommended for the Generation and Increase of Faith, *viz.* the Study of the Word and Works of God, and a sincere Endeavour to discharge the Whole of our Duty.

That the last is necessary to keep up the Fear of God, may appear, inasmuch as those who continue to disobey, must, by degrees, fall into Insensibility and Callosity ; the frequent Returns of the Ideas of Guilt and Fear make them sit easier upon the Mind, at the same time that the remaining Uneasiness keeps these Ideas, with all their Associates, out of View, in great measure, as has been mentioned already.

Of Gratitude towards God.

Gratitude or Thankfulness to God arises from the Recollection of Benefits received, just as that to Men. And if we could see and feel practically and perpetually, that God is the sole Spring of all Action, our Gratitude to God would absorb all Kinds and Degrees of it paid to Men. Could we also look with the Eye of Faith into Futurity, and be convinced really, that *Eye hath not seen, nor Ear heard, neither hath it entered into the Heart of Man to conceive, what things God has prepared for such as love him,* that *all things work together for their Good,* Trials and Affli-

ctions

ctions as much, or more than any thing eife, that
every Creature fhall love, and blefs, and praife God
at laft, and every one partake of the Happinefs of
all the reft, whilft yet we all, who are thus Heirs of
an Excefs of Glory, Perfection, and Happinefs, are
Creatures of Yefterday, called forth from nothing by
God's Almighty Word ; if, farther, we confider, that
the Son of God became Flefh, took our Infirmities and
Sorrows, and at laft died for us, God condefcending
thus to recommend and evidence his infinite Love
to us ; our Hearts could not but overflow with fuch
Gratitude, as even to overpower our Faith for a
while.   We fhould then acknowlege, that all we are,
and have, and hope for, are from him ; we fhould
praife him for all the Bleffings paft, prefent, and future, which we receive in our own Perfons, or in
thofe of our Fellow-Creatures ; and defire nothing fo
ardently, as to be admitted into his Prefence, and
the Society of thofe happy Beings, who reft not Day
and Night, faying *Holy, Holy, Holy, Lord God Almighty, which was, and is, and is to come.*

Of Hope and Truft in God, and Refignation to his Will.

Hope and Truft in God differ only in Degree, the
laft being a firmer Hope, and, as it were, an Affurance of the Favour of God to ourfelves in particular ; and that he will provide for all our Wants.
Refignation is the fame Hope and Truft exerted, notwithftanding that prefent Appearances may be contrary thereto : It is the Submiffion of our own Wills
and Judgments to God's, with an intire Confidence in
his Care and Goodnefs.   Let us endeavour to place
this Hope, Truft, and Refignation, upon a fure Foundation, laid in the Word and Works of God.

Firft, then, The Scriptures give the ftrongeft and
plaineft Affurances, that all thofe who love and obey
God here, will be admitted to pure, exalted, and
eternal Happinefs at the Expiration of this Life.   If
therefore

therefore *our Hearts do not condemn us*, we *may have this Confidence in him* ; we may have an intire Hope and Truſt in him, as to the moſt weighty of all Points, our eternal Salvation. And though natural Reaſon could not have diſcovered this ineſtimable Hope to us, though it was not able *to bring Life and Immortality to Light*, Chriſt being the only *ſure and ſtedfaſt Anchor* of that Hope, which reaches *beyond the Veil* of Death ; yet it readily concurs with all the Scripture Declarations of this Kind, and even affords a comfortable Probability of itſelf, after we have once been enlightened by Revelation.

Secondly, the Scriptures, The Voice of Reaſon, and careful Obſervation, all concur to aſſure us, that a ſecret Providence attends upon the Good ; protects and bleſſes them in the Events of the preſent Life, ordinary and extraordinary ; delivers them in great Trials and Afflictions ; and diſpoſes every Incident and Circumſtance in ſuch a manner, as they would wiſh and deſire for themſelves, could they judge aright, and take the Whole of Things into their View. Now the full Perſuaſion of this would be a moſt endearing Motive to Truſt and Confidence in God. For the Things of this Life, however inconſiderable when compared to thoſe of another, do moſt ſenſibly affect even good Men ; and, till they can arrive at a due Indifference to this World, it is highly requiſite, that they ſhould turn their Exceſs of Senſibility into a Motive to Gratitude and Truſt.

Thirdly, The Aſſurance that all our Afflictions are the Chaſtiſements of our heavenly Father, and equally productive of Happineſs with th other Events of our Lives, as mentioned in the laſt Paragraph, enables us to reſign ourſelves. The higheſt Act of this Kind is, for the moſt part, in the Article of Death, when we are ſurrounded with Infirmity, Pain, and Darkneſs, and when all inferior Comforts muſt be given up. Now this Theopathetic Affection of

Reſignation

Refignation, though it is in its firft State painful, and difficult to corrupt Nature; yet in its Progrefs it becomes eafy, and at laft affords the deepeft Peace and Satisfaction. By refigning all, we are delivered from every Anxiety and Difquietude, and enter upon the next Period of our Exiftence, with an Impartiality and Freedom, that qualifies us to enjoy whatever the Order of Providence beftows. And unlefs we were exercifed with fome Trials and Temptations of this Kind, unlefs our Wills were fometimes difappointed, we fhould at laft be fwallowed up by mere Wilful-nefs, and purfue every Object of Defire with an unconquerable Eagernefs and Obftinacy: We fhould alfo idolize ourfelves, as the Authors of our Succefs and Bleffings; or, at the utmoft, fhould look no farther than the Courfe of Nature, and blind unmeaning Fate: Whereas by learning a ready Compliance with the Will of God, however unexpected, we become Partakers of his Happinefs; for his Will can never be difappointed.

Fourthly, Thofe Perfons who believe the Goodnefs of God, according to the Third of the Suppofitions before-mentioned, *i. e.* who believe that he will advance all his Creatures to unlimited Happinefs ultimately, may much more eafily refign themfelves to God, in all refpects, fpiritual as well as temporal, on that Account. But it appears, that very pious Perfons have an intire Refignation without any diftinct Conception or Belief of this Hypothefis. They know and feel, as it were, that God is infinitely good, and that *the Judge of all the Earth muft do right*; and, in this Confidence, they leave the Myfteries of his Providence, his unfearchable Judgments, to be unfolded in his own time, preferving themfelves from Difquietude by an humble religious Scepticifm. But if it fhould pleafe God to difplay the Riches of his Mercy in the full Difcovery and Eftablifhment of the Doctrine of univerfal Reftora-

tion,

tion, in the latter times, which are now approaching, it will become us firſt to receive it with the higheſt Gratitude, and then to uſe it as a Means of accelerating our Progreſs towards the abſolute Reſignation of ourſelves, and all ourFellow-Creatures, into the Hands of God.

Fifthly, As the Conſiderations contained in the Four laſt Paragraphs may contribute to beget Hope, Truſt, and Reſignation in us, ſo all the foregoing Theopathetic Affections, and particularly Gratitude, with all the Means of obtaining them, conſpire to the ſame Purpoſe, as will be eaſily ſeen.

Of the Love of God.

The Love of God may be conſidered as the laſt of the Theopathetic Affections, as before remarked ; for they all end in it, and it is the Sum total of them all. In its firſt Riſe, it muſt, like all the reſt of them, reſemble the ſympathetic one of the ſame Name ; and thus it differs from the reſt in *their* firſt Riſe, and is, as it were, contrary to Fear. In its firſt Riſe it is often tinctured with Fondneſs and Familiarity, and leans much towards Enthuſiaſm ; as, on the other hand, the Fear is often at firſt a ſlaviſh ſuperſtitious Dread. By degrees the Fear and Love qualify each other ; and, by uniting with the other theopathetic Affections, they all together coaleſce into a reverential, humble, filial Love, attended with a Peace, Comfort, and Joy, that paſs all Belief of thoſe who have not experienced it ; ſo that they look upon the Diſcourſes and Writings of thoſe who have, to be either Hypocriſy, or romantic Jargon. The Book of *Pſalms* affords the ſublimeſt and moſt correct Expreſſions of this Kind, and can never be too much ſtudied by thoſe who would cheriſh, purify, and perfect in themſelves a devout Frame of Mind. And this ſingle Circumſtance, excluſive of all other Conſiderations, appears to me a moſt convincing Proof of the Divine Authority of this Book, and confequently of the reft of the Books of the Old and New Teftament. But they have all the fame Evidence in their Favour, in their refpective Degrees ; they are all Helps to beget in us the Love of God, and Tefts whether we have it or no ; and he who *meditates Day and Night in the Law of God,* joining thereto the practical Contemplation of his Works, as prefcribed by the Scriptures, and the *Purification of his Hands and Heart,* will foon arrive at that devout and happy State, which is fignified by the Love of God. I will here add fome practical Confequences refulting from what has been advanced concerning the theopathetic Affections.

Firft, then, Though an Excefs of Paffion of every Kind, fuch as is not under the Command of the voluntary Power, is to be avoided, as dangerous and finful ; yet we muft take care to ferve God with our Affections, as well as our outward Actions ; and indeed, unlefs we do the firft, we fhall not long continue to do the laft, the internal Frame of our Minds being the Source and Spring, from whence our external Actions flow. God, who gives us all our Faculties and Powers, has a Right to all ; and it is a fecret Difloyalty and Infidelity, not to pay the Tribute of our Affections. They are evidently in our Power, immediately or mediately ; and therefore he who goes to his Profeffion, Occupation, or Amufements, with more Delight and Pleafure than to his Exercifes of Devotion, his Reading and Meditation upon divine Subjects, and his Prayers and Praifes, whofe *Soul is not athirft for the living God,* and *the Water of Life,* may affuredly conclude, that he is not arrived at the requifite Degree of Perfection ; that he ftill hankers after *Mammon,* though he may have fome real Defires, and earneft Refolutions, with refpect to God.

Secondly,

Secondly, Though this be true in general, and a Truth of the greateſt practical Importance ; yet there are ſome Seaſons, in which all the theopathetic Affections, and many, in which thoſe of the delightful Kind, are languid, and that even in Perſons that are far advanced in Purity and Perfection. Thus the enthuſiaſtic Raptures, which often take place in the Beginning of a religious Courſe, by introducing an oppoſite State, diſqualify ſome ; a *Judaical* Rigour and Exactitude in long Exerciſes, bodily Diſorders, *&c.* others, from feeling God to be their preſent Joy and Comfort. So that the Fervours of Devotion are by no means in exact Proportion to the Degree of Advancement in Piety ; we can by no means make them a Criterion of our own Progreſs, or that of others. But then they are always ſome Preſumption ; and it is far better, that they ſhould have ſome Mixture even of Enthuſiaſm, than not take place at all. As to thoſe, who are in the dry and dejected State, the Fear of God is, for the moſt part, ſufficiently vivid in them. Let them therefore frequently recollect, that the Fear of God is a Scripture Criterion and Seal of the Elect, as well as Love. Let them conſider, that this Trial muſt be ſubmitted to, as much as any other, till *Patience have her perfect Work* ; that it is more purifying than common Trials; that the State of Fear is far more ſafe, and a much ſtronger Earneſt of Salvation, than premature and ecſtatic Tranſports; and that, if they continue faithful, it will end in Love, probably during this Life, certainly in another. Laſtly, That no feeble-minded Perſon may be left without Comfort, if there be any one who doubts whether he either loves or fears God, finding nothing but Dulneſs, Anxiety, and Scrupuloſity, within him, he muſt be referred to his external Actions, as the ſureſt Criterion of his real Intentions, in this confuſed and diſorderly State of the Affections ; and at the ſame time admonished not to depend upon his external Righteousness, which would breed an endless Scrupulosity, and an Endeavour after an useless Exactitude, but to take Refuge in the Mercy of God through Jesus Christ.

Lastly, The Cultivation of the Love of God in ourselves by the Methods here recommended, and all others that suit our State and Condition, with a prudent Caution to avoid Enthusiasm on one hand, and Superstition on the other, is the principal Means for preserving us from Dejection of every Kind, and freeing us, if we be fallen into it. Worldly Sorrows must by degrees die away, because worldly Desires, their Sources, will. And this Progress will be much accelerated by the Impressions of a contrary Nature, which Gratitude, Hope, Love towards God, will make upon the Mind. As to the Dejection, which relates to another World, it generally ends, as has been frequently remarked already, in the opposite State, being its own Remedy and Cure; but all direct Endeavours after the true and pure Love of God must assist. It is much to be wished, that low-spirited Persons of all Kinds would open themselves without Reserve to religious Friends, and particularly to such as have passed through the same dark and dismal Path themselves, and, distrusting their Judgments, would resign themselves for a time to some Person of approved Experience and Piety. These would be like guardian Angels to them; and as our Natures are so communicative, and susceptible of Infection good and bad, they would by degrees infuse something of their own peaceable, chearful, and devout Spirit into them. But all human Supports and Comforts are to be at last resigned; we must have no *Comforter, no God, but one* ; and happy are they who make haste towards this central Point, in which alone we can *find Rest to our Souls.*

S C H O-

SCHOLIUM.

If we confider the Love of the World, the Fear of God, and the Love of God, in the firft Ratio which they bear to each other, it will appear, that the Love of the World is infinitely greater than the Fear of God, and the Fear infinitely greater than the Love; fo that the Fear of God is a middle Proportional between the Love of the World and the Love of God, in the firft or nafcent Ratio of thefe Affections. In like manner, if we take their laft Ratio, or that in which the Love of the World, and the Fear of God, vanifh into the Love of God, the Love of the World will be infinitely lefs than the Fear of God, and the Fear infinitely lefs than the Love; fo that the Fear of God will ftill be a middle Proportional between the Love of the World and the Love of God. Let us fuppofe the Fear of God to be a middle Proportional between the Love of the World and the Love of God in all the intermediate States of thefe Affections, from their firft Rife in Infancy, till their ultimate Abforption and Evanefcence in the Love of God; and fee how this Suppofition will tally with Experience, and how each Affection varies in refpect of the other two. Call therefore the Love of the World W, the Fear of God F, and the Love of God L. Since then $W : F :: F : L$, $W = \frac{1^2}{L}$. If now F be fuppofed to remain the fame $W :: L$, *i. e.* every Diminution of the Love of the World will increafe the Love of God, and *vice verfa*; fo that, if the Love of the World be nothing, the Love of God will be infinite, alfo infinitely greater than the Fear, *i. e.* we fhall be infinitely happy. If, on the contrary, the Love of the World be greater than the Love of God, the Fear will alfo be greater than it, and our Religion be chiefly Anxiety and Superftition. If, farther, F, fuppofed ftill to remain the fame, be greater than W, it is our trueft trueſt Intereſt to diminiſh W as much as we can, becauſe then the Gain in L is far greater than the Loſs in W. If L remain the ſame, then $W = F^2$; *i. e.* every Increaſe of W will increaſe F alſo, *i. e.* every Increaſe of the Love of the World will increaſe the Fear of God, which therefore, ſince the Love is not increaſed by Suppoſition, muſt incline to a ſuperſtitious Dread : As, on the contrary, if W vaniſhes, F muſt vaniſh alſo ; *i. e.* the Love of the World and Fear being both annihilated, we ſhall receive pure Happineſs, of a finite Degree, from the Love of God. If W remain the ſame, then F^2 : : L ; *i. e.* every Acceſſion made to the Fear of God will be the Cauſe of a greater Acceſſion to the Love, and every Acceſſion to the Love the Cauſe of only a leſs Acceſſion to the Fear ; *i. e.* we ſhall be Gainers upon the Whole by all Motives either to the Fear or Love of God, Loſers by all contrary Motives. For if F be ſuppoſed even infinite, L will be infinito-infinite, *i. e.* will abſorb it infinitely ; and, if F be infiniteſimal, L will be infinito-infiniteſimal ; *i. e.* we ſhall become mere ſelfiſh Worldlings ; which is the Caſe with thoſe practical Atheiſts, who ſucceed in their Endeavours to put God, and a future State, out of their Thoughts, that they may give themſelves up to this World. W now occupies the Place of L, and extinguiſhes both F and it ; *i. e.* Self and the World are their God. Upon the Whole, it follows from this Speculation concerning the Quantities W, F, and L, that W ought to be diminiſhed, and F and L to be increaſed, as much as poſſible, that ſo W may be indefinitely leſs than F, and F indefinitely leſs than L ; *i. e.* we ourſelves indefinitely happy in the Love of God, by the previous Annihilation of Self and the World. And it may not perhaps be quite unuſeful to have repreſented this moſt important of all Concluſions, with the Steps that lead to it, in this new and compendious Light.

P R O P.

PROP. 73.

To deduce practical Rules concerning the Manner of expressing the theopathetic Affections by Prayer, and other religious Exercises.

THERE cannot be a more fatal Delusion, than to suppose, that Religion is nothing but a Divine Philosophy in the Soul; and that the foregoing theopathetic Affections may exist and flourish there, tho' they be not cultivated by devout Exercises and Expressions. Experience, and many plain obvious Reasons, shew the Falshood and mischievous Tendency of this Notion; and the Theory of these Papers may furnish us with other Reasons to the same Purpose, of a deeper and more subtle Nature. It follows from this Theory, that no internal Dispositions can remain long in the Mind, unless they be perpetually nourished by proper Associations, *i. e.* by some external Acts. This therefore may be considered as a strong Argument for frequent Prayer.

But, Secondly, Though God be in himself infinite in Power, Knowlege, Goodness, and Happiness, *i. e.* acquainted with all our Wants, ready and able to supply them, and incapable of Change through our Intreaties and Importunities; yet, as he represents himself to us both in his Word and Works in the Relation of a Father and Governor, our associated Nature compels us, as it were, to apply to him in the same way as we do to earthly Fathers and Governors; and, by thus compelling us, becomes a Reason for so doing. If God's incomprehensible Perfection be supposed to exclude Prayer, it will equally exclude all Thoughts and Discourses concerning him; for these are all equally short and unworthy of him; which is direct Atheism.

I

Thirdly,

Thirdly, Though the Hypothefis of Mechanifm may feem at firft Sight to make Prayer fuperfluous and ufelefs; yet, upon farther Confideration, it will be found quite otherwife. For if all Things be conducted mechanically, *i. e.* by Means; then Prayer may be the Means of procuring what we want. Our Ignorance of the Manner in which Things operate, is not the leaft Evidence againft their having a real Operation. If all be conducted mechanically, fome Means muft be made ufe of for procuring our Wants. The Analogy of all other Things intimates, that thefe Means muft proceed in part from Man. The Analogy taken from the Relations of Father and Governor fuggefts Prayer. It follows therefore, according to the mechanical Hypothefis, that Prayer is one of the principal Means, whereby we may obtain our Defires.

Fourthly, If all thefe Reafons were fet afide, the preffing Nature of fome of our Wants would extort Prayers from us, and therefore juftify them.

Fifthly, In like manner, the theopathetic Affections, if they be fufficiently ftrong, will break forth into Prayers and Praifes, as in the Authors of the *Pfalms*, and other devout Perfons.

Laftly, The Scriptures direct and command us to pray, *to pray always, in every thing to give Thanks*; and fupport the foregoing and fuch-like Reafons for Prayer and Praife. And this removes all Doubt and Scruple, if any fhould remain from the infinite Nature and Majefty of God. We may be fatisfied from the Scriptures, that we have the Privilege to pray, to expofe all our Wants, Defires, Joys, and Griefs, to our Creator; and that he will hear us, and help us.

As to the Time, Manner, and Requifites of Prayer, we may make the following Obfervations.

Firft, That Words are of great Ufe in the moft private Prayer, becaufe of the Affociations transferred upon them, and which therefore they excite in the Mind.

Mind. But then, as there are internal Sentiments and Combinations of thefe, to which no Words can correfpond, we muft not confine the noble Privilege of Prayer and Praife to our Languages, which are the Offspring of the Confufion at *Babel.* There are therefore proper Seafons and Occafions for mental Prayer, for the Tendency and Afpiration of the Heart to God without Words, as well as for vocal Prayer. And indeed all private vocal Prayer feems to admit of and require mental Prayer, at fhort Intervals, in order to fix our Attention, and exalt our Affections, by giving Scope to the fecondarily automatic Workings of a devout Heart.

Secondly, Forms of Prayer, compofed by Perfons of a devout Spirit, are of Ufe to all at certain times, for affifting the Invention, and exciting Fervency; and in the Beginning of a religious Courfe they feem to be neceffary, as they certainly are for Children. But it would be a great Hindrance to the Growth and Perfection of our Devotion, always to keep to Forms. The Heart of every particular Perfon alone knows its own Bitternefs, its Defires, Guilt, Fears, Hopes, and Joys; and it will be impoffible to open ourfelves without Referve, and with a filial Love and Confidence in God, unlefs we do it of ourfelves, in fuch Words as the then prefent State of Mind, when under a vigorous Senfe of the Divine Prefence, fhall fuggeft.

Thirdly, A Regularity as to the Times of private Devotion helps to keep Perfons fteady in a religious Courfe, and to call them off again and again from purfuing and fetting their Hearts upon the Vanities of the World. And we may affirm in particular, that the Morning and Evening Sacrifice of private Prayer and Praife ought never to be difpenfed with, in ordinary Cafes, not even by Perfons far advanced in the Ways of Piety. It feems alfo very confonant to the true Spirit of Devotion, to have fet Hours of Prayer

Prayer in the Courfe of the Day, as Memorials and Means of begetting this Spirit, which, however, cannot be obferved by the Bulk of the World with Exactnefs. Laftly, It will be of great Ufe to accuftom ourfelves to certain Ejaculations upon the various particular Occafions, that occur in the daily Courfe of each Perfon's Bufinefs and Profeffion. It is true indeed, that all thefe Rules are of the Nature of *Judaical* Rites and Ceremonies; but then let it be confidered, that even in Chriftian Countries every Man muft be a *Jew* in Effect, before he can arrive at *Chriftian* Liberty, and be able to worfhip God *in Spirit, and in Truth,* and indeed in order to arrive thither. Times, Forms, and Rules of Devotion, are Schoolmafters that ferve to bring us to Chrift. As for thofe Perfons who are fo far advanced, as to walk with God continually, who fanctify the minuteft Actions by a perpetual Dedication of them to God, I do not prefume to inftruct them. *Their Anointing teaches them all Things.*

Fourthly, The Matter of our Prayers muft be different, according to the State that we are in; for in Prayer we ought always to lay our real Cafe, whatever it be, before God. Confeffion of Sins, and Petition for Graces, are the moft ufeful and requifite for young Penitents, and muft always have a confiderable Share in thofe who are farther advanced. But when the Heart overflows with Joy and Gratitude to God, and tender Love to others, which is more frequently the Cafe with thofe, who have *kept* their *firft Love* for fome time, it is eafy to fee, that Praife and Interceffion muft be moft natural and fuitable. Temporal Wants ought not to be forgotten. We are to acknowlege God in every thing; confider him as our Father, and only Friend, upon all Occafions; place no Confidence in our own Wifdom or Strength, or in the Courfe of Nature; have moderate Defires, and be ready to give up even thefe. Now Prayer, with
exprefs

exprefs Acts of Refignation, in refpect of external Things, has a Tendency to beget in us fuch Difpofitions. However, I do not extend this to fuch Perfons as are refigned to God in all Things, temporal and fpiritual, for themfelves as well as for others, who, defiring nothing but that the Will of God may be done, fee alfo that it is done, acquiefce and rejoice in it.

Fifthly, Prayer muft always be accompanied by Faith; *i. e.* we muft not only look up to God, as our fole Refuge, but as an effectual one. He that believes the Exiftence and Attributes of God really and practically, will have this intire Confidence, fo as to be affured, that the Thing defired of God will be granted, either precifely as defired, or in fome way more fuitable to his Circumftances; an Act of Refignation being here joined to one of Faith. How far our Saviour's Directions, concerning Faith in Prayer, are an Encouragement and Command to expect the precife Thing defired, is very doubtful to me. However, we may certainly learn from his Example, that Refignation is a neceffary Requifite in Prayer; that we ought always to fay, *Neverthelefs not my Will, but thine be done.*

Sixthly, Public Prayer is a neceffary Duty, as well as private. By this we publicly profefs our Obedience to God through Chrift; we excite and are excited by others to Fervency in Devotion, and to Chriftian Benevolence; and we have a Claim to the Promife of Chrift to thofe who are affembled together in his Name. The Chriftian Religion has been kept alive, as one may fay, during the great Corruption and Apoftafy, by the public Worfhip of God in Churches; and it is probable, that religious Affemblies will be much more frequent than they now are, whenever it fhall pleafe God to put it into the Hearts of Chriftians to proceed to the general Converfion of all Nations. We ought therefore to prepare ourfelves for, and

haften

haften unto, this glorious Time, as much as poffible, by joining together in Prayers for this Purpofe; and *fo much the more, as we fee the Day approaching.*

Laftly, Family Prayer, which is fomething between the public Prayers of each Church, and the private ones of each Individual, muft be neceffary, fince thefe are. The fame Reafons are eafily applied. And I believe it may be laid down as a certain Fact, that no Mafter or Miftrefs of a Family can have a true Concern for Religion, or be a Child of God, who does not take care to worfhip God by Family Prayer. Let the Obfervation of the Fact determine.

SECT.

SECT. VIII.

Of the Regard due to the Pleasures and Pains of the Moral Sense in forming the Rule of Life.

PROP. 74.

The Moral Sense ought to be made the immediate Guide of our Actions on all sudden Emergencies; and therefore its Pleasures may be considered as making Part of our primary Pursuit.

IN deducing Rules for social Conduct above, I laid down the Moral Sense as one, which ought to have great Influence in the most explicit and deliberate Actions. Now this is, in some measure, sufficient to prove, that its Pleasures make Part of our primary Pursuit. I here propose to shew, that the Moral Sense ought not only to have some, but the sole Influence, on emergent Occasions; and this will be a farther Recommendation of its Pleasures.

That the Moral Sense is such an immediate Guide, will appear for the following Reasons.

First, Because it offers itself in the various Occurrences of Life, at the same time producing its Credentials. For it warns us beforehand, and calls us to Account afterwards; it condemns or acquits; it rewards by the Pleasures of Self-approbation, or punishes by the Pains of Self-condemnation. It appears therefore with the Authority of a Judge, and also of one who knows the Hearts; and, by Consequence, it claims to be God's Vicegerent, and the Forerunner of the Sentence which we may hereafter expect from him.

Secondly, The Moral Sense is generated chiefly by Piety, Benevolence, and rational Self-interest; all which are explicit Guides of Life in deliberate Actions. Since therefore thefe are excluded on fudden Occafions, through the Want of Time to weigh and determine, it feems highly reafonable to admit the Moral Senfe, which is their Offspring, and whofe Dictates are immediate, for their Subftitute.

Thirdly, The Greatnefs, the Permanency, and the calm Nature of the Pleafures of the Moral Senfe, with the Horrors, and conftant Recurrency, of the Senfe of Guilt, are additional Arguments to fhew, that thefe Pleafures and Pains were intended for the Guides of Life, and the Pleafures for a primary Purfuit.

Fourthly, The mechanical Generation of the Pleafures and Pains of the Moral Senfe may by fome be thought an Objection to the Reafoning here ufed; but it will appear otherwife, upon due Confideration. For all the Things which have evident final Caufes, are plainly brought about by mechanical Means; fo that we may argue either way, *viz.* either from feeing the mechanical Means, to the Exiftence of a final Caufe, not yet difcovered; or from the Exiftence of a final Caufe, to that of the mechanical Means, not yet difcovered. Thus a Perfon who fhould take notice, that Milk always appeared in the Breafts of the Dam at the proper Seafon for the young Animal, might conclude that this was effected mechanically; or, if he firft faw, that Milk muft be brought mechanically into the Breafts, foon after the Birth of the Young, he might conclude, that this Milk would be of fome Ufe; and, from a very little farther Recollection, might perceive that it was for the Nourifhment of the newborn Animal. In like manner, if any one fees, that a Power, like that of Confcience, muft be generated in the human Mind, from the Frame of it, compared

I

with

with the Impreſſions made upon it by external Objeĉts, he may be aſſured, that this Power muſt have ſome Uſe ; and a very little Refleĉtion upon the Divine Attributes, and the Circumſtances of Mankind, will ſhew that its peculiar Uſe muſt be that of a Guide and Governor.

If we could ſuppoſe the Moral Senſe to be either an Inſtinĉt impreſſed by God, or the neceſſary Reſult of the eternal Reaſons and Relations of Things, in-dependent of Aſſociation, it ought ſtill to be conſidered as a Guide of Life. For ſince the Favourers of each of theſe Suppoſitions maintain, that the Moral Senſe is intirely coincident with the Precepts of Benevolence and Piety ; it muſt, according to them, be made their Subſtitute upon emergent Occaſions.

P R O P. 75.

To deduce praĉtical Rules for the Regulation and Improvement of the Moral Senſe.

THERE are Three Things principally neceſſary in the Conduĉt of the Moral Senſe. Firſt, That it extend to all the Aĉtions of Moment, which occur in the Intercourſes of human Life ; and be a ready Monitor to us on ſuch Occaſions. Secondly, That it ſhould not deſcend to minute and trifling Particulars ; for then it would check Benevolence, and turn the Love of God into a ſuperſtitious Fear. And, Thirdly, That its Informations be in all Caſes agreeable to Pie-ty and Benevolence, whoſe Subſtitute it is.

Now it will be eaſily ſeen, that, for the right Con-duĉt of our Moral Senſe in all theſe Particulars, it will be neceſſary for us to be much employed in the praĉtical Study of the Scriptures, and of the Writings of good Men of all Denominations, in obſerving the living Examples of ſuch, in calling ourſelves to Ac-count frequently, in Prayer, and other Exerciſes of

Devotion,

Devotion, in endeavouring to convert all the fympathetic and theopathetic Affections into the Love of
God, in aiming at a truly catholic and charitable Spirit, and in walking faithfully, according to the Dictates
of Benevolence, Piety, and the Moral Senfe, fuch as
they are at prefent. For *to him that hath fhall be
given, and he fhall have Abundance.* Some of thefe
Directions are more particularly fuited to correct one
Defect in the Moral Senfe, fome another; but they
will all confpire in purifying and perfecting it.

General COROLLARIES *to the laſt Seven*
SECTIONS.

COR. I. WE may now, by reviewing·the Seven
laſt Sections, judge how much the
Chriſtian Morality is ſuperior to the Pagan, in Sublimity and Purity. The Pagan Morality was comprehended under the Four Cardinal Virtues of Prudence,
Juſtice, Fortitude, and Temperance; and theſe were
ſo explained and underſtood by the Pagans, as to omit
many neceſſary Chriſtian Virtues, and allow. or even
recommend, ſome great Enormities. I will claſs a
few Particulars of this Kind under the reſpective Heads
of Senſation, Imagination, Ambition, Self-intereſt,
Sympathy, Theopathy, and the Moral Senſe.

The Pagan. Virtue of Temperance prohibited all
groſs Exceſſes in Eating and Drinking, and many Acts
of Lewdneſs. But it fell far ſhort of the Chriſtian
Precepts, in regard to the external Actions; and ſeems
no-ways to have extended to the Regulation of the
Thoughts.

The Pagan Fortitude injoined great Patience and
Perſeverance in Difficulties, Pains, and Dangers. But
it was, in part, founded in Pride; and ſo was oppo
ſite to the Chriſtian Fortitude, whoſe Strength lies in
its Weakneſs, in a Diffidence in ourſelves, and Confidence in God. And how much the Chriſtian was ſuperior in Degree, as well as Kind, may appear from
the Examples of the Martyrs and Confeſſors in the
primitive times, who were of all Ranks, Profeſſions,
Ages, and Sexes, and of innumerable private Perſons
in the preſent, as well as all paſt Ages of the Church,
who are able to *rejoice in Tribulation*, and to do all
Things, through Chriſt that ſtrengtheneth them.
They do not make a Shew of themſelves to the
World; that would be Oſtentation, and Vain-glory:

But thofe who defire to be animated by, and to imitate, fuch living Examples, may find them in every Chriftian Country in the World.

As to the Pleafures of Imagination, there feems to have been no Reftraint laid upon them by the Pagan Morality. Curiofity, and the Study of the Arts and Sciences for their own fakes, were even recommended.

Ambition was, in like manner, efteemed virtuous; and many Kinds and Degrees of Humility were treated with Reproach and Contempt.

Grofs Self-intereft was allowed in a much greater Degree by the Pagans, than it is amongft Chriftians. The Pagans fcarce knew what refined Self-intereft was; and they did not at all apprehend, that any Objection lay againft rational Self-intereft, or that a purer Motive to Action was neceffary.

Their Benevolence was chiefly a Love of Relations, Benefactors, and their Country. They fell far fhort of univerfal unlimited Benevolence, equal to Self-love; and they allowed, and even recommended, taking Vengeance on Enemies, as an heroic, noble Action.

As to the theopathetic Affections of Faith, Fear, Gratitude, Hope, Truft, Refignation, and Love, with the Expreffions of thefe in Prayer and Praife, they knew nothing of them in general. Polytheifm, and impure Notions of their Deities, had quite depraved and ftarved all their theopathetic Affections. They were deftitute of Love, and their Fear was Superftition.

Laftly, The Confequence of all this muft be, and accordingly was, a proportional Imperfection in the Moral Senfe. It was deficient in moft Things, erroneous in many, and needlefly fcrupulous in fome. It occupied the Place of the Deity; for the beft amongft the Pagans idolized the innate Senfe of *Honefty*, and the independent Power of the Mind, the *Senfus Honefti*, and the τὸ ἐφ' ἡμῖν.

I

I do not deny but that fome Heathen Moralifts may now-and-then have exprefled themfelves in a manner fuperior to what I have here defcribed. But I fpeak of the general Tenor of their Writings, and defire that may be compared with the general Tenor of the Scriptures, of the Fathers, and of the Chriftian Divines of all Ages.

Cor. 2. By a like Review of the Seven laft Sections, we may difcern more clearly and fully the relative Nature of the Virtues and Vices, which has been already taken notice of; and thus both learn to be more candid and charitable in our Judgments on the Actions of others, and more earneft and unwearied after Perfection in ourfelves.

Cor. 3. Since it now appears fully, that the Pleafures and Pains of the Four firft Claffes are to be fubjected to thofe of the Three laft, *i. e.* the Pleafures of thofe foregone, and the Pains accepted; whereas the Pleafures of thefe are to be chofen, and the Pains avoided; I will here give, in one View, fome principal Motives to engage us thus to regulate our Affections and Actions.

Firft, then, The great Compofure and Peace of Mind, which thofe Perfons enjoy, who make Benevolence, Piety, and the Moral Senfe, the Rule of their Lives, is a ftrong Inducement to us to imitate their Example. As we defire to learn all other Arts from thofe who practife them in the greateft Perfection, fo ought we the Art of Living. The Perfons in whom this Peace is moft obfervable, were the Authors of the Books of the Old and New Teftaments; and thefe Books may be diftinguifhed from all other Books by this remarkable Circumftance, that the Authors appear to have been quite free from that Diffatisfaction, Doubt, Care, and Fear, which are fo obvious in the Difcourfes and Writings of other Perfons. However, the fame Thing appears, in a lefs Degree, in the Difcourfes of all good Men, even Heathens; as

Z 4 in

in the Difcourfes of *Socrates* preferved by *Plato* and *Xenophon*; and may be obferved in the Conduct and Behaviour of all fuch, by thofe who are converfant with them. Eminently pious and benevolent Perfons feem to be in Poffeffion of fome great Secret, fome *Catholicon*, or Philofophers Stone. They pafs through Life unhurt, as to the Peace of their Minds, by the Evils of it; and find abundant Matter for Praife and Thankfgiving to God in it. All which appears to be owing to their being guided by the true Principle of Action.

Secondly, Death is certain, and neceffarily attended with many terrifying Affociations; and a future State muft, even upon the flighteft Prefumption of its Reality, be a Matter of the greateft Concern to all thinking Perfons. Now the frequent Recurrency of thefe Fears and Anxieties muft embitter all guilty Pleafures, and even the more innocent trifling Amufements; which, though not glaringly oppofite to Duty, are yet befides it, and foreign to it. And thus Men live in Bondage all their Lives through the Fear of Death; more fo than they are aware of themfelves (for Men often neglect the fair Examination of themfelves, fo much as not to know their real State, though obvious enough upon a due Inquiry); and ftill much more fo, than they own and exprefs to others. But nothing can deliver Men from this great Evil, befides intire Rectitude of Heart. While there is a Confcioufnefs of any wilful Failure, of any Unfairnefs, of Prevarication with God, or a Defire and Defign to deceive one's felf, the Terrors of Religion rage with greater Fury than in a State of utter Negligence, and Difregard to Duty. A Man cannot reft, while he is double-minded, while he ftrives and hopes to ferve God and *Mammon* together; but muft either go forward in order to obtain true lafting Peace, or backward to infatuate and ftupefy himfelf. And this
helps

helps us to account for the foregoing Obſervation on
the Behaviour of truly good Men.

Thirdly, It appears from the very Frame of our
Natures, that we are not qualified for any great Degrees of Happineſs here, nor for an uninterrupted
Continuance of any Degree, nor for the frequent Returns of any particular Pleaſure, bodily or mental.
From all which it will follow, that a general Hope,
mixed with the Cares, Fears, and Sorrows of Compaſſion and Contrition, is the only Pleaſure, that is
attainable, laſting, or ſuitable to our preſent Circumſtances.

Fourthly, Beſides the Fears relating to Death, and
a future State, all Perſons who ſerve the World, muſt
have very great ones in reſpect of the Things of the
World. A Man muſt be *crucified to the World*, before his Heart can be at Eaſe concerning its Pleaſures,
Honours, and Profits. And as our Pains are, in
general, more exquiſite than our Pleaſures; ſo is
Fear, worldly Fear, the Offspring of the Firſt, greater
in Degree, than worldly Hope, the Offspring of the
Laſt; and, if it recurs often, will overbalance it; and
muſt make a great Deduction, upon all Suppoſitions.
Now Devotion to God, though it does leſſen the
Hopes of this World, as well as the Fears; yet it
ſeems to leſſen the Fears in a much quicker Ratio;
however, it certainly takes off their Edge, and leaves
ſo much Hope and Pleaſure, as to be a Foundation
for the Duty of Thankfulneſs to God.

Fifthly, An upright Heart is neceſſary to our having a real influencing Senſe and Conviction of the
Divine Amiableneſs and Benevolence, and, conſequently, to our Peace and Comfort. When any Dread, or
ſlaviſh Fear, attends the Conception of the Divine
Nature, a Man can never think himſelf ſafe; but will
always have Anxieties and Miſgivings. And our
Ideas of God muſt always be thus tainted with Superſtition, whatever our Theory be, if our Hearts be

not right before him. We fhall weakly and wickedly fuppofe and fear, that he *is fuch a one as we ourfelves are*, whatever Declarations we make, whatever Demonftrations we poffefs, to the contrary. And as this cannot but caft a Gloom upon the whole Courfe of Nature to the Wicked, fo the contrary Perfuafion is the principal Source of Joy and Comfort to the Good. They do in earneft believe God to be their Friend and Father; they love him with a fincere, though imperfect Love; and are eafily led, from the Confcioufnefs and inward Feeling of this, to confider him as pure and infinite Love. And all thefe Four laft Obfervations, put together, but efpecially that of this Paragraph, account for the Facts mentioned in the Firft.

SECT.

SECT. IX.

Of the Rule of Faith.

PROP. 76.

To inquire what Faith in Natural and Revealed Religion, or in the particular Tenets of Christian Churches, is necessary for the Purification and Perfection of our Natures.

HAving now shewn, that Benevolence, Piety, and the Moral Sense, are to be the Guides of Life, and the Compass by which we are to steer our Course through the Difficulties and Dangers of this mixed, imperfect State, it remains that we inquire, whether there be any Rule of Faith, resulting or distinct from the foregoing Rule of Life, that is necessary to our present Duty, or future Salvation.

First, then, Since Piety is Part of the foregoing Rule of Life, it is evident, that no one can comply with this Rule, unless he be a sincere Deist at least, *i. e.* unless he believe the Existence and Attributes of God, his Providence, a future State, and the Rewards and Punishments of it.

Secondly, The Evidence for the Christian Religion seems to be so clear and strong in all Christian Countries, and that with respect to all Ranks and Conditions of Men, that no Person, who is previously qualified by Benevolence, Piety, and the Moral Sense, in the manner described in the Seven last Sections, can refuse his Assent to it. This I take to be a plain Matter of Observation, supported by the universal Testimony of those Persons, that attend to it; meaning, by the Christian Religion, the Belief of the divine Mission of *Moses* and the Prophets, of Christ

and

and his Apostles, or the Truth of the Scriptures. Whoever therefore conducts himself by the foregoing Rule, must believe Revealed Religion, as well as Natural, if born in a Christian Country. All Unbelievers, where there is so much Evidence, I had almost said all Doubters, seem to be culpable in a very high Degree.

Thirdly, As Faith in Christ is the Result of a right Disposition of Mind in Christian Countries ; so is this right Disposition, in its Turn, the Result of believing in Christ ; and they increase one another reciprocally without Limits. And though some Persons in the Heathen World were conducted to great Degrees of Benevolence, and Uprightness of Mind, and even to some Degrees of Piety ; yet were these Persons exceedingly rare, and the Degrees far inferior to what is ordinarily to be found in Christian Countries. This therefore is a strong Proof of the Necessity of Faith in Revealed Religion. All Things else being alike, the Person who believes in Christ will become superior to him who does not, in proportion to the Vigour of his Faith. Which is also a plain and cogent Reason, why those, that are already Christians, should labour to the utmost of their Abilities in converting the barbarous Nations, even though their present Ignorance of Revealed Religion be excusable in them. But there is far more Reason to alarm and awaken, if possible, those who disbelieve in the midst of Light and Evidence, *the lost Sheep of the House of Israel*; since they not only want these Motives and Assistances to Perfection, but are guilty of great Prevarication and Unfairness with themselves, and shut their Eyes against *the Light, because their Deeds are evil.* If any Unbeliever thinks this Censure too severe, let him examine his own Heart. Is he previously qualified by Love to God, and to all the World, by a sincere Regard for, and Observance of, Natural Religion ? Is he chaste, temperate, meek,
humble,

humble, juft, and charitable? Does he delight in God,
in contemplating his Providence, praying to him,
and praifing him? Does he believe a future State,
and expect it with Hope and Comfort? Is he not fo
fond of the Praife of Men, or fo fearful of Cenfure
and Ridicule, as to be afhamed to own Chrift? If
the Chriftian Religion be true, it muft be of great
Importance; and, if of great Importance, it is a
Duty of Natural Religion to inquire into it. The
Obligation therefore to examine ferioufly fubfifts in
fome Degree, as long as there is any Evidence for,
any Doubt of, the Truth of Revelation. For, if true,
it muft be of Importance, whether we fee that Importance or not. He who determines, that it is of
no Importance, determines at once, that it is falfe.
But it is too evident to all impartial Obfervers, that
thofe who difbelieve, or affect to difbelieve, have not
made a ferious accurate Inquiry; fuch a one as they
would make about a worldly Concern of Moment;
but content themfelves, and endeavour to perplex
others, with general Objections, mixed, for the moft
part, with Ridicule and Raillery, things that are manifeft Hindrances in the Search after Truth. However, this may be perhaps, too fevere a Cenfure, in
refpect of fome; nay, we ought not to condemn
any, but to confider, that *to their own Mafter they
ftand or fall.*

Fourthly, A nominal, or even a real, but merely
hiftorical and fpeculative Faith, is quite infufficient,
and falls infinitely fhort of that which the foregoing
Rule of Duty requires. And yet it is of fome probable Ufe to be reckoned among the Number of Believers, though a Man be, for the prefent, inatten-
tive; becaufe fuch a one lies more in the way of
Conviction and Influence; and is free from that great
Objection and Difficulty to human Nature, a Reluctance to change even a nominal Opinion. As to the
Perfon, who has a real, hiftorical, fpeculative Faith,

i. e.

i. e. who fees that the Old and New Teftaments have the fame and in many refpects greater Evidences for their Truth and Genuinenefs, than other Books univerfally allowed, who is ready to acknowlege this, and to give Reafons for it of the fame kind with thofe that are admitted in fimilar Cafes, he poffeffes one of the principal Requifites for generating the true, practical, internal Faith, *that overcomes the World*; and if he be not with-held by Pride and Self-conceit, fo as to reft in this hiftorical Faith, as fufficient of itfelf, will make much quicker Advances, *cæteris paribus*, towards the true living Faith, than a Perfon deftitute of the hiftorical one. For the true living Faith is that vivid Senfe and Perception of God, our Saviour, a future State, and the other related Ideas, that make them appear at once as Realities, and become powerful and inftantaneous Motives to Action. But it is very evident, that an hiftorical Faith muft, by impreffing and uniting thefe Ideas during the time that they are confidered, and reflected upon, produce the Effects, the Reality, above-defcribed, in the fame manner as the interefted Love of God does at laft generate the pure difinterefted Love. And the Calamities and Sorrows of human Life will be much more likely to ftrike him who is poffeffed of an hiftorical Faith, than a Perfon ignorant of the Subject.

It muft, however, be acknowleged, that the real practical Faith is by no means in exact Proportion to the hiftorical. Perfons of good Difpofitions, of humble Minds, who *pray without ceafing*, who have been much afflicted, *&c.* have Impreffions of the religious Kind excited in them with more Vigour and Facility than others. Yet ftill no Man can have the practical Faith without fome Degree of the hiftorical; and thofe who have little of the hiftorical are liable to be fhaken, to *be turned about by every Wind of Doctrine*, and to be carried into Extravagancies

cies by the Zeal without Knowlege. *What God hath joined together, let no Man put afunder.* It is the Duty of every Man, whether he have the practical Faith or not, to inquire, to read the Scriptures, and to meditate thereon; the neceffary Confequence of which is an Increafe of the hiftorical Faith. It is alfo the Duty of every Chriftian to give a Reafon for his Faith, to preach the Gofpel (for true Chriftians are a Nation of Priefts in this Senfe); which cannot be done without fome Knowlege of the hiftorical Evidences. Admitting therefore, that mere internal Faith (if fuch a thing be poffible) did fuffice to all other Purpofes, it will, however, be defective in this one moft neceffary Duty of the Chriftian Life. Though a mere good Example will do much Good, yet the fame good Example, accompanied with Knowlege, and a rational Faith, will do more.

Fifthly, It feems intirely ufelefs to all good Purpofes, to the Promotion of Piety and Benevolence, in the prefent State of Things, to form any Creeds, Articles, or Syftems of Faith, and to require an Affent to thefe in Words or Writing. Men are to be influenced, even in refpect of the principal Doctrines of God's Providence, a future State, and the Truth of the Scriptures, by rational Methods only, not by Compulfion. This feems acknowleged on all hands. Why then fhould harfher Methods be ufed in things of confeffedly lefs Importance? It is true, that Magiftrates have a Power from God to inflict Punifhment upon fuch as difobey, and to confine the natural Liberty of acting within certain Bounds, for the common Good of their Subjects. But all this is of a Nature very foreign to the Pretences for confining Opinions by Difcouragements and Punifhments.

Thofe who believe neither Natural nor Revealed Religion practically, will be held by no Reftraints; they will appear to confent to any thing, juft as

their

their Intereſt leads them. And this is the Caſe of a great Part of the Subſcribers in all Chriſtian Communities. They have a mere nominal Faith only, at the time of ſubſcribing, not even a ſpeculative or hiſtorical one : Or if they have any Degree of Seriouſneſs, and good Impreſſions, they muſt do proportional Violence to theſe by performing a religious Act out of a mere intereſted View.

If the Perſon be an earneſt Believer of Natural Religion, but an Unbeliever in reſpect of Revealed (to ſuppoſe this poſſible for Argument's ſake), he will not attempt any Office in the Chriſtian Miniſtry. However, he ought not to be deprived of *civil* Privileges, whilſt ſo many wicked nominal Chriſtians are ſuffered to enjoy them.

Suppoſe the Perſon required to ſubſcribe to be a ſpeculative hiſtorical Believer, why ſhould his future Inquiries be confined ? How can he inquire honeſtly, if they be ? How can a Perſon be properly qualified to ſtudy the Word of God, and to ſearch out its Meaning, who finds himſelf previouſly confined to interpret it in a particular Manner ? If the Subject-matter of the Article be of great Importance to be underſtood and believed, one may preſume, that it is plain, and needs no Article ; if of ſmall Importance, why ſhould it be made a Teſt, or infiſted upon ? If it be a difficult, abſtruſe Point, no one upon Earth has Authority to make an Article concerning it. We are all Brethren ; there is no Father, no Maſter, amongſt us ; we are Helpers of, not Lords over, each other's Faith. If we judge from other Branches of Learning, as Natural Philoſophy, or Phyſic, we ſhall there find, that the pure Evidence of the Things themſelves is ſufficient to overcome all Oppoſition, after a due time. The Doctrines of Gravitation, of the different Refrangibility of the Rays of Light, of the Circulation of the Blood, &c. can never be believed to any uſeful practical Purpoſe, till
they

they be examined and underſtood ; and thoſe, who now believe them, affirm, that this is all that is ne-ceſſary for their univerſal Reception. If they ſhould be miſtaken in this, free Examination would be ſo much the more requiſite.

The Apoſtles Creed is ſo plain and clear, except in the Three Articles concerning the Deſcent of Chriſt into Hell, the holy Catholic Church, and the Com-munion of Saints, that no one who believes the Truth of the Scriptures, can heſitate about it ; not even how to interpret the Three forementioned Ar-ticles, in a Senſe agreeable to the Scriptures. It is quite uſeleſs therefore to require an Aſſent even to theſe Articles. As to the metaphyſical Subtleties, which appear in the ſubſequent Creeds, they can at beſt be only human Interpretations of Scripture Words ; and therefore can have no Authority. Words refer to Words, and to grammatical and lo-gical Analogies, in an endleſs Manner, in theſe Things ; and all the real Foundation which we have is in the Words of Scripture, and of the moſt antient Writers, conſidered as Helps, not Authorities. It is ſufficient therefore, that a Man take the Scriptures for his Guide, and apply himſelf to them with an honeſt Heart, and humble and earneſt Prayer ; which things have no Connexion with Forms and Subſcriptions.

Nay, it ſeems needleſs, or enſnaring, to ſubſcribe even to the Scriptures themſelves. If to any parti-cular Canon, Copy, &c. enſnaring, becauſe of the many real Doubts in theſe things. If not, it is quite ſuperfluous from the Latitude allowed. Yet ſtill it appears to me inconteſtable, that no careful impartial Inquirer can doubt of the great Truths of the Scrip-tures, ſuch as the miraculous Birth, Life, Death, Reſurrection, and Aſcenſion of Chriſt, &c. or of the practical Conſequences thence ariſing ; and ſurely it cannot be neceſſarily requiſite, that a Man ſhould be-lieve more than theſe.

For, Laftly, Let us fuppofe the Perfon required to affent, or fubfcribe, to be a real earneft Believer. It can fcarce be fuppofed, that fuch a Perfon fhould affent to any Set of Articles, fo as honeftly to affirm, that he would choofe to exprefs his own Senfe of the Scripture Language in thefe Words. To ftrain either the Scriptures, or the Articles, muft be a very ungrateful Tafk to an ingenuous Man ; and perhaps there may be fo wide a Difference in fome Inftances in his Opinion, that no Straining can bring them together. And thus fome of the moft earneft Believers are excluded from the Chriftian Miniftry, and from certain common Privileges of Society, by a Method, which fuffers nominal wicked Chriftians to pafs without Difficulty.

If it be objected, that, unlefs Preachers fubfcribe, they may teach different Doctrines ; I anfwer, that they do this, though they do fubfcribe ; and that in the moft important practical Points. If the Scriptures cannot yet produce a true Unity of Opinion on account of our prefent Ignorance, and the Weaknefs and Wickednefs of our Natures, how fhould Articles do this ? Men can put as different Senfes upon Articles, as upon Texts, and fo difpute without End. Which evidently appears to have been the Cafe in the primitive Church. Every Decifion, as foon as fettled, became the Source of a new Divifion between Perfons, who yet ftill agreed to the foregoing Decifion in Words ; till at laft the whole Efficacy and Spirit of Chriftianity was loft in mere verbal Difputes. But the beft Anfwer is, That Preachers ought intirely to confine themfelves to practical Subjects, the Defcriptions of the Virtues and Vices, with the Motives for and againft each, the Directions to attain the Virtues, and avoid the Vices ; and this in all the various real Circumftances of human Life. Learned Inquiries have their Ufe undoubtedly ; but they are much better communicated

cated to the learned World by the Prefs, than to a mixed Affembly by the Pulpit. It is a kind of Sacrilege to rob God's Flock of the Nourifhment due to them from public Preachings, and, in its ftead, to run out upon Queftions, that minifter no Profit to the Hearers, at leaft to far the greateft Part.

As to the Prefs, fince all other Men have the Liberty of conveying their Thoughts to the Public that way, it is furely unfitting, that the Minifters of the Gofpel fhould be deprived of it. And, indeed, to lay any Reftraints, looks like diftrufting the Caufe. There is undoubtedly a very bad Ufe made of the Prefs, and *Wo to thofe by whom Offences come* to the Little-ones that believe in Chrift! But it is to be hoped and prefumed, that the Power of the Wicked to do Harm is not equal to the Power of the Good to do Good, in this or any other fuch neutral Method of communicating Infection good and bad to the Public. This would be to prefer Barbarity and Ignorance to the Inftruction and Civilization of Mankind. Learning, Arts, and Improvements of all Kinds, are fubfervient both to good and bad Purpofes; and yet ftill the Balance is probably on the Side of Good upon the Whole, fince God is all-powerful, all-wife, and all-good. Thefe Attributes muft ever turn the Scale to their own Side, finitely in every finite Portion of Time, infinitely in infinite Time. We need not fear therefore, but that true Knowlege will at laft be increafed and prevail, that the Wife and Good will underftand, the Wicked be filenced and converted, and the Church of Chrift fill the whole Earth. It is a great Infult offered to the Truths of Religion, to fuppofe that they want the fame kind of Affiftance as Impoftures, human Projects, or worldly Defigns. Let every Man be allowed to think, fpeak, and write, freely; and then the Errors will combat one another, and leave Truth unhurt.

A a 2　　　　　　　Sixthly.

Sixthly, Though Creeds, Articles, *&c.* feem to have no Ufe now, but even to be prejudicial to the Caufe of Truth in themfelves; yet it may be neceffary to fubmit to fome Forms of this Kind in certain Cafes; at leaft, it no-ways becomes a Chriftian to declaim againft them in violent Terms, or oppofe them with Bitternefs, but merely, in a plain difpaffionate Way, to reprefent the Truth of the Cafe, fo as by degrees to draw Mens Zeal from thefe leffer Matters, and transfer it upon greater. *Let not him that eateth, defpife him that eateth not; and let not him which eateth not, judge him that eateth.* There may be good relative Reafons in both Cafes. And it may be, and probably is the Truth, that in the early Ages of the Church, whilft Chriftians were Judaizers, entangled in Externals, grofs in their Conceptions, *&c.* thefe Forms were neceffary, *cæteris manentibus.* But now they grow old, and feem ready to die away, and to give place to the Worfhip of God *in Spirit, and in Truth*; in which there is no *Papift, Proteftant, Lutheran, Calvinift, Trinitarian, Unitarian, Myftic, Methodift,* &c. but all thefe Diftinctions are carried away like the Chaff of the Summer Threfhing-floors. We are all Chriftians, we received this Denomination in Apoftolic Times, and ought to feek no other. Only let us take care to depart from Iniquity, to have the true Seal of God in our Foreheads, not the Mark of the Beaft. The real Converfion of the Heart from the idolatrous Worfhip of Pleafure, Honour, and Profit, of Senfation, Imagination, Ambition, and Self-intereft, to ferve the living God, is the only Thing of Importance; *Circumcifion and Uncircumcifion are equally nothing. Let every Man abide in the fame Calling wherein he was called.* Only, where a plain Act of Infincerity is required, this approaches to the Cafe of eating in the Idol's Temple, and gives great Offence to others.

4

Seventhly,

Seventhly, If we examine the Doctrines which are chiefly contested among Christians by the opposite Parties, it will appear, that the Disputes are, in great measure, verbal, and proceed from Mens not knowing the true Nature and Use of Words. Thus, if we consider the Doctrine of Infallibility, the Nature of Words shews at once, that this could be of no Use, since the Decisions of the infallible Judge must be expressed in Words, and consequently be liable to be misunderstood by some or other of the Readers, for the same Reasons as the Scriptures are.—To say that Christ's Body and Blood are in the Bread and Wine so as that the sensible Qualities of one become the sensible Qualities of the other, would be to appeal to the Senses for Assent, where they instantly reject the Proposition. To say that Christ's mystical or glorified Body is present in some way or other, is what no one can deny, because nothing is really affirmed. The Words seem to coalesce into a verbal Truth; but, when we attempt to realize the Proposition, it vanishes. The Scripture Expressions concerning the mystical Body of Christ, and his Union with the Church, contain within them some most important and wonderful Truths undoubtedly; but they are yet sealed up from us.—In the Disputes concerning the Trinity, and Incarnation of Christ, if the Words *Person, Substance, Nature,* &c. be used as in other Cases, or any way defined, the most express Contradictions follow : Yet the Language of the Scriptures is most difficult, sublime, and mysterious, in respect of the Person of Christ ; so that one cannot fall short of paying all that Honour to Christ, which the most Orthodox believe to be required.—As to the Doctrine of the Satisfaction of Christ, it appears that he has done all for us that one Being can do for another ; and that it would be a most unjustifiable and narrow Way of expressing ourselves, to confine the Benefits received from Christ to that of mere Example. But the firſt and moſt literal Senſe of the Words *Sacrifice*, *Redemption*, &c. when realized, is evidently impoſſible ; and we do not ſeem to be able to give any better general Senſe to theſe Words, than by ſaying, that they ſignify, that the Sufferings of one Being are, by the Order of God, made the Means of Happineſs to another. To adopt the Ideas of *Debt*, *Wrath of God*, &c. in a ſtrict Senſe, is Anthropomorphitiſm. —— The Introduction of new, unſcriptural, technical Terms ſeems ſcarce juſtifiable, unleſs as far as one Chriſtian Brother may thereby endeavour to make the Harmony and Analogy of the Scripture Language to itſelf, and to the Courſe of Nature, more evident to another. But this is all *private Interpretation*. And it often happens in theſe Caſes, that an Hypotheſis is taken up haſtily, in order to reconcile the Scripture to itſelf, like thoſe philoſophical ones, which are not drawn from a Number of concurring Facts, but merely accommodated to a few particular Appearances.

C H A P.

CHAP. IV.

Of the Expectations of Mankind, here and hereafter, in Consequence of their Observance or Violation of the Rule of Life.

SECT. I.

Of the Expectations of Individuals in the present Life.

PROP. 77.

It is probable, that most or all Men receive more Happiness than Misery in their Passage thro the present Life.

SOME Evidences for this Proposition have been given above, where it was alleged as one of the Proofs of the Goodness of God. Here we may consider it, both as deducible from those Evidences, and from the Goodness of God, previously established upon independent Principles.

For if we suppose God to be both infinitely benevolent, and the sole Cause of all Things; if, farther, the relative Appellations of Governor, Friend, and

Father,

Father, may with Propriety be made the Foundation of our Inquiries into his Difpenfations in general (all which I have endeavoured to prove above); we can fcarce fuppofe, but that the remarkable Period of our Exiftence, which commences at our Birth, and ends with the Death of the Body, which we then brought into the World with us, will, upon the Whole, afford us more Pleafure than Pain. This is, at leaft, our firft and moft natural Prefumption, in the View of Things here confidered. However, it muft always be remembred, that we are not proper Judges of fuch high Speculations; and that an Over-balance of Mifery in this Life, or any other, is perfectly confiftent with the infinite Goodnefs of God, even according to our Ways of Reafoning, upon Suppofition that all his Creatures become happy upon the Whole at laft, finitely or infinitely.

I choofe therefore to reft this Propofition chiefly upon certain Intimations, and indirect Evidences thereof, which are fcattered up and down in the Scriptures. Such are the Blefling of God conferred upon *all* his Creatures at their Creation, his Covenant with them *all* at the Flood, the Precepts to *all* to praife him, the Mention of his being *loving to every Man*, *of remembring Mercy in Judgment*, not being *extreme to mark what is done amifs*, &c. Thefe are no direct Proofs of the Propofition here advanced; but they leave fuch Impreffions of Love and Mercy upon the Mind, and feem intended to put us into fuch a Way of Thinking and Reafoning, as lead to it. They afford therefore fome Prefumption in its Favour, fince nothing contrary thereto is to be found any-where either in the Word or Works of God.

The Murmurings, and bitter Outcries, of Men in a State of Suffering, are no more an Evidence againft this Propofition, than the extravagant Mirth, and chimerical Hopes, of unexperienced Perfons, during

Health

Health and Prosperity, are for it. Neither of these take in the Whole of the Case.

PROP. 78.

The Balance cannot be much in Favour even of the most happy, during the present Life.

FOR, First, This is agreeable to the general Experience of Mankind. It is obvious, that Life is chequered with Good and Evil in such Degrees and Varieties, as that the First cannot prevail much. Agreeably to this, the Experienced and Dispassionate, in reviewing their past Life, will at least affirm, that the Happiness has not greatly exceeded the Misery. And indeed the Difficulty of proving the foregoing Proposition is a very sufficient Evidence for this.

Secondly, The disorderly State of the external World, and the Imperfection of our Bodies, with their Tendency to Corruption, do not permit, that Happiness should much exceed Misery in the present Life; and may be considered as the efficient instrumental Cause of this. Bodily Pain must in many Cases be impressed upon us by external Objects; both this, and bodily Pleasure, lay the Foundation for intellectual Pains, and for irregular Passions, which lead back again to Pain, bodily and mental; our Bodies must return to Dust, and every manifest Approach thereto must be attended with Suffering; and the unknown internal Structure of the Brain, the great Instrument of Sense and Thought, is such, as subjects us, from innumerable secret unavoidable Causes, to pass into the Limits of Pain. All which is only saying in other Words, that we are fallen Creatures.

Thirdly, In our present Circumstances, all other Things remaining as they are, it is requisite for us not to have any great Over-balance of Happiness in this Life; and this may be considered as the final Cause.

For

For we may hope, by this perpetual Mixture of Mifery with our Happinefs, to be the fooner and the more perfectly freed from that Self-love, grofs or refined, which every Kind and Degree of Happinefs, even the moft fpiritual, contributes to generate in us; and to make the greater Progrefs in learning the Virtues of Benevolence, Compaffion, Humility, Fear of God, Submiffion to his Will, earneft Application to him, Faith, Hope, Love towards him.

Fourthly, The whole Tenor of the Scriptures fhews both in a direct and indirect way, that we ought not, cannot expect any great or lafting Happinefs in this Life.

We ought therefore, whenever falfe flattering Hopes, with relation to our future Condition in this Life, rife up to View in our Imaginations, and tempt us, inftantly to reject them; and, in the Language of the Scriptures, *to rejoice as though we rejoiced not*; to remember that we *are Strangers and Pilgrims here*, that we only *dwell in Tabernacles, have no continuing City*, but *expect one to come, the New Jerufalem*, of which we are Denizens, *where our Treafure and Hearts ought to be*. The beft and moft religious Perfons ought to expect, and even to defire, this *daily Bread* of Sorrow and Affliction, this *Bleffednefs of thofe that mourn*, and *to watch and pray* againft the Temptations of Profperity, left the Day of Death fhould come upon them unawares, *as a Thief in the Night, while they are eating and drinking, marrying and giving in Marriage*.

Cor. We might fhew, by a like Method of Reafoning, that if the Mifery of this Life fhould, in certain Cafes, outweigh the Happinefs, it cannot, however, do this in any great Degree. There muft, from the Nature of our Frame and Circumftances here, be many Intervals of Eafe, Chearfulnefs, and even pofitive Pleafure. Dejection and Defpondency are therefore as unfuitable to our prefent Situation, as

z

a vain Confidence, and foolish Hope, of uninterrupted Happiness. We may learn also hence not to be terrified at any Self-denials or Sufferings for the sake of Religion, exclusively of those Arguments, which shew in a direct way, that Religion promotes our present Happiness, as well as our future. Our very Natures prevent the long Continuance of exquisite Misery. Misery by Continuance declines, and even passes into Happiness; and there must be, in every State of long Continuance, the frequent Intervention of grateful Sensations and Ideas.

PROP. 79.

Virtue has always the fairest Prospect, even in this Life; and Vice is always exposed to the greatest Hazards.

THIS has been the Business of the last Chapter to shew. But it is a Truth, which is sufficiently evident from common Observation. Particular Acts of Virtue and Vice often fail of their due Reward and Punishment, if we take in no more than a small Period of Time after the Act is performed. But then, if we take in the indefinite Extent of this Life, and estimate the natural Expectations, it can scarce be doubted, but that every Act of Virtue is our greatest Wisdom, even in respect of this World, every Act of Vice our greatest Folly. Now this general Tendency of Virtue and Vice respectively may be considered as the principal Evidence, which the Light of Nature, not subtilized or refined by deep Speculations, affords for the moral Character of the Deity. The Rewards which the Course of Nature bestows upon Virtue in general, and the Fairness of the Prospect which it affords to the Virtuous, shew that the Virtuous are acceptable to the Deity; and we may conclude for like Reasons, that Vice is odious in his Sight.

PROP.

P R O P. 80.

It does not seem at all probable, that Happiness is exactly proportioned to Virtue in the present Life.

FOR, First, Those who suffer Martyrdom for the sake of Religion cannot be said to receive any Reward in this Life for this their last and greatest Act of Fidelity.

Secondly, Many good Men are exercised with severe Trials, purified thereby, and removed into another State in the Course of this Purification, or soon after it. Diseases which end in Death, are a principal Means of such Purifications.

Thirdly, There are frequent Instances of Persons free indeed from gross Vices, but void of great Virtues, who from a favourable Conjuncture of Circumstances in this World, such as we may suppose attended the rich Man in the Parable, *fare sumptuously every Day*, and live in a State of comparative Ease and Pleasure.

Fourthly, The same Thing seems to hold in certain rare Instances, even of very vicious Persons; and one might almost conjecture, that Providence exposes some Instances of this Kind to View in a notorious manner, that the apparent Inequality of its Dispensations here, in a few Cases, and the Argument for a future State thence deducible, may make the greater Impression upon us.

The Reader may observe, that this Proposition is not contrary to the foregoing; and that the foregoing must be established previously, before we can draw an Argument for a future State from this, and the moral Character of the Deity, put together.

It

It is to be obferved alfo of the Reafoning made ufe of under all the Four Propofitions of this Section, that it is rather probable, and conclufive, in a general way only, than demonftrative and precife. However, the Probability and Precifion are as great as is neceffary in practical Matters. The practical Inferences would remain the fame, though thefe were lefs.

S E C T.

SECT. II.

Of the Expectation of Bodies Politic, the Jews *in particular, and the World in general, during the present State of the Earth.*

PROP. 81.

It is probable, that all the present Civil Governments will be overturned.

THIS may appear from the Scripture Prophecies, both in a direct way, *i. e.* from express Passages; such as those concerning the Destruction of the Image, and Four Beasts, in *Daniel*; of Christ's *breaking all Nations with a Rod of Iron, and dashing them in Pieces like a Potter's Vessel,* &c. and from the Supremacy and universal Extent of the Fifth Monarchy, or Kingdom of the Saints, which is to be set up.

We may conclude the same Thing also from the final Restoration of the *Jews*, and the great Glory and Dominion promised to them, of which I shall speak below.

And it adds some Light and Evidence to this, that all the known Governments of the World have the evident Principles of Corruption in themselves. They are composed of jarring Elements, and subsist only by the alternate Prevalence of these over each other. The Splendor, Luxury, Self-interest, Martial Glory, &c. which pass for Essentials in Christian Governments, are totally opposite to the meek, humble, self denying Spirit of Christianity; and whichsoever of these finally prevails over the other, the present

Form

Form of the Government muſt be diſſolved. Did true Chriſtianity prevail throughout any Kingdom intirely, the Riches, Strength, Glory, *&c.* of that Kingdom would no longer be an Object of Attention to the Governors or Governed ; they would become a Nation of Prieſts and Apoſtles, and totally diſregard the Things of this World. But this is not to be expected : I only mention it to ſet before the Reader the natural Conſequence of it. If, on the contrary, worldly Wiſdom and Infidelity prevail over Chriſtianity, which ſeems to be the Prediction of the Scriptures, this worldly Wiſdom will be found utter Fooliſhneſs at laſt, even in reſpect of this World ; the Governments, which have thus loſt their Cement, the Senſe of Duty, and the Hopes and Fears of a future Life, will fall into Anarchy and Confuſion, and be intirely diſſolved. And all this may be applied, with a little Change, to the *Mahometan* and *Heathen* Governments. When Chriſtianity comes to be propagated in the Countries where theſe ſubſiſt, it will make ſo great a Change in the Face of Affairs, as muſt ſhake the Civil Powers, which are here both externally and internally oppoſite to it ; and the Increaſe of Wickedneſs, which is the natural and neceſſary Conſequence of their Oppoſition, will farther accelerate their Ruin.

The Diſſolution of antient Empires and Republics may alſo prepare us for the Expectation of a Diſſolution of the preſent Governments. But we muſt not carry the Parallel too far here, and ſuppoſe that as new Governments have ariſen out of the old ones, reſembling them in great meaſure, ſubſiſting for a certain time, and then giving place to other new ones, ſo it will be with the preſent Governments. The Prophecies do not admit of this ; and it may be eaſily ſeen, that the Situation of Things in the Great World is very different from what it has ever been before. Chriſtianity muſt now either be proved true, to the intire Conviction of Unbelievers ; or, if it be an Impoſture,

posture, it will soon be detected. And whichsoever of these turns up, must make the greatest Change in the Face of Affairs. I ought rather to have said, that the final Prevalence and Establishment of Christianity, which, being true, cannot but finally prevail, and be established, will do this. But it may perhaps be of some Use just to put false Suppositions.

How near the Dissolution of the present Governments, generally or particularly, may be, would be great Rashness to affirm. Christ will come in this Sense also *as a Thief in the Night.* Our Duty is therefore to watch, and to pray; to be faithful Stewards; to give Meat, and all other Requisites, in due Season, to those under our Care; and to endeavour by these, and all other lawful Means, to preserve the Government, under whose Protection we live, from Dissolution, seeking the Peace of it, and submitting to every Ordinance of Man for the Lord's sake. No Prayers, no Endeavours of this Kind, can fail of having some good Effect, public or private, for the Preservation of ourselves or others. The great Dispensations of Providence are conducted by Means that are either secret, or, if they appear, that are judged feeble and inefficacious. No Man can tell, however private his Station may be, but his fervent Prayer may avail to the Salvation of much People. But it is more peculiarly the Duty of Magistrates thus to watch over their Subjects, to pray for them, and to set about the Reformation of all Matters Civil and Ecclesiastical, to the utmost of their Power. Good Governors may promote the Welfare and Continuance of a State, and wicked ones must accelerate its Ruin. The sacred History affords us Instances of both Kinds, and they are recorded there for the Admonition of Kings and Princes in all future Times.

It may not be amiss here to note a few Instances of the Analogy between the Body Natural, with the Happiness of the Individual to which it belongs, and the

the Body Politic, composed of many Individuals, with its Happiness, or its flourishing State in respect of Arts, Power, Riches, &c. Thus all Bodies Politic seem, like the Body Natural, to tend to Destruction and Dissolution, as is here affirmed, through Vices public and private, and to be respited for certain Intervals, by partial, imperfect Reformations. There is no complete or continued Series of public Happiness on one hand, no utter Misery on the other; for the Dissolution of the Body Politic is to be considered as its Death. It seems as romantic therefore for any one to project the Scheme of a perfect Government in this imperfect State, as to be in Pursuit of an universal Remedy, a Remedy which should cure all Distempers, and prolong human Life beyond Limit. And yet as Temperance, Labour, and Medicines, in some Cases, are of great Use in preserving and restoring Health, and prolonging Life; so Industry, Justice, and all other Virtues, public and private, have an analogous Effect in respect of the Body Politic. As all the Evils, which Individuals suffer through the Infirmity of the mortal Body, and the Disorders of the external World, may, in general, contribute to increase their Happiness even in this Life, and also are of great Use to others; and as, upon the Supposition of a future State, Death itself appears to have the same beneficial Tendency in a more eminent Degree than any other Event in Life, now considered as indefinitely prolonged; so the Distresses of each Body Politic are of great Use to this Body itself, and also of great Use to all neighbouring States; and the Dissolutions of Governments have much promoted the Knowlege of true Religion, and of useful Arts and Sciences, all which seem, in due time and manner, intended to be intirely subservient to true Religion at last. And this affords great Comfort to benevolent and religious Persons, when they consider the Histories of former

Times, or contemplate the probable Confequences of Things in future Generations.

PROP. 82.

It is probable, that the prefent Forms of Church-Government will be diffolved.

THIS Propofition follows from the foregoing. The Civil and Ecclefiaftical Powers are fo interwoven and cemented together, in all the Countries of *Chriftendom*, that if the firft fall, the laft muft fall alfo.

But there are many Prophecies, which declare the Fall of the Ecclefiaftical Powers of the Chriftian World. And though each Church feems to flatter itfelf with the Hopes of being exempted; yet it is very plain, that the prophetical Characters belong to all. They have all left the true, pure, fimple Religion; and teach for Doctrines the Commandments of Men. They are all Merchants of the Earth, and have fet up a Kingdom of this World, abounding in Riches, temporal Power, and external Pomp. They have all a dogmatizing Spirit, and perfecute fuch as do not receive their own Mark, and worfhip the Image which they have fet up. They all neglect Chrift's Command of preaching the Gofpel to all Nations, and even that of going to *the loft Sheep of the Houfe of Ifrael*, there being innumerable Multitudes in all Chriftian Countries, who have never been taught to read, and who are, in other refpects alfo, deftitute of the Means of faving Knowlege. It is very true, that the Church of *Rome* is *Babylon the Great, and the Mother of Harlots, and of the Abominations of the Earth*. But all the reft have copied her Example, more or lefs. They have all received Money, like *Gehazi*; and therefore the Leprofy of *Naaman* will cleave to them, and to their Seed for ever. And this Impurity may be confidered not only as juftifying the Application of the Prophecies to all the Chri-

I

ftian

ftian Churches, but as a natural Caufe for their Downfal. The corrupt Governors of the feveral Churches
will ever oppofe the true Gofpel, and in fo doing will
bring Ruin upon themfelves.

The Deftruction of the Temple at *Jerufalem*, and
of the Hierarchy of the *Jews*, may likewife be confidered as a Type and Prefage of the Deftruction of
that *Judaical* Form of Rites, Ceremonies, and human Ordinances, which takes place, more or lefs, in
all Chriftian Countries.

We ought, however, to remark here,

Firft, That though the Church of Chrift has been
corrupted thus in all Ages and Nations, yet there
have been, and will be, in all, many who receive
the Seal of God, and worfhip him *in Spirit, and in
Truth*. And of thefe as many have filled high Stations, as low ones. Such Perfons, though they
have concurred in the Support of what is contrary
to the pure Religion, have, however, done it inno-
cently, with refpect to themfelves, being led thereto
by invincible Prejudices.

Secondly, Neverthelefs, when it fo happens, that
Perfons in high Stations in the Church have their
Eyes enlightened, and fee the Corruptions and Deficiences of it, they muft incur the prophetical Cenfures in the higheft Degree, if they ftill concur, nay,
if they do not endeavour to reform and purge out
thefe Defilements. And though they cannot, according to this Propofition, expect intire Succefs; yet
they may be bleffed with fuch a Degree, as will
abundantly compenfate their utmoft Endeavours, and
rank them with the Prophets and Apoftles.

Thirdly, As this Corruption and Degeneracy of
the Chriftian Church has proceeded from the fallen
State of Mankind, and particularly of thofe Nations
to whom the Gofpel was firft preached, and amongft
whom it has been fince received; fo it has, all other
things being fuppofed to remain the fame, fuited our

Circum-

Circumstances, in the best Manner possible, and will continue to do so, as long as it subsists. God brings Good out of Evil, and draws Men to himself in such manner as their Natures will admit of, by external Pomp and Power, by things not good in themselves, and by some that are profane and unholy. He makes use of some of their Corruptions, as Means of purging away the rest. The Impurity of Mankind is too gross to unite at once with the strict Purity of the Gospel. The *Roman* Empire first, and the *Goths* and *Vandals* afterwards, required, as one may say, some Superstitions and Idolatries to be mixed with the Christian Religion; else they could not have been converted at all.

Fourthly, It follows from these Considerations, that good Men ought to submit to the Ecclesiastical *Powers that be*, for Conscience-sake, as well as to the Civil ones. They are both from God, as far as respects Inferiors. Christ and his Apostles observed the Law, and walked orderly, though they declared the Destruction of the Temple, and the Change of the Customs established by *Moses*. Both the *Babylonians*, who destroyed *Jerusalem* the first time, and the *Romans*, who did it the second, were afterwards destroyed themselves in the most exemplary Manner. And it is probable, that those who shall hereafter procure the Downfal of the Forms of Church-Government, will not do this from pure Love, and Christian Charity, but from the most corrupt Motives, and by Consequence bring upon themselves, in the End, the severest Chastisements. It is therefore the Duty of all good Christians to obey both the Civil and Ecclesiastical Powers under which they were born, *i. e.* provided Disobedience to God be not injoined, which is seldom the Case; to promote Subjection and Obedience in others; gently to reform and rectify, and to pray for the Peace and Prosperity of, their own *Jerusalem*.

P R O P

PROP. 83.

It is probable, that the Jews *will be restored to* Palæstine.

THIS appears from the Prophecies, which relate to the Restoration of the *Jews* and *Israelites* to their own Land. For,

First, These have never yet been fulfilled in any Sense agreeable to the Greatness and Gloriousness of them. The Peace, Power, and Abundance of Blessings, temporal and spiritual, promised to the *Jews* upon their Return from Captivity, were not bestowed upon them in the Interval between the Reign of *Cyrus*, and the Destruction of *Jerusalem* by *Titus*; and ever since this Destruction they have remained in a desolate State.

Secondly, The Promises of Restoration relate to the Ten Tribes, as well as the Two of *Judah* and *Benjamin*. But the Ten Tribes, or *Israelites*, which were captivated by *Salmaneser*, have never been restored at all. There remains therefore a Restoration yet future for them.

Our Ignorance of the Place where they now lie hid, or Fears that they are so mixed with other Nations, as not to be distinguished and separated, ought not to be admitted as Objections here. Like Objections might be made to the Resurrection of the Body; and the Objections both to the one, and the other, are probably intended to be obviated by *Ezekiel's* Prophecy concerning the dry Bones. It was one of the great Sins of the *Jews* to call God's Promises in Question, on account of apparent Difficulties and Impossibilities; and the *Sadduces*, in particular, erred concerning the Resurrection, because *they knew not the Scriptures, nor the Power of God.* However, it is our Duty to inquire, whether the Ten

B b 3   Tribes

Tribes may not remain in the Countries where they were firſt ſettled by *Salmaneſer*, or in ſome others.

Thirdly, A double Return ſeems to be predicted in ſeveral Prophecies.

Fourthly, The Prophets who lived ſince the Return from *Babylon*, have predicted a Return in ſimilar Terms with thoſe who went before. It follows therefore, that the Predictions of both muſt relate to ſome Reſtoration yet future.

Fifthly, The Reſtoration of the *Jews* to their own Land ſeems to be predicted in the New Teſtament.

To theſe Arguments, drawn from Prophecy, we may add ſome concurring Evidences, which the preſent Circumſtances of the *Jews* ſuggeſt.

Firſt, then, The *Jews* are yet a diſtinct People from all the Nations amongſt which they reſide. They ſeem therefore reſerved by Providence for ſome ſuch ſignal Favour, after they have ſuffered the due Chaſtiſement.

Secondly, They are to be found in all the Countries of the known World. And this agrees with many remarkable Paſſages of the Scriptures, which treat both of their Diſperſion, and of their Return.

Thirdly, They have no Inheritance of Land in any Country. Their Poſſeſſions are chiefly Money and Jewels. They may therefore transfer themſelves with the greater Facility to *Palæſtine*.

Fourthly, They are treated with Contempt and Harſhneſs, and ſometimes with great Cruelty, by the Nations amongſt whom they ſojourn. They muſt therefore be the more ready to return to their own Land.

Fifthly, They carry on a Correſpondence with each other throughout the whole World; and conſequently muſt both know when Circumſtances begin to favour their Return, and be able to concert Meaſures with one another concerning it.

Sixthly,

Sixthly, A great Part of them fpeak and write the *Rabbinical Hebrew*, as well as the Language of the Country where they refide. They are therefore, as far as relates to themfelves, actually poffeffed of an univerfal Language and Character; which is a Circumftance that may facilitate their Return, beyond what can well be imagined.

Seventhly, The *Jews* themfelves ftill retain a Hope and Expectation, that God will once more reftore them to their own Land.

COR. 1. May not the two Captivities of the *Jews*, and their two Reftorations, be Types of the firft and fecond Death, and of the firft and fecond Refurrections?

COR. 2. Does it not appear agreeable to the whole Analogy both of the Word and Works of God, that the *Jews* are Types both of each Individual in particular, on one hand, and of the whole World in general, on the other? May we not therefore hope, that, at leaft after the fecond Death, there will be a Refurrection to Life eternal to every Man, and to the whole Creation, which groans, and travails in Pain together, waiting for the Adoption, and glorious Liberty, of the Children of God?

COR. 3. As the Downfal of the *Jewifh* State under *Titus* was the Occafion of the Publication of the Gofpel to us Gentiles, fo our Downfal may contribute to the Reftoration of the *Jews*, and both together bring on the final Publication and Prevalence of the true Religion; of which I fhall treat in the next Propofition. Thus the Type, and the Thing typified, will coincide; the Firft-fruits, and the Lump, be made holy together.

P R O P.

PROP. 84.

The Christian Religion will be preached to, and received by, all Nations.

THIS appears from the exprefs Declarations of Chrift, and from many of his Parables, alfo from the Declarations and Predictions of the Apoftles, and particularly from the *Revelation*. There are likewife numberlefs Prophecies in the Old Teftament, which admit of no other Senfe, when interpreted by the Events which have fince happened, the Coming of Chrift, and the Propagation of his Religion.

The Truth of the Chriftian Religion is an Earneft and Prefage of the fame Thing, to all who receive it. For every Truth of great Importance muft be difcuffed and prevail at laft. The Perfons who believe can fee no Reafons for their own Belief, but what muft extend to all Mankind by degrees, as the Diffufion of Knowlege to all Ranks and Orders of Men, to all Nations, Kindred, Tongues, and People, cannot now be ftopped, but proceeds ever with an accelerated Velocity. And, agreeably to this, it appears that the Number of thofe who are able to give a Reafon for their Faith increafes every Day.

But it may not be amifs to fet before the Reader in one View fome probable Prefumptions for the univerfal Publication and Prevalence of the Chriftian Religion, even in the way of natural Caufes.

Firft, then, The great Increafe of Knowlege, literary and philofophical, which has been made in this and the Two laft Centuries, and continues to be made, muft contribute to promote every great Truth, and particularly thofe of Revealed Religion, as juft now mentioned. The Coincidence of the Three remarkable Events, of the Reformation, the Invention of Printing, and the Reftoration of Letters, with each other, in Time, deferves particular Notice here.

Secondly,

Secondly, The Commerce between the several Nations of the World is inlarged perpetually more and more. And thus the Children of this World are opening new Ways of Communication for future Apostles to spread the glad Tidings of Salvation to the uttermost Parts of the Earth.

Thirdly, The Apostasy of nominal Christians, and Objections of Infidels, which are so remarkable in these Days, not only give Occasion to search out and publish new Evidences for the Truth of Revealed Religion, but also oblige those who receive it, to purify it from Errors and Superstitions; by which means its Progress amongst the yet Heathen Nations will be much forwarded. Were we to propagate Religion, as it is now held by the several Churches, each Person would propagate his own Orthodoxy, lay needless Impediments and Stumbling-blocks before his Hearers, and occasion endless Feuds and Dissensions amongst the new Converts. And it seems as if God did not intend, that the general Preaching of the Gospel should be begun, till Religion be discharged of its Incumbrances and Superstitions.

Fourthly, The various Sects, which have arisen amongst Christians in late Times, contribute both to purify Religion, and also to set all the great Truths of it in a full Light, and to shew their practical Importance.

Fifthly, The Downfal of the Civil and Ecclesiastical Powers, mentioned in the 81st and 82d Propositions, must both be attended with such public Calamities, as will make Men serious, and also drive them from the Countries of *Christendom* into the remote Parts of the World, particularly into the *East* and *West-Indies*; whither consequently they will carry their Religion now purified from Errors and Superstitions.

Sixthly, The Restoration of the *Jews*, mentioned in the last Proposition, may be expected to have the greatest Effect in alarming Mankind, and opening
their

their Eyes. This will be fuch an Accomplifhment of the Prophecies, as will vindicate them from all Cavils. Befides which, the careful Survey of *Palæſtine*, and the neighbouring Countries, the Study of the *Eaſtern* Languages, of the Hiſtories of the preſent and antient Inhabitants, *&c.* (which muſt follow this Event) when compared together, will caſt the greateſt Light upon the Scriptures, and at once prove their Genuine-neſs, their Truth, and their Divine Authority.

Seventhly, Mankind ſeem to have it in their Power to obtain fuch Qualifications in a natural way, as, by being conferred upon the Apoſtles in a ſupernatural one, were a principal Means of their Succeſs in the firſt Propagation of the Goſpel.

Thus, as the Apoſtles had the Power of Healing miraculouſly, future Miſſionaries may in a ſhort time accompliſh themſelves with the Knowlege of all the chief practical Rules of the Art of Medicine. This Art is wonderfully ſimplified of late Years, has received great Additions, and is improving every Day, both in Simplicity and Efficacy. And it may be hoped, that a few theoretical Poſitions, well aſcer-tained, with a moderate Experience, may enable the young Practitioner to proceed to a conſiderable Va-riety of Caſes with Safety and Succeſs.

Thus alſo, as the Apoſtles had the Power of ſpeak-ing various Languages miraculouſly, it ſeems poſſible from the late Improvements in Grammar, Logic, and the Hiſtory of the human Mind, for young Per-ſons, by learning the Names of viſible Objects and Actions in any unknown barbarous Language, to im-prove and extend it immediately, and to preach to the Natives in it.

The great Extenſiveneſs of the *Rabbinical Hebrew*, and of *Arabic*, of *Greek* and *Latin*, of *Sclavonic* and *French*, and of many other Languages, in their re-ſpective ways, alſo of the *Chineſe* Character, ought to be taken into Conſideration here.

And

And though we have not the Gift of Prophecy, yet that of the Interpretation of Prophecy seems to increase every Day, by comparing the Scriptures with themselves, the Prophecies with the Events, and, in general, the Word of God with his Works.

To this we may add, that when Preachers of the Gospel carry with them the useful manual Arts, by which human Life is rendered secure and comfortable, such as the Arts of Building, tilling the Ground, defending the Body by suitable Cloathing, &c. it cannot but make them extremely acceptable to the barbarous Nations; as the more refined Arts and Sciences, Mathematics, natural and experimental Philosophy, &c. will to the more civilized ones.

And it is an additional Weight in favour of all this Reasoning, that the Qualifications here considered may all be acquired in a natural way. For thus they admit of unlimited Communication, Improvement, and Increase; whereas, when miraculous Powers cease, there is not only one of the Evidences withdrawn, but a Recommendation and Means of Admittance also.

However, far be it from us to determine by Anticipation, what God may or may not do! The natural Powers, which favour the Execution of this great Command of our Saviour's, to preach the Gospel to all Nations, ought to be perpetual Monitors to us to do so; and, as we now live in a more adult Age of the World, more will now be expected from our natural Powers. The *Jews* had some previous Notices of Christ's First Coming, and good Persons were thereby prepared to receive him; however, his Appearance, and intire Conduct, were very different from what they expected; so that they stood in need of the greatest Docility and Humility, in order to become Disciples and Apostles. And it is probable, that something analogous to this will happen at Christ's Second Coming. We may perhaps say, that some
Glimmerings

Glimmerings of the Day begin already to ſhine in the Hearts of all thoſe, who ſtudy and delight in the Word and Works of God.

P R O P. 85.

It is not probable, that there will be any pure or complete Happineſs, before the Deſtruction of this World by Fire.

THAT the Reſtoration of the *Jews*, and the uni-verſal Eſtabliſhment of the true Religion, will be the Cauſes of great Happineſs, and change the Face of this World much for the better, may be inferred both from the Prophecies, and from the Nature of the Thing. But ſtill, that the great Crown of Glory promiſed to Chriſtians muſt be in a State ulterior to this Eſtabliſhment, appears for the following Rea-ſons.

Firſt, From the expreſs Declarations of the Scrip-tures. Thus St. *Peter* ſays, that the Earth muſt be burnt up, before we are to expect *a new Heaven, and new Earth, wherein dwelleth Righteouſneſs*; and St. *Paul*, that *Fleſh and Blood cannot inherit the Kingdom of God*; the celeſtial, glorious Body, made like unto that of Chriſt, at the Reſurrection of the Dead, being requiſite for this Purpoſe.

Secondly, The preſent diſorderly State of the natu-ral World does not permit of unmixed Happineſs; and it does not ſeem, that this can be rectified in any great Degree, till the Earth have received the Baptiſm by Fire.

But I preſume to affirm nothing particular in rela-tion to future Events. One may juſt aſk, whether Chriſt's Reign of a Thouſand Years upon Earth does not commence with the univerſal Eſtabliſhment of Chriſtianity; and whether the Second Reſurrection,

the

the new Heavens, and new Earth, *&c.* do not coincide with the Conflagration.

One ought also to add, with St. *Peter*, as the practical Consequence of this Proposition, that the Dissolution of this World by Fire is the strongest Motive to an Indifference to it, and to that holy Conversation and Godliness, which may fit us for *the new Heavens, and new Earth.*

———————————————————

S E C T.

S E C T. III.

Of a Future State after the Expiration of this Life.

P R O P. 86.

It is probable from the mere Light of Nature, that there will be a Future State.

I Do not here mean, that Mankind in antient Times did difcover a Future State, and reafon themfelves into it. This, I apprehend, is contrary to the Faƈt, a Future State having been taught all Mankind by Patriarchal Revelations before or after the Flood. Nor do I mean, that Men could have done this without any Affiftance, primarily or fecondarily, from Revelation, and by mere unaffifted Reafon. This is a Problem of too deep a Nature to be determined conclufively ; or, if it can, we fhall determine for the oppofite Side, as it feems to me, as foon as our Knowlege of the Powers of the human Mind is arrived at a fufficient Height. My Defign is only to fhew, that the Works of God are fo far opened to us in the prefent Age, that, when the Queftion concerning a Future State is put, we ought to determine for the Affirmative, though the Authority of his Word be not taken into Confideration. Here then I obferve,

Firft, That it is not poffible to produce any Evidence againft a Future State ; fo that the Probability for it muft at leaft be equal to that againft it, *i. e.* to the Fraƈtion $\frac{1}{2}$, if we fpeak according to the precife Language ufed in the Doƈtrine of Chances. We are apt indeed to conclude, that, becaufe what we fee *is*, fo what we fee not, *is not* ; and confequently that there

there is no Future State; *i. e.* we make our Ignorance of the Means by which our Exiftence is preferved after Death, and of the Manner in which we are to exift, an Argument againft it. But this is utterly incon-clufive. Our Ignorance is a Nothing, and therefore can be no Foundation to go upon; and we have every Day Inftances of the Miftakes which Reafoning from it would lead us into. If there be really a Future State, it feems very poffible, that its Connexion with other Realities in this State may afford Prefumptions for it; and that it does fo, I fhall fhew in the Para-graphs that follow: But, if there be no Future State, this Non-entity cannot have any Properties or Con-nexions, upon which to erect an Argument for it. We muft therefore, previoufly to all probable Argu-ments for a Future State, own that we are ignorant whence we came, and whither we go; and that our not being able to penetrate into the dark Regions be-yond Death, were that abfolutely the Cafe, would not be an Evidence, that there is nothing in thofe Regions. That we can both penetrate thither, and difcover fomething in thefe Regions, is my next Bufi-nefs to fhew. For,

Secondly, The fubtle Nature of Senfation, Thought, and Motion, afford fome pofitive Pre-fumptions for a Future State. The Connexion of thefe with Matter, and their Dependence on it, are perhaps more fully feen in the foregoing Account of Vibrations and Affociation, than in any other Syftem that has yet been produced. However, there remains one Chafm ftill, *viz.* that between Senfation, and the material Organs, which this Theory does not attempt to fill up. An immaterial Subftance may be required for the fimpleft Senfation; and, if fo, fince it does not appear how this Subftance can be affected by the Diffolution of the grofs Body at Death, it remains probable, that it will fubfift after Death, *i. e.* that there will be a Future State.

Or

Or if we take the Syftem of the Materialifts, and fuppofe Matter capable of Senfation, and confequently of
Intellect, Ratiocination, Affection, and the voluntary
Power of Motion, 'we muft, however, fuppofe an
elementary infinitefimal Body in the Embryo, capable of vegetating *in Utero*, and of receiving and retaining fuch a Variety of Impreffions of the external
World, as correfponds to all the Variety of our Senfations, Thoughts, and Motions; and, when the
Smalnefs and wonderful Powers of this elementary
Body are confidered in this View, it feems to me, that
the Depofition of the grofs Cruft at Death, which
was merely inftrumental during the whole Courfe of
Life, is to be looked upon as having no more Power
to deftroy it, than the Accretion of this Cruft had a
Share in its original Exiftence, and wonderful Powers;
but, on the contrary, that the elementary Body will
ftill fubfift, retain its Power of vegetating again, and,
when it does this, fhew what Changes have been
made in it by the Impreffions of external Objects here;
i. e. receive according to the Deeds done in the *grofs*
Body, and reap as it has fowed.

Or, if thefe Speculations be thought too refined,
we may, however, from the evident Inftrumentality
of the Mufcles, Membranes, Bones, *&c.* to the
nervous Syftem, and of one Part of this to another,
compared with the fubtle Nature of the Principle of
Senfation, Thought, and Motion, infer in an obvious
and popular, but probable Way, that this Principle
only lofes its prefent Inftrument of Action by Death.
And the Reftitution of our mental and voluntary
Powers, after their Ceffation or Derangement by Sleep,
Apoplexies, maniacal and other Diforders, prepares
for the more eafy Conception of the Poffibility and
Probability of the fame Thing after Death. As
therefore, before we enter upon any Difquifitions of
this Kind, the Probability for a Future State is juft
equal to that againft it, *i. e.* each equal to the Fraction
$\frac{1}{2}$;

$\frac{1}{2}$; fo it feems, that the firft Step we take, though it be through Regions very faintly illuminated, does, however, turn the Scale, in fome meafure, in favour of a Future State; and that, whether the Principle of Thought and Action within us be confidered in the moft philofophical Light to which we can attain, or in an obvious and popular one.

Thirdly, The Changes of fome Animals into a different Form, after an apparent Death, feem to be a ftrong Argument of the forementioned Power of elementary animal Bodies; as the Growth of Vegetables from Seeds apparently putrefied is of a like Power in elementary vegetable Bodies. And all thefe Phæ-nomena, with the Renewals of the Face of Nature, Awaking from Sleep, Recovery from Difeafes, &c. feem in the vulgar, moft obvious, and moft natural way of confidering thefe Things, to be Hints and Prefumptions of a Life after the Extinction of this.

Fourthly, The great Defire of a future Life, with the Horror of Annihilation, which are obfervable in a great Part of Mankind, are Prefumptions for a future Life, and againft Annihilation. All other Appetites and Inclinations have adequate Objects prepared for them: It cannot therefore be fuppofed, that this Sum total of them all fhould go ungratified. And this Argument will hold, in fome meafure, from the mere Analogy of Nature, though we fhould not have recourfe to the moral Attributes of God; but it receives great additional Force from confidering him as our Father and Protector.

If it be faid, that this Defire is factitious, and the neceffary Effect of Self-love; I anfwer, That all our other Defires are factitious, and deducible from Self-love, alfo; and that many of thofe which are gratified proceed from a Self-love of a groffer Kind. Befides, Self-love is only to be deftroyed by, and for the fake of, the Love of God, and of our Neighbour. Now the ultimate Prevalency of thefe is a ftill ftronger Argument for a future Life, in which we may firft love God, and then our Neighbour in and through him.

Fifthly, The Pain which attends the Child during its Birth or Paffage into this World, the Separation and Death of the *Placenta*, by which the Child received its Nourifhment *in Utero*, with other Circumftances, refemble ' what happens at Death. Since therefore the Child, by means of its Birth, enters upon a new Scene, has new Senfes, and, by degrees, intellectual Powers of Perception, conferred upon it, why may not fomething analogous to this happen at Death? Our Ignorance of the Manner, in which this is to be effected, is certainly no Prefumption againft it; as all who are aware of the great Ignorance of Man, will readily allow. Could any Being of equal Underftanding with Man, but ignorant of what happens upon Birth, judge beforehand that Birth was an Introduction to a new Life, unlefs he was previoufly informed of the Suitablenefs of the bodily Organs to the external World? Would he not rather conclude, that the Child muft immediately expire upon fo great a Change, upon wanting fo many things neceffary to his Subfiftence, and being expofed to fo many Hazards and Impreffions apparently unfuitable? And would not the Cries of the Child confirm him in all this? And thus we may conclude, that our Birth was even intended to intimate to us a future Life, as well as to introduce us into the prefent.

Sixthly, It would be very diffonant to the other Events of Life, that Death fhould be the laft; that the Scene fhould conclude with Suffering. This can fcarce be reconciled to the Beauty and Harmony of the vifible World, and to the general Prepollency of Pleafure over Pain, and Subferviency of Pain to Pleafure, before-mentioned. All the Evils of Life, of which we are Judges, contribute fome way to improve and perfect us. Shall therefore the laft which we

fee,

fee, and the greateft in our Apprehenfions, quite extinguifh our Exiftence? Is it not much more likely,
that it will perfect all fuch as are far advanced, and
be a fuitable Correction and Preparatory to the reft?
Upon Suppofition of a future eternal Life, in which
our Happinefs is to arife from the previous Annihilation of ourfelves, and from the pure Love of God,
and of our Neighbour, it is eafy to fee how Death
may contribute more to our Perfection, than any
other Event of our Lives; and this will make it
quite analogous to all the others. But that our
Lives fhould conclude with a bitter Morfel, is fuch
a Suppofition, as can hardly confift with the Benevolence of the Deity, in the moft limited Senfe, in
which this Attribute can be afcribed to him.

Seventhly, All that great *Apparatus* for carrying
us from Body to Mind, and from Self-love to the
pure Love of God, which the Doctrine of Affociation
opens to View, is an Argument that thefe great Ends
will at laft be attained; and that all the imperfect
Individuals, who have left this School of Benevolence
and Piety at different Periods, will again appear no
the Stage of a Life analogous to this, though greatly different in particular Things, in order to re-
fume and complete their feveral remaining Tafks,
and to be made happy thereby. If we reafon upon
the Defigns of Providence in the moft pure and perfect Manner, of which our Faculties are capable; *i. e.*
according to the moft philofophical Analogy, we
fhall be unavoidably led to this Conclufion. There
are the moft evident Marks of Defign in this *Apparatus*, and of Power and Knowlege without Limits
every-where What then can hinder the full Accomplifhment of the Purpofe defigned? The Confideration of God's infinite Benevolence, compared with
the Profpect of Happinefs to refult to his Creatures
from this Defign, adds great Strength to the Argument.

Eighthly,

Eighthly, Virtue is, in general, rewarded here, and has the Marks of the Divine Approbation ; Vice, the contrary. And yet, as far as we can judge, this does not always happen ; nay, it feems to happen very feldom, that a good Man is rewarded here in any exact Proportion to his Merit, or a vicious Man punifhed exactly according to his Demerit. Now thefe apparent Inequalities in the Difpenfations of Providence, in fubordinate Particulars, are the ftrongeft Argument for a future State, in which God may fhew his perfect Juftice and Equity, and the Confiftency of all his Conduct with itfelf. To fuppofe Virtue in general to be in a fuffering State, and Vice in a triumphant one, is not only contrary to obvious Facts, but would alfo, as it appears to me, deftroy all our Reafoning upon the Divine Conduct. But if the contrary be laid down as the general Rule, which is furely the Language of Scripture, as well as of Reafon, then the Exceptions to this Rule, which again both Scripture and Reafon atteft, are irrefragable Evidences for a future State, in which Things will be reduced to a perfect Uniformity. Now, if but fo much as one eminently good or eminently wicked Perfon can be proved to furvive after the Paffage through the Gulph of Death, all the reft muft be fuppofed to furvive alfo from natural Analogy. The Cafe of Martyrs for Religion, Natural or Revealed, deferves a particular Confideration here. They cannot be faid to receive any Reward for that laft and greateft Act of Obedience.

Ninthly, The Voice of Confcience within a Man, accufing or excufing him, from whatever Caufe it proceed, fupernatural Impreffion, natural Inftinct, acquired Affociations, &c. is a Prefumption, that we fhall be called hereafter to a Tribunal ; and that this Voice of Confcience is intended to warn and direct us how to prepare ourfelves for a Tryal

at

at that Tribunal. This, again, is an Argument, which Analogy teaches us to draw from the Relation in which we ftand to God, compared with earthly Relations. And it is a farther Evidence of the Juftnefs of this Argument, that all Mankind in all Ages feem to have been fenfible of the Force of it.

Tenthly, The general Belief of a future State, which has prevailed in all Ages and Nations, is an Argument of the Reality of this future State. And this will appear, whether we confider the efficient or the final Caufe of this general Belief. If it arofe from Patriarchal Revelations, it confirms the Scriptures, and confequently eftablifhes itfelf in the manner to be explained under the next Propofition. If it arofe from the common Parents of Mankind after the Flood, it appears at leaft to have been an Antediluvian Tradition. If Mankind were led into it by fome fuch Reafons and Analogies as the foregoing, its being general is a Prefumption of the Juftnefs of thefe Reafons. The Truth of the Cafe appears to be, that all thefe things, and probably fome others, concurred (amongft the reft, Apparitions of the Dead, or the Belief of thefe, Dreams of Apparitions, and the feeming Paffage to and from another World during Sleep, the Body being alfo, as it were, dead at the fame time); and that, as the other Parts of the fimple, pure, Patriarchal Religion degenerated into Superftition and Idolatry, fo the Doctrine of a future State was adulterated with Fictions and Fables, as we find it among the *Greeks* and *Romans,* and other Pagan Nations.

As to the *Jews,* their high Opinion of themfelves on account of the Covenant made with their Father *Abraham,* and repeated at *Sinai,* which in its firft and literal Senfe was merely temporal, contributed probably to make the more grofs and carnal amongft them overlook the Doctrine of a future State, as at-

tefted

tefted either by Reaſon or Tradition. But when their Captivity by *Nebuchadnezzar*, and other Calamities, rendered this World contemptible and bitter to them, many, as the *Phariſees* and *Eſſenes*, had recourſe in earneſt to this great Source of Comfort; whilſt others, adhering ſervilely to the Letter of the Law, expected only temporal Proſperity under a victorious *Meſſiah*. However, it is not to be doubted, but that, before this, good *Jews*, particularly ſuch as did, or were ready to lay down their Lives for the ſake of Religion, had the Support of this Belief; and it appears to me, that there are many things in the Old Teſtament, which both ſhew, that the Doctrine of a future State was the current Opinion among the *Jews*; and alſo that it was attended with far leſs Expectations, than amongſt Chriſtians; whence it might eaſily be overlooked and neglected by carnal Minds, as above noted. Their Hearts were ſet upon temporal Proſperity, for themſelves conſidered ſeparately, for their Nation, for their Poſterity: All which we muſt, however, ſuppoſe to be more ſuitable to their other Circumſtances, and to thoſe of the World in general, when the Whole of Things is taken into Conſideration, than if they had had more full and magnificent Expectations after Death.

As to the final Cauſes of the Belief of a future State amongſt Mankind, if we ſuppoſe, that theſe are either the better Regulation of States, and the public Happineſs, or the private Happineſs of each Individual, they would be ſtrong Arguments for the Divine Benevolence, and conſequently for a future State; even though it be ſuppoſed, that the efficient Cauſe was only the Invention of thoſe Men, who ſaw that this Doctrine would be uſeful publicly and privately. For God muſt, at leaſt, have permitted this; according to the Doctrine of theſe Papers, muſt have cauſed it.

But,

But, without entering into this Examination of the efficient or final Caufes, we may affirm, that the mere general Prevalence of the Doctrine of a future State is of itfelf a ftrong Prefumption of its Truth. If it be true, it is natural, *i. e.* analogous to other things, to fuppofe that we fhould have fome general Expectation of it, juft as in other Cafes, where we are nearly concerned; alfo that as Mankind advance in Knowlege and Spirituality by the advanced Age of the World, this Doctrine fhould be more and more opened to them. Now this is the Fact; the Doctrine of a future State has, from the firft Memory of Things in the Poftdiluvian World, been thus perpetually opened more and more. Therefore, *e converfo*, it is probable, that the Doctrine itfelf is true.

It may be objected to fome of the Arguments here alleged for a future State, that they are applicable to Brutes; and therefore that they prove too much. To this we may anfwer, that the future Exiftence of Brutes cannot be difproved by any Arguments, as far as yet appears: Let therefore thofe which favour it be allowed their due Weight, and only that. There are, befides thofe common to all Animals, many which are peculiar to Man, and thofe very forcible ones. We have therefore much ftronger Evidence for our own future Exiftence, than for that of Brutes; which, again, is a Thing very analogous to our Circumftances. It is fomething more than mere Curiofity, that makes benevolent Perfons concerned for the future Welfare of the Brute Creation; and yet they have fo much to do nearer home, for themfelves, and their Relatives, by way of Preparation for a future State, that it would be a great Mifufe of Time to dwell upon fuch foreign Speculations.

The Doctrine of Tranfmigration may be confidered as an Argument for the future Exiftence of

all

all Animals in one View; though a moſt pernicious
Corruption of the practical Doctrine of a future State
in another.

It may farther be objected to ſome Part of the
foregoing Reaſoning, That the Deſtruction of Vegetables in ſo many various Ways, that few, relatively
ſpeaking, come to Perfection, with the many Irregularities of the Natural World, ſhew that God does
not, in fact, bring all his Works to Perfection. I
anſwer, That if vegetable Life be not attended with
Senſation (and we do not at all know, that it is),
this, with infinite other Phænomena of a like kind,
may be no Irregularity at all. The inanimate World
may, according to the preſent Conſtitution of Things,
however irregular that may ſeem to us, ſerve, in the
beſt poſſible manner, to promote the Happineſs of
the animate. We are apt to eſtimate Maturity in
natural Productions according to very narrow relative Conſiderations. But, in Truth, that Herb or
Fruit is mature, which has anſwered its End in reſpect of animal Life, the Support, for Inſtance, of a
peculiar Set of Inſects ; and, if the Particles of inanimate Matter thus paſs through the Bodies of Vegetables and Animals in an endleſs Revolution, they
may perform all the Offices intended by God : Or
he may have fitted them for infinite other Uſes and
Offices, of which we know nothing.

But if Vegetables have Senſation, which may indeed be a Speculation very foreign to us, but is
what we cannot diſprove, then Vegetables may be
provided for in the ſame manner as Animals. Or,
if we ſuppoſe the Argument to fail here, ſtill Animals, *i. e.* thoſe allowed by all to be ſo, may live
hereafter, though no Vegetables do identically, and
few according to the ordinary Courſe of Propagation by their Seeds or Shoots : Or the Argument
may fail in reſpect of Brute Animals, and extend
to Man alone,

P R O P.

PROP. 87.

The Christian Revelation gives us an absolute Assurance of a future State.

THAT the Reader may see more fully the Degree of Evidence afforded by the Scriptures to this most important Doctrine, I will here make the following Observations.

First, then, A future State is the plain and express Doctrine of the New Testament, in the obvious and literal Sense of the Words. It rests therefore upon the Authority of the Revelation itself. Hence all the Miracles of Christ and his Apostles, and, by consequence, of *Moses* and the Prophets, all the Prophecies of the Scriptures, whose Accomplishment is already past, and visible to us, become Pledges and Attestations of the Truth of this Doctrine. We cannot suppose, that God would have given such Powers and Evidences, as must necessarily propagate and establish this Doctrine, was it not true. For this is the grand, and, as we may say, the only Doctrine of the New Testament, and even of the Old, when interpreted by the New, as it ought to be.

And, as this is the most convincing Evidence even to philosophical Persons, so it is almost the only one which can affect and satisfy the Vulgar. But indeed what Resource can any Man have in things above his Capacity, besides resting on those who have evidently more Power, Knowlege, and Goodness, than himself, who have worked Miracles, foretold Things to come, preached and practised Righteousness?

All the Miracles of both the Old and New Testament were performed by Christ in Effect, *i. e.* by his Power and Authority. He therefore must be able

to

to preserve us from perishing utterly; and the Predictions of future States in this World, which God gave to him, and he to his Servant *John* and others, both before and after his Coming, shew by their Accomplishment, that all his other Predictions, and especially the great one of a Resurrection to Life eternal, will also be accomplished in due time.

Secondly, The Persons brought back to Life again in the Old and New Testaments, and, above all, the Resurrection of Christ himself, have a great Tendency to strengthen the foregoing Argument, and to remove all our Doubts, Fears, and Jealousies, concerning the Reality of a future State. The same may be said of the Histories of *Enoch* and *Elijah*, and of the Appearance of *Moses* and *Elijah* at Christ's Transfiguration. As there are no Footsteps back again from the Grave to Life, our Imagination staggers, and our Faith stands in need of a sensible, as well as a rational Support.

Thirdly, The great Readiness of the Prophets and Apostles, and of other good *Jews* and *Christians* after their Example, to suffer Death for the sake of their Religion, is a singular Comfort and Encouragement to us. We are sure from hence, that they believed a future State themselves; and they could not but know whether or no they had the Power of working Miracles, had seen Christ after his Death, had received Divine Communications, &c. They must therefore have been possessed of these undeniable Evidences for a future State; they could neither be deceived themselves in this Matter, nor deceive others.

Fourthly, The whole History and Institutions of the *Jewish* People, when interpreted by Christianity, are Types and Prophecies of a future State. And here the Old and New Testaments confirm and illustrate each other in the strongest manner: And the Old Testament, when interpreted by the New, be-

comes

comes intirely fpiritual, and equally expreffive, with
the New, of the Doctrine of a future State.   It may
be obferved of the *Pfalms* particularly, that the fpiritual Interpretation is to us, in the prefent Times,
more eafy and natural upon the Whole, than the literal and temporal one.

Fifthly, If we compare what was advanced above,
concerning the elementary infinitefimal Body, with
the Scripture Doctrine of the Refurrection of the
Body, and particularly with St. *Paul's* Account of it,
1 *Cor.* xv. there will appear fuch a Harmony and Coincidence between the Evidences from Reafon, and
thofe from Scripture, as will greatly confirm both.

PROP. 88.

*The Rewards and Punifhments of a future Life
will far exceed the Happinefs and Mifery of
this, both in Degree and Duration.*

HERE I will firft confider the Suggeftions of the
Light of Reafon; fecondly, the Declarations
of the Scriptures.

Firft, then, As Man appears, according to the
Light of Reafon, to be in a progreffive State, it may
be conjectured, or even prefumed, that the Rewards
and Punifhments of a future Life will exceed that
Happinefs and Mifery, which are here the natural
Confequences of Virtue and Vice.   However, the
Light of Reafon is not clear and certain in this
Point: Neither can it determine, whether the Happinefs and Mifery of the next Life will be pure and
unmixed, or no.   It may indeed fhew, that each
Man will receive according to his Deferts; but then,
fince there is no pure Virtue or Vice here, fince
alfo there may be room for both Virtue and Vice
hereafter, the Rewards and Punifhments of the next
Life may fucceed each other at fhort Intervals, as

in

in the prefent : Or, if we adopt the mechanical Syftem throughout, then we can only hope and prefume, that God will ultimately make the Happinefs
of each Individual to outweigh his Mifery, finitely
or infinitely ; and fhall be intirely uncertain, whether or no, at the Expiration of this Life, we fhall
pafs into another, in like manner, chequered with
Happinefs and Mifery : And thus one of the principal Motives to Virtue and Piety would be loft.

It is true indeed, that the Heathens had their *Ely-
fium* and *Tartarus* ; but then thefe Doctrines were
probably the corrupted Remains of fome traditionary Revelation ; and fo contribute to ftrengthen the
real Doctrine of the Scriptures on this Head, which
I am to fet forth in the next Place.

The Scriptures then reprefent the State of the
Good hereafter, as attended with the pureft and greateft Happinefs ; and that of the Wicked as being ex-
quifitely and eternally miferable.   And though the
Words tranflated *eternal* and *for ever*, in the Old and
New Teftaments, do not feem to ftand for an abfolute metaphyfical Infinity of Duration, as we now
term it, yet they certainly import a Duration of a
great relative Length, and may import any long
Period of Time, fhort of an abfolute Eternity.   The
Scriptures therefore, in their Declarations concerning
the Degree and Duration of future Rewards and Punifhments, lay before us the ftrongeft Motives to Obedience ; fuch as, if duly confidered, would roufe and
alarm our Hopes and Fears, and all our Faculties, to
the utmoft ; excite to the moft earneft Prayers ; and
mortify inftantly to the Things of this World.

Now, though Reafon cannot difcover this to us,
or determine it abfolutely, as juft now remarked ;
yet it approves it, when difcovered and determined
previoufly.   At leaft, it approves of the pure and
indefinite Happinefs of the Good, and acquiefces in
the indefinite Punifhment of the Wicked.   For we
always

always feem ready to expect a State of pure Holinefs
and Happinefs from the infinite Perfection of the
Deity; and yet the prefent Mixture of Happinefs
with Mifery, and of Virtue with Vice, alfo any future
Degree of Vice and Mifery, may be reconciled to infinite Perfection and Benevolence, upon Suppofition
that they be finally overpowered by their Oppofites:
Or, if we confult the Dictates of the Moral Senfe
alone, without entering into the Hypothefis of Mechanifm, the pure Mifery of the Wicked, under certain Limitations as to Degree and Duration, may be
reconciled to the Mercy of God, and will be required
by his Juftice. But the Moral Senfe was certainly
intended to warn us concerning Futurity.

It will not be improper here to remark, that the
Scriptures favour our firft Notions concerning pure
Virtue and Happinefs, by the Mention of a Paradifiacal State, as the original one, in which Man was
placed; and by reprefenting our future Happinefs, as
a Reftoration to this State. They take notice therefore of that greateft of all Difficulties, the Introduction of Evil into the Works of an infinitely benevolent Being; and by afcribing it to Sin, the Thing
which is moft oppofite to God, raife an Expectation,
that it muft be intirely overcome at laft.

P R O P. 89.

It is probable, that the future Happinefs of the
Good will be of a fpiritual Nature; but the
future Mifery of the Wicked may be both cor-
poreal and mental.

THESE are Points in which the Scriptures have
not been explicit. It is therefore our Duty to
beware of vain Curiofity, and to arm ourfelves with a
deep Humility. We are not Judges, what Degree
of Knowlege is moft fuited to our Condition. That
there

there will be a future State at all, has not been difcovered, with Certainty, to a great Part of Mankind;
and we may obferve in general, that God conceals
from us all particular Things of a diftant Nature, and
only gives us general Notices of thofe that are near;
and fometimes not even fo much as this, where a peculiar Duty, or Defign of Providence, requires otherwife. However, as we are obliged to read and meditate upon the Scriptures, to examine our own Natures, and to compare them with the Scriptures, we
feem authorized to make fome Inquiry into this high
and interefting Point.

Now it appears from the foregoing Theory, as
well as from other Methods of Reafoning, that the
Love of God, and of his Creatures, is the only Point,
in which Man can reft; and that the firft, being generated by means of the laft, does afterwards purify,
exalt, and comprehend it. In like manner, the
Scriptures place our ultimate Happinefs in finging
Praifes to God, and the Lamb; in becoming one
with God, and Members of Chrift, and of each other;
which Phrafes have a remarkable Agreement with the
foregoing Deductions from Reafon: And we feem
authorized to conclude from both together, that the
future Happinefs of the Bleffed will confift in contemplating, adoring, and loving God; in obeying his
Commands; and, by fo doing, miniftring to the Happinefs of others; rejoicing in it, and being Partakers
of it.

It feems probable alfo, both from fome Paffages of
the Scriptures, and from the Analogy of our Natures,
that our Attachments to dear Friends and Relations,
for whom we are *not to forrow as they that have no
Hope*, and our Efteem and Affection for eminently
pious Perfons in former Ages, for *Abraham, Ifaac,*
and *Jacob,* and *the Spirits of* other *juft Men made
perfect,* will ftill fubfift on our Arrival at the true
Mount Sion, and *the heavenly Jerufalem.*

2   It

It may be conjectured farther, that the glorified Body will not be capable of Pleasures that may be called corporeal, in the same Sense as the present bodily Pleasures are; but only serve as the Eye and Ear do to spiritual religious Persons; *i. e.* be a mere Instrument and Inlet to the refined Pleasures of Benevolence and Piety.

Is it not probable, that this Earth, Air, *&c.* will continue to be the Habitations of the Blessed? It seems to me, that a very wonderful Agreement between philosophical Discoveries, and the Scriptures, will appear hereafter. Some Instances, and many Hints, of this Agreement may be seen in Mr. *Whiston*'s Works. Only let us always remember, that we must think and speak upon the Things of another World, much more imperfectly than Children do concerning the Pleasures, Privileges, and Occupations of Manhood.

With respect to the Punishments of the Wicked in a future State, we may observe, that these may be corporeal, though the Happiness of the Blessed should not be so. For Sensuality is one great Part of Vice, and a principal Source of it. It may be necessary therefore, that actual Fire should feed upon the elementary Body, and whatever else is added to it after the Resurrection, in order to burn out the Stains of Sin. The elementary Body may also perhaps bear the Action of Fire for Ages, without being destroyed, like the *Caput mortuum*, or *Terra damnata*, of the Chemists. For this *Terra damnata* remains after the Calcination of vegetable and animal Substances by intense and long-continued Fires. The Destruction of this World by Fire, spoken of both in the Scriptures, and in many profane Writings, the Phænomena of Comets, and of the Sun and fixed Stars, those vast Bodies of Fire, which burn for Ages, the great Quantity of sulphureous Matter contained in the Bowels of the Earth, the Destruction of *Sodom* and *Gomorrah* by Fire and Brimstone, alluded to in the New Testament,

the

the Reprefentation of future Punifhment under the Emblem of the Fire of *Gehenna*, and, above all, the exprefs Paffages of Scripture, in which it is declared, that the Wicked fhall be punifhed by Fire, even everlafting Fire, confirm this Pofition concerning the corporeal Nature of future Punifhment, as well as give Light to one another.

The fame Confiderations confirm the long Duration of future Punifhment. For if the Earth be fuppofed to be fet on Fire, either by the near Approach of a Comet, or by fome general Fermentation in its own Bowels, juft as the Deluge was caufed partly by Waters from the Heavens, partly by thofe of the great Deep, it may burn for many Revolutions, either in a planetary or a cometary Orbit; and thefe may be the *Ages of Ages*, fpoken of in the *Apocalypfe*. Farther, if the Duration of Chrift's Reign upon Earth for a Thoufand Years be eftimated, as Interpreters have with apparent Reafon eftimated other Durations in the prophetical Writings, by putting a Day for a Year, then will this Reign continue for 360,000 Years. And fince it appears to be previous to the Punifhment in the Lake of Fire, and limited, whereas that Punifhment is to endure *for Ages of Ages*, that is, for an indefinitely long Period of Time, one may perhaps conjecture, that this Punifhment is to be of longer Duration than the Reign of Chrift upon Earth for 360,000 Years. But thefe Things are mere Conjectures. God has not been pleafed to difcover the Kind, Degree, or Duration of future Punifhment in explicit Terms. However, the facred Writings concur every-where with the Voice of Reafon in alarming us to the utmoft Extent of our Faculties, left we come into that Place of Torment. The Punifhments threatened to the Body Politic of the *Jews* have fallen upon it in the heavieft and moft exemplary Manner. The *Jews*, confidered as a Body Politic, have now been in a State of Suffering, without any Interval of

of Relaxation, for almoſt 1700 Years; during which
Time they have been like *Cain* the elder Brother, who
ſlew *Abel*, becauſe he was more righteous than himſelf,
and his Sacrifice more acceptable than his own, Fugitives
and Vagabonds over the Face of the Earth: They
have been perſecuted and ſlain every-where, having
the indelible Mark of Circumciſion ſet upon them,
to which they ſtill adhere moſt tenaciouſly, and which
has been a principal Means of preventing their apoſtatizing from their own Religion, after they grow up to
adult Age. And this may ſerve as a Type and Evidence of the Certainty and Greatneſs of future Puniſhment, ſhewing that it will be greater, and more laſting, than human Foreſight could poſſibly have conjectured; juſt as their final Reſtoration ſeems to pre-
ſage the final Redemption and Salvation of the moſt
Wicked. And therefore, according to that earneſt
and affectionate Admonition of our Saviour, *He that
hath Ears to hear, let him hear.*

But if the Puniſhments of another World ſhould be
corporeal in ſome meaſure, there is ſtill the greateſt
Reaſon to believe, that they will be ſpiritual alſo; and
that by Selfiſhneſs, Ambition, Malevolence, Envy,
Revenge, Cruelty, Profaneneſs, Murmuring againſt
God, Infidelity, and Blaſphemy, Men will become
Tormenters to themſelves, and to each other; deceive, and be deceived; infatuate, and be infatuated,
ſo as not to be able to repent, and turn to God, till
the appointed Time comes, if that ſhould ever be.

But we are not to ſuppoſe, that the Degree, probably not the Duration of future Puniſhment, corporeal or mental, will be the ſame to all. It may alſo
perhaps be, that there may be ſome alleviating Cir
cumſtances, or even ſome Admixture of Happineſs.
Only the Scriptures do not authorize any ſuch Conjectures; and therefore we ought to proceed with the
utmoſt Caution, leſt we lead ourſelves or others into
a fatal Miſtake. And indeed, if the Happineſs of

the Bleffed be pure and unmixed, as the Scriptures feem to declare, and Reafon to hope, then may the Mifery of the Wicked be unmixed alfo. Neverthelefs, fince the Goodnefs of God has no Oppofite, Analogy does not here require that Conclufion.

PROP. 90.

It feems probable, that the Soul will remain in a State of Inactivity, though perhaps not of Infenfibility, from Death to the Refurrection.

SOME religious Perfons feem to fear, left by allowing a State of Infenfibility to fucceed immediately after Death, for fome Hundreds, or perhaps Thoufands of Years, the Hopes and Fears of another World fhould be leffened. But we may affirm, on the contrary, that they would be increafed thereby. For Time, being a relative Thing, ceafes in refpect of the Soul, when it ceafes to think. If therefore we admit of a State of Infenfibility between Death and the Refurrection, thefe two great Events will fall upon two contiguous Moments of Time, and every Man enter directly into Heaven or Hell, as foon as he departs out of this World, which is a moft alarming Confideration.

That the Soul is reduced to a State of Inactivity by the Depofition of the grofs Body, may be conjectured from its intire Dependence upon the grofs Body for its Powers and Faculties, in the Manner explained in the foregoing Part of this Work. It feems from hence, that neither the elementary Body, nor the immaterial Principle, which is generally fuppofed to prefide over this, can exert themfelves without a Set of fuitable Organs. And the Scriptures of the New Teftament, by fpeaking of the Refurrection of the Body as fynonymous to a future Life, favour this Conjecture. There are alfo many Paffages in the Old

Teftament,

Testament, and some in the New, which intimate
Death to be a State of Rest, Silence, Sleep, and Inactivity, or even of Insensibility. However, there
are other Passages of Scripture, which favour the
opposite Conjecture. It seems also, that Motion,
and consequently Perception, may not cease intirely in
the elementary *Body* after Death; just as in the Seeds
of *Vegetables* there is probably some small intestine
Motion kept up, during Winter, sufficient to preserve
Life, and the Power of Vegetation, on the Return of
the Spring. And thus the Good may be in a State of
Rest, Tranquillity and Happiness, upon the Whole rather pleasant than painful, and the Wicked in a contrary State. Some imperfectly good Persons may also
receive what remains of the necessary Purification,
during the Interval between Death and the Resurrection. And, upon the Whole, we may guess, that
tho' the Soul may not be in an insensible State, yet it
will be in a passive one, somewhat resembling a Dream;
and not exert any great Activity till the Resurrection,
being perhaps roused to this by the Fire of the Conflagration. For Analogy seems to intimate, that the
Resurrection will be effected by Means strictly natural.
And thus every Man may rise in his own Order,
agreeably to the Words of St. *Paul*.

However, let it be remembred, that all our Notions
concerning the intermediate State are mere Conjectures.
It may be a State of absolute Insensibility on one hand,
or of great Activity on the other. The Scriptures are
not explicit in this Matter, and natural Reason is utterly
unequal to the Task of determining in it. I have just
hinted a middle Opinion, as being more plausible perhaps than either Extreme. Such Inquiries and Disqui-
sitions may a little awaken the Mind, and withdraw it
from the magical Influences of this World: And, if the
Children of this World find a Pleasure and Advantage
in ruminating upon their Views and Designs in it, much
more may the Children of another World, by making
that the Subject of their Meditations and Inquiries.

S E C T. IV.

Of the Terms of Salvation.

WE have feen in the foregoing Section the Greatnefs of the Rewards and Punifhments of a future Life. Now this is a Point of infinite Importance to us to be practically and duly confidered. It is of infinite practical Importance to come within the Terms of Salvation at the Day of Judgment. Though all God's Creatures fhould be made happy at laft indefinitely, yet ftill there is in the Way in which we do, and muft, and ought to conceive of thefe things, an infinite practical Difference, whether at the Refurrection we enter into the *New Jerufalem,* and *the Kingdom of Heaven,* or whether we be caft into *the Lake of Fire, whofe Smoke afcendeth up for ever and ever.* Let us inquire therefore, what are the Terms of Salvation after this fhort Life is ended, *i e.* what Degree of Purity and Perfection is required of us here, in order to be refcued from the Miferies of another World, and advanced into the glorious Manfions of the Bleffed.

P R O P. 91.

It follows from the foregoing Theory of our intellectual Pleafures and Pains, that the Bulk of Mankind are not qualified for pure unmixed Happinefs.

FOR the Bulk of Mankind are by no means fo far advanced in Self-annihilation, and in the Love of God, and of his Creatures in and through him, as appears, from the Tenor of the foregoing Obfervations, to be required for the Attainment of
pure

pure Happineſs. There are few, even in Chriſtian Countries, that ſo much as know what the true Religion and Purity of the Heart is; at leaſt, that attend to it with Care and Earneſtneſs; and in Pagan Countries ſtill fewer by far. How exceedingly few then muſt that *little Flock* be, whoſe Wills are broken and ſubjected to the Divine Will, who delight in Happineſs where-ever they ſee it, who look upon what concerns themſelves with Indifference, and are perpetually intent upon their Father's Buſineſs, in any proper Senſe of theſe Words! And as Experience ſhews us, that Men are not carried from Worldly mindedneſs to Heavenly-mindedneſs, nor advanced from lower Degrees of the laſt to higher in general, but by paſſing through Pain and Sorrow; ſo there is the greateſt Reaſon from the mere Light of Nature to apprehend, that the Bulk of Mankind muſt ſuffer after Death, before they can be qualified for pure and ſpiritual Happineſs. If what we have felt here does not cure us of Senſuality, Selfiſhneſs, and Malevolence, there is the greateſt Reaſon from Analogy to apprehend, that ſeverer Puniſhments will be applied hereafter for that Purpoſe.

PROP. 92.

It follows from the Declarations of the Scriptures, that the Bulk of Mankind are not qualified for the Manſions of the Bleſſed.

FOR, according to the Scriptures, *The Gate that leadeth to Life is ſtreight, and there are few who find it,* even though they *ſeek to enter in.* The Righteouſneſs of the Scribes and Phariſees, of the formal Profeſſors, who yet are no Adulterers, Extortioners, &c. will not be in any-wiſe ſufficient. *Many are called, and but few choſen;* and, agreeably hereto, the Firſt-fruits, which are a Scripture Type

D d 3 of

of the Chofen or Elect, are fmall in Comparifon of
the Lump.   In like manner, the *Jews* are few in
Comparifon of the Gentiles; the 144, 000, in Comparifon of all the Tribes; the *Ifraelites*, in Comparifon of all *Abraham*'s Seed; *Elijah*, and the 7000,
in Comparifon of the Priefts and Worfhipers of *Baal*.
Thus alfo *Noah*, and his Family, alone, were preferved at the Deluge; and of the *Ifraelites* a Rem-
nant only is faved, whilft the reft are rejected.   And
the Reafon of this Smalnefs of the Elect, the Thing
here typified, appears from the Conditions.   For
we muft take up our Crofs daily, hate Father and
Mother, and even our own Lives; elfe we cannot
be Chrift's Difciples.   We cannot ferve God and
Mammon together.   We muft feek the Kingdom of
God, and his Righteoufnefs, firft; hunger and thirft
after it; and leave all to follow Chrift.   We muft
be born again, *i. e.* have quite new Difpofitions,
and take Pleafure in Works of Piety and Charity,
as we formerly did in fenfual Enjoyments, in Honour and Profit; we muft be transformed by the
Renewal of our Minds, walk according to the Spirit, have our Hearts in Heaven, and do all to the
Glory of God.   We muft pray always; rejoice in
Tribulation; count all things as Dung in Comparifon of the Knowlege of Chrift, and him crucified;
cloath the Naked, feed the Hungry, vifit the Sick,
preach the Gofpel in all Nations.   If there be Strife
or Vain-glory, Schifms or Divifions, amongft us, we
are ftill carnal.   If there be Wrath, Clamour, Evil-
fpeaking, Covetoufnefs, we cannot inherit the Kingdom of God.   If we govern not our Tongues, we
deceive ourfelves; our Religion is vain.   The Luft
of the Flefh, the Luft of the Eye, and the Pride
of Life, are inconfiftent with the Love of the Father,
i. e. with Happinefs, with Freedom from torment-
ing Fear.   Though we give all our Goods to feed
the Poor, and our Bodies to be burnt, even fuffer
Martyrdom,

Martyrdom, it profiteth nothing, unlefs we have that Charity, that Love, which feeketh not her own, but rejoiceth in the Truth, *&c. i. e.* unlefs we become indifferent to ourfelves, and love God, and his Truth, Glory, and Goodnefs, manifefted in his Creatures, alone. This World, with the Bulk of its Inhabitants, is all along in Scripture reprefented as doomed to Deftruction, on account of the Degeneracy, Idolatry, Wickednefs, which every-where prevail in it. The true *Jews* and Chriftians are a feparate People, in the World, not of the World, but hated and perfecuted by it, becaufe they fhine as Lights *in the midft of a crooked and perverfe Generation,* which cannot bear the Light, *&c. &c.* for it would be endlefs to tranfcribe Texts to this Purpofe. If a Man has but Courage to fee and acknowlege the Truth, he will find the fame Doctrine expreffed or implied in every Part of the Bible.

P R O P. 93.

To apply the foregoing Doctrine, as well as we can, to the real Circumftances of Mankind.

HERE we may obferve, Firft, That, left the beft of Men, in confidering the Number and Greatnefs of their Sins, and comparing them with the Purity of the Scripture-Precepts, and the Perfection of God, fhould not dare to look up to him with a filial Truft and Confidence in him, left their Hearts fhould fail, Chrift our Saviour is fent from Heaven, God manifeft in the Flefh, that whofoever believeth in him fhould not perifh, but have everlafting Life; that, though our Sins be as Scarlet, they fhould by him, by means of his Sufferings, and our Faith, be made as white as Wool; and the great Punifhment, which muft otherwife have been inflicted upon us according to what we call the Courfe of Nature, be averted. Faith then in Chrift the Righteous will fup-

D d 4　　　　　ply

ply the Place of that Righteoufnefs, and finlefs Perfection, to which we cannot attain.

Secondly, And yet this Faith does not make void
the Law, and ftrict Conditions, above defcribed ;
but, on the contrary, eftablifhes them.   For no Man
can have this Faith in Chrift, but he who complies
with the Conditions.   To have a Senfe of our Sins,
to be humble and contrite, and in this State of
Mind to depend upon Chrift as the Mediator between God and Man, as able and willing to fave us,
which is true Faith, argues fuch a Difpofition, as
will fhew itfelf in Works.   And if our Faith falls
fhort of this, if it does not overcome the World,
and fhew itself by Works, it is of no Avail ; it is
like that of the Devils, who *believe and tremble.*
Men muft labour therefore after this Faith as much
as after any other Chriftian Grace, or rather as much
as after all the others ; elfe they cannot obtain it. For
it contains all the other Chriftian Graces ; and we can
never know, that we have it, but by our having the
Chriftian Graces, which are its Fruits.

Thirdly, Hence it follows, that a mere Affurance,
or ftrong Perfuafion, of a Man's own Salvation, is
neither a Condition, nor a Pledge of it.   The Faith
above defcribed *is* ; and fo are all other Chriftian Graces, Love, Fear, Truft, Repentance, Regeneration,
&c. when duly advanced and improved, fo as to
beget and perfect each other.   But there is great
Reafon to fear, both from the foregoing Theory of
the human Mind, and from plain Experience, that
fuch a ftrong Perfuafion may be generated, whilft
Men continue in many grofs Corruptions ; and that
efpecially if they be firft perfuaded, that this ftrong
Perfuafion or Affurance of Salvation is a Condition
and Pledge of it, and be of fanguine Tempers. For,
if they be of fearful and melancholy ones, a contrary
Effect may be expected.   All this appears from the
foregoing Theory of Affent and Diffent.   Eager Defires

fires are attended with Hope in the Sanguine, the Vain-glorious, and the Self conceited ; and this Hope, as it increafes, becomes a comfortable Aſſurance and Per-ſuaſion, drawing to itſelf by degrees the inward Sen-timents, that attend upon Aſſent. On the contrary, eager Defires in the Scrupulous, Superſtitious, and Dejeċted, end in Fear and Diſſent. But if this De-jeċtion ſhould paſs into the oppoſite State, then the anxious Diffidence may at once, as it were, paſs in-to its Oppoſite, a joyful Perſuaſion.

But the chief thing to be obſerved here is, that the Scriptures no-where make an Aſſurance of Salvation the Condition or Pledge of it. Unleſs therefore it could be ſhewn to be included in Faith, Love, Fear, and other Scripture-Conditions, the Doċtrine of Aſſu-rance, at it ſeems to be taught by ſome Perſons, can-not be juſtified by the Scriptures. But all the Chri-ſtian Graces may exiſt without an explicit Aſſurance of, or even Refleċtion upon, a Man's own Salva-tion ; and Fear, in particular, does not admit of this Aſ-ſurance. At the ſame time it ought to be remembred, that all Aċts of Faith, Love, Truſt, Gratitude, exer-ciſed towards God, leave Peace and Comfort in the Mind ; and that the frequent Meditation upon the Joys of another Life, as our Hope and Crown, will excite us powerfully to Obedience. We ought there-fore to labour and pray moſt earneſtly for the per-petual Increaſe of the Hope of Salvation ; yet waiting patiently for it, if it ſhould be delayed through bo-dily Indiſpoſition, or any other Cauſe.

Fourthly, If it be aſked, where the Privilege and Advantage of Faith lies, ſince Works are neceſſary alſo, according to the foregoing Account of it ; I an-ſwer, Firſt, That the Righteouſneſs and Suffer-ings of Chriſt, with our Faith in them, are neceſſary to ſave us from our Sins, to enable us to perform our imperfeċt Righteouſneſs ; and, Secondly, That Faith is propoſed by the Scriptures as the Means ap-

pointed

pointed by God for rendering imperfect Righteoufnefs equivalent, in his Sight, to perfect. and even of
transforming it into perfect, as foon as we are freed
from that Body of Flefh and Death, which wars
againft the Law of our Minds. And, as Faith thus
improves Righteoufnefs, fo every Degree of Righteoufnefs is a proportional Preparative for Faith; and,
if it does not produce Faith, will end in Self-Righte-
oufnefs, and *Satanical* Pride.

Fifthly, If it be alleged, in favour of the Doctrine of Juftification by Faith alone, and exclufively of Works, that if the greateft Sinner fhould, in
the Midft of his Sins and Impieties, ftop at once,
and, with a deep Senfe of them, earneftly defire Forgivenefs of God through Chrift, firmly believing in
him as his Saviour, we cannot fuppofe, that God
would reject him; I anfwer, That this deep Senfe of
Sin, this earneft Prayer, and firm Belief, are things
not to be attained in a fhort Space of Time, according to the ufual Courfe of Nature. A Sinner cannot be ftopped at all in the Career of his Sins, but
by fuffering; and there may indeed be a Degree
of Suffering fo great, as to work the due Contrition
in any given fhort Interval of Time, according to
the Courfe of Nature. But it does not appear from
Experience, that an effectual Reformation is generally wrought in great Sinners by common Calamities, nor even by very fevere ones; though the Suffering, one may hope, is not loft; but will here or
hereafter manifeft its good Effects. However, fome
few there are, who, recovering from a dangerous
Sicknefs, or other great Affliction, fhew that their
Change of Mind was of a permanent Nature; that
they were made *new Creatures*; and that they had
a real practical Faith, fufficient to overcome the
World, generated in them. Now, fuch a Faith,
though it have not time to evidence itfelf by Works,
will

will undoubtedly be accepted by God; since he knows, that Time alone is wanting.

Sixthly, It will be asked then, What are we to do for those unhappy Persons, who have neglected to make use of the Means of Grace in due time, and who are seized by some fatal Disease in the midst of their Sins? I answer, That we must exhort them to strive to the utmost, to pray that they may pray with Faith, with Earnestness, with Humility, with Contrition. As far as the dying Sinner has these Graces, no doubt they will avail him, either to alleviate his future Misery, or to augment his Happiness. And it seems plainly to be the Doctrine of the Scriptures, that all that can be done, must be done in this Life. After Death we enter into a most durable State of Happiness or Misery. We must here, as in all other Cases, leave the Whole to God, who judgeth not as Man judgeth. Our Compassion is as imperfect and erroneous, as our other Virtues, especially in Matters where we ourselves are so deeply concerned. The greatest Promises are made to fervent Prayer. Let therefore not only the dying Person himself, but all about him, who are thus moved with Compassion for him, fly to God in this so great Distress; not the least devout Sigh or Aspiration can be lost. God accepts the Widow's Mite, and even a Cup of cold Water, when bestowed upon a Disciple and Representative of Christ. And if the Prayer, Love, Faith, &c. either of the Sinner himself, or of any one else, be sufficiently fervent, he will give him Repentance unto Salvation. But how shall any of us say this of ourselves? This would be to depend upon ourselves, and our own Abilities, instead of having Faith in Christ alone.

These awakening Considerations may be thought to lead to Despair. But the Despair arising from them appears to be infinitely safer, than that enthusiastic Faith, or rather Presumption, which is sometimes

times the Confequence of the Doctrine of Juftification by Faith alone. If indeed a Man's Defpair
fhould make him neglect God in his laft Moments,
put away the Thoughts of his Sins, and harden himfelf in a carelefs Stupidity with refpect to his future
Condition, this would be the worft State on this
Side the Grave. But it is evident, that the foregoing Confiderations have no fuch Tendency. Where
a Man is fo terrified, that, like *David,* his Heart
fails him, or, like the Publican, he dares not look
up; that he does not think himfelf worthy of the
high Title of the Child of God, or of Admiffion into
the Kingdom of Heaven, all thefe Emotions, all the
Agonies of this Kind of Defpair, have a great Tendency to better him, to purify and perfect him, to
humble him, to break his ftubborn Will; and, though
he fhould not be able to pray but by the *Groanings
that are unutterable,* God, who knows the Mind of
the Spirit, which is now working in him *a Repentance not to be repented of,* i. e. if thefe Groanings be
fufficiently earneft, will accept him. If they fall
fhort of the Gofpel-Terms, whatever thefe be, he
will, however, be beaten with fewer Stripes. And
it muft be remembred, that the Queftion is not whether a Man fhall die here in apparent Peace, fo as
to comfort the Friends and Byftanders under their
alarming Senfe of Fear for themfelves, and Compaffion for him, but whether he fhall awake in Joy or
Torment. The Defpair, which arifes from a Fear,
left our remaining Difpofition to Sin be fo great, our
Faith and Love fo weak, and our Prayer fo languid,
as that we do not come up to the Gofpel-Terms,
is no Offence againft the Divine Goodnefs. We are
to eftimate this Goodnefs in its particular Manifefta-
tions by God's Promifes alone; and to do otherwife,
would be to open a Door to all Wickednefs, and lead
ourfelves into the moft fatal Miftakes. The Scriptures declare in the moft exprefs Terms, that Works
are

are neceffary to Salvation. Faith is never faid to be effectual, when not attended by Works; but, on the contrary, the true Faith is emphatically characterized by its producing Works. This Faith is itfelf a Work, as much as any other, the Caufe and the Effect of the others, all proceeding from one univerfal Caufe thro' Chrift. How then can we flatter ourfelves, that a mere ftrong Perfuafion or Affurance of Salvation, of the Application of Chrift's Merits to a Man's Self in particular, will be of any Avail? Efpecially fince it is evident, from the Nature of the Mind, that fuch a Perfuafion may be generated in a wicked Man; and alfo from Experience, that it is fometimes found in fuch.

I have here endeavoured to treat this moft important Subject with the greateft Fidelity, and Regard to Truth. God's Ways are indeed infinitely above our Ways, *i. e.* infinitely more merciful in reality, ultimately, than we can exprefs or conceive. But all the Threatenings of the Scriptures have been fulfilled hitherto, as well as the Promifes. *There is no Peace to the Wicked.* The Faith, which removeth Mountains, availeth nothing without Charity. *Not he that faith unto* Chrift, *Lord, Lord,* i. e. merely applies to him for Mercy and Affiftance, *but he that doth the Will of* God, *fhall enter into the Kingdom of Heaven.* And we muft not, we cannot, explain away thefe exprefs Paffages.

As in the Body, fo in the Mind, great and lafting Changes are feldom wrought in a fhort time; and this the Hiftory of Affociation fhews to be the neceffary Confequence of the Connexion between Body and Mind. And yet he who made the Blind to fee, the Lame to walk, the Deaf to hear, the Lepers clean, and the Maimed whole, by a Word, can as eafily perform the analogous Things, the Antitypes, in the Mind. But then it is to be obferved, that the bodily Changes by Miracles were not made by our Saviour, except in confequence of previous Changes in the Mind.

Mind. And thus indeed *to him that hath shall be given, and he shall have more abundantly.* Love, Faith, Fear, Prayer, will carry Men on in a very rapid Progress. But then the Work of Regeneration is already advanced in them. It is of infinite Consequence not to lay a Stumbling-block, or Rock of Offence, in our own way, or in that of others; not to *break the least Commandment, or teach others so to do.* Let us *not be deceived, God is not mocked; what a Man soweth, that shall he also reap. Indignation and Wrath, Tribulation and Anguish,* must come *upon every Soul of Man that does Evil, upon every Child of Disobedience.*

Seventhly, It follows from the Purity of the Scripture-Precepts, that even the better Sort of Christians may be under considerable Uncertainties as to their own State; and that in many Cases, as a Man grows better, and consequently sees more distinctly his own Impurity, he will have greater Fears for himself, and perhaps think, that he grows worse. Now the final Cause of this is undoubtedly, that we may make our Calling and Election sure, and left he that thinketh he standeth should fall. And yet, as wicked Persons, let them endeavour ever so much to stupefy themselves, must have frequent Forebodings of the Judgment that will be past upon them at the last Day; so good Persons will generally have great Comforts in the midst of their Sorrows. The Scripture-Promises are so gracious and unlimited, the Precepts for loving God, and rejoicing in him, so plain and express, and the Histories of God's Mercies towards great Sinners and the great Sins of good Men, are so endearing, that whoever reads and meditates upon the Scripture daily, will find *Light spring up* to him *in the midst of Darkness; will hope against Hope,* i. e. will hope for the Mercy of God, though he has the greatest Doubts and Fears in relation to his own Virtue, Faith, Love, Hope; and fly to him, as his Father and Saviour, for that very Reason. This will beget earnest and inceffant

ceffant Prayer, a perpetual Care not to offend, and a Reference of all Things to God. When fuch a Perfon furveys his own Actions, and finds that he does in many Inftances of Thought, Word, and Deed, govern himfelf by the Love and Fear of God, by a Senfe of Duty, by the Gofpel-Motives of future Reward and Punifhment, &c. thefe are to him evident Marks, that the Spirit of God works with his Spirit; he is encouraged to have Confidence towards God; and this Confidence fpurs him on to greater Watchfulnefs and Earneftnefs, if he does not dwell too long upon it. When, on the other hand, he finds many unmortified Defires, and many Failings in his beft Words and Actions, with fome grofs Neglects perhaps, or even fome Commiffions, this terrifies and alarms him; adds Wings to his Prayers, and Zeal to his Endeavours. And it is happy for us, in this World of Temptations, to be thus kept between Hope and Fear. Not but that very good Perfons, who have been conftant and earneft for a long Courfe of Time, who have paffed through fevere Trials, who live, as the firft Chriftians did, in perpetual Apprehenfions of Sufferings and Death, or who, like their bleffed Lord and Mafter, go about doing Good, and preaching the Gofpel to the Poor, may be always favoured with the Sight of the Promifed Land; and feveral of thefe may date the Rife of this happy State from fome remarkable Point in their Lives. But there is great Danger of being impofed upon here by the wonderful Subtlety of the natural Operations of the Mind. When a Man begins to fanfy, that an inward Sentiment, much or long defired by him, fuch as the Affurance of his Salvation, has happened or will happen to him, this impofes upon his Memory by imperceptible Degrees in one Cafe; and begets the Sentiment itfelf, the Affurance, in the other. Such a factitious Affurance can therefore be no Evidence for itfelf. It is a mental Affection, of the fame Kind with

4   the

the reft; and can lefs be depended upon, as a Teft, than plain Actions.   Mere Ideas, and internal Feelings, muft be lefs certain Marks of the prevailing, permanent Difpofition of our Hearts, than the Tenor of our Actions, which is the natural and neceffary Fruit of it.   And we ought to judge of ourfelves by our Fruits, as well as of thofe who pretend to be Prophets.   *A good Tree cannot bring forth evil Fruit, nor an evil Tree good Fruit.*   Here we may lay our Foundation, as upon a Rock.   When indeed this Perfuafion, or Affurance, is the Refult of an earneft impartial Examination into our Fruits, and of our Confcience not condemning us, it may reafonably afford Confidence towards God; becaufe our Confcience was intended by God to inform us of our State; as appears both from Scripture and Reafon.   But a conftant abfolute Affurance, *i. e.* Appearance thereof (for it can be no more, till we have efcaped all the Hazards of this Life, and our Judge has paffed his Sentence upon us in another), may be dangerous even to good Men, and render them by infenfible Degrees fecure, neglectful of neceffary Duties, and felf-conceited.   However, fince a Hope, free from all anxious Fears, feems to be often given by God as a Comfort in great Trials, and a Reward for behaving well under fuch, and perfevering faithfully, as I obferved juft now; we have the greateft Encouragement to do and to fuffer every thing that God requires of us, to be *fervent in Spirit, ferving the Lord,* to *watch and pray always,* &c. fince we may expect to obtain this Hope thereby, and in it an Hundredfold for all that we give up in this World, as well as everlafting Life in the World to come.

And though it be proper to comfort religious Perfons under bodily or mental Diforders, which fill their Minds with difproportionate Fears and Scruples, by informing them, that a Solicitude about our Salvation is the fure Means of obtaining it; that this Affliction is to
be

be endured with Patience, and Confidence in God, as much as any other; that it is attended with the fame Advantages as common Afflictions, and alfo with fome peculiar to itfelf, fuch as putting us upon a thorough Examination of our Hearts; and that this fevere Chaftening in the prefent World is the ftrongeft Mark, that we are loved by God, and therefore fhall be faved in the World to come; yet the fame Perfons are to be admonifhed, that a great Degree of Fearfulnefs and Scrupulofity often proceeds from fome Self deceit and Prevarication at the Bottom. There is probably fome fecret Sin, fome Sin that circumvents them more eafily and frequently than the reft, of which they may not perhaps be fully aware, and yet about which they have great Sufpicions and Checks, if they would hearken to them fully and fairly. They ought therefore, with all Earneftnefs and Honefty, to defire God to try and examine them, and to feek the Ground of their Hearts; and, in confequence of this Prayer, to fet about it themfelves in the Prefence of God. And if this be neceffary for the fcrupulous and feeble-minded, even for the Children of God, how much more for the carelefs, voluptuous, profane World! How ought they to be alarmed and exhorted to hear the Voice of Wifdom in the prefent Life, during *the accepted Time, left Fear come upon them as Defolation, and Deftruction as a Whirlwind!*

Laftly, We may obferve, that as undue Confidence leads to Security, and confequently to fuch Sins, as deftroy this Confidence, unlefs we be fo unhappy, as to be able to recal the internal Feeling of this Confidence without fufficient Contrition; and as the difproportionate Fearfulnefs, which is its Oppofite, begets Vigilance, and thus deftroys itfelf alfo; whence Perfons in the Progrefs of a religious Courfe are often paffing from one Extreme to another; fo it is difficult for ferious Perfons, in thinking or fpeaking about the Terms of Salvation, to reft in any particular Point;

they are always apt to qualify the laft Decifion, what-ever it be, either with fome alarming Caution, or comfortable Suggeftion, left they fhould miflead themfelves or others. This is Part of that Obfcurity and Uncertainty, which is our chief Guard and Security in this State of Probation, and the *daily Bread* of our Souls. Let me once more add this neceffary Obfer-vation ; *viz.* That future eternal Happinefs is of in-finitely more Weight than prefent Comfort ; and there-fore that we ought to labour infinitely more after Purity and Perfection, than even after fpiritual De-lights. We are only upon our Journey through the Wildernefs to the Land of *Canaan*; and, as we can-not want Manna from Day to Day for our Support, it is of little Concernment, whether we have more deli-cious Food. Let us therefore *hunger and thirft after Righteoufnefs* itfelf ; that fo we may firft *be filled* with it, and afterwards, in due time, may obtain that *eter-nal Weight of Glory*, which will be the Reward of it.

SECT.

SECT. V.

Of the final Happiness of all Mankind in some distant future State.

PROP. 94.

It is probable from Reason, that all Mankind will be made happy ultimately.

FOR, First, It has been observed all along in the Course of this Work, that all the Evils that befal either Body or Mind in this State, have a Tendency to improve one or both. If they fail of producing a peculiar, appropriated, intermediate good Effect, they must, however, necessarily contribute to the Annihilation of that *Self*, carnal or spiritual, gross or refined, which is an insuperable Bar to our Happiness in the pure Love of God, and of his Works. Now, if we reason at all concerning a future State, it must be from Analogies taken from this; and that we are allowed to reason, that we are able to do it with some Justness, concerning a future State, will appear from the great Coincidence of the foregoing natural Arguments for a future State, and for the Rewards and Punishments of it, with what the Scriptures have delivered upon the same Heads; also because a similar kind of Reasonings in respect of the future States, which succeed in order from Infancy to old Age, is found to be just, and to afford many useful Directions and Predictions. We ought therefore to judge, that the Evils of a future State will have the same Tendency, and final Cause, as those of this Life, *viz.* to meliorate and perfect our Natures, and to prepare them for ultimate unlimited Happiness in the Love of God, and of his Works.

Secondly,

Secondly, The Generation of Benevolence, by the natural and neceſſary Tendency of our Frames, is a ſtrong Argument for the ultimate Happineſs of all Mankind. It is inconſiſtent to ſuppoſe, that God ſhould thus compel us to learn univerſal unlimited Benevolence; and then not provide Food for it. And both this and the foregoing Argument ſeem concluſive, though we ſhould not take in the Divine Benevolence. They are both ſupported by the Analogy and Uniformity apparent in the Creation, by the mutual Adaptations and Correſpondencies of Things exiſting at different Times, and in different Places: But they receive much additional Force from the Conſideration of the Goodneſs of God, if that be firſt proved by other Evidences; as they are themſelves the ſtrongeſt Evidences for it, when taken in a contrary Order of Reaſoning.

And as the Benevolence of one Part of the Creation is thus an Argument for the Happineſs of the other; ſo, ſince Benevolence is itſelf Happineſs, a Tendency to learn it in any Being is alſo an Argument for his own Happineſs. And, upon the Whole, ſince God has commanded his beloved Sons, the Good, to love and compaſſionate every Being, that comes within their Cognizance, by the Voice of their Natures ſpeaking within them, we cannot ſuppoſe, that theſe his Favourites (to ſpeak according to preſent Appearances, and our neceſſary Conceptions, which with this Caution is juſtifiable) will fail of their proper Reward in the Gratification of this their Benevolence.

Thirdly, The infinite Goodneſs of God is an Argument for the ultimate Happineſs of all Mankind. This appears without any particular Diſcuſſion of this Attribute. But it may not be amiſs for the Reader juſt to review the Evidences for it above exhibited, and their Tendency to prove the ultimate Happineſs of all God's Creatures.

Fourthly,

Fourthly, The infinite Happineſs and Perfection of God is an Argument for, and, as it were, a Pledge of, the ultimate Happineſs and Perfection of all his Creatures. For theſe Attributes, being infinite, muſt bear down all Oppoſition from the Quarters of Miſery and Imperfection. And this Argument will be much ſtronger, if we ſuppoſe (with Reverence be it ſpoken!) any intimate Union between God and his Creatures; and that, as the Happineſs of the Creatures ariſes from their Love and Worſhip of God, ſo the Happineſs of God conſiſts, ſhews itſelf, &c. (for one does not know how to expreſs this properly) in Love and Beneficence to the Creatures. As God is preſent every-where, knows and perceives every thing, he may alſo, in a way infinitely ſuperior to our Comprehenſion, feel every-where for all his Creatures. Now, according to this, it would ſeem to us, that all muſt be brought to ultimate infinite Happineſs, which is, in his Eye, preſent infinite Happineſs.

Fifthly, The Impartiality of God, in reſpect of all his Creatures, ſeems to argue, that, if one be made infinitely happy upon the Balance, all will be made ſo. That Benevolence, which is infinite, muſt be impartial alſo; muſt look upon all Individuals, and all Degrees of Happineſs, with an equal Eye; muſt ſtand in a Relation of Indifference to them all. Now this is really ſo, if we admit the Third of the foregoing Suppoſitions concerning the Divine Benevolence. If all Individuals be at laſt infinitely happy upon the Balance, they are ſo at preſent in the Eye of God; *i. e.* he is perfectly impartial to all his Creatures. And thus every intermediate finite Degree of Miſery, how great ſoever, may be conſiſtent with the Impartiality of God. But to ſuppoſe, before the Creatures *A* and *B* exiſted, that *A* was made by God to be eternally happy, and *B* made to be eternally miſerable, ſeems as irreconcileable to God's Impartiality, as to his Benevolence. That both ſhould be made for eternal

and

and infinite Happiness, one to enjoy it in one way, the other in another, one by paffing through much Pain, the other by paffing through little or per- haps none, one by an Acceleration in one Period of his Exiftence, the other in another, *&c. &c.* is perfectly confiftent with God's Impartiality; for, the Happiness of each being infinite at prefent in the Eye of God, his Eye muft regard them equally. And, even in the Eye of finite Beings, if *A*'s Happiness feems lefs than *B*'s, in one refpect, becaufe *A* paffes through more Pain, it may feem greater in another, becaufe he arrives at greater Degrees of it in lefs Time. But this is all Appearance. Different finite Beings form different Judgments according to their different Experiences, and ways of Reafoning. Who therefore fhall be made the Standard? Not the inferior Orders certainly. And, if the fuperior, we fhall not be able to reft, till we conclude, that all that appears to all finite Beings, is falfe and delufive; and that the Judgment of the infinite Being is the only true real Judgment. Now I have endeavoured to fhew, according to the Method of ultimate Ratio's, how, allowing the Third Suppofition concerning the Divine Goodnefs, all Individuals are equally happy in the Eye of God. And thus the Impartiality of God is vindicated, according to the Truth and Reality of Things, in the Judgment of his own infinite Under- ftanding.

Sixthly, All the foregoing Reafoning feems to be fomewhat more fhort and clear upon the Hypothefis of Mechanifm; but it is not invalidated by that of Free-will. For Free-will muft be confidered as the Production of infinite Power, and therefore as be- ing fuited to the reft of the Divine Attributes, his Benevolence, Happinefs, and Impartiality, and to all the Methods, by which God conducts Men to Benevo- lence and Happinefs. Or, if the Hypothefis of Free- will be a Bar to the foregoing Reafonings in their full
Extent.

Extent, it cannot, however, account for Mifery upon the Whole, much lefs for eternal Mifery. To fuppofe that God wills and defires the Happinefs of all his Creatures, and yet that he has given them a Power, by which many of them will, in fact, make themfelves eternally miferable, alfo that he forefees this in general, and even in each particular Cafe, is either to fuppofe God under fome fatal Neceffity of giving fuch a Power; or elfe to take away his unlimited Benevolence in Reality, after that it has been allowed in Words. If therefore God has given Men Free-will in fuch a meafure, as that they may bring upon themfelves finite Mifery thereby in the prefent State, or in any future intermediate one, we .muft, however, fuppofe it to be fo reftrained, as that it fhall not occafion infinite and eternal Mifery. *The Caufe of the Caufe is alfo the Caufe of the Thing caufed*; which is furely as evident in the Application of it to the prefent Subject, as in any other Inftance, where it can be applied.

Seventhly, There are many obvious and undeniable Arguments, taken from the relative Attributes of God, which firft exclude the eternal Mifery of his Creatures, and then eftablifh their ultimate Happinefs by neceffary, or, at leaft, by probable Confequence. Thus the whole Tenor of Nature reprefents God to us as our Creator, Preferver, Governor, Friend, and Father. All Ages and Nations have fallen into this Language; and it is verified every Day by the wonderful Beauty, Harmony, and Beneficence, manifefted in the Works of the Creation, and particularly in the exquifite Make of our Bodies and Minds. Shall then a Creator, who is a Friend and Father, create for eternal infinite Mifery? Can any intermediate Suppofitions, Free-will, Perverfenefs, Reprobatenefs, &c. reconcile and unite Extremes fo utterly difcordant? Will he preferve an Exiftence, which ceafes to afford Happinefs, and can now only produce

Mifery

Mifery without End? Will not the Governor and Judge of all the Earth do right? In whatever manner Sin be eftimated, it muft be finite, becaufe it is the Work of a finite Mind, of finite Principles and Paffions. To fuppofe therefore a Sinner to be abfolutely condemned to infiniite irreverfible Mifery, on account of the finite Sins of this Life, feems moft highly injurious to the Juftice of God. And to fay, that this infinite irreverfible Mifery is not merely the Confequence of the Sins of this Life, but alfo of thofe to be committed in another, is to give a Power of repenting, and becoming virtuous, as well as of finning, in another Life; whence the Sentence might be reverfed, contrary to the Suppofition.

The worft Man of thofe who go to Heaven, and the beft of thofe who go to Hell, feem to us, if we will reafon upon thefe Subjects, as we do upon others, to differ but by an infinitefimal Difference, as one may fay; and yet the Reward of the firft, being eternal, however fmall in each finite Portion of Time, muft at laft become infinite in Magnitude; and the Punifhment of the laft in like manner. There would therefore be a double infinite Difference in the Reward and Punifhment, where the Virtue and Vice, caufing thefe refpectively, have only an infinitely fmall one. To fay, that, in fuch Cafes, the Rewards and Punifhments of another Life may be fo conducted by a Mixture of Happinefs and Mifery in each, as that the Balance fhall not become ultimately infinite in either, is to take away all Hopes and Fears relating to a future State; *i. e.* morally and practically to take away the State itfelf.

Again, Can it be fuppofed, that an infinitely merciful Father will caft off his Son utterly, and doom him to eternal Mifery, without farther Trials than what this Life affords? We fee numberlefs Inftances of Perfons at prefent abandoned to Vice, who yet, according to all probable Appearances, might be reformed

formed by a proper Mixture of Correction, Inſtruction, Hope, and Fear. And what Man is neither able nor willing to do, may and muſt, as ſhould ſeem, be both poſſible to God, and actually effected by him. He muſt have future Diſcipline of a ſeverer Kind for thoſe whom the Chaſtiſements of this Life did not bring to themſelves. Yet ſtill they will all be fatherly Chaſtiſements, intended to amend and perfect, not to be final and vindictive. That the Bulk of Sinners are not utterly incorrigible, even common Obſervation ſhews; but the Hiſtory of Aſſociation makes it ſtill more evident; and it ſeems very repugnant to Analogy to ſuppoſe, that any Sinners, even the very worſt that ever lived, ſhould be ſo, ſhould be hardened beyond the Reach of all Suffering, of all Selfiſhneſs, Hope, Fear, Good-will, Gratitude, &c. For we are all alike in Kind, and do not differ greatly in Degree here. We have each of us Paſſions of all Sorts, and lie open to Influences of all Sorts; ſo as that the Perſons *A* and *B*, in whatever different Proportions their intellectual Affections now exiſt, may, by a ſuitable Set of Impreſſions, become hereafter alike.

These and many ſuch-like Reaſonings muſt occur to attentive Perſons upon this Subject, ſo as to make it highly unſuitable to the Benevolence of the Deity, or to the Relations which he bears to us, according to the mere Light of Nature, that infinite irreverſible Miſery, to commence at Death, ſhould be the Puniſhment of the Sins of this Life. And, by purſuing this Method of Reaſoning, we ſhall be led firſt to exclude Miſery upon the Balance, and then to hope for the ultimate unlimited Happineſs of all Mankind.

PROP.

PROP. 95.

It is probable from the Scriptures, that all Mankind will be made ultimately happy.

IN confidering the Doctrine of the Scriptures upon this Head, it will firft be requifite to fhew, that the Texts alleged to prove the abfolutely eternal and irreverfible Mifery of the Wicked in another Life, may juftly be interpreted in a different Senfe.

Now the *Greek* Words tranflated *eternal, everlafting,* and *for ever,* in the New Teftament, do not by Derivation ftand for an abfolute Eternity, neither are they always ufed in this Senfe in the New Teftament, the *Septuagint,* or Pagan Authors. The fame may be faid of the correfponding *Hebrew* Words. It is true indeed, that they generally reprefent a long Duration; and this is fometimes limited by the Context, or Nature of the Subject, fometimes not. Now, according to this Interpretation, the Punifhments of the Wicked will be of great Duration, fuppofe of one or more long Ages or Difpenfations. But one might rather conclude from the Words of the Original, if their Derivation be confidered, that they will end at the Expiration of fome fuch long Period, than that they will be abfolutely eternal.

If it be faid, That the Eternity of God is expreffed by the fame Words; I anfwer, That here the Nature of the Subject gives a Senfe to the Words, whereof they are otherwife incapable. It may be urged in like manner, that the Duration of future Rewards is expreffed by the fame Words; but then the abfolute Eternity of this Duration is not perhaps deducible at all from thefe or any other Words. We muft in this intirely refer ourfelves to the Bounty and Benevolence of our Creator, and depend upon him for all our Expectations. Befides, the Nature of the Subject differs widely here. To fuppofe the

Mifery

Mifery of the Wicked to be, in every refpect, equal
and parallel to the Happinefs of the Good, is quite
contrary to the general Tenor of the Scriptures;
and looks like fetting up the *Manichean* Doctrine of
two oppofite infinite Principles, a Doctrine every-
where condemned in effect, though not in exprefs
Words, both by the Old and New Teftament. We
may add, that the Happinefs of the Good is alfo de-
noted in Scripture by Incorruption, Indiffolubility,
&c. as well as by the Words applied to the Punifhments of the Wicked.

The Words of our Saviour, *Where their Worm
dieth not, and their Fire is not quenched,* are thought
by fome to be a ftrong Argument for the abfolute
Eternity of future Punifhment. But as thefe Words
are taken from *Ifaiah,* and allude to the Punifhment
of the Malefactors, whofe Carcafes were fuffered to
rot upon the Ground, or burnt in the Valley of *Hin-
nom,* they appear to be too popular and figurative
to juftify fuch an Interpretation. And yet they feem
plainly intended to declare the very long Duration of
future Punifhment; and that, as the Worms, which
feed upon a putrefied Body, or the Fire, which burns
it in this World, do themfelves come to a certain and
known Period, the Mifery of another World, and
the Fire of Hell, will have no definite one; but
continue till they have confumed the Sin and Guilt
which feed them. In this Way of Interpretation,
the Paffage under Confideration would agree with
that concerning the *Payment of the laft Farthing.*

Our Saviour's Expreffion concerning *Judas,* viz.
*That it had been good for him, that he had not been
born,* cannot indeed be alleged for the Proof of the
Eternity of future Punifhment; but it feems to oppofe the Suppofition of the ultimate Happinefs of
all. However, this Expreffion may be popular and
proverbial; or it may perhaps denote, that his laft
Agonies, or his Sufferings in another World, fhould
outweigh

outweigh all his preceding Happineſs, or ſome way admit of an Interpretation conſiſtent with the Propoſition under Conſideration. For it does not appear to be ſufficiently clear and preciſe for an abſolute Diſproof of it. We may add, that as every Man, who at his Death falls ſhort of the Terms of Salvation, whatever theſe be, *crucifies the Son of God afreſh*, according to the Language of St. *Paul*; ſo he will have Reaſon, according to his then neceſſary Conceptions, to wiſh with *Judas*, that he had never been born. *O that they were wiſe, that they underſtood this, that they would conſider their latter End!*

Now, as the Words of the New Teſtament do not neceſſarily infer the abſolute Eternity of Puniſhment; ſo the general Tenor of Reaſoning there uſed, with numberleſs Paſſages both of the Old and New Teſtaments, concerning the Mercy of God, his Readineſs to forgive, *&c.* favour the contrary Opinion. And this is a farther Reaſon for interpreting theſe Texts of an indefinitely long Duration only; and that eſpecially if the ſmall Number of them, and the infinite Importance of the Doctrine, which they are ſuppoſed to contain, be alſo taken into Conſideration.

To the ſame Purpoſe we may obſerve, that there is nothing in all St. *Paul*'s Epiſtles, from whence the abſolute Eternity of future Puniſhment can be at all inferred, except the Words, *Everlaſting Deſtruction from the Preſence of our Lord*, 2 Theſſ. i. 9. though the Epiſtles to the *Romans* and *Hebrews* are both of them general Summaries of the Chriſtian Religion, and though he ſpeaks in both of future Puniſhment. In the Epiſtle to the *Romans*, he ſays, *Tribulation and Anguiſh* (not eternal Tribulation) ſhall be *upon every Soul of Man, that doth Evil*; alſo that the *Wages of Sin is Death*, not eternal Death, or eternal Puniſhment; *whereas the Gift of God is eternal Life*. In the Epiſtle to the *Hebrews*, he aſks, Of how much ſorer Puniſhment than temporal Death, an Apoſtate

is

is to be thought worthy ? Which feems not likely for
him to do, had he believed it eternal. In like manner, there is nothing of this Kind in St. *Luke*'s Gofpel, or his *Acts of the Apostles*, in St. *John*'s Gofpel,
or his Epiftles, or in the Epiftles of St. *James*, St.
Peter, or St. *Jude*. And yet good Men now, who
believe the Eternity of Punifhment, fcarce ever fail
to infift upon it moft earneftly in their Difcourfes and
Exhortations. For, if it be a Doctrine of the Chriftian Religion, it is fo effential a one, as that it could
not have been omitted by any infpired Writer, nor
fail to have been declared in the moft exprefs Terms,
which certainly cannot be faid of any of the Texts
alleged to prove the Eternity of Punifhment. The
Words tranflated *eternal*, and *for ever*, muft have
been ambiguous to the *Jews*, i. e. to the firft Chriftians ; and the figurative Expreffion, *Their Worm dieth not*, &c. is far lefs determinate than many Phrafes, which our Saviour might have chofen, had it
been his Intention to denounce abfolutely eternal
Mifery.

To this we may add, that it does not appear
from the Writings of the moft antient Fathers, that
they put fuch a Conftruction upon the Words of
the New Teftament ; and the Omiffion of this Doctrine in the antient Creeds fhews, that it was no
original Doctrine, or not thought effential ; which
yet could not be, if it was believed ; or that many
eminent Perfons for fome Centuries were of a contrary Opinion. And indeed the Doctrine of Purga-
tory, as now taught by the Papifts, feems to be a
Corruption of a genuine Doctrine held by the antient
Fathers concerning a purifying Fire.

It may perhaps be, that the abfolute Eternity of
Punifhment was not received, till after the Introduction of metaphyfical Subtleties relating to Time,
Eternity, &c. and the Ways of expreffing thefe ; *i. e.*
not

not till after the Pagan Philofophy, and vain Deceit, had mixed itfelf with and corrupted Chriftianity.

Still farther, It does by no means appear to be confonant to the Nature of the Chriftian Religion to interpret the New Teftament in a ftrict literal Manner, or adhere to Phrafes in Oppofition to the general Tenor of it. Our Saviour in many Places appeals to the natural equitable Judgments of his Auditors. The Evangelifts and Apoftles all enter into the Reafons of Things; the Gofpels are fhort Memoirs; the Epiftles were written to Friends, and new Converts; and the Nature of fuch Writings muft be very different from that of a precife determinate Law, fuch as that of *Mofes*, or the Civil Law of any Country. And indeed herein lies one material Difference between the rigid *Jewifh* Difpenfation, and the Chriftian, which laft is called by St. *James* the *perfect Law of Liberty*. From all which it follows, that we are rather to follow the general Tenor, than to adhere to particular Expreffions. And this will appear ftill more reafonable, when it is confidered, that we are yet but Novices in the Language of the Old and New Teftaments, the Relations which they bear to each other, and their Declarations concerning future Events.

Another Argument againft interpreting the Paffages above referred to, in the Senfe of abfolutely eternal Mifery, is, that there are many other Paffages, whofe ftrict and literal Senfe is contrary thereto. And in fuch a Cafe it feems, that the infinite Goodnefs of God, fo many ways declared in the Scriptures, muft foon turn the Scale. For the Scriptures muft be made confiftent with themfelves; and the Veracity and Goodnefs of God feem much rather to oblige him to perform a Promife, than to execute a Threatening. I will mention a few Paffages, fome of which it may be obferved even eftablifh the contrary Doctrine of the ultimate Happinefs of all Mankind.

Thus the moft natural, as well as the moft ftrict
and

and literal Senfe of the Words, *As in Adam all die,
fo in Chrift fhall all be made alive,* is the ultimate
Happinefs of all the Children of *Adam,* of all Mankind. God's *Mercy* is declared to *endure for ever*;
and he is faid *not to keep his Anger for ever*: Which
Expreffions, in their firft and moft obvious Senfe,
are quite inconfiftent with the abfolute Eternity of Punifhment. Our Saviour fays, that the
Perfon who is not reconciled to his Brother, *fhall
not be difcharged till he has paid the laft Farthing*;
which intimates, that there is a Time when he will
be difcharged. In like manner the Debtor, who
owed his Lord 10,000 Talents, is delivered over to
the Tormentors, till he pay thefe. To fay that he
can never pay them, becaufe as we have all our Faculties from God, fo we can merit nothing from
God, is to embrace the Mechanical Hypothefis, which,
in the Judgment of all, muft be utterly inconfiftent
with the Eternity of Punifhment. For, if a Man
cannot have Merit, he cannot have Demerit. To
fuppofe a Creature any-way brought into Being upon
fuch Terms, as to be only capable of Demerit,
feems moft highly injurious to the Attributes of God,
by whatever means this be effected, the Fall of our
firft Parents, or any other.

Again, *God in Judgment remembers Mercy.* This
is faid in general; and therefore it ought not to be
confined to the Judgments of this World. And to
do fo, when all the Pleafures and Pains of this World
are every-where in the New Teftament declared unworthy of our Regard in comparifon of thofe of another, is highly unfuitable to the Goodnefs of God.
But indeed this cannot be done without departing
from the moft obvious literal Senfe. The fame may
be faid of the Paffages, *God is not extreme to mark
what is done amifs; that he is loving to every Man;
that his Mercy, his tender Mercy, is over all his
Works,* &c. Can it be faid with any Appearance of

4 Truth,

Truth, that God will give an infinite Overbalance of Mifery to thofe Beings whom he loves?

It may very well be fuppofed, that though the Punifhments of a future State be finite; yet this fhould not be declared in fo many Words in the Scriptures. For fuch a Procedure would be analogous to the gradual Opening of all God's Difpenfations of Mercy. Mankind in their Infant State were not able to receive fuch Kind of Nourifhment; neither are all perhaps yet able. But, if future Punifhments be abfolutely eternal, it is hard to conceive why this fhould not have been declared in the moft exprefs Terms, and in many Places of Scripture; alfo how there fhould be fo many Paffages there, which are apparently inconfiftent therewith.

There remains one Argument more, and of great Weight in my Opinion, againft interpreting any Paffages of Scripture fo as to denounce abfolutely eternal Mifery. This is, the Declarations of the Scriptures concerning the Smalnefs of the Number of the Elect, and the great Difficulty of entering in at the ftreight Gate, already taken notice of. To fuppofe future Punifhments to be abfolutely eternal, is to fuppofe, that the Chriftian Difpenfation condemns far the greater Part of Mankind to infinite Mifery upon the Balance, whilft yet it is every-where declared to be a Difpenfation of Mercy, to be *Glory to God*, and *Good-will to Men*; which is a great apparent Inconfiftency. And indeed, unlefs the Doctrine of abfolutely eternal Punifhment be taken away, it feems impracticable to convince the World of the great Purity and Perfection required by the Gofpel in order to our Entrance into the Kingdom of Heaven. If there be no Punifhment in another State, befides what is abfolutely eternal, Men of very low Degrees of Virtue will hope to efcape this, and confequently to efcape with Impunity: Whereas, if there be a purging Fire, into which all the Wicked are to be caft, to

remain

remain and suffer there according to their Demerits,
far beyond what Men generally suffer in this Life;
and if there be only few, that are admitted to Happiness after the Expiration of this Life, without such
farther Purification; what Vigour and Earnestness
should we use to escape so great a Punishment, and
to be of the happy Number of those, whose Names
are written in the Book of Life!

This may suffice to shew, that the absolute Eternity of future Punishment cannot be concluded from
the Scriptures. We are next to inquire what Evidences they afford for the ultimate Happiness of all
Mankind. I have already mentioned some Passages, which favour this Doctrine; but I intend
now to propose two Arguments of a more general
Nature.

First, then, It may be observed, That the Scriptures give a Sanction to most of the foregoing Arguments, taken from the Light of Nature, for this Doctrine, by reasoning in the same Manner. Thus the
Punishments of the *Jews* and others are represented
as Chastisements, *i. e.* as Evils tending to produce a
Good greater than themselves. Our Benevolence to
our Children is represented by Christ, as an Argument of the infinitely greater Benevolence of God
our Heavenly Father. God promises to make *Abraham* happy by making his Posterity happy, and
them happy by making them the Instruments of Happiness to all the Nations of the Earth (which they
are still to be probably in a much more ample
Manner, than they have ever yet been). Now this
shews, that the Happiness, intended for us all, is
the Gratification of our Benevolence. The Goodness of God is every-where represented as prevailing
over his Severity; he remembers good Actions to
Thousands of Generations, and punishes evil ones
only to the Third and Fourth. Not a Sparrow is
forgotten before him; he giveth to all their Meat

in due Seafon ; pities us, as a Father does his Children ; and fets our Sins as far from us, as Heaven is from Earth, &c. All which Kind of Language furely implies both infinite Mercy in the Forgiveness of Sin, and infinite Love in advancing his purified Children. We are all the Offspring of God, and, by confequence, agreeably to other Phrafes, are *Heirs of all Things, Heirs of God, and Coheirs with Chrift, Members of the myftical Body of Chrift, and of each other*, i. e. we are all Partakers of the Happiness of God, through his Bounty and Mercy. God is the God of the *Gentiles*, as well as of the *Jews* ; and has *concluded* them *all in Unbelief, only that he might have Mercy upon all.* And, in general, all the Arguments for the ultimate Happiness of all Mankind, taken from the Relations which we bear to God, as our Creator, Preferver, Governor, Father, Friend, and God, are abundantly attefted by the Scriptures.

Secondly, There are in the Scriptures fome Arguments for the ultimate Reftoration and Happiness of all Mankind, which now feem fufficiently full and ftrong, and which yet could not be underftood in former Ages ; at leaft we fee, that, in fact, they were not. Of this kind is the Hiftory of the *Jewish* State, with the Prophecies relating thereto. For we may obferve, that, according to the Scriptures, the Body Politic of the *Jews* muft be made flourifhing and happy, whether they will or no, by the Severities which God inflicts upon them. Now the *Jewish* State, as has been already remarked, appears to be a Type of each Individual in particular, on one hand ; and of Mankind in general, on the other.

Thus, alfo, it is foretold, that Chrift will *fubdue all things to himfelf.* But Subjection to Chrift, according to the figurative prophetic Style of the Scriptures, is Happiness, not merely Subjection by Compulfion, like that to an earthly Conqueror. Agreeably to this, all things are to be *gathered together in one in Chrift,*
both

both thofe which are *in Heaven*, and thofe *on Earth:* And St. *John* faw *every Creature in Heaven, in Earth, under the Earth, and in the Sea, and all that were in them, praifing God.*

The Prayer of Faith can remove Mountains; all Things are poffible to it; and, if we could fuppofe all Men defective in this Article, in praying with Faith for the ultimate Happinefs of Mankind, furely our Saviour muft do this; his Prayer for his Crucifiers cannot furely fail to obtain Pardon and Happinefs for them.

We are commanded to love God with our whole Powers, to be joyful in him, to praife him evermore, not only for his Goodnefs to us, but alfo for that to all the Children of Men. But fuch Love and Joy, to be unbounded, prefuppofe unbounded Goodnefs in God, to be manifefted to all Mankind in due time; elfe there would be fome Men, on whofe Accounts we could not rejoice in God. At the fame time, the Delay of this Manifeftation of God's Goodnefs, with the Severity exercifed towards Particulars, in their Progrefs to Happinefs, beget Submiffion, Refignation, *Fear and Trembling*, in us, till at laft we come to that *perfect Love that cafts out Fear.*

It may perhaps be, that the Writers of the Old and New Teftaments did not fee the full Meaning of the glorious Declarations, which the Holy Spirit has delivered to us by their means; juft as *Daniel*, and the other Prophets, were ignorant of the full and precife Import of their Prophecies, relating to Chrift. Or perhaps they did; but thought it expedient, or were commanded, not to be more explicit. The Chriftian Religion, in converting the various Pagan Nations of the World, was to be corrupted by them; and the fuperftitious Fear of God, which is one of thefe Corruptions, may have been neceffary hitherto on account of the reft. But now the Corruptions of the true Religion begin to be difcovered, and removed, by the

earneft

earneſt Endeavours of good Men of all Nations and Sects, in theſe latter Times, by their *comparing ſpiritual Things with ſpiritual.*

How far the Brute Creation is concerned in the Redemption by Chriſt, may be doubted ; and it does not ſeem to be much or immeditately our Buſineſs to inquire, as no relative Duty depends thereon. However, their Fall with *Adam*, the Covenant made with them after the Deluge, their ſerving as Sacrifices for the Sins of Men, and as Types and Emblems in the Prophecies, their being commanded to praiſe God (for every thing that hath Breath is thus commanded, as well as the Gentiles), ſeem to intimate, that there is Mercy in Store for them alſo, more than we may expect, to be revealed in due time. The *Jews* conſidered the *Gentiles* as Dogs in compariſon of themſelves. And the Brute Creatures appear by the foregoing Hiſtory of Aſſociation to differ from us in Degree, rather than in Kind.

It may be objected here, That, if this Opinion of the ultimate Happineſs of all Mankind be true, it is not, however, proper to publiſh it. Men are very wicked, notwithſtanding the Fear of eternal Puniſhment ; and therefore will probably be more ſo, if that Fear be removed, and a Hope given to the moſt wicked of attaining everlaſting Happineſs ultimately. I anſwer, Firſt, That this Opinion is already publiſhed ſo far, that very few irreligious Perſons can be ſuppoſed to believe the contrary much longer : Or, if they do believe abſolutely eternal Puniſhment to be the Doctrine of the Scriptures, they will be much induced thereby to reject Revealed Religion itſelf. It ſeems therefore to be now a proper Time to inquire candidly and impartially into the Truth. The World abounds ſo much with Writers, that the mere Opinion of a ſingle one cannot be ſuppoſed to have any great Weight. The Arguments produced will themſelves be examined, and a Perſon can now do little more

than

than bring Things to View for the Judgment of others. The Number of Teachers in all Arts and Sciences is fo great, that no one amongft them can or ought to have Followers, unlefs as far as he follows Truth.

But, Secondly, It does not feem, that even the Motives of Fear are leffened to confiderate Perfons, by fuppofing the Fire of Hell to be only a purifying one. For it is clear from the Scriptures, that the Punifhment will be very dreadful and durable. We can fet no Bounds either to the Degree or Duration of it. They are therefore practically infinite.

Thirdly, The Motives of Love are infinitely enhanced by fuppofing the ultimate unlimited Happinefs of all. This takes off the Charge of Enthufiafm from that noble Expreffion of fome myftical Writers, in which they refign themfelves intirely to God, both for Time and Eternity. This makes us embrace even the moft wicked with the moft cordial, tender, humble Affection. We pity them at prefent, as *Veffels of Wrath*; yet live in certain Hopes of rejoicing with them at laft; labour to bring this to pafs, and to haften it; and confider, that every thing is good, and pure, and perfect, in the Sight of God.

CON-

CONCLUSION.

I HAVE now gone through with my Obfervations on the Frame, Duty, and Expectations of
MAN, finifhing them with the Doctrine of
ultimate, unlimited Happinefs to All. This Doctrine,
if it be true, ought at once to difpel all Gloominefs,
Anxiety, and Sorrow, from our Hearts; and raife
them to the higheft Pitch of Love, Adoration, and
Gratitude towards God, our moft bountiful Creator,
and merciful Father, and the inexhauftible Source of all
Happinefs and Perfection. Here Self-intereft, Benevolence, and Piety, all concur to move and exalt our
Affections. How happy in himfelf, how benevolent
to others, and how thankful to God, ought that Man
to be, who believes both himfelf and others born to
an infinite Expectation! Since God has bid us rejoice,
what can make us forrowful? Since he has created us
for Happinefs, what Mifery can we fear? If we be
really intended for ultimate unlimited Happinefs, it
is no Matter to a truly refigned Perfon, when, or
where, or how. Nay, could any of us fully conceive,
and be duly influenced by, this glorious Expectation,
this infinite Balance in our Favour, it would be fufficient to deprive all prefent Evils of their Sting and
Bitternefs. It would be a fufficient Anfwer to the
πόθεν τὸ κακὸν, to all our Difficulties and Anxieties from
the Folly, Vice, and Mifery, which we experience in
ourfelves, and fee in others, to fay, that they will all
end

end in unbounded Knowlege, Virtue, and Happineſs; and that the Progreſs of every Individual in his Paſſage through an eternal Life is from imperfect to perfect, particular to general, leſs to greater, finite to infinite, and from the Creature to the Creator.

But, alas! this is chiefly Speculation, and muſt be to the Bulk of Mankind. Whilſt we continue entangled in the Fetters of Sin, we cannot enjoy the glorious Liberty and Privileges of the Children of God. We cannot exalt ourſelves to Heaven, and make a right Eſtimate of Things, from the true Point of View, till we get clear of the Attraction, and magic Influences, of the Earth. Whence it follows, that this Doctrine, however great and glorious in itſelf, in the Eye of a Being ſufficiently advanced in Purity and Comprehenſion, muſt be to us like the Book given to St. *John, bitter in the Belly,* though *ſweet in the Mouth.* The firſt general View cannot but charm us, however groveling and corrupt our Minds may be. But when we begin to digeſt it, when, after mature Deliberation, we come to ſee its ſeveral Evidences, Connexions, and Conſequences, our Self-intereſt, our Benevolence, and our Piety, in proportion to their Strength and Purity, will all riſe up, and join their Forces, and alarm us to the utmoſt Extent of our Faculties. When we conſider the Purity required of thoſe, who are ſo happy as to eſcape the Second Death, and the purifying Lake of Fire, whoſe Smoke aſcendeth up for ever and ever, *i. e.* for Ages of Ages, we cannot but be in Pain for ourſelves, and work out our own Salvation with Fear and Trembling. When we view the Sin and Wickedneſs, with which the World every-where abounds, our Hearts cannot but melt with Compaſſion for others, for the Tortures that are prepared for them, after the Expiration of this Life, in order to fit them for pure and ſpiritual Happineſs, to burn out the Stains of Senſuality and Self-love, and exalt them to the unbounded

Love

Love of God, and his Works. When we confider farther, that God has Mercy on whom he will, and hardens whom he will, and that we, with all our Pleafures and Pains, are abfolute Nothings in comparifon of him, we muft, like St. *John* again, fall down at his Feet dead with Aftonifhment. And yet we need not fear ; from the Inftant that we thus humble ourfelves, he will lay his Hand upon us, and exalt us ; he has the Keys of Death and Hell, in every poffible Senfe of thofe Words.

There is alfo another Confideration, which, though of lefs Moment than the foregoing, is yet abundantly fufficient to move the Compaffion of the Good, and alarm the Fears of the Wicked ; I mean the temporal Evils and Woes, which will probably fall upon the nominally Chriftian States of thefe Weftern Parts, the Chriftian *Babylon*, before the great Revolution predicted in the Scriptures, before the Kingdoms of this World become the Kingdoms of our Lord, and of his Chrift. Thefe Evils will be brought upon us by our Excefs of Wickednefs, juft as the Deluge was upon the old World, and the Deftruction of *Sodom* upon its lewd Inhabitants, through theirs ; they may alfo be fomewhat delayed, or alleviated, by Reformations public or private, even partial and temporary ones. 1 will therefore make a few fhort Remarks concerning fuch Things, as feem more particularly to call for the Attention of the prefent Chriftian World ; at leaft of thofe good *Philadelphians*, who are defirous to keep themfelves and others from that Hour of Temptation, which is coming upon us all. My Remarks muft be fuppofed to relate chiefly to this Kingdom ; to be fuggefted by what occurs in it ; and to be calculated, as far as my poor, but fincere and earneft Endeavours can have any Weight, to ftem for a while that Torrent of Vice and Impiety, which feem ready to fwallow us up, and, if poffible, to protract the Life of the Body Politic. But

I

I prefume, that the Refemblance between all the States of *Chriftendom* is fo great in all the Points here confidered, that the practical Confequences are the fame upon the Whole.

There are Six Things, which feem more efpecially to threaten Ruin and Diffolution to the prefent States of *Chriftendom*.

Firft, The great Growth of Atheifm and Infidelity, particularly amongft the governing Part of thefe States.

Secondly, The open and abandoned Lewdnefs, to which great Numbers of both Sexes, efpecially in the high Ranks of Life, have given themfelves up.

Thirdly, The fordid and avowed Self-intereft, which is almoft the fole Motive of Action in thofe who are concerned in the Adminiftration of public Affairs.

Fourthly, The Licentioufnefs and Contempt of every Kind of Authority, divine and human, which is fo notorious in Inferiors of all Ranks.

Fifthly, The great Worldly-mindednefs of the Clergy, and their grofs Neglects in the Difcharge of their proper Functions.

Sixthly, The Careleffnefs and Infatuation of Parents and Magiftrates with refpect to the Education of Youth, and the confequent early Corruption of the rifing Generation.

All thefe Things have evident mutual Connexions and Influences; and, as they all feem likely to increafe from time to time, fo it can fcarce be doubted by a confiderate Man, whether he be a religious one or no, but that they will, fooner or later, bring on a total Diffolution of all the Forms of Government, that fubfift at prefent in the Chriftian Countries of *Europe*. I will note down fome of the principal Facts of each Kind, and fhew their utter Inconfiften-

cy

cy with the Welfare of a Body Politic, and their neceffary Tendency to Anarchy and Confufion.

I begin with the Atheifm and Infidelity which prevail fo much among the governing Part of thefe Weftern Kingdoms. That Infidelity prevails, efpecially in thefe Kingdoms, will readily be acknowleged by all. But the fame Perfons, who treat the Chriftian Religion, and its Advocates, with fo much Scorn, will probably, fome of them at leaft, profefs a Regard to Natural Religion ; and it may feem hard to queftion their Sincerity. However, as far as has occurred to my Obfervation, thefe Perfons either deceive themfelves, or attempt to deceive others, in this. There appears in them no Love or Fear of God, no Confidence in him, no Delight in meditating upon him, in praying to him, or praifing him, no Hope or Joy in a future State. Their Hearts and Treafures are upon this Earth, upon fenfual Pleafures, or vain Amufements, perhaps of Philofophy or Philology, purfued to pafs the Time, upon Honour or Riches. And indeed there are the fame Objections, in general, to Natural Religion as to Revealed, and no ftronger Evidences for it. On the contrary, the hiftorical and moral Evidences for the general Truth of the Scriptures, which thefe Perfons deny, are more convincing and fatisfactory to philofophical as well as to vulgar Capacities, than the Arguments that are ufually brought to prove the Exiftence and Attributes of God, his Providence, or a future State: Not but that thefe laft are abundantly fufficient to fatisfy an earneft and impartial Inquirer.

If now there really be a God, who is our natural and moral Governor, and who expects, that we fhould regard him as fuch, thofe Magiftrates who care not to have him in their Thoughts, to fuffer him to interfere in their Scheme of Government, who *fay in their Hearts, that there is no God*, or wifh it, or even bid open Defiance to him (though I hope and believe
this

this laft is not often the Cafe), cannot profper; but muft bring down Vengeance upon themfelves, and the wicked Nations over whom they prefide. In like manner, if God has fent his beloved Son Jefus Chrift to be an Example to the World, to die for it, and to govern it, it cannot be an indifferent Thing whether we attend to his Call or no. The Neglect of Revealed Religion, efpecially in Perfons of Authority, is the fame thing as declaring it to be falfe; for, if true, the Neglect of it is, as one may fay, High Treafon againft the Majefty of Heaven. He that honours not the Son, cannot honour the Father, who has fent him with fufficient Credentials. And accordingly, if we confider the Second Pfalm as a Prophecy relating to Chrift, which it certainly is, thofe Kings and Magiftrates, who rife up againft God and his Chrift, intending to fhake off the Reftraints of Natural and Revealed Religion, muft expect to be broken in Pieces like a Potter's Veffel. Since they will not *kifs the Son*, and *rejoice before him with Reverence*, they muft expect, that he will *rule over them with a Rod of Iron*.

Nay, we may go farther, and affirm, that if there were no fatisfactory Evidence for Natural or Revealed Religion, ftill it is the Intereft of Princes and Governors to improve that which there is to the beft Advantage. The Happinefs of their People, their own Intereft with them, their Power, their Safety, their All, depend upon it. Neither is this any intricate, far-fetched, or doubtful Pofition, but a Truth which lies upon the Surface of Things, which is evident at firft Sight, and undeniable after the moft thorough Examination. So that for Governors to render Religion contemptible in the Eyes of their Subjects, by Example or Infinuation, and much more by directly ridiculing or vilifying it, is manifeft Infatuation; it is feeing without perceiving, and hearing without underftanding, through the Groffnefs and

Carnality

Carnality of their Hearts. And it may be part of the Infatuation predicted to come upon the Wicked in the latter Ages of the World. For then *the Wicked shall do wickedly, and none of the Wicked shall understand.*

Religion is often said by Unbelievers to have been the Invention of wise Law-givers, and artful Politicians, in order to keep the vicious and headstrong Multitude in Awe. How little does the Practice of the present Times suit with this! The Administrators of public Affairs in the present Times are not even wise or artful enough to take Advantage of a pure Religion, handed down to them from their Ancestors, and which they certainly did not invent; but endeavour to explode it at the manifest Hazard of all that is dear to them. For Mankind can never be kept in Subjection to Government, but by the Hopes and Fears of another World; nay, the express Precepts, Promises, and Threatenings of the Gospel are requisite for this Purpose. The unwritten Law of Nature is too pliable, too subtle, and too feeble; a dishonest Heart can easily explain it, or its Motives, away; and violent Passions will not suffer it to be heard; whereas the Precepts of Revealed Religion are absolute and express, and its Motives alarming to the highest Degree, where the Scriptures are received and considered, in any measure, as they ought to be.

The *Greek* and *Roman* Philosophy and Morality was not indeed equal to ours; but we may have a sufficient Specimen from thence, how little very good Doctrines, when taught without Authority, are able to check the growing Corruption of Mankind. Had not Christianity intervened at the Declension of the *Roman* Empire, and put a Stop to the Career of Vice, the whole Body Politic of the civilized Nations of that Empire must have been dissolved from the mere Wickedness and Corruption of its several Parts. And much rather may the same come

upon

upon us, if after fuch Light and Evidence we caft off the Reftraints and Motives of Revealed Religion.

I would not be underftood to fpeak here to thofe alone, who are legally the Governors of the Nations of *Chriftendom*, i. e. who have a particular legiflative or executive Power vefted in them by the Conftitutions or Cuftoms of their refpective Countries ; but alfo to all fuch as by their Eminence in any way, their Learning, their Titles, their Riches, &c. draw the World after them. And it feems requifite to remind the two learned Profeffions of Law and Phyfic, that though they are no-ways qualified to judge of the Evidence for Religion, unlefs they have examined it carefully, *i. e.* with the fame Attention and Impartiality, as they would do a Matter of Law or Phyfic, where it is their Intereft to form a right Judgment (in which Cafe there feems to be no Doubt but they will determine for it) ; yet the illiterate Part of Mankind will eafily catch the Infection from them on account of their general, confufed Reputation of being learned, and by means of the plaufible Way of haranguing and defcanting upon Topics, to which they are formed by their Educations and Profeffions. And thus, whether they attend to it or no, they become the Seducers of Mankind, and Rocks of Offence to the Weak and Ignorant, and load themfelves with the Guilt of other Mens Sins. This Caution is fo much the more neceffary, as it is common for young Students in thefe Profeffions to lift themfelves on the Side of Irreligion, and become nominal Infidels of courfe, and from Fafhion, as it were ; and without pretending, as indeed there could be no reafonable Pretence, to have examined into the Merits of the Caufe. Which blind and implicit Faith in the Blind, in one does not know what or whom, would be moft unaccountable in thofe who profefs Infidelity, were it not, that this is in every other Inftance a Contradiction to itfelf, and muft be fo, on

account

account of the wilful Infatuation from which it arifes.

I will now fhew briefly how the Prevalence of Infidelity increafes, and is increafed by, the other Evils here mentioned. That it opens a Door to Lewdnefs, cannot be doubted by any one; and indeed the Strictnefs and Purity of the Chriftian Religion, in this refpect, is probably the chief Thing, which makes vicious Men firft fear and hate, and then vilify and oppofe it. The unwritten Law of Nature cannot fix precife Bounds to the Commerce between the Sexes. This is too wide a Field, as I have obferved above; and yet it highly approves of Chaftity in Thought, Word, and Deed. If therefore Men reject only Revealed Religion, great Libertinifm muft enfue; but if they reject Natural alfo, which is generally the Cafe, we can expect nothing but the moft abandoned Diffolutenefs.

As to Self-intereft, we may obferve, that thofe who have no Hopes in Futurity, no Piety towards God, and confequently no folid or extenfive Benevolence towards Men, cannot but be engroffed by the moft fordid and groveling Kind, that which refts in prefent Poffeffions and Enjoyments. And, converfly, when fuch a Self-intereft has taken Root, they muft be averfe to Religion, becaufe it opens diftant and ungrateful Views to them, and inculcates the pure and difinterefted Love of God, and their Neighbour; to them an enthufiaftic and impoffible Project.

In like manner Infidelity muft difpofe Men to fhake off the Yoke of Authority, to unbounded Licentioufnefs; and reciprocally is itfelf the natural Confequence of every Degree of Licentioufnefs. Thofe who do not regard the fupreme Authority, can be little expected to regard any of his Vicegerents; thofe who do not fear God, will not honour the King. If the Infatuation of Princes was not of the deepeft Kind,
they

they could not but fee, that they hold their Dominions intirely by the real Chriftianity, that is left amongft us ; and that, if they do fucceed in taking away this Foundation, or weakening it much farther, their Governments muft fall, like Houfes built upon Sand. Befides the great Influence which Chriftianity has to make Men humble and obedient, it is to be confidered, that our Anceftors have fo interwoven it with the Conftitutions of the Kingdoms of *Europe,* that they muft ftand or fall together. Chriftianity is the Cement of the Buildings.

It is alfo evident, that the Infidelity of the Laity muft have an ill Effect in refpect of the Clergy. Many of thefe muft be the Sons of Infidels, thruft into the Church by their Parents for Subfiftence, or with a View to great Honours and Profits ; and muft carry with them a deep Tincture of the Corruption and Infidelity, which they imbibed in their Infancy and Youth. And it is not lefs evident, that the Worldly-mindednefs and Neglect of Duty in the Clergy is a great Scandal to Religion, and Caufe of Infidelity ; the chief probably after the Impatience of Reftraint in refpect of Chaftity in the Laity. It is alfo to be confidered, that unbelieving Magiftrates will have little Regard to the Piety of the Perfons, whom they promote to the higheft Stations of the Church, but rather to their Flattery, Subferviency, and apparent political Ufefulnefs.

Laftly, As to the perverted Education of Youth, Atheifm and Infidelity are both the Caufe and Effect of this in fo obvious a manner, that it feems fuperfluous to inlarge upon it.

The Lewdnefs which I have mentioned above, as a Second Caufe of the future Diffolution of thefe Weftern Kingdoms, is now rifen to fuch a Height, as almoft to threaten utter Confufion. Men glory in their Shame, and publicly avow what in former Ages was induftrioufly concealed. Princes are juftly chargeable

3

able

able with a great Part of this public Guilt. Their Courts will imitate them, in what is bad at leaſt; and be led on thereby from one Degree of Shamelef-ſneſs to another. The Evil increaſes gradually; for neither Courts, nor private Perſons, become quite profligate at once; and this may make ſome almoſt perſuade themſelves, that the preſent Times are not worſe than the preceding. The Sins of this Kind are, for the moſt part, joined with Idolatry in the prophetical Writings, and made the Types thereof. So that the open and avowed Practice of them is an open Renunciation of our Allegiance to God and Chriſt; and, agreeably to this, is, as has been obſerv-ed above, the principal Cauſe why ſo many Perſons reject Revealed Religion. But, if we renounce our Allegiance and Covenant, we can be no longer under the Protection of God.

The groſs Self-intereſt, which is now the principal Motive in moſt Marriages in High-Life, is both a Cauſe and Conſequence of this Libertiniſm. The ſame may be obſerved of the great Contempt, in which Marriage is held, and which almoſt threatens promiſcuous Concubinage among the higher Ranks, and the profeſſed Unbelievers.

As to the Clergy, if they neglect to admoniſh Princes and great Men through Fear, and ſervile In-tereſt, a great Part of the national Guilt will lie at their Doors; and, if they become, in general, infect-ed with this Vice (which indeed is not the Caſe now; but may perhaps hereafter, as all things grow worſe), it will ſoon be the intire Subverſion of the external Form of Church Government; however certain it be, that the Church of thoſe, who *worſhip God in Spirit, and in Truth*, will prevail againſt the Gates of Hell.

The Third great Evil likely to haſten our Ruin is the Self-intereſt, which prevails ſo much amongſt thoſe, to whom the Adminiſtration of public Affairs

is

is committed. It feems that Bodies Politic are in this Particular, as in many others, analogous to Individuals, that they grow more felfish, as they decline. As Things now are, one can fcarce expect, that, in any impending Danger, thofe who have it in their Power to fave a falling State, will attempt it, unlefs there be fome Profpect of Gain to themfelves. And, while they barter and caft about for the greateft Advantages to themfelves, the Evil will b come paft Remedy. Whether or no it be poffible to adminifter public Affairs upon upright and generous Principles, after fo much Corruption has already taken place, may perhaps be juftly queftioned. However, if it cannot be now, much lefs can it be hereafter; and, if this Evil increafes much more in this Country, there is Reafon to fear, than an independent Populace may get the upper hand, and overfet the State. The Wheels of Government are already clogged fo much, that it is difficult to tranfact the common neceffary Affairs, and almoft impoffible to make a good Law.

The Licentioufnefs of Inferiors of all Ranks, which is the Fourth great Evil, runs higher in this Country perhaps, than in any other. However, the Infection will probably fpread. The Inferiors in other Countries cannot but envy and imitate thofe in this; and that more and more every Day, as all mutual Intercourfes are inlarged. The Self-intereft juft fpoken of contributes greatly to this Evil, the Infolence of the Populace againft one Party of their Superiors being fupported, and even encouraged, by the other, from interefted Views of difplacing their Oppofites. Let it be obferved alfo, that the Laity of high Rank, by ridiculing and infulting their Superiors in the Church, have had a great Share in introducing the Spirit of univerfal Difobedience, and Contempt of Authority, amongft the inferior Orders, in this Nation.

The wicked and notoriously false Calumnies, which are spread about concerning the Royal Family by the disaffected Party in this Country, may be ranked under this Evil. Those who scruple to take the Oaths required by the present Government, ought at least to seek the Peace of the Country, where they live in Peace, and the quiet Enjoyment of their Possessions. However, the Crime of such as take the Oaths, and still vilify, is much greater, and one of the highest Offences that can be offered to the Divine Majesty.

That Worldly-mindedness, and Neglect of Duty, in the Clergy, must hasten our Ruin, cannot be doubted. These are *the Salt of the Earth*, and *the Light of the World*. If they lose their Savour, the whole Nation, where this happens, will be converted into one putrid Mass; if their Light become Darkness, the whole Body Politic must be dark also. The Degeneracy of the Court of *Rome*, and Secular Bishops abroad, are too notorious to be mentioned. They almost cease to give Offence, as they scarce pretend to any Function or Authority, besides what is temporal. Yet still there is great Mockery of God in their external Pomp, and Profanation of sacred Titles; which, sooner or later, will bring down Vengeance upon them. And as the Court of *Rome* has been at the Head of the great Apostasy and Corruption of the Christian Church, and seems evidently marked out in various Places of the Scriptures, the severest Judgments are probably reserved for her.

But I rather choose to speak to what falls under the Observation of all serious, attentive Persons in this Kingdom. The superior Clergy are, in general, ambitious, and eager in the Pursuit of Riches; Flatterers of the Great, and subservient to Party Interest; negligent of their own immediate Charges, and also of the inferior Clergy, and their immediate Charges. The inferior Clergy imitate their Superiors, and, in

general,

general, take little more Care of their Parishes, than barely what is neceffary to avoid the Cenfure of the Law. And the Clergy of all Ranks are, in general, either ignorant; or, if they do apply, it is rather to profane Learning, to philofophical or political Matters, than to the Study of the Scriptures, of the Oriental Languages, of the Fathers, and Ecclefiaftical Authors, and of the Writings of devout Men in different Ages of the Church. I fay this is, in general, the Cafe; *i. e.* far the greater Part of the Clergy of all Ranks in this Kingdom are of this Kind. But there are fome of a quite different Character, Men eminent for Piety, facred Learning, and the faithful Difcharge of their Duty, and who, it is not to be doubted, mourn in fecret for the crying Sins of this and other Nations. The Clergy, in general, are alfo far more free from open and grofs Vices, than any other Denomination of Men amongft us, Phyficians, Lawyers, Merchants, Soldiers, &c. However, this may be otherwife hereafter. For it is faid, that in fome foreign Countries the fuperior Clergy, in others the inferior, are as corrupt and abandoned, or more fo, than any other Order of Men. The Clergy in this Kingdom feem to be what one might expect from the Mixture of good and bad Influences that affect them. But then, if we make this candid Allowance for them, we muft alfo make it for Perfons in the high Ranks of Life, for their Infidelity, Lewdnefs, and fordid Self-intereft. And though it becomes an humble, charitable, and impartial Man, to make all thefe Allowances; yet he cannot but fee, that the Judgments of God are ready to fall upon us all for thefe things; and that they may fall firft, and with the greateft Weight, upon thofe, who, having the higheft Office committed to them in the fpiritual Kingdom of Chrift, neglect it, and are become mere *Merchants of the Earth*, and *Shepherds, that feed themfelves, and not their Flocks.*

How

How greatly might the Face of things be changed in this Kingdom, were any Number of the fuperior, or even of the inferior Clergy, to begin to difcharge their refpective Functions with true Chriftian Zeal, Courage, and Fidelity! The Earneftnefs of fome might awaken and excite others, and the whole Lump be leavened. At leaft, we might hope to delay or alleviate the Miferies, that threaten us. Why are not all the Poor taught to read the Bible, all inftructed in the Church Catechifm, fo as to have fuch Principles of Religion early inftilled into them, as would enable them to take Delight in, and to profit by, the Bible, and practical Books of Religion? Why are not all the Sick vifited, the Feeble-minded comforted, the Unruly warned? And why do not Minifters go about, thus doing Good, and feeking out thofe who want their Affiiftance? Why do not the fuperior Clergy inquire into thefe things, punifh and difcourage all negligent Parifh-Minifters, reward and promote thofe that are pious and diligent? Let thofe worthy Clergymen, who lament the Degeneracy of their own Order, inform the Public what is practicable and fitting to be done in thefe things. I can only deliver general Remarks, fuch as occur to a By-ftander.

There are great Complaints made of the Irregularities of the Methodifts, and, I believe, not without Reafon. The fureft Means to check thefe Irregularities is, for the Clergy to learn from the Methodifts what is good in them, to adopt their Zeal, and Concern for loft Souls: This would foon unite all that are truly good amongft the Methodifts to the Clergy, and difarm fuch as are otherwife. And if the Methodifts will hearken to one, who means fincerely well to all Parties, let me intreat them to reverence their Superiors, to avoid fpiritual Selfifhnefs, and Zeal for particular Phrafes and Tenets, and not to fow Divifions in Parifhes and Families, but to be

Peace-

Peace-makers, as they hope to be called the Children of God. The whole World will never be converted, but by thofe who are of a truly catholic Spirit. Let me intreat all Parties, as a fincere Friend and Lover of all, not to be offended with the great, perhaps unjuftifiable Freedom, which I have ufed, but to lay to Heart the Charges here brought, to examine how far they are true, and reform where-ever they are found to be fo.

If the State of Things in this and other Nations be, in any meafure, what I have above defcribed, it is no wonder, that the Education of Youth fhould be grofsly perverted and corrupted, fo that one may juftly fear, that every fubfequent Generation will exceed that which went before it in Degeneracy and Wickednefs, till fuch time as the great Tribulation come. Vicious Parents cannot be fenfible of the Importance and Neceffity of a good and religious Education, in order to make their Children happy. They muft corrupt them not only by their Examples, but by many other Ways, direct as well as indirect. As Infidelity now fpreads amongft the Female Sex, who have the Care of both Sexes during their Infancy, it is to be feared, that many Children will want the very Elements of Religion; be quite Strangers to the Scriptures, except as they fometimes hear them ridiculed; and be Savages as to the internal Man, as to their moral and religious Knowlege and Behaviour; and be diftinguifhed from them chiefly by the feeble Reftraints of external Politenefs and Decorum. It is evident from common Obfervation, and more fo from the foregoing Theory, that Children may be formed and moulded as we pleafe. When therefore they prove vicious and miferable, the Guilt lies at our Doors, as well as theirs; and, on the contrary, he who educates a Son, or a Daughter, in the Ways of Piety and Virtue, confers the higheft Obligation both upon his Child, and upon the rifing Generation;

and

and may be the Inſtrument of Salvation, temporal and eternal, to Multitudes,

There are two things here, which deſerve more particular Attention ; *viz.* the Education of the Clergy, and that of Princes.

As to the Firſt, one cannot but wonder, how it is poſſible for the many ſerious and judicious Clergymen, who have the Care of Youth in public Schools and Univerſities, to be ſo negligent of the principal Point, their moral and religious Behaviour ; and that eſpecially as the Regulation of this would make all other Parts of Education go on with ſo much more Eaſe and Succeſs : How Schoolmaſters can ſtill perſiſt to teach lewd Poets after the Remonſtrances of pious Men againſt this Practice, and the evident ill Conſequences : How the Tutors in the Univerſities can permit ſuch open Debauchery, as is often practiſed there : And how ſacred Learning, which ſurely is the chief Thing for Scholars intended for the Chriſtian Miniſtry, can be allowed ſo ſmall a Share of Time and Pains, both in Schools, and in the Univerſities. But, as I ſaid before of the Clergy in general, Let thoſe Schoolmaſters and Tutors, who have Religion at Heart, ſpeak fully to this Point. I ſhall ſubmit my own Judgment, in both Caſes, intirely to the better Judgment of pious Men, that are converſant in theſe things.

As to the Education of Princes, the Caſe is every thing but deſperate ; ſo that one could ſcarce think of mentioning it, were it not for the great Change in the Face of Things, which would immediately enſue, if but ſo much as one Sovereign Prince would ſet aſide all Self-regards, and devote himſelf intirely to the Promotion of Religion, and the Service of Mankind. I do not at all mean to intimate, that Princes are worſe than other Men, proper Allowances being made. On the contrary, I ſuppoſe they are juſt the ſame. And they have an undoubted

Right

Right to the greateſt Candour, and Compaſſion from their Subjeꞔts, on account of the extraordinary Difficulties and Temptations, with which they are beſet, as well as to the moſt profound Reverence, and intire Obedience.

Theſe are my real and earneſt Sentiments upon theſe Points. It would be great Raſhneſs to fix a Time for the breaking of the Storm that hangs over our Heads, as it is Blindneſs and Infatuation not to ſee it; not to be aware, that it may break. And yet this Infatuation has always attended all falling States. The Kingdoms of *Judah* and *Iſrael*, which are the Types of all the reſt, were thus infatuated. It may be, that the Prophecies concerning *Edom, Moab, Ammon, Tyre, Egypt,* &c. will become applicable to particular Kingdoms before their Fall, and warn the Good to flee out of them. And *Chriſtendom,* in general, ſeems ready to aſſume to itſelf the Place and Lot of the *Jews,* after they had rejeꞔted their Meſſiah the Saviour of the World. Let no one deceive himſelf or others. The preſent Circumſtances of the World are extraordinary and critical, beyond what has ever yet happened. If we refuſe to let Chriſt reign over us, as our Redeemer and Saviour, we muſt be ſlain before his Face, as Enemies, at his ſecond Coming.

F I N I S.

AN

I N D E X

TO

Both PARTS.

A.

Affo-

INDEX.

INDEX.

INDEX.

INDEX.

INDEX.

K.

INDEX.

INDEX.

Retor-

INDEX.

INDEX.

Types

INDEX.

CPSIA information can be obtained at www.ICGtesting.com
Printed in the USA
LVOW11s1045080616

R10991500001B/R109915PG490878LVX2B/2/P